Students!
Information for HM Video Cases and Online Resources That Accompany This Book

Are you interested in what *really* happens in the classroom? Do you want to know how teachers handle challenging situations? Watch the Houghton Mifflin Video Cases and see how new and experienced teachers apply concepts and strategies in real K–12 classrooms. These 4- to 6-minute video clips cover a variety of different topics that today's teachers face and allow you to experience real teaching in action.

To access the Houghton Mifflin Video Cases and other premium, online resources, look for your passkey, packaged with your new text.

ENHANCE YOUR LEARNING EXPERIENCE.

Houghton Mifflin Video Cases are integrated into your new copy of Koch, *So You Want to Be a Teacher?* throughout the text and assignments. The cases include video clips and a host of related materials to provide a comprehensive learning experience. See the complete list of Video Case topics on page xix.

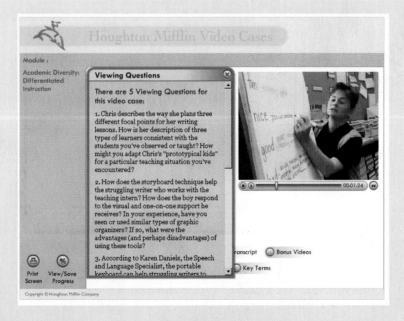

Reflect on the teacher's approach and assess how you might handle the situation by considering the **Viewing Questions**.

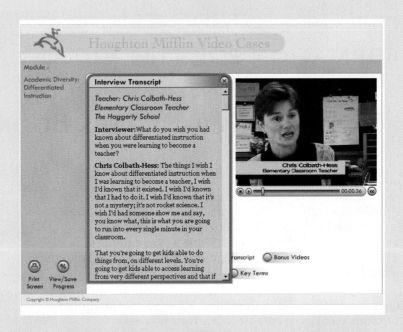

Read detailed **interviews with the teachers** as they explain their approach, how they engage students, and how they resolve issues.

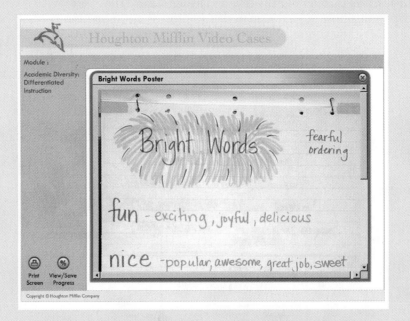

View **handouts and materials used in the class**, and gain ideas for your own portfolio.

So You Want to Be a Teacher?

TEACHING AND LEARNING IN THE 21ST CENTURY

Janice Koch

<small>HOFSTRA UNIVERSITY</small>

<small>Houghton Mifflin Company   Boston   New York</small>

Executive Publisher: Patricia Coryell
Editor in Chief: Carrie Brandon
Sponsoring Editor: Shani Fisher
Marketing Manager: Amy Whitaker
Senior Development Editor: Lisa Mafrici
Senior Project Editor: Samantha Ross
Art and Design Manager: Jill Haber
Cover Design Manager: Anne S. Katzeff
Senior Photo Editor: Jennifer Meyer Dare
Senior Composition Buyer: Chuck Dutton
New Title Project Manager: James Lonergan
Editorial Assistant: Amanda Nietzel
Marketing Assistant: Samantha Abrams
Editorial Assistant, Production: Anne Finley

Cover images: © Andersen Ross/Blend Images/Corbis; © Image Source Pink/Getty Images

Credits begin on page 325, which constitutes an extension of the copyright page.

Printed in the U.S.A.

Library of Congress Control Number: 2007928278

ISBN-10: 0-618-84200-4
ISBN-13: 978-0-618-84200-1

123456789-CRK-11 10 09 08 07

Brief Contents

So You Want to Be a Teacher?
Teaching and Learning in the 21st Century

CONTENTS

CHAPTER 4
Principles of Teaching and Learning:
Exploring Pedagogy, Curriculum, and Instruction   91

CHAPTER **6**   Contemporary Trends and Issues in Education   154

Houghton Mifflin Video Cases— A Special Feature in the Text

Dear Reader,

Here are a few thoughts to consider as you begin this book.

Learning to teach is like taking a trip. Taking an introductory education course is like setting out on a journey, a lengthy process that requires you to explore the inner workings of education as well as *your* inner workings. One stop on this journey is to examine the nature of teaching and learning as processes that are wedded to each other. Another stop is to listen to the experiences of teachers, both past and present. Still another stop is the study of American public education from historical, legal, and social perspectives.

Learning to teach requires self-reflection. Looking inward to discover your own strengths and weaknesses will help you understand the personal attributes that make you suited for teaching—as well as the personality areas you need to develop further.

Learning to teach is about understanding diversity. Gaining an appreciation of the wide variety of students who enter our public schools includes recognizing not just diverse ethnicities, religions, and cultural beliefs, but also recognizing the needs of students with disabilities and those of students whose learning styles differ widely from what you may consider typical.

Learning to teach requires honoring the learner. Understanding who your students are, what their lives are like, how they experience the world, and what types of families they belong to is one way to address being a good teacher. Honoring the learner means that you have a feeling for each student's readiness to learn and the ways in which he or she will be most successful.

Learning to teach is about getting connected. Creating community in your classroom gives students a sense of belonging that transcends the classroom walls. You create community through real-time, face-to-face encounters with your students and also through electronic encounters— on a class website, for example.

Learning to teach is about becoming generous of spirit. This text will help you see how the joy of teaching derives from doing on behalf of others. In the following pages we will explore the many wonderful possibilities for meeting the needs of future students—and the future of our world depends on doing just that.

Janice Koch

PREFACE

For the college or graduate student, making the decision to become a teacher is often fraught with uncertainty, complexity, and confusion. What should I know? What courses do I take? How do I get certified? How can I be certain that this career choice is right for me?

Although some aspiring teachers approach this journey with more personal confidence than others, most find it a challenge to make the transition from the college classroom to their own classrooms. *So You Want to Be a Teacher? Learning and Teaching in the 21st Century* is designed to help them meet that challenge. I wrote the book in response to colleagues who felt that I could speak to future teachers plainly and clearly.

FOCUS AND ORGANIZATION OF THIS BOOK

In the early chapters, I begin a conversation with education students that invites them to look inward and outward, backward and forward, as they analyze their personal strengths and weaknesses in light of their choice to become a teacher. The text challenges the reader by asking if there is a "good fit" between the reader's personal and cognitive attributes and the demands of the teaching profession. Since this is not a simple question, I encourage future teachers to think sincerely about the complex aspects of a "good fit."

Later chapters focus on subjects common in introductory texts—such as the history of American education, principles of teaching and learning, the characteristics of today's students, the legal rights of students and teachers—but I continue prompting readers to think about what these topics mean for them and their conception of teaching. The final chapter returns to the readers' career decision and offers practical advice for those who do choose the teaching profession.

One overarching idea of the text can be summed up in this statement: "We teach who we are." By this I mean that a teacher's entire self is present in the classroom. Who we are, what we believe, what we think about ourselves and our students—all these are exposed through the dynamic processes of teaching and learning. By the time a reader finishes this book, he or she should have a clearer *personal* sense of what it will mean to be a teacher.

IMPORTANT THEMES OF THIS BOOK

Believing that we teach who we are, I should confess that I write who I am. Though this book is meant as a broad introduction to the field of education, it certainly reflects some of my own strong beliefs:

▶ **Diversity and Community.** Never have American students been more diverse in their ethnicities, social classes, religious affiliations, and learning styles and abilities. The increasing diversity in the United States amounts to a cultural and social revolution. As a consequence, the teacher's role in building a learning community has never before been as important as it is today. This book addresses diversity with all of its challenges and opportunities and examines how teachers can foster a respectful community of learners.

▶ **The Internet Revolution.** Another contemporary revolution is the rise of the Internet with its extraordinary communication technologies. The Internet has profoundly changed the ways in which our students think, work, act, communicate, and go about their daily lives. Never before has so much information been accessible so quickly. Never before has collaborating with others been less defined by the boundaries of a classroom. We can communicate with students and teachers across the world in fractions of a second. This text explores in depth the implications of our connectivity for both teaching and learning in the 21st century.

▶ **Meaningful, Active Learning.** Though I discuss older philosophies and their contributions, my approach draws most heavily on contemporary constructivist theory and research. Meaningful learning, this book contends, is an active process of developing and building on existing ideas. Teachers also need to be learners who actively listen to their students in order to create optimal learning environments.

LEARNING FEATURES OF THE TEXT

This book relies on several key elements to engage the reader: (1) the use of authentic stories about teachers and students; (2) video cases of real classrooms at all grade levels; (3) frequent prompts to write and reflect on the stories and video cases; (4) learning projects and Chapter Challenges; (5) a portfolio-building feature; (6) a Join the Discussion section in each chapter that invites the readers to comment on the reading in an online blog; and (7) a self-assessment questionnaire at the end of each part.

Becoming a Teacher: Stories to Learn By

TEACHING STORIES
COMMUNICATING WITH A CLASS ACROSS THE OCEAN

Recently students in a fifth-grade class on the Eastern Shore of Maryland used their handheld Palm computers and keyboards to communicate with students in a fifth-grade class in South Africa. Each student e-mailed a message to a student "buddy" in the class in South Africa. The students exchanged information about their personal interests and about what they were learning in mathematics.

Then the teachers set up an international telephone link between the classrooms using Skype, a free Internet phone service. The Maryland students used their math skills to calculate what time it would be in South Africa during their call. In this Skype conversation and in further communications, both classes learned about life and culture in each place, the languages spoken and understood, and the role of homework and studying in their lives.

As a result of the prodding of colleagues and friends who have used my earlier book, *Science Stories,* for preservice science teachers, I have again included narratives to gain the confidence and empathy of readers. Numerous teachers—wonderful and smart people with whom I have been privileged to work—share their stories, providing context for the reader and bringing to life the many facets of teaching. My own experiences also dot the landscape of this book as I draw on years of teaching middle and high school students.

The longer narratives, called "Teaching Stories," are often followed by a section titled "The Teaching Ideas Behind This Story" that helps the reader assess the content. Besides contextualizing the philosophies, strategies, and teaching approaches described throughout the book, the stories are intended to "interrogate" readers' thinking, challenging prospective teachers to imagine themselves in similar settings.

Video Cases

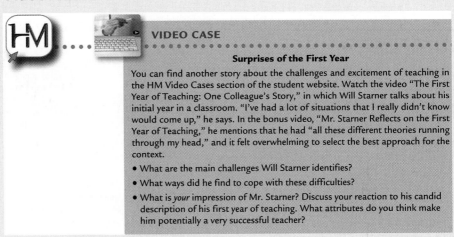

VIDEO CASE

Surprises of the First Year

You can find another story about the challenges and excitement of teaching in the HM Video Cases section of the student website. Watch the video "The First Year of Teaching: One Colleague's Story," in which Will Starner talks about his initial year in a classroom. "I've had a lot of situations that I really didn't know would come up," he says. In the bonus video, "Mr. Starner Reflects on the First Year of Teaching," he mentions that he had "all these different theories running through my head," and it felt overwhelming to select the best approach for the context.

- What are the main challenges Will Starner identifies?
- What ways did he find to cope with these difficulties?
- What is *your* impression of Mr. Starner? Discuss your reaction to his candid description of his first year of teaching. What attributes do you think make him potentially a very successful teacher?

To take the reader even more directly into classrooms, I make extensive use of Houghton Mifflin's award-winning series of Video Cases. At least once in each chapter—and more often in later chapters—a Video Case feature invites readers to visit the student website and watch a short video pertinent to the topics under discussion. The cases show teachers in real classrooms interacting with students and discussing the methods they are using. The text provides questions to stimulate reflection, and the cases themselves offer Viewing Questions, Key Terms, Bonus Videos, and more. Prospective teachers will find these glimpses of teachers at work both fascinating and instructive.

Prompts for Writing and Reflection

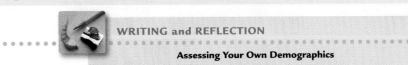

WRITING and REFLECTION

Assessing Your Own Demographics

- *Demographics* is a general term for the kind of statistics we have been discussing so far in this chapter—the characteristics of human populations. How would you describe your demographics?
- Did you attend a neighborhood school? If so, how did it reflect the composition of your neighborhood? What do you think are the advantages of attending the local neighborhood school?
- Why might a diverse student body make a greater contribution to the entire group's learning than would a homogeneous group?

To encourage readers to engage actively with the material, the text has frequent sections called "Writing and Reflection." Like the questions after the Video Cases, these brief interludes prompt readers to think about what they have just read and put their conclusions into their own words. The Writing and Reflection prompts can form the basis for entries in a teaching journal, or they can be used for class discussions, either in class or online.

Throughout the book, these sections reinforce the idea that a good teacher must be a reflective practitioner who consistently modifies her or his own teaching practices in response to events in the classroom.

Learning Projects and Chapter Challenges

LEARNING PROJECT

Gaining Entry to the Profession: Developing a Timeline

Becoming a teacher requires at least a bachelor's degree, usually related to the field in which you plan to teach. Beyond that, however, requirements for becoming a teacher vary from state to state. In most states, some form of advanced training is also needed. If you are seriously considering teaching as a career, it is important to find out exactly what you need in order to become a teacher in the state in which you want to work.

As a start, visit this webpage provided by the AFT: http://www.aft.org/teachers/jft/becoming.htm. As you do your research, look for answers to the following questions:

- In your state, can you begin teaching with just a bachelor's degree?
- Do you have to take and pass tests to gain a teaching certificate or license? How many tests? In which areas of study?
- Are you required to obtain a master's degree? If so, what disciplines are accepted as leading to certification?
- Some states require attendance at special seminars in addition to completing the requirements for your academic degree. Is that the case in your state? If so, what seminars are required?

Finally, develop a timeline for your professional preparation. What courses will you take and when will you take them? When will you complete your requirements? Make a checklist of tests, seminars, courses, and application dates for gaining entry into teaching in your state.

The text includes a number of Learning Projects that engage the reader in research on specific topics, ranging from certification requirements to curriculum structure to issues surrounding inclusion.

CHAPTER CHALLENGE

Learning About a Local School District

At this time, you'll find it useful to visit a local public school district's website. See what you can learn about the history of schooling in the area, the mission of the district, how the schools in the district are funded, and the biggest challenges facing the district today.

Write a description of this school district as if you were a real estate agent advertising the district to a future homeowner or apartment dweller. Here are some questions to guide your district profile:

- What are the key elements of the district's mission statement?
- Is the school district known for outstanding projects? What are they? How are they presented?
- Has a student or teacher from this district recently distinguished herself or himself in any special way?
- How many schools are in the district?
- How many students attend the schools?
- When was the district formed?
- How is the central administration of the district organized?

• Is there a "state of the district" report? What does it say?

• Is there a board of education for the district? If so:

• How many members are on it? What is the duration of their terms?

• What are the board's responsibilities? (In some states, boards are responsible for establishing the policies governing the operation of the schools.)

At the end of each chapter, the Chapter Challenge presents a more extended project to increase the reader's understanding and appreciation of teaching. The Challenges include such activities as observing and writing about a school's culture and climate; interviewing a classroom teacher; and developing a student survey.

Building a Professional Portfolio

FROM THE COLLEGE CLASSROOM TO YOUR OWN CLASSROOM

The Trends You Find Appealing

There is so much to think about as you continue your professional portfolio! Write about the current educational trends you find most appealing as a future teacher. Explore the ways you can see yourself involved in this type of change.

Following the Chapter Challenge, each chapter includes a section called "From the College Classroom to Your Own Classroom." In addition to encouraging readers to reflect on what they have read, this feature guides them in building a portfolio to present when they apply for a job.

Join the Discussion: Using the Edublog

JOIN THE DISCUSSION

Visit the student website and locate the Edublog for Chapter 3. Continue the discussion by responding to the following questions:

➥ Why is it important to diversify the teaching workforce? Why does it matter, for example, that a typical kindergarten teacher is a white female?

➥ How would you characterize your personal teaching philosophy at this point? Are you an essentialist? a progressive? a social reconstructionist? a mix of several types? How and why?

This book's student website includes a link to the Edublog, an ongoing weblog in which I engage students in discussing ideas and issues raised in the text. This online component is an exciting and truly interactive way for students to learn about the teaching profession. At the end of the text in each chapter, a short feature called "Join the Discussion" invites readers to take part in the Edublog and suggests topics for discussion.

Taking Stock: Self-Assessment Questionnaires

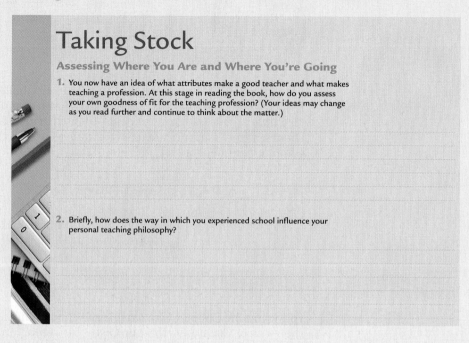

After each of the book's four parts, readers will find a section called "Taking Stock," which invites them to assess where they are and where they are going. The questions here will help them decide on their own teaching philosophies, their "goodness of fit" for the profession, and how they will meet typical challenges that today's teachers face.

ACCOMPANYING TECHNOLOGY SUPPORT

Several electronic ancillaries support and extend the learning experiences offered in the text.

HM TeacherPrepSPACE™ Student and Instructor Websites

In addition to the Edublog and the Video Cases, the textbook's companion websites (accessible from **college.hmco.com/pic/koch**) include a multitude of other resources for both students and instructors.

On the students' site, your class members will find a self-assessment tool to help them reflect on their aptitude for teaching, called *Becoming a Teacher: A Tool for Personal Reflection*; glossary flashcards; direct links to the websites mentioned in the text; portfolio resources and a portfolio building tutorial; and additional ideas for research and reflection. Students can access HM TeacherPrepSPACE™ content at any time via the Internet. Some content may be passkey protected.

The HM TeacherPrepSPACE Instructors' website includes a sample course syllabus, an Instructor's Resource Manual, a PowerPoint slide program, and more.

HM Testing CD

This CD-ROM for instructors includes a full test bank of assessment items consisting of multiple-choice, short answer, and essay questions for each chapter.

HM TeacherPrepSPACE with Eduspace

For instructors who use a course management system, Eduspace®, Houghton Mifflin's Course Management System, offers a flexible, interactive online platform to help them communicate with students, organize material, evaluate student work, and track results in a powerful grade book. In addition to the grade book and other course management tools, Eduspace includes special interactive components to aid students in studying and reflecting on what they have learned.

ACKNOWLEDGMENTS

This work is a result of the kind of contemporary collaboration that could only be possible in a wired world. Communication with contributors and researchers via the Internet, blogs, podcasts, and email resulted in rich sources of information for this text. My research assistants, Josephine Potucek and Betsy Koch, contributed mightily to helping me sort and manage the relevant data on each of the topics.

As you will see, the voices of my former Hofstra University students who became teachers and shared their stories—Amanda Prinz, Jessica Powers, Pearl Halegua, Jane Boyd, Meredith Landau, Winelle Outerbridge, James Ufier, Danny Wittich, Sharyn Liebowtitz, and Laura Marvullo—were central to the development of the book. Many thanks, too, to Adam Weisler, whose work in high school social studies continues to be a model, and to Christine Schroder Nichols and Jaime Barron, whose warm and wonderful work in building classroom community sets the tone for much of Chapter 9. My Hofstra colleagues Maureen Miletta and Jane Goldman and my assistant Eloise Gmur provided the kind of emotional support that every writer hopes for.

My sincere appreciation goes to Lisa Mafrici at Houghton Mifflin, along with Mary Finch and Shani Fisher. Their unending support for my work is a constant source of encouragement. Of course, there could be no book without my developmental editor, Doug Gordon, whose insight and humor are unequaled.

The Advisory Board for this text and ancillary program included a large group of reviewers who offered excellent guidance along the way, and their suggestions have proved extremely valuable. They include:

Cindi Deagen Bluhm, Northwest Vista College

Ginny A. Buckner, Montgomery College

Dominique Charlotteaux, Broward Community College

Susan H. Christian, Patrick Henry Community College

David E. Coffman, Bridgewater College

Beth Day-Hairston, Winston Salem State University

Erskine S. Dottin, Florida International University

Jill Flygare, University of Utah

Constance J. Goodman, The University of Central Florida

Samuel Hinton, Eastern Kentucky University

Charles Howell, Minnesota State University

Brenda J. Kennedy, Winston-Salem University

Arnold Munroe, University of Central Florida

Phillip Masila Mutisya, North Carolina Central University

Thom O'Mara, Eastern Shore Community College

Michael H. Parsons, Hagerstown Community College

Jocelyn Lee Payne, Northeastern State University

Melvin J. Pedras, University of Idaho

Rochelle Pozner, Pima Community College

Michael Pregot, Iona College

Nancy Reedy, Pulaski Technical College

Marjorie Schiller, Central Arizona College

Marvin A. Seperson, Nova Southeastern University

Paul Shore, St. Louis University

Shelia L. Skahan, Three Rivers Community College

Karen R. Trainor, University of Northern Colorado

Karen A. Vuurens, South Texas College

Merrill Watrous, Lane Community College

Anna Weidhofer, Springfield College

Karen Whitaker, Martinson Elementary School

Diana Yeager, Hillsborough Community College

Many thanks to all of these expert commentators.

Clearly, my two favorite digital natives, my granddaughters Kayley and Sydney Tarantino, were my inspiration for addressing twenty-first-century skills in Chapters 7 and 8. They and their parents, my daughter Robin and son-in-law Brian, continue to inspire me with their understanding of the possibilities of life in a digital age. My daughter Betsy worked very hard on the research for many of the chapters, and her mental lens was a huge help.

Finally, I dedicate this book to my husband, Bob Koch, who has always made it possible for me to pursue my dreams. Thanks, Bobby.

Janice Koch

So You Want to Be a Teacher?

PART I

Thinking About Teaching: Making the Decision

This book invites you on a personal journey of reflection about education—your own education, the education of people you know, and the education of children who will become America's future. It is a journey of self-exploration, during which you will be asked to look inside your mind and heart and consider what it takes, emotionally and intellectually, to become a teacher who experiences joy and satisfaction through service to others.

Part I of this book invites you to explore the teaching profession by hearing the voices of teachers in the field and by examining the role of teachers in your life. It also challenges you to think about teaching in new ways. You have spent many years in classrooms. You have had many experiences, and you have tacitly held beliefs about what it means to teach and to learn. Welcome to a journey that will help you expand your thinking and explore your aptitude for this career.

One caution: Reading this book can be hazardous to a closed mind. If there is one thing we all need, it is to open our minds to multiple ways of thinking about teaching!

PART OUTLINE

CHAPTER 1
Becoming a Teacher: Looking Forward and Backward at the Same Time

CHAPTER 2
Teaching Stories

Becoming a Teacher: Looking Forward and Backward at the Same Time

FOCUSING QUESTIONS

▶ How did you feel about school?

▶ Do you think you'll teach as you have been taught?

▶ Who was your favorite teacher?

▶ What special qualities do teachers need?

▶ Can you picture yourself teaching a class?

This book is designed to guide your thinking about entering the field of education. It is about schools and schooling, teachers and teaching, learners and the process of learning. It is also about you. What do you already know about classrooms, and how can you apply that knowledge to the complex experience of being a classroom teacher? Your answers to these questions will play a big role in deciding the kind of teacher you will become.

You have within you everything you need to create the kind of teacher you want to be. This book challenges you to identify the attitudes, skills, and dispositions that are required by the field of teaching. You will need to make a commitment to being a lifelong learner—that is, expanding your ideas by what you learn from your students, your research, and your own personal growth. Donald Schön (1983), an educational researcher, used the term **reflective practitioner** to refer to a teacher who consistently and consciously modifies her or his own teaching practice based on the active consideration of events in her or his classroom. This book invites you to conceptualize teaching as a personal activity requiring a large capacity for reflective thought and deliberate action and experimentation.

reflective practitioner
A teacher who consistently reflects on classroom events (both successes and problems) and modifies teaching practices accordingly.

The field of teaching, which requires such a heightened sense of self and a commitment to the social good, demands nothing less of its professionals than an ongoing examination of their authentic motives for teaching. Hence, in addition to *knowledge* about schools, curriculum, and instruction, this text provides a *venue* through which you can actively consider your skills, attitudes, and dispositions as they relate to becoming a teacher.

We begin by examining your interest in the field of education. This chapter is subtitled "Looking Forward and Backward at the Same Time" because it will encourage you to reflect on your own educational background as you explore the possibility of forging a career as a teacher.

LOOKING BACKWARD: TALKING ABOUT TEACHING

When I recently asked a number of new teachers what made them decide to enter teaching, some of them remarked that they had always loved school. School was, for them, their happiest place to be. But several others shared not-so-glorious stories about their experiences. They decided to go into teaching to make a difference, to teach others in ways they wish they themselves had been taught.

Yet other teachers had no specific personal calling to teach. They "fell into" teaching because they needed a job and teaching presented itself. Still others are trying to figure out if teaching is for them. Whichever of these categories you feel you may fit into, this book will help you explore the field of education and discover for yourself if teaching is for you.

Laura and Sharyn pursued teaching careers because they loved school and loved learning. Laura explained that from her earliest years in school, she was excited when the school year began and sad when it ended. School was her happiest place, so she decided to pursue a career that would keep her there. Sharyn described similar feelings:

> As a child, I could not wait for summer camp to be over because I wanted to go back to school. In high school, I participated in a peer tutoring program in my school and also privately tutored friends and classmates. When they did well, I was happier than when I did well because I had helped them succeed. My love for school and learning, combined with the joy I felt when my friends whom I tutored succeeded, led me to want to teach. I wanted to enable children to love learning as much as I did.

A third teacher I interviewed, Derrick, told me that most of his teachers were female. Not until sixth grade did he experience his first male teacher—the music teacher. He gained an appreciation of music from this teacher and started to imagine that he might teach as well. He played school with his younger brother and began to consider a career in education. Later, a male history teacher encouraged him to study that subject, and he majored in history in college while also pursuing a professional program in elementary education. A kindergarten teacher today, Derrick is firmly convinced that men are needed in early childhood education so that children can see that men are able caretakers.

Are you like Laura, Derrick, or Sharyn in your conviction that teaching is a career you clearly want to pursue? Or are you more ambivalent? The following Writing and Reflection activity will help you think about ways in which your educational past, and your thoughts and feelings about it, may influence your future career.

WRITING and REFLECTION

Draw Yourself as a Teacher

Take a pencil and paper and draw a picture of yourself teaching a lesson. You do not have to be an artist; stick figures are fine (see Figure 1.1). Just imagine yourself in a classroom and draw the images you see. Be sure to include the students! This is a way to explore your images of teaching.

Close the book while you work! When you finish your drawing, return to this section.

As you analyze your drawing, you may want to reflect on the following questions:

- How is your classroom arranged?
- Are there desks in rows? Or are tables grouped around the room?
- What are you doing? What are your students doing?
- Are you standing in front? in the middle? to the side?
- Are students raising their hands?
- Judging from your drawing, what mental models do you have of yourself as a teacher?

continued

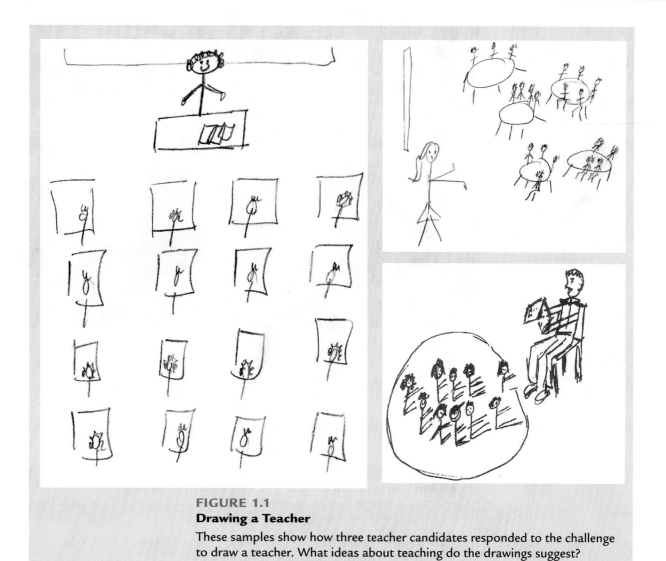

FIGURE 1.1
Drawing a Teacher
These samples show how three teacher candidates responded to the challenge to draw a teacher. What ideas about teaching do the drawings suggest?

Your Educational Autobiography

What was school like for you? What kind of a student were you? When you think of teaching, which teacher or teachers do you conjure up?

You may think questions like these are irrelevant at this stage of your life. But examining your early experiences as a student is an important task:

> *Who you are as a person, the kinds of experiences you had inside and outside of school, your values, beliefs and aspirations shape what you will be as a teacher and how you will teach and how you will respond to the changing contexts of teaching (Bullough & Gitlin, 2001, p. 45).*

Thinking about your own story, and telling it, is an important step in looking backward.

Think back from your earliest school experiences up to the present—what was going to school like for you?

educational autobiography Your own educational history, told by you.

An **educational autobiography** is your own story of your life as a student. It has no definite length but usually responds to the following questions:

- What do you think of when you think of school?

- Where did you attend school?

- When you walked in the building, did you have a sense of comfort? fear? anxiety?

- Close your eyes and imagine you are back in elementary, middle, or high school. What was school like for you? Do you remember what school *smells* like? *sounds* like?

- Try to imagine specific teachers. What grades did they teach? Who were your friends in those grades?

My own first story begins with kindergarten:

I remember starting kindergarten at the age of four years and six months. Arbitrary calendar cut-off dates, typical of many public school districts, allowed me to enter school well before my fifth birthday. Neighbors would say, "She made the year." That referred to being allowed to commence kindergarten prior to turning five. Other children, born four weeks later, had "missed the year" and began kindergarten after their fifth birthday. They would be the oldest in the grade, while I was the youngest.

I remember being frightened and throwing up every day for the first two months of kindergarten. But I also recall my kindergarten teachers' accepting and welcoming me each day, regardless of my physiological reaction to separating from my home. I was a very "young" four-and-a-half year old and would probably have been better served by "missing the year." How patient and kind my two kindergarten teachers were! They saw me coming and intuitively knew that I was not ready for school. After helping me get over being sick each morning (they had a pail ready), they guided me gently to my seat. Their understanding that I had to become comfortable at my own pace enabled me to make an adjustment without shame and embarrassment.

I shall always remember their acceptance of me and my lack of readiness. How lucky I was to have these two teachers as I acclimated myself to being away from home.

Christine, too, felt some pain in her early school years. Her story begins in first grade:

Christine's first-grade teacher never smiled and often yelled. One day she accused Christine of talking on line, sent her back to the classroom instead of letting her go to art, and then yelled at her. Christine was shy and quiet and never told her parents about the incident. The next day, however, she locked herself in the bathroom of her home and would not go to school.

When she finally did return to school, she was silent for the rest of the school year. It would be years later when her parents learned why she locked herself in the bathroom.

The following year, second grade, turned school around for Christine. She had a second-grade teacher who was loving and nurturing and who took a genuine interest in every child. This teacher developed a classroom environment in which students were encouraged to explore their own interests, and she made a personal connection with each child. From second grade on, Christine loved learning. It was, for her, that love of learning that motivated her to become a teacher.

WRITING and REFLECTION

Beginning Your Educational Autobiography

To begin your educational autobiography, describe your early school experiences. Start with some basic facts: where you went to school, how you traveled there, how it felt to be in the classroom, and when (if at all) you thought about becoming a teacher.

For example, I remember walking to school with my older sister, and after getting used to kindergarten I loved first grade. I remember starting to read and loving my first-grade teacher. I thought school was neat. My elementary school was a wonderful old building in the Bronx in New York City. There was a swimming pool in the school, and every week we had swimming lessons with Mrs. Doyle. I felt special because my school had a swimming pool.

continued

What similar—or dissimilar—memories do you have?

So start your educational autobiography with some similar facts: How old were you when you started school? Did you attend a nursery school or pre-school? Where did you live? Was the school within walking distance, did you take a bus, or did someone drive you? What is your earliest memory of being in a classroom? What grade were you in?

Now you are on your way to describing your educational experience through your own lens.

What Is Your Metaphor? Establishing a Personal Philosophy

"Being a teacher feels like being a dentist—we are always pulling teeth," a new teacher remarked to me recently. "Ouch," I responded. "Is it that hard?"

"Well," she replied, "when they don't give me what I am looking for, I feel like that."

Aha, I think—some metaphor! One of the most important misconceptions about the teaching profession is that it is a solitary activity—something you do *in order to have control over someone else.* In fact, teaching and learning is an interaction, a conversation, a collaborative process involving you, the teacher, and all of your students. Teaching is about the students, *their* needs, not *your* needs for them. The teacher who feels like a dentist is focusing on what her needs are, not on the needs of her students.

It is true that sometimes we wish students would respond in certain ways and they just don't. Yet there are much better metaphors than pulling teeth. Much of the time teaching is like:

▶ **Being a tour guide.** According to one teacher, a good tour guide takes travelers to new places, interprets experiences and sites, helps travelers understand and appreciate these new experiences, and develops a group atmosphere to maximize positive experiences for the travelers. A good tour guide has general goals in mind but is flexible and allows for exploration of ideas that arise from the group.

Indeed, there are many times when teaching is like being a tour guide. The teacher sets the itinerary and takes the students through the lessons to many new places. Yet there are other times when being a teacher is like:

▶ **Being a sailor.** Sometimes when you go sailing, you think you're going to reach a certain island. You set out for that island, but you find it doesn't have a dock. The dock is simply not there. So you need to have an alternative plan.

On other days, you have a destination in mind, but the wind is blowing in the wrong direction and the sailboat just will not go there.

Yes, on many days, teaching is like sailing, and the teacher changes course in midstream as he or she determines a better direction and a more feasible destination. Still on most days, teaching is a lot like:

▶ **Being a sculptor.** Sculptors are fond of saying that they don't "make" their art, they uncover what is already hidden in the material. Similarly, teachers uncover the ideas emerging in the minds of their students.

▶ **Climbing a hill.** Jo explains that teaching is a constant process of ascending an incline. Every once in a while you stop, take a breather, make sure everyone is comfortable, and then you start climbing again.

As I talked with young teachers, yet another metaphor emerged. Chris imagined teaching as a *thing:* a toolbox. He believed that teaching was about providing students with the tools to be lifelong learners: a set of skills and dispositions to help them enjoy learning on their own. Have *you* ever thought of teaching that way?

When I asked him what would be in this toolbox, Chris gave several examples: the ability to do research, use the Internet to find reliable sources, access data from the library, and make decisions about the information one finds. These indeed are valuable skills. Another skill Chris hopes for is that students will learn to interact with their peers—talking about their ideas and putting information into their own words.

The following Writing and Reflection activity will help you come up with your own metaphor for teaching. There is an important reason for exploring your metaphor: It gets you started on developing your personal philosophy of teaching statement. A **philosophy of teaching statement** outlines your ideas about teaching and learning, sets out techniques for being reflective about your practice, and describes how you will teach. It may also include your goals for yourself as a teacher. If you decide to pursue a career in teaching, your philosophy of teaching statement will form an important part of your teaching portfolio, as you'll see at the end of this chapter.

philosophy of teaching statement A description of your ideas about teaching and learning and how those ideas will influence your practice. It should be based on your knowledge of educational research.

Your teaching philosophy should be backed up by evidence from research. For many decades, educators have studied how people learn and have compiled evidence about successful teaching strategies. As you read this book, you will encounter some of that research; the more you learn about it, the better prepared you will be to state your own teaching philosophy. But it is never too early to begin this kind of thinking. Take a few moments to do the following activity.

WRITING and REFLECTION

Find Your Favorite Metaphor

Think of one or more metaphors for teaching. If you need some leads, visit the website "Metaphorically Speaking" from the Annenberg Media Learner Interactive Workshops (http://www.learner.org/channel/workshops/nextmove/metaphor/). You may come up with several metaphors that seem apt. As you choose metaphors, explain why you think each of them is a good description of teaching.

Hold on to these metaphors and return to them as you continue to consider teaching as a career. The best teachers usually have a strong sense of who they are and of what attributes of their personality are expressed in their teaching role. Your metaphors for teaching will probably change many times as your professional education continues, but they all will help build your personal philosophy of teaching.

Some teachers stand out in our memories because they were innovative and creative.

WRITING and REFLECTION

Your Favorite Teacher

Describe a teacher or teachers who had a profound influence on you. These questions will help focus your thinking:

- What was the nature of this teacher's influence? How did he or she change your thinking about yourself, school, or learning?
- In what grade did you have your favorite teacher? What was special about that year?
- Construct a list of attributes the teacher had. What particular qualities made him or her your favorite?
- How can this memory serve you as you explore the field of education?

A Favorite Teacher

Is there a teacher who stands out in your mind as having influenced you in a positive way? How did this teacher make an impact, and what was the result of her or his connection to you? Answering these questions is another good way to reflect on your educational past. Here's my own recollection:

I had a seventh-grade teacher, Mrs. Fisher, in JHS 117 in the Bronx, New York. I was, as you read in the early part of my educational autobiography, a really young seventh grader; I was eleven years old. Mrs. Fisher was my science teacher, and in those days, much of general science revolved around learning how the internal combustion engine of an automobile worked.

I really liked science, but I was shy, young, and from a poor neighborhood. I had little self-confidence. Mrs. Fisher took me aside one day and said,

"You know, Janice, you are very good in science; you should go to the Bronx High School of Science." This high school is one of the specialized schools in New York City requiring that students pass an entrance exam. Mrs. Fisher brought the application and helped me complete it.

I passed the exam, was admitted, and began attending the Bronx High School of Science at the age of twelve. My experience at this distinctive high school changed the course of my future education and career. Years later, I went back to visit Mrs. Fisher and thanked her for having taken an interest in me. I determined that one day I, too, would make a difference for students.

What Qualities Are Needed to Be a Good Teacher?

After completing the reflection on your favorite teacher, you may want to compare the attributes of this teacher with a list of some general qualities of good teachers. Read the sidebar "Attributes of Good Teachers." How do these qualities match up with the ones you just listed for your favorite teacher?

goodness of fit   A term generally used in descriptive statistics to describe the match between a theory and a particular set of observations; in this book, it means the match between a teacher candidate's personal attributes, values, and dispositions and the demands of teaching.

In making this comparison, think about whether you possess these qualities. As we proceed in this text, we will often return to the concept of **goodness of fit**. This term refers to how good a match there may be between your qualities as a person and the demands of teaching.

Don't be discouraged if you don't find a perfect match between yourself and the ideal characteristics listed in the sidebar. You are always growing and changing as a person, and you certainly may develop qualities you don't have now. You may also recognize areas of weakness that you want to work on.

VIDEO CASE

Advice from the Field

When you actually find yourself teaching in a classroom, will you be able to put all your knowledge—everything you've learned and planned and hoped for—into practice? The answer may depend not only on your dedication to the job, but also on fundamental qualities of your personality and character.

Watch the short video "Becoming a Teacher: Voices and Advice from the Field," available in the HM Video Cases section of the student website. In this video you will meet several teachers, some new to the field and some who have been teaching for years. Pay special attention to their ideas about what is needed to be a successful teacher. After the main video, view the bonus video called "Essential Qualities That Teachers Must Possess."

As you view these video cases:

- Jot down the various qualities the teachers mention as essential. How many of them overlap with the attributes listed in the sidebar "Attributes of Good Teachers"? How many are new?

- Begin thinking about whether you yourself have these qualities. Are there some you don't have currently but could work to develop? The following Writing and Reflection activity offers some further questions to consider.

WRITING and REFLECTION

Thinking About Your Strengths and Weaknesses

When you begin to think about a career in teaching, one of your tasks is to analyze your own strengths and weaknesses. Take a few minutes to do that now.

- What are some of your strengths as a person? as a student? as a future professional?
- How do these strengths serve you as you look forward to becoming a teacher?
- What are some of your weaknesses? Will they be problematic if you choose teaching as a profession?

One teacher described himself as compassionate, considerate, helpful, and determined. How would those qualities affect his role as a teacher? His weakness, he said, was his need for perfection. How would that affect his career choice?

Attributes of Good Teachers

A good teacher needs to be:

Knowledgeable. A sound understanding of the fields of teaching and learning and your own content area is essential. Students know when you are knowledgeable.

Alive! A good teacher has a healthy balance of warmth and strictness and an enthusiasm for being with young people, evidenced by her or his ability to share students' interests. Enthusiasm does not mean boisterousness but teaching requires a *presence* in the classroom that is both personal and professional.

Articulate. A good teacher has good communication skills and expresses herself or himself clearly. This includes having a sense of humor.

Innovative. A good teacher constantly seeks new and exciting ways to interest and engage students in the topic at hand. Novel methods and techniques leave a lasting impression on students and demonstrate that the teacher has taken the time to prepare for the lesson.

Patient. A good teacher is not easily overwhelmed or distressed and has the capacity to be a good listener. There are times you will need to repeat lessons or remind students of the classroom rules, not to mention the occasions when you will have to help students overcome their doubts and fears. These times require patience and stamina.

Committed. A good teacher is dedicated to furthering the learning experiences of young people and fostering a love of learning. A certain amount of selflessness is required.

Able to find joy in teaching. A good teacher derives a great deal of pleasure from teaching. You cannot make learning a joy for students unless you love the teaching profession and find joy in it.

LOOKING FORWARD: THE PROFESSION

N ow it's time to begin looking forward. What is special about teaching as a career? What do you need to know about this profession you are considering?

An Essential Profession

Every child needs—and deserves—dedicated, outstanding teachers who know their subject matter, are effectively trained, and know how to teach to high standards and to make learning come alive for students.

— President Bill Clinton, 1998

In a U.S. Department of Education report, *Promising Practices: New Ways to Improve Teacher Quality* (1998), teaching is referred to as "the essential profession, the one that makes all other professions possible." What do you think is meant by that?

The report further declares that

> *without well-qualified, caring, and committed teachers, neither improved curricula and assessments, nor safe schools—not even the highest standards in the world— will ensure that our children are prepared for the challenges and opportunities in America's third century. More than ever before in our history, education will make the difference between those who will prosper in the new economy and those who will be left behind. Teaching is the profession that is shaping this education and therefore America's future—molding the skills of our future workforce and laying the foundation for good citizenship and full participation in community and civic life.*

Hence, it is you, the teacher, who will bring to life the ideals, the attitudes, the learning experiences, and the joy that are possible in a classroom. The curriculum, which we will explore later in this text, is a lifeless document in itself. It is the classroom teacher who enables the curriculum materials to have personal meaning for each learner.

Does this sound like a tall order? It is! Because what teachers know and are able to do has such a profound impact on the future of education, you need to understand how it is that people come to learn. You need to spend time in classrooms to become familiar with different contexts for teaching and the diversity of students in our schools.

We would not expect that a future doctor would be able to examine a patient or perform surgery with just a few months' training. Yet we often expect students to become teachers after a period of only several weeks of in-classroom training. This is why many teacher education programs (and yours may be one) require early field experiences during which you observe and participate in the life of a classroom at the grade level you are thinking about teaching.

People have debated for years whether teaching is technically a *profession* in the same sense that, say, medicine and law are. On one hand, teachers do not get paid as much as doctors and lawyers, nor is teachers' training as extensive. Also, to many people, the knowledge that teachers possess about teaching and learning does not seem as complicated and technical as what a neurologist knows about the nervous system. On the other hand, teaching does share a number of attributes with other professions. Look at the questionnaire "Is Teaching a Profession?" and decide for yourself how many of the statements are true about teaching.

A Code of Ethics

National Education Association (NEA) The largest organization of teachers and other education professionals, headquartered in Washington, DC.

The **National Education Association (NEA)** is the nation's largest professional employee organization. It has 2.8 million members who work in educational settings from preschools through universities. With affiliate organizations in all fifty states and in more than 14,000 U.S. communities, the NEA provides local services such as workshops and collective bargaining for teachers. On a state and national scale, it acts as a lobbying group for educational issues.

Later chapters will have much more to say about professional organizations for teachers. I bring up the NEA here because, as far back as 1929, NEA members adopted a code of ethics for the profession. The most recent revision of the code is shown in Table 1.1. Look at the first paragraph of the code's preamble. Let's take this statement apart and see what it means.

▶ **"Believing in the worth and dignity of each human being."**
This phrase refers to a teacher's commitment to all of her or his students.

Is Teaching a Profession?

If the following were the criteria for a line of work to be judged a "profession," would teaching make the cut?

1. Professions provide essential services to the individual and society.

    ☐ **True of Teaching**   ☐ **Not True of Teaching**

2. A profession is concerned with a specific area of need in society.

    ☐ **True of Teaching**   ☐ **Not True of Teaching**

3. A profession has a unique body of content knowledge and skills.

    ☐ **True of Teaching**   ☐ **Not True of Teaching**

4. Professional decisions are based on valid knowledge, principles, and theories.

    ☐ **True of Teaching**   ☐ **Not True of Teaching**

5. Professional associations control the admissions, standards, and licensing for the profession.

    ☐ **True of Teaching**   ☐ **Not True of Teaching**

6. Practitioners have to meet performance standards to become part of and continue in the profession.

    ☐ **True of Teaching**   ☐ **Not True of Teaching**

7. Preparation for the profession requires a formal program, usually in a college or university professional school.

    ☐ **True of Teaching**   ☐ **Not True of Teaching**

8. The public has a high level of trust and confidence in the profession and in its members.

    ☐ **True of Teaching**   ☐ **Not True of Teaching**

9. Individual practitioners are characterized by a strong and lifelong commitment to the social good.

    ☐ **True of Teaching**   ☐ **Not True of Teaching**

10. The individual practitioner has a relatively large amount of freedom from direct or public job supervision.

    ☐ **True of Teaching**   ☐ **Not True of Teaching**

WRITING and REFLECTION

Teaching as a Profession

The question of teaching's status as a profession dates back at least as far as Myron Lieberman's 1956 book *Education as a Profession*. Using Lieberman as a source, Robin Ann Martin (2000) discusses several attributes of a profession. Let's focus on three key ones:

- A profession offers a unique, definite, and essential service.
- A profession places an emphasis on intellectual techniques in performing its service.
- A profession requires a long period of specialized training.

Think about these attributes and explain how they apply to teaching:

- In teaching, what is the unique and essential "service"?
- For teaching, what do you think the "intellectual techniques" are?
- Though Lieberman and Martin say a profession requires a long period of specialized training, just how much time is needed to prepare teachers is a hotly debated topic. What do *you* think?

TABLE 1.1   Code of Ethics of the Education Profession

Preamble

The educator, believing in the worth and dignity of each human being, recognizes the supreme importance of the pursuit of truth, devotion to excellence, and the nurture of the democratic principles. Essential to these goals is the protection of freedom to learn and to teach and the guarantee of equal educational opportunity for all. The educator accepts the responsibility to adhere to the highest ethical standards.

The educator recognizes the magnitude of the responsibility inherent in the teaching process. The desire for the respect and confidence of one's colleagues, of students, of parents, and of the members of the community provides the incentive to attain and maintain the highest possible degree of ethical conduct. The Code of Ethics of the Education Profession indicates the aspiration of all educators and provides standards by which to judge conduct.

The remedies specified by the NEA and/or its affiliates for the violation of any provision of this Code shall be exclusive and no such provision shall be enforceable in any form other than the one specifically designated by the NEA or its affiliates.

PRINCIPLE I: Commitment to the Student

The educator strives to help each student realize his or her potential as a worthy and effective member of society. The educator therefore works to stimulate the spirit of inquiry, the acquisition of knowledge and understanding, and the thoughtful formulation of worthy goals.

In fulfillment of the obligation to the student, the educator—

1. Shall not unreasonably restrain the student from independent action in the pursuit of learning.
2. Shall not unreasonably deny the student's access to varying points of view.

continued

3. Shall not deliberately suppress or distort subject matter relevant to the student's progress.

4. Shall make reasonable effort to protect the student from conditions harmful to learning or to health and safety.

5. Shall not intentionally expose the student to embarrassment or disparagement.

6. Shall not on the basis of race, color, creed, sex, national origin, marital status, political or religious beliefs, family, social or cultural background, or sexual orientation, unfairly—

   a. Exclude any student from participation in any program

   b. Deny benefits to any student

   c. Grant any advantage to any student

7. Shall not use professional relationships with students for private advantage.

8. Shall not disclose information about students obtained in the course of professional service unless disclosure serves a compelling professional purpose or is required by law.

PRINCIPLE II: Commitment to the Profession

The education profession is vested by the public with a trust and responsibility requiring the highest ideals of professional service.

In the belief that the quality of the services of the education profession directly influences the nation and its citizens, the educator shall exert every effort to raise professional standards, to pro-

mote a climate that encourages the exercise of professional judgment, to achieve conditions that attract persons worthy of the trust to careers in education, and to assist in preventing the practice of the profession by unqualified persons.

In fulfillment of the obligation to the profession, the educator—

1. Shall not in an application for a professional position deliberately make a false statement or fail to disclose a material fact related to competency and qualifications.

2. Shall not misrepresent his/her professional qualifications.

3. Shall not assist any entry into the profession of a person known to be unqualified in respect to character, education, or other relevant attribute.

4. Shall not knowingly make a false statement concerning the qualifications of a candidate for a professional position.

5. Shall not assist a noneducator in the unauthorized practice of teaching.

6. Shall not disclose information about colleagues obtained in the course of professional service unless disclosure serves a compelling professional purpose or is required by law.

7. Shall not knowingly make false or malicious statements about a colleague.

8. Shall not accept any gratuity, gift, or favor that might impair or appear to influence professional decisions or action.

Adopted by the National Education Association Representative Assembly in 1975.

A teacher's authentic desire to make a connection with *every* student and to consider each individual's needs is the essence of good teaching. For some further thoughts about the meaning of this clause in the NEA code of ethics, see the sidebar "Honoring Diversity."

▶ **"Recognizes the supreme importance of the pursuit of truth, devotion to excellence."** This phrase assumes different meanings in the twenty-first century than it did in the past. We live in the context of an information technology revolution, a time when the amount of information available to us and to our students is exploding. Hence, our commitment might better be stated as recognizing the importance of *multiple* truths and *multiple expressions* of excellence.

▶ **"Nurture of the democratic principles."** This phrase reminds us to honor individual expression, capitalize on special student interests, and expand students' abilities to explore and critique multiple ideas and values.

▶ **"Responsibility to adhere to the highest ethical standards."** Figure 1.2 shows statistics indicating that the public considers teachers to be highly trustworthy. This is very positive as far as it goes. But your ethical responsibility as a teacher goes beyond telling the truth. Your responsibility is to place the needs of students at the center of your work and to give them priority over your own needs. Hence, your constant question is, "What is in the best interests of my students?" This is important as you consider a career in teaching. Many people enter the profession and discover that it is difficult to be as generous of spirit as the profession demands. That would not make you a bad person, but you need to consider how it relates to the "goodness of fit" between this profession and your personal attributes.

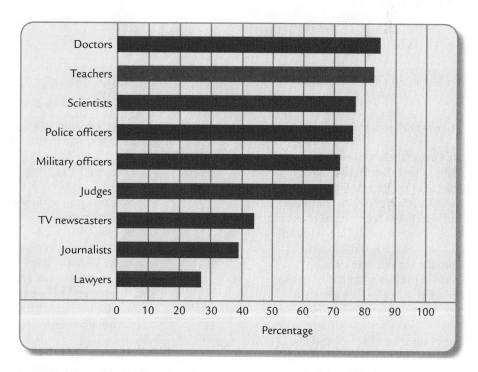

FIGURE 1.2

Public Trust in Various Professions

Pollsters asked, "Would you generally trust each of the following types of people to tell the truth, or not?" The bars show the percentage of respondents who said they would trust each type of person.

Source: Statistics from *The Harris Poll* #61, August 8, 2006; based on telephone interviews of 1,002 U.S. adults, July 10–16, 2006.

Teaching requires a desire to help others by creating meaningful learning experiences.

Honoring Diversity

Read the following poem by Lew Gardner.

My Great Uncle's Horse
My mother's uncle had a horse.
The best time of a deadly relatives' Sunday
was to walk with him to the stable
and watch him feed the quiet animal,
to give it sugar from my own hand
and jump back away
from the big warm tongue,
to smell the hay and manure, to see
the white horse in the next stall,
with tail and mane like yellow silk.

If my mother and I ran into him
as he and the horse were making their rounds,
buying up the wonderful junk
they heaped and hauled in the wagon,
he'd lift me up to the seat
and let me hold the reins and yell "Giddy-up!"

In the spring of 4th grade,
one afternoon of silent division
we heard a clanking and looked outside.
My great-uncle! I could tell them all
how I had held those reins!

"My Great Uncle's Horse" reproduced by permission of Lewis Gardner.

But everyone laughed at the hunched old man,
the obsolete wagon and horse,
the silly, clattering junk.
I did not tell them.

Reading this poem, do you see that students, coming as they do from diverse backgrounds and knowledge bases, may be hidden to you unless you create "spaces" for them in the classroom? Respect for diversity must become part of every classroom teacher's agenda, regardless of grade level and subject matter and regardless of whether the teacher looks and sounds like his or her students.

Honoring diversity means accepting that we are all products of our own culture, our own biases, and our own beliefs. You must constantly ask, "Who are my students? What are their lives like? What are their stories? . . . and knowing these things, how can I help them learn?" This is all part of respecting the learner and ultimately respecting ourselves as learners. Chapter 5 addresses the issue of the wide diversity of students in today's schools and its implications for teaching and learning. If we think of diversity as an opportunity, we will grow from the challenge and become better teachers.

An Organized Profession

American Federation of Teachers   An international union, affiliated with the American Federation of Labor and Congress of Industrial Organizations, representing teachers and other school personnel as well as many college faculty and staff members, health-care workers, and public employees.

Overall, teaching is a highly organized profession. In addition to the NEA, the **American Federation of Teachers (AFT)**, created in 1916 and affiliated with the American labor movement, boasts more than 1.3 million members. Both the NEA and the AFT provide legal services and collective bargaining representation as well as a network of support for teachers, including professional development resources for your growth as a teacher. These large groups also wield a great deal of political influence on behalf of educators and schools.

When you enter the teaching profession, you may decide to join one or both of these organizations. We will visit them again in this book's final chapter, but it is not too early to think about becoming a member.

A National Board

National Board for Professional Teaching Standards (NBPTS)   A nonprofit organization that aims to advance the quality of teaching by developing professional standards for teachers.

In 1987 the **National Board for Professional Teaching Standards (NBPTS)** was created to set forth a vision for what accomplished teachers might "look like." These principles were developed in response to the report *A Nation Prepared: Teachers for the 21st Century* (Carnegie Forum on Education and the Economy, 1986). Besides being an advocacy organization, the National Board sets standards for what accomplished teachers should know and be able to do and offers a national system to certify teachers who meet these standards.

The Board intends this certification to be a symbol of professional teaching excellence; it is entirely voluntary (National Board for Professional Teaching Standards, 2002). State licensing systems for teachers set entry-level standards, but National Board certification establishes more advanced standards. Out of approximately 2.9 million newly hired teachers in the United States, only about 50,000 will have achieved National Board certification.

Later in this book, we will visit the standards set forth by this National Board as well as some of the components of the certification test. For now, I

Am I a Professional If I Join a Union?

Although teachers cannot be forced to join a union, both the NEA and the AFT have local affiliates all over the country, and there are more than 2.5 million people who belong to one or both of them. Because they are labor unions (the NEA became a union in the 1960s, and the AFT was founded as a union in 1912), many individuals challenge the professionalism of teaching, arguing that other professions do not have unions. In fact, many people see the unions' ability to call strikes as a potential means of victimizing the very people teachers serve, students.

Union advocates respond that teachers, unlike members of some of the wealthier professions, need collective bargaining to secure better working conditions and higher salaries. In negotiating contracts on teachers' behalf, unions have certainly helped teachers gain power over their workload expectations, class sizes, pay scales, and benefits.

The unions' role in school reform also provokes debate. As powerful national organizations, the NEA and AFT can lobby for educational improvements. But some people argue that teacher contracts can be so specifically written that it becomes difficult to enact meaningful school reform—that is, the contracts merely serve to maintain the current system.

You will need to form your own opinion about the role of teacher unions and their effect on teachers' professionalism. When you start your first teaching job, you should inquire about the local union affiliation of your school or district and the union's connection to the NEA, AFT, or both. Teachers' unions can provide tremendous support to the new teacher as well as resources for his or her professional development.

hope you will see the Board and its work as yet another indication of the professionalism of the field of teaching and the exciting prospects you have in entering the field.

More Than a Profession

We have been talking about teaching as a profession, but is that all it is? Carl Jung, the noted Swiss psychiatrist, said:

> *An understanding heart is everything in a teacher. One looks back with apprecia-tion at the brilliant teachers, but with gratitude to those who touched our human feeling. The curriculum is so much necessary raw material, but warmth is the vital element for the growing plant and for the soul of the child (McGuire, 1954, paragraph 249).*

So much is said about the skills and knowledge that are needed for the profession of teaching. The unspoken requirement, however, has to do with your dispositions, your own ability to understand your students and to connect with them in ways that help them to become better learners.

More than in most other professions, your personality and your belief in yourself shine through the techniques and strategies you employ. Your authentic self—that part of you that wants to make a contribution to the social good—is evident in the way you address the students, in your smile, in your level of preparedness for class, in the questions you ask, and in the respect you demonstrate for students as individuals.

As you work with this text, be sure to explore your innermost hopes and dreams, and keep asking yourself, "Is teaching really for me?"

LEARNING PROJECT

Gaining Entry to the Profession: Developing a Timeline

Becoming a teacher requires at least a bachelor's degree, usually related to the field in which you plan to teach. Beyond that, however, requirements for be-coming a teacher vary from state to state. In most states, some form of advanced training is also needed. If you are seriously considering teaching as a career, it is important to find out exactly what you need in order to become a teacher in the state in which you want to work.

As a start, visit this webpage provided by the AFT: http://www.aft.org/teachers/jft/becoming.htm. As you do your research, look for answers to the following questions:

- In your state, can you begin teaching with just a bachelor's degree?

- Do you have to take and pass tests to gain a teaching certificate or license? How many tests? In which areas of study?

- Are you required to obtain a master's degree? If so, what disciplines are accepted as leading to certification?

continued

- Some states require attendance at special seminars in addition to completing the requirements for your academic degree. Is that the case in your state? If so, what seminars are required?

Finally, develop a timeline for your professional preparation. What courses will you take and when will you take them? When will you complete your requirements? Make a checklist of tests, seminars, courses, and application dates for gaining entry into teaching in your state.

THE WORKPLACE: SCHOOL CLIMATE AND SCHOOL CULTURE

The day-to-day workings of a school influence how you enact your philosophy of teaching. Schools are constantly in flux, depending on student enrollment, collaboration among colleagues, pressures from the local community, and the vision of the school leader.

As you think about applying a teacher's professional commitments and values in a particular school setting, there are two terms you should know: **school climate** and **school culture**. These phrases refer to "the sum of the values, cultures, safety practices, and organizational structures within a school that cause it to function and react in particular ways" (McBrien & Brandt, 1997, p. 87).

Often the two terms are used interchangeably, but some educators make a distinction between them: *school climate* referring to the way students experi-

school climate and **school culture** The values, cultures, practices, and organization of a school.

Some classroom climates can be experienced even by a casual observer.

ence the school and *school culture* meaning the way teachers and administrators interact and collaborate.

Still other educators think about *school climate* as the general social atmosphere or environment in a school. This is my preferred way of using the term. The social environment in this sense includes the relationships among students, between students and teachers, among teachers themselves, and between teachers and administrators. Students experience their environment differently depending on the rules and protocols set up by school administrators and teachers. *School climate* also includes the orderliness of the environment, the clarity of the rules, and the strictness of the teachers in enforcing the rules (Moos, 1979, p. 96).

Think back to your educational autobiography. According to the definition of *school climate* as the general social atmosphere, how would you describe the climate of your elementary school, middle school, and high school? A school climate may be described as *nurturing, authoritarian,* or somewhere in between. For example, I experienced my high school as nurturing *and* strict, caring *and* rigorous. We can also ask whether a school has a *healthy* climate, one in which students are made aware of expectations for their behavior toward one another and their teachers. In your own elementary school, middle school, and high school, was the student body diverse in terms of ethnicity, race, and social class, and if so, was there evidence of prejudice or racism? How was that expressed? What did school officials do to make students feel like valued members of the educational community?

Can You Feel the School Climate?

Frequently, you can tell if a school's climate is nurturing by the feeling you get in the halls—if the principal and other administrators are readily visible, and if teachers smile and greet students by name. In such a school, students are treated as individuals.

At the other extreme, in a school with an authoritarian climate the halls are very quiet, there are strict "no talking" rules, doors are closed tight, and there is a feeling of tension in the air.

Teaching practices, student and teacher diversity, and the relationships among administrators, teachers, parents, and students all contribute to school climate.

Although no single, universally accepted definition of *school culture* has been established, there is general agreement that it involves deep patterns of values, beliefs, and traditions formed over the course of the school's history (Deal & Peterson, 1990). A school culture may have, for instance, a reputation for being very academic. My high school did. The culture of my high school could be described as academically driven, college preparatory, nonathletic, and very cerebral. We were thought of as "geeks" because we attended this very serious-minded high school whose culture had been forged since its inception. Other high schools in my area had a culture that was more social, athletic, and active in the community, though also academic.

A school's culture is evident in its shared values, heroes, rituals, ceremonies, stories, and cultural networks. For example, if a school's leaders believe that motivation and academic achievement are a definitive part of the school's culture, they communicate and celebrate those values in as many ways as possible. In my high school, students were made to feel proud of the academic productivity of their classmates. Achievement was rewarded in the school newspaper and in organized assemblies.

When you think back to the ways in which the schools you attended functioned, how would you describe the school culture of your elementary, middle, and high schools? What did the schools stand for? How was that communicated?

CONCLUDING THOUGHTS

Although teaching is an important and essential profession, ideas about it are often oversimplified. Our memories of our teachers are sometimes selective and misleading. However, the interpersonal nature of teaching demands that those interested in the profession take account of their own attributes and dispositions, their personal school experiences, and their future goals for themselves as teachers.

It is never too soon to consider yourself a reflective practitioner. The Chapter Challenge will help you imagine yourself as a classroom teacher.

JOIN THE DISCUSSION

Visit the student website and locate the Edublog for Chapter 1. Begin your Edublog by responding to the following questions:

➡ Did anything about your personal educational autobiography surprise you? Share it here with other beginning education students.

➡ For you, what is the most intimidating aspect of becoming a teacher?

CHAPTER CHALLENGE

Observing a School: Culture and Climate

Now that you have developed a feeling for your own educational history and taken a peek at the profession of teaching, it is time to visit a school of your choice and shadow one or more teachers for part of the school day.

Before you visit, you will need to secure permission from the principal or head of school. Schedule your visit on a day that is convenient for the teacher or teachers you will be shadowing. It is probably best to visit more than one teacher's class. Be sure to select a school that houses the grade or grades you are interested in teaching. Dress appropriately and professionally: no jeans or T-shirts; no very short skirts; no recreational or casual attire.

During your visit you will notice many things, but pay particular attention to the school's culture and climate. Of course, it is difficult to learn the culture of a school from a brief visit, but the checklist in Figure 1.3 can help. Use this checklist before, during, and after your visit to focus your thinking about the school.

Write an essay about this experience. Include responses to the above questions as well as your observations of the teacher(s). If you were a student, would you be happy in this school and in these classrooms? Can you imagine yourself in any of the classes you observed? What was most surprising for you?

Finally, and most important, how do you feel about pursuing a teaching career as a result of this visit? What, if anything, has changed for you?

FROM THE COLLEGE CLASSROOM TO YOUR OWN CLASSROOM

Beginning Your Professional Portfolio

A professional portfolio is a collection of documents and other artifacts that represent your personal philosophy and your research and accomplishments. For

teaching portfolio A collection of documents and other items that represent your work as a teacher, your goals, and your philosophy.

teachers, this kind of collection is known as a **teaching portfolio**. It is your own personal brag book, a place where you document multiple aspects of your teaching ability.

You should create a teaching portfolio for at least two reasons:

- The act of compiling a portfolio asks you to reflect on your abilities and accomplishments as they relate to becoming a teacher. As you explore the field of education and your place in it, your portfolio can become a valuable resource for developing your thinking.

- Once compiled, your portfolio is an excellent tool when you seek a teaching position. Many school districts expect you to present a portfolio when you apply for a job. The NBPTS uses portfolios in its certification process, as do many states.

A portfolio can be presented in a traditional physical case, like an artist's portfolio, or it can be electronic, stored on your computer and submitted to a potential employer via any convenient electronic medium.

Eventually your portfolio will include items like lesson plans, samples of students' work, and videos of your teaching. Right now, as we conclude Chapter 1, you

---

School Climate

☐ When you enter the school, how does it feel?

☐ How does it smell?

☐ Are you happy to be there?

☐ Does the school feel welcoming? In what way(s)?

☐ Do you have to sign in?

☐ Are there security guards?

☐ Do you have to be buzzed into the building?

☐ Are there students in the halls? teachers? parents?

☐ Is there evidence of student and faculty diversity? What do you notice?

☐ Do you get a sense of the social class(es) of the students? What evidence do you have for this?

☐ Do you have the chance to meet the principal or another administrator?

☐ Do you see students' work hanging in the halls? What types of work do you see?

☐ Is there a mission statement for the school? Are any quotes posted?

☐ Are you able to spend any time in the faculty or staff room? If so, what are the conversations like?

The Classroom(s)

☐ What grade(s) are you visiting?

☐ What is it like to be in the classroom? How does it feel?

☐ In what types of activities does the teacher engage the students?

☐ Do you notice any interruptions during teaching time? If so, what is the nature of the interruptions?

FIGURE 1.3
School Visit Checklist

may want to begin your portfolio with your educational autobiography, a list of your strengths and weaknesses, and notes about your experience as you undertook the Chapter Challenge of visiting a school and describing its climate.

As you continue reading this text, you will add more documentation to your collection. By the end of your course, you will be able to decide which documents are most important for you to keep in the portfolio.

RESOURCES FOR FURTHER EXPLORATION

American Federation of Teachers http://www.aft.org/   The AFT's website has news and reports about issues of professional interest, resources for both practicing and aspiring teachers, and a legislative action center.

Sylvia Ashton-Warner, *Teacher* (New York: Simon & Schuster, 1963).   This is a moving story of a New Zealand teacher's extraordinary work teaching Maori children; it exposes one teacher's thinking processes about placing her students' needs at the center of her practice.

National Board for Professional Teaching Standards, *The Five Core Propositions* http://www.nbpts.org/the_standards/the_five_core_propositions   Five basic principles, each with several subordinate points, that form the foundation of the National Board's mission.

National Education Association http://www.nea.org/   In addition to the code of ethics reproduced in this chapter, the NEA's website has a wide variety of useful resources and information for teachers.

Parker Palmer, *The courage to teach: Exploring the inner landscape of a teacher's life* (San Francisco: Jossey-Bass, 1998).   This exciting book addresses the ways in which teachers' lives, values, personal beliefs, and goals shape their practice.

Donald Schön, *Educating the reflective practitioner* http://educ.queensu.ca/~ar/schon87.htm   An article encapsulating some of Schön's thinking about reflective practice in teaching.

Teaching Stories

FOCUSING QUESTIONS

▶ Why do you think most teachers enter the field?

▶ What do you think might be the most exciting aspects of teaching?

▶ What might be the most difficult challenges for teachers?

▶ Who do you suppose offers teachers the most support?

This chapter gives you a glimpse at the ways teachers from grades K–12 make their decisions to enter the field and what they experience as the most exciting and challenging aspects of teaching. Their stories are designed to help you explore what Parker Palmer (1998) calls the "inner landscape of a teacher's life."

Being a teacher requires an emotional and intellectual engagement. By this I mean that, in a typical school day, teachers can experience excitement and frustration, pleasure and angst, great leaps of joy as well as sadness. How ready you are to navigate these emotions—while at the same time staying focused on your goals for the day—is something only you can know. The stories in this chapter may remind you of yourself or of a teacher you may have had. But before we hear the stories of several actual teachers, let's take a brief look at who our teachers are, statistically speaking.

WHO ARE OUR TEACHERS?

Figure 2.1 presents various statistics about U.S. public school teachers that give us a glimpse of the teaching workforce.

The majority of public school teachers in the U.S. workforce are over forty years old, with the average age in the mid-forties. About 90 percent are white, and despite all the social changes in the past generation, that percentage has stayed approximately the same (Snyder, Tan, & Hoffman, 2006; National Education Association, 2003). What do you think of these statistics? Given the increasing diversity of U.S. students (see Chapter 5), many educators be-

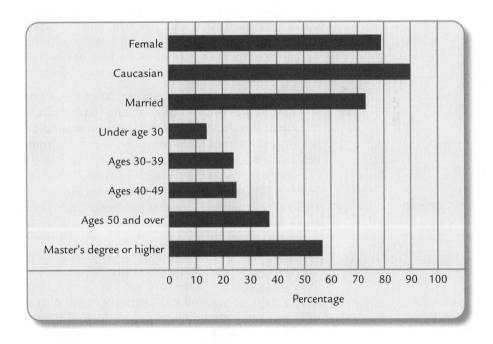

FIGURE 2.1

U.S. Public School Teachers, by the Numbers

Source: Data from Snyder, T. D., Tan, A. G., & Hoffman, C. M. (2006). *Digest of Education Statistics 2005* (NCES 2006-030), U.S. Department of Education, National Center for Education Statistics, Washington, DC: U.S. Government Printing Office; National Education Association (2003), *Status of the American Public School Teacher 2000–2001,* Washington, DC: Author.

lieve that American schools have an urgent need for young teachers from varied ethnic backgrounds.

One figure that has changed in recent decades is the proportion of males in the teaching force. It has *declined* from 31 percent in 1961 to about 21 percent today (Snyder, Tan, & Hoffman, 2006). Some researchers suspect that the declining number of male teachers has had negative consequences for students and for the profession, as we will see in some of the stories later in this chapter.

DECIDING TO BECOME A TEACHER

In my entire life as a student, I remember only twice being given the opportunity to come up with my own ideas, a fact I consider typical and terrible.

— Eleanor Duckworth (1991)

Over the years, I have asked teachers from all grades and all backgrounds to talk about themselves and their attitudes toward the profession. Let's begin with what some of them said about their reasons for becoming teachers.

TEACHING STORIES
HOW DID YOU DECIDE TO BECOME A TEACHER?

JESSICA   Jessica is a sixth-grade English teacher in a suburban school district on the East Coast. Her first love was dance, and she still teaches dance at a private dance school after regular school hours. She is also a regular choreographer of school plays. She has been teaching for three years. This is how she answers the question about deciding to become a teacher.

I had always wanted to be a teacher. When I was growing up, I loved to play school with the children I babysat, and I would give the neighborhood children free dance lessons. After college, I decided that I didn't want to be a dancer full time, so I turned to my other love—English. From the very first day of my very first graduate class in education, I knew I had chosen the right career.

I attribute my interest in teaching to several things: (1) a lifelong love of learning; (2) I had always loved going to school, even when I wasn't the best student (I did better in school as I got older); and (3) the fact that my mother is also a teacher, and I grew up watching her grade papers and plan her instruction.

AMANDA   Amanda is a third-grade teacher in the northwest corner of the country. When I first entered her classroom, I was struck by how quiet it was. She apologized profusely for the silence, remarking that the students were usually noisier and more actively engaged in groups, but this time they were just finishing independent reading. She promised that soon I would see the *real* class! So often we think of good classes as silent, but learning often happens in social exchanges with others, as we will see in later chapters. When asked why she entered teaching, Amanda said:

Teaching has always been my calling. Ever since my first week of kindergarten, I knew that teaching would be my chosen path. That first day, I came home exclaiming to my mom, "I want to be a teacher just like Mrs. Seguin!" I spent the rest of my elementary school days playing teacher with my sister, my friends, and even my stuffed animals when no one was available. I had grade books, lesson plans, and homemade worksheets, and I made signs for my door that indicated my room was now "Miss Riggs's 1st grade class."

Even though I have always been drawn to the profession, it wasn't until my first year of college when I was taking an education course that I began to fully understand why I wanted to be a part of education. My dad was never what one might call a reader or a writer. The only book that I saw him read was the Bible, and I remember him asking me for help in spelling different words starting in second grade. Yet it was my dad who showed me the responsibility of being an educator. I was talking with him about a literacy lesson that I needed to prepare for class. I shared the many techniques that I had learned and how I was going to have the kids first participate in a hands-on activity and then draw the knowledge out from the activity. My father changed my outlook on education forever when he said, "I would have learned how to read and write if my teachers had taught like you." It was then that I realized I wanted to be a teacher to reach those kids who couldn't learn through traditional teaching methods. I wanted to find a way so that every student "clicked" with literacy and gained the skills to make his or her life one of continuous learning.

JAMES   James is in his fourth year teaching middle school in a midwestern suburban area. He was always involved in sports until he broke his leg in high school and could no longer play football. Many months of physical therapy and then working as an aide to a physical therapist helped him think about those who struggle with adversity.

The person who shaped my goal to become a teacher entered my life in the fourth grade. My fourth-grade teacher, a six-foot-four-inch man who was my first male teacher, was also my inspiration to become a learner. I wanted to be just like him, and I saw in him a genuine enthusiasm for teaching and for learning. I began to love school.

As fate would have it, I had him again in the sixth grade and then as the assistant principal of the high school I attended. He had taken me under his wing, and I was always grateful for his guidance. He is currently the assistant superintendent of the school district I attended. I attribute my desire to teach to his model of what that can look like.

My teaching style is derived from a patient mother and a very interested and involved father. Both positive and negative experiences in school shaped my thinking about how to speak sensitively to students. I enjoy the rapport I have with my students more than any other aspect of my teaching life. I attend their sporting events and try to encourage them in the ways that I was encouraged as a youngster. I really enjoy watching the students succeed and helping them overcome personal adversity.

I am very aware of the importance of being a positive role model for kids; they do not always have that at home.

PEARL   Pearl is a veteran elementary school teacher of twenty-five years in an urban area of New York City. She has been both the mathematics

continued

specialist and the social studies specialist in her school as well as a mentor to countless student teachers. Her intellectual love is mathematics, and she is also committed to issues of social justice. She relentlessly celebrates women and people of color.

My parents were immigrants; my mom was born in Russia in 1905. In her little corner of the world, education for girls was not thought of as a necessity. She was never sent to school. When she came to the United States, she worked in sweatshops on the Lower East Side and cooked and cleaned for people to support herself. She cherished the educational opportunities that were afforded to children in this country—"God bless America," she would say. She especially cherished the opportunity afforded me, her daughter, to go to school. In my mother's eyes teaching was ranked as the most highly important and respected profession.

My paternal grandfather was a theologian and a sought-after teacher in his town, known for his knowledge of religious texts. My father thought the world of him and respected him for his knowledge and ability to communicate ideas. So the teaching profession was well respected in my home.

Then there came Miss Rochford, my sixth-grade teacher. I loved Miss Rochford. She made math fun; she introduced us to musicals; she taught us how to write scripts and then we produced our own play; she showed us slides of her trips to Europe; and she exposed us to poetry. She introduced me to Mark Twain, Shakespeare, and Robert Frost. Miss Geraldine Rochford opened doors for me to a world beyond East New York, Brooklyn. I wanted to do the things she did. I wanted to travel, enjoy the arts, and share the wonders of learning with kids like myself. That is why I never wanted to leave the public school system. She was one of the people who made me into a lifelong learner. As early as the sixth grade, I knew that I wanted to teach.

JANE   Jane has been teaching eighth-grade mathematics in an urban area on the East Coast for five years. Her decision to enter teaching came after her own children had gone off to college. The wife of a minister, she had taught religious classes in her church, and she wanted to choose a career she thought she would be good at. Jane is now a mentor teacher and very well thought of by students and faculty.

I feel like I entered teaching for all the wrong reasons. I wanted retirement benefits and good working hours, and I wanted to use skills that I believed I had developed as a mother and a minister's wife. I thought you should enter teaching because you had always wanted to be a teacher, but for me, it was really an afterthought that came later in life—that is why I think of it as being for the wrong reasons.

When I self-assessed, though, I recognized that I was a good listener and genuinely excited about math. I had majored in math in college, and I thought that was a good start. I also have a lot of self-knowledge, so I am able to recover from my mistakes. I have the ability to say "I'm sorry" when I have made a mistake, and I have a lot of respect for young people.

I knew when I entered my first education course that I had made the right decision since teaching would ensure that I was a lifelong learner. I am very focused on my own and my students' education. Teaching for me is like water walking; if you keep your eyes on the goals, you will not sink.

ALEX   Alex is in his tenth year teaching history in a northeastern suburb. He was a perpetual student. He loved learning and loved the study of history, and he decided to get his PhD in history at the ripe old age of twenty-seven.

I entered teaching when my university advisor told me I was ready to defend my dissertation. A perennial student, I realized I needed a job! My advisor told me of a local college that needed instructors in history, and I started my teaching career with no formal education training.

Once in the classroom, I immediately realized that I really liked making complex concepts understandable to students. I was excited about teaching. I knew that I had a lot to learn, so I entered a program to earn a teaching certificate. I wound up becoming a secondary school history teacher. It gave me the opportunity to connect current events with the history curriculum and to join the faculty of a high-pressured, academically oriented school where we work hard and feel a lot of pressure to meet a high level of quality teaching.

I love it. I could not imagine becoming a high school teacher when I was younger, and now cannot imagine doing anything else with my life's work.

THE TEACHING IDEAS BEHIND THESE STORIES

Over the years, I have asked many teachers from all grades and all backgrounds to talk about why they decided to enter teaching. Often teachers say, "I love children" or "I love kids." These answers echo the findings of formal studies. Figure 2.2, for instance, summarizes the most recent responses from a broad-based survey that has been conducted periodically for many years. In this survey, the proportion of teachers who say they decided to teach because of a "desire to work with young people" has consistently been over 65 percent, and it reached 73 percent in the latest results (National Education Association, 2003).

Yet the most successful teachers I know—like the ones featured in this chapter—respond somewhat differently. They typically talk about how they "loved learning." That is not to say they do not also love children, but teaching is a very complex activity. In the words of Jackie Grennon Brooks (2002), from whom we will hear more in a later chapter,

> Common thinking is that teaching is simple. But teaching isn't simple. It's a highly sophisticated intellectual activity that requires, among other things, a centered presence in the classroom, good negotiation skills, understandings of pedagogy and psychology that inform one another, and sensitivity to sociological factors in learning.

When beginning education students talk about entering teaching because they love kids, I learn from talking with them that they have been babysitters and camp counselors and that they have enjoyed these responsibilities. That is a fine start, but these informal experiences with children or adolescents are different from the more structured experiences found in classrooms and the demands of teaching. At this point in your reading, you may have already visited one or more classrooms and observed teaching in action, so you are aware of the vast differences between the formal and informal settings in which we interact with youngsters.

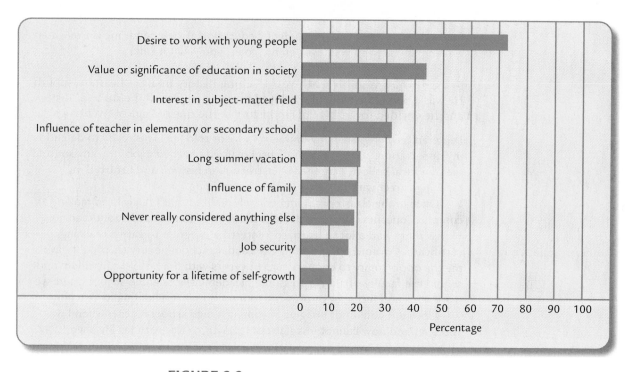

FIGURE 2.2
Reasons for Originally Deciding to Become a Teacher
This graph shows responses by almost 1,500 public school teachers who were asked, "What are the three main reasons you originally decided to become a teacher?"
Source: Data from National Education Association, *Status of the American Public School Teacher 2000–2001* (Washington, DC: Author, 2003), Table 49, p. 68, and Appendix B, pp. 357–358.

"I Like the Hours"

Sam wakes up one morning and says, "I want to be a teacher." When asked why, Sam answers, "I like the hours."

This is an uninspiring reason, and it's misguided as well. Did you know that teachers work much longer than the traditional 9:00 to 3:00 daily? Look at the following data the National Education Association (2006a) gathered from its teacher members:

Twenty-first century teachers:

- Spend an average of fifty hours per week on all teaching duties.
- Teach an average of twenty-one pupils in a class at the elementary level, twenty-eight pupils per class at the secondary level.
- Spend an average of $443 per year of their own money to meet the needs of their students.
- Enter the teaching profession to help shape the next generation.

In Figure 2.2, notice that only 21 percent of teachers cited the "long summer vacation" as a principal reason for entering teaching. If that is your best reason for teaching, then the profession is probably not a good fit for you.

Another study, conducted with thirty-six secondary teacher candidates (Younger et al., 2004), found that their reasons for wanting to teach often stemmed from their own positive experiences in school. That matches what we heard from Jessica, Amanda, Pearl, and James in this chapter as well as from Laura and Sharyn in Chapter 1. Notice especially what James said about the inspiration provided by a male teacher. Recent research, though controversial, suggests that male teachers may have a significant positive impact on the achievement of male students (Dee, 2005, 2006).

Another major reason cited in the study of secondary teacher candidates was prior experiences as a high school tutor or peer teacher. Like Jane, some were motivated to teach because of positive experiences in informal teaching settings. And like Jane, some had early religious training that affected their desire to serve others and teach.

What about Alex's story? His description of what we might call "falling into" teaching may resonate with you if you have just lately considered the idea of becoming a teacher. Not everyone who enters the field has had a life-long calling to teach. Yet life as a teacher becomes fulfilling when there is a good match between the person and the demands of the profession. This is what I referred to as *goodness of fit* in Chapter 1. For Alex, teaching offered an

Teachers are important role models for their students.

WRITING and REFLECTION

How Do You Feel About Teaching and Learning?

- Was there a time when you felt you were intellectually engaged to a high degree? Was that a result of an in-school or out-of-school experience?

- Can you describe a "learning experience"? What was the subject or topic? What did you learn? Why does it stand out in your memory? Who functioned as your teacher in this experience?

- What is the major appeal of teaching for you?

- Which of the foregoing stories, if any, resonates best with your story?

- Why is it important to understand your own thinking about this career?

excellent fit with his personality and his desire to share knowledge and foster his students' success.

In the study of secondary teacher candidates, one pervasive idea was that teaching involved commitment to "more than a job." For some, it was a "calling" to make a difference in students' lives and contribute to society (Younger et al., 2004). These notions should give you plenty to mull over as you reflect on the following questions.

EXCITEMENT AND CHALLENGES IN TEACHING

Every September, every teacher proceeds into foreign territories.
— Maxine Hong Kingston, 1986

When teachers are asked about the most exciting aspects of their work, invariably their answers relate to student learning. In this section we explore what some teachers say really excites them about their work, and then we examine some difficult challenges.

TEACHING STORIES
WHAT ARE THE MOST EXCITING ASPECTS OF YOUR WORK?

AMANDA

Contrary to popular belief, I do not find it exciting when my students get 100 percent on their tests. It is the process that is exciting—the look on a student's face when he or she finally gets it, watching a student move from confusion to understanding, fielding a question you did not expect and do not know the answer to. It has been my greatest joy to see that student who struggled so much in an area work hard and become successful.

There are many times when I struggle with presenting difficult material so that all students can grasp the "big idea" of the lesson. I can go through four or five activities in my room, and sometimes there are a handful of kids who just cannot make sense of the material. Finally finding a way to reach those kids—now *that* is exciting.

The classroom is a complex roller-coaster ride in the dark; you never know what will happen next. From scheduling changes to student needs, environmental factors (try teaching about fractions in 90-degree weather!), and even your own moods, no plan is ever left in its original state. An educator must roll with the needs of his or her students, and those needs are everchanging, every day. I find that exciting.

JESSICA

The most exciting aspects of being a teacher are the possibilities that come with each new day. Of course, school brings a set routine, so that I know what to expect in terms of scheduling and planning most of the time. On the other hand, I teach young adolescents, and they truly are different people every day. Watching them change and grow from the first day of sixth grade to the last day of sixth grade is like watching a transformation right in front of your own eyes, and it is very exciting and challenging.

Though it seems like a cliché, the most rewarding part of the day is the "aha" that I see on students' faces when they understand something they didn't understand before. These moments happen daily, but some are bigger than others. The best times are when students uncover new meaning for themselves, because their reactions are so much bigger.

JANE

To me, meeting a brand new group of students each year is the most exciting part of teaching. Because every group of students is unique, I am challenged

A wide variety of classroom activities is necessary to engage students' minds and bodies.

continued

to address my teaching strategies in an entirely new way than I did the previous year. It is like starting a new job every year. There is so much to learn from each new set of students. It is so exciting and challenging to understand each class's strengths and to tailor your teaching strategies to help them be all they can be in mathematics.

PEARL

Teaching has made me a lifelong learner. In order to keep things new and interesting, I am always reading, studying, and thinking of new ways to teach a concept.

As a classroom teacher, I have the opportunity to wear many hats: storyteller, dream weaver, mathematician, scientist, poet, author, playwright, producer, director, choreographer, historian, and social worker. You name it, a classroom teacher has to play each of those roles, and sometimes all in one day. I get so immersed in my work very often that I forget to go to the bathroom until it is time to go home.

Teaching makes you aware of process—for instance, coming up with a rubric for writing a good biographical report and teaching kids how to take notes, organize their materials, and pay attention to the editing and presentation. It is exciting, too, to put together the "problems of the day" for my gifted math class, work on some of the challenging ones myself, and feel my brain churning. There's the frustration in trying to solve a problem and then that satisfaction when you "get it" and then, to top it all off, the opportunity to go through all those feelings again with the students—knowing how to coax them when they are ready to give up and being able to shed some light on a stumbling block so that they can feel that joy of accomplishment when they "get it" themselves.

THE TEACHING IDEAS BEHIND THESE STORIES

■ For these teachers, the idea of meeting new students every year and, in Jessica's case, feeling like there are new students almost daily, is a stimulating aspect of being a teacher. Each day is different, requiring a sharp and attentive adult presence in the classroom. These teachers enjoy the challenge.

■ Amanda notes that the process of teaching is more exciting than the outcomes. Like Amanda, many teachers try different approaches to content material to make sure they reach the various types of learners in their classes.

■ Pearl, Amanda, and Jessica talk about the excitement of reaching the children and recognizing that they "got it" as it related to new knowledge construction. Pearl gets so immersed in the activities with her students that she forgets to take a bathroom break.

■ These teachers, typical of most, work actively on their teaching preparations and constantly challenge themselves to come up with novel ways to engage students in their own learning. They remind me that "to teach is to learn." Pearl illustrates this idea when she explains her own process in solving a difficult mathematics problem as a learner and then going through it again as a teacher.

WRITING and REFLECTION

The Most Exciting Moments

- Why do you think Amanda is not very excited when her students all get 100 percent on a test?
- Jessica states that the best times are when students "uncover new meaning" on their own. What do you think she means?
- Do you remember an "aha" moment as a student? Can you describe it?
- What do *you* anticipate will be the most exciting part of teaching?

TEACHING STORIES
WHAT ARE THE MOST DIFFICULT CHALLENGES FOR TEACHERS?

AMANDA

I find that the most difficult challenge is staying focused on my purpose. I am not in the room to raise test scores, to be a child's best friend, or to follow every theory I learned in school. I am there to help students go beyond their potential and gain skill sets needed for a successful, learning life. Many distractions are found in the school environment—often created by those who are well meaning. Stick to what you know is best for your students despite what others around you might think.

This year my room was across the hall from a teacher whom you might refer to as burned out. Every morning she arrived at the same time as the kids. By the time the children began to enter her room, my classroom was busy with morning learning activities. At least four times a week, our classroom was disrupted with her rants of "Why do Mrs. P's students get right to work and you are out here talking! I am tired of my class not being ready for the day!" These outbursts not only damaged her class but mine as well.

A good educator knows how to instruct students about expected behaviors and not shout about bad behaviors. No matter how frustrated, disappointed, or exhausted I become, I am here as a teacher and a learner, and learning happens mostly by my example—a good example or a poor one.

JAMES

If I had one wish about the profession, it would be that it was higher paying—that, for me, is the greatest downside of teaching. To raise a family, I must work a second job, and that is often a burden.

THE TEACHING IDEAS BEHIND THESE STORIES

- By a "learning life," Amanda refers to a desire to know more and to have the skills to acquire new knowledge when the need and desire arises. Amanda herself has a "learning life," and by example and through practice, she engages her students in what it means to be a learner.

- Earlier in this chapter, the quote from Jackie Grennon Brooks introduced the concept of the teacher as a "centered presence" in the classroom. Amanda's understanding of her role in the classroom and her goals for her students helps her establish this centered presence. She is prepared and capable and has high expectations for her students.

- When Amanda says that learning happens by example, she means that she models to her students—demonstrates through her own behavior—what it looks like to be a learner. She learns about the content areas she teaches through her own research; she learns about her students through the interactions she has with them; and she learns about herself as she strives to refine her practice and to discover what works best for her students.

teacher burnout The condition of teachers who have lost their motivation, desire, sense of purpose, and energy for being effective practitioners.

- Amanda's teacher neighbor appears to be "burned out," meaning that she has lost the motivation to excel in her work and is no longer able to be an effective teacher. Teacher burnout, a reaction to prolonged high stress, commonly results either in withdrawing and caring less, or in working harder, often mechanically, to the point of exhaustion (Farber, 1991). As in any other field, burnout can have serious consequences for the health and happiness of teachers, their students, and the families with which they interact. There are many causes of teacher burnout, the most common being working conditions that are unsupportive and stressful interactions with parents and students.

- New teachers may experience burnout when the work of teaching requires a different set of skills from what they had anticipated. Teachers who have been in the profession longer and have not taken advantage of opportunities to renew their skills through formal and informal professional development may also experience burnout.

- Table 2.1 lists some symptoms of burnout and steps you can take to combat it. One of the most important protections from burnout is being reflective. Remember what Chapter 1 said about being a reflective practitioner. Often a teaching journal—an idea we will discuss later in this chapter—is helpful in this respect. Writing in the journal is a way to monitor your work and your emotional availability for the tasks ahead of you.

- In a remark not unconnected to the idea of burnout, James complains about teachers' salaries. Many educators believe that the feminization of the teaching profession—the decline in the percentage of male teachers—has helped reduce the pressure for better pay and benefits.

Yet teachers' salaries have, in fact, risen considerably over the past few decades. Elementary and secondary school teachers now make an average of about $49,000 per year. Starting salaries for new teachers average about $32,000 per year (National Education Association, 2006a,b). These figures do vary considerably from district to district and state to state, but more than half of U.S. public school teachers report being satisfied with their salaries (Snyder, Tan, & Hoffman, 2006, Table 72).

JESSICA

One of the most difficult challenges for teachers stems from paperwork! I had no idea going into the profession how much paperwork there is to manage. I assumed that lesson plans, student handouts, and student work would be all the paperwork I'd come into contact with. In addition to those items, there are constant requests for information from the office, the nurse, the psychologists, special education teachers, parents, administrators, and even people in the community that must be dealt with promptly and regularly. The amount of paperwork required for a classroom observation, or a field trip, or a school play, can be mind boggling.

Another major difficulty I didn't anticipate was dealing with parents. Although the majority of parents are on your side because both you and they are trying to achieve the goal of education for their children, there are parents who hold you responsible for things that are out of your control, who will blame you when a child fails even when you've done everything in your power to help the child. When parents see you as the adversary and not as their partner, it can be very painful.

A third difficulty is navigating relationships with in-building and district administration. When you are not tenured, you are advised to walk on eggshells, so to speak. This can create problems when you need assistance or when you disagree with a district policy or with the way a parent issue is being

continued

TABLE 2.1   Recognizing and Dealing with Teacher Burnout

Signs of Burnout	What Teachers Can Do	What Schools Can Do
Your expectations for becoming a teacher and your experience are in conflict.	Consult with other teachers about your feelings and such matters as curriculum planning.	Create networks for new teachers and set up regular group meetings.
You do not feel like going to work.	Maintain a teacher journal in which you record your experiences and feelings.	Provide adequate resources and facilities to support teachers.
You have difficulty concentrating and feel inadequate in your role as a teacher.	Join new-teacher networks at your school or at the district level. Share your experiences, and keep journaling.	Provide clear job descriptions and expectations for new teachers.
You feel overwhelmed by the paperwork and the workload.	Find a mentor or seek the one to whom you have been assigned. Talk about your feelings!	Establish and maintain open communications between the school administration and the teachers.
You withdraw from your colleagues or enter into conflicts with them.	You may be emotionally exhausted. Find a professional to talk with.	Allow for and encourage professional development activities that help new teachers find mentors and become part of networks.

Source: Adapted from Kyraciou (2001) and Wood & McCarthy (2002).

handled. Some administrators are more supportive than others, and it is important to know whom you can go to for help or guidance when you need it.

These things shouldn't dissuade people from becoming teachers. You learn how to deal with them effectively and appropriately soon after you begin teaching. They represent difficulties I didn't know about before I entered teaching, but the benefits of this career far outweigh the challenges in the workplace.

Completing paperwork is one of many responsibilities for a teacher.

THE TEACHING IDEAS BEHIND THIS STORY

■ Jessica's comment about paperwork excluded some other areas in the daily life of the classroom where paper needs to be managed. These include attendance reports, progress reports for each student, and evidence of student work. Elementary school teachers often keep work folders for each student, while in the middle and upper grades student work is often handled using computer software programs. Science teachers usually have lengthy lab reports to evaluate, while language arts and social studies teachers evaluate analytical essays, term reports, book responses, and creative writing. In a 2001 survey, paperwork combined with "heavy workload," "extra responsibilities," and "meetings" to form the category that teachers said hurt them the most in their efforts to provide the best service in their teaching positions (National Education Association, 2003, Table 55).

■ Dealing with parents is part of a teacher's responsibility. We serve the children, but they are not ours. Jessica is conflicted about her communication with parents. Of course, parents are affected by what happens at their child's school and in their child's classroom. Communication between teachers and parents is important, and it is fostered through school practices that we will explore later in this text. Not only can parents influence decisions made about their child's education at school, but they can also contribute to the governance of the school though a parent teacher association (PTA) or similar group.

■ It is always a good idea to reach out to parents and invite them to become part of your classroom community as helpers and contributors. In some school districts, parents are a frequent presence in classrooms. In other communities, parents are not available as often because of work responsibilities, but it is still important to invite them to contribute whenever possible.

■ Many people experience schools as "little villages," where the principal is the mayor and other individuals have varying amounts of importance or privilege. In all jobs, the politics of the environment can affect each of the workers. It is a good idea to learn about the expectations and norms of the school environment in which you will be working. You may already have had jobs where the politics of the environment affected your work. Although workplace politics may annoy or sometimes discourage you, keep in mind how important it is that schools function as learning communities where all the professionals share a core set of common goals.

JANE

For me, the greatest challenge is having to implement the eighth-grade mathematics curriculum at a pace determined by the date of the standardized test. Instead of asking myself, "Should I linger longer on this topic since the students seem to need more time?" I speed along because I know there is so much to cover for the test.

This is a frustration in my teaching career since I am interested in how the students can make their math learning personal and relate it to their lives. This may take time, but it is important, and it always leaves me behind my colleagues in getting the curriculum done. I know that "teaching for the test" does not help the students make personal meaning for themselves.

THE TEACHING IDEAS BEHIND THIS STORY

■ Jane feels she is constantly challenged to "cover" math topics rapidly to prepare students for the standardized test they must take. With today's emphasis on standards—and on the tests that determine whether students meet those standards—many teachers feel similar pressures.

■ Yet a large number of educators, like Jane, believe that merely "covering" curriculum is the wrong approach. It leads to a shallow form of learning. Instead, these educators say, we need to *uncover* the curriculum by engaging students in exploring ideas and developing a deeper, more meaningful understanding. Remember what Jessica said earlier in the chapter: "The best times are when students uncover new meaning for themselves."

PEARL

As a new elementary school teacher, I found one of the most difficult challenges was engaging with the curriculum. I had to familiarize myself with a lot of topics that I was not sure about. I spent hours each weekend planning for the upcoming weeks by going to the library, finding the right books or the right motivational poems, leafing through magazines for the right pictures to support a lesson or illustrate a word, making visual aids, buying materials, and marking papers. As I became more experienced, I continued to plan on the weekends, but it became more a source of pleasure than of anxiety.

THE TEACHING IDEAS BEHIND THIS STORY

- Pearl describes a major challenge for teachers at all levels: the preparation required to engage students in meaningful learning experiences. Many people, like Sam earlier in this chapter, are unaware of the number of hours beyond the school day that teachers spend in preparation.

- The term *curriculum,* as we will explore later in this text, refers to a plan of studies that includes the ways in which the instructional content is organized and presented at each grade level. Even if you have studied a subject area extensively, you may need to deepen your knowledge of certain topics in the curriculum. Teachers can never be overprepared.

- Students know when a teacher is prepared for the school day. It is evident in the materials the teacher has assembled and the activities the teacher is ready to implement. It contributes to Brooks's "centered presence" in the classroom.

WRITING and REFLECTION

The Challenges of Teaching

- As we will see in a later chapter, meaningful learning takes time. So how do teachers reconcile the pressure to "get through" the curriculum with meaningful learning? Do you have any ideas?

- Jane believes that, given time, her students can find "personal meaning" in the math topics she teaches. Can you think of a math topic that has personal meaning for you?

- Do you remember a teacher who made connections between topics in the curriculum and your life outside of school? How did those connections help you find personal meaning in the subject you were studying?

- How do you feel about the number of hours you will need to spend preparing to teach effective lessons? Will that time be a burden or what Pearl calls a "source of pleasure"?

- Knowing that you will have to deal with lots of paperwork, and possibly with unhelpful administrators and difficult parents, do you still believe firmly that the rewards of teaching outweigh the troubles? If so, why?

VIDEO CASE

Surprises of the First Year

You can find another story about the challenges and excitement of teaching in the HM Video Cases section of the student website. Watch the video "The First Year of Teaching: One Colleague's Story," in which Will Starner talks about his initial year in a classroom. "I've had a lot of situations that I really didn't know would come up," he says. In the bonus video, "Mr. Starner Reflects on the First Year of Teaching," he mentions that he had "all these different theories running through my head," and it felt overwhelming to select the best approach for the context.

- What are the main challenges Will Starner identifies?

- What ways did he find to cope with these difficulties?

- What is *your* impression of Mr. Starner? Discuss your reaction to his candid description of his first year of teaching. What attributes do you think make him potentially a very successful teacher?

TEACHING AND VISION

Research has found that all teachers carry in their head a vision of what they want to be as a teacher (Hammerness, 2006). That is, all teachers have their own sense of what a classroom should "look like" and how it should function. Yet these visions of teaching are as variable as are the individuals who choose to teach.

Our beliefs and images concerning teaching are often difficult to enact; there is often a disconnect between what we imagine and what we can practice. For example, when I walked into a second-grade classroom early one morning, the teacher had the children in the center of the room and was engaging them in hand motions and movement routines to a popular rock song blasting from her boom box. The children were loving it! When it was all done, Ms. Outerbridge said, "OK, girls and boys, we are now ready to work!" When I asked her about this activity, she said that (like Jessica, whom you met earlier) she had been a dancer, and her life in dance had taught her that releasing the energy in our bodies was an important way to stimulate the thinking in our minds. She worried that when her students came to class, they were too docile, having learned by grade 2 how to "be quiet." She wanted them to be active in their bodies so they could be active thinkers about the topics of study.

"How wonderful!" I thought. I knew, however, that try as I might, I could never get myself or my youngsters to learn and then enact this intricate movement routine. I do not have that set of skills. I admired Ms. Outerbridge's vision but could not enact it. It is in this way that *who we are* comes to bear upon *what we do* with children and how we engage them in learning.

Throughout your teacher education, you will be asked about your personal vision. It is a goal of teacher preparation programs that you develop a personal educational philosophy informed not only by the scholars and research you have learned about in your program but also by your own beliefs, metaphors, personal vision, and values. The combination of self-knowledge and scholarly knowledge will assist you in developing your own philosophy. You started to do this in Chapter 1 when you described your personal metaphor for teaching.

The mantra that "we teach who we are" permeates this text. Ms. Outerbridge is a dancer; that background has served her as a learner, and she shares her passion with her second graders. Similarly, in the story that follows, my life as a scientist found its way into a third-grade classroom not long ago.

Every week, I was visiting a local elementary school classroom and exploring different topics in physical science with them. One weekend prior to a visit, I was in another state celebrating the seventh birthday of my first granddaughter. Her mother, my daughter, discovered that the batteries in her digital camera appeared to be dead and asked if I had batteries in my camera that she could use. We made the switch; I handed the "dead" batteries to my husband, and my daughter was able to use her camera.

Some hours later, when we arrived back home after the party, my husband noticed that his right pocket was very warm—uncomfortably so. "What do you have in there?" I asked. "Just the batteries and my loose change," he replied. Delighted, I shrieked, "The batteries are not dead, and there is an electrical circuit in your pocket. It is generating all this heat!"

It is a family joke now that my thrill at finding "science in our daily life" seemed to overcome my empathy for his discomfort. However, I recognized that this was another opportunity to make the topic relevant to the third graders who were making circuits for an electricity unit. I told the story to them that week and stopped short of an explanation. "If my husband had the dead batteries and some loose coins in his pocket, why would it be warm? Can you draw a picture of the contents of his pocket?" Eagerly students drew coins and batteries and understood that the metal coins acted as a wire and conducted electricity.

This story illustrates how our personal lives meet our professional lives in the classroom. Your students will learn a lot about you, and you will learn about them.

The stories we tell students about our lives and experiences outside of school are one small part of what may be considered the **hidden curriculum**: what students learn as they participate in the act of going to school, being part of a classroom community, and relating to their peers and their teachers. The phrase *hidden curriculum* was coined by the sociologist Phillip Jackson (1968), who described ways in which schools become arenas for socialization and transmit messages to students about how to be in the world. Long before that, educational philosopher John Dewey (1916) explored the hidden curriculum in schools as he examined the social values inherent in the experience of school. Hence, the hidden curriculum includes how we interact with students, how we enact the rules of the school culture, and how we communicate our expectations for student achievement and demeanor and our own passion for teaching and learning.

By telling the batteries-in-the-pocket story to young students, I gave them a glimpse of what it is like to be an adult with a curious, scientific mind

hidden curriculum What students learn, beyond the academic content, from the experience of attending school.

(and a family eager to make fun of my propensities). Perhaps the story helped some students in the class feel that science is fun, interesting, and relevant to daily life—and that certainly matches my vision of what I want to do in the classroom.

Every day, through countless similar incidents, teachers contribute positively to their school's hidden curriculum. However, teachers can also affect the hidden curriculum in negative ways. If you and other teachers are bored and cynical, for instance, you convey those feelings to your students. No matter how dutifully you slog through the subject matter, students will sense that it doesn't interest you, and they will absorb that message.

SUPPORT FOR TEACHERS

When asked who gave them the most support in their teaching careers, Jessica, Amanda, and Jane all agreed that their colleagues were the strongest source of support. This matches the findings of a survey in which teachers rated cooperative and competent colleagues and mentors as the factor that helped them most in their teaching positions (National Education Association, 2003, Table 55). But the teachers I interviewed mentioned other sources of support as well. As you read the following stories, think about how these teachers interacted with their colleagues and others in the school and the community.

TEACHING STORIES
WHO PROVIDES THE MOST SUPPORT IN YOUR WORK AS A TEACHER?

AMANDA

I have found it supportive to listen to fellow teachers and the administrators, students, parents, and community members. You can learn a vast amount from conversations with others. In a crowded teachers' room, I am the one who is content to sit alone and listen in on others' conversations. As you listen, you can learn so much about the expectations, the culture, the negatives, and the positives, and ways to connect to the school and community in which you teach. I find keeping a teaching journal and jotting down what I discover about the students and the school to be very helpful. I try to make entries at least two or three times a week.

I jumped into school activities when I started and found that others who like to get involved were very supportive. My first year, I became a member of the Staff Development Committee, and I have never regretted that decision. I did not speak up as often as the other members, but I did listen and learn a great deal about the district that I was making my home. I am on various districtwide committees and involved in many school-based activities that have given me insight for understanding the context in which I teach.

Working with colleagues to plan curriculum and class projects and to bounce ideas off of one another is an important part of the teaching profession.

WRITING and REFLECTION

Learning from Others

- As Amanda discovered, being a good listener is often a good way to learn about a school's environment. How are your listening skills?

- As you enter teaching, what do you think are the benefits of jumping right into school committees as Amanda did?

- Have you ever kept a personal journal or diary? Have you thought about keeping a teaching journal like Amanda's as you begin your career—writing down your reflections on the day or the week?

JESSICA

In the first years of teaching, much of my support came from my fellow teachers in the building. They were the ones who knew the answers to difficult situations and who would give encouraging words. I have found that to be true even now that I am a few years into the profession. Other educators can give you ideas, advice, and a sympathetic ear when needed, and this help can come from other new teachers as well as from veterans in the profession.

I also accessed my education professors, keeping in contact with them through e-mail. I was assigned a mentor at school, and this teacher was very helpful in acclimating me to the routines and procedures that I needed to understand at the very beginning. As time went on, she became an important role model for me.

THE TEACHING IDEAS BEHIND THIS STORY

- Many schools and school districts are adopting mentor teacher programs. Mentor teachers are specially trained to work with new teachers and support them in understanding the school culture, the curriculum, and the resources available to them as professionals.

- You may want to ask if there is a mentor program where you begin teaching. Mentoring has been a trend over the last ten years as the teaching profession has recognized the need to develop a special transition period during which new teachers acclimate to their profession. This period as a whole is often called *induction*.

- Good mentors have a broad range of skills and are able to help new teachers apply their professional knowledge in the classroom. They are generally master teachers who have demonstrated a love of teaching and learning and are eager to share their experiences with others.

JANE

I gain the most support for my teaching from my colleagues, the school and district committees on which I serve, communication with my peers and my students, and my church.

Each Sunday, I teach a course in religion to adults, and I am struck by how much the enrollment in this class has increased over time. I employ teaching strategies similar to those I use with my eighth-grade mathematics students. I am organized and prepared, I respect their ideas and who they are, and I try to forge goals with them for our work together.

I also look inward for support. I evaluate my goals and reflect on my week in school and ask myself, "What should I change?"

THE TEACHING IDEAS BEHIND THIS STORY

- Once again, teacher peers play an important role in supporting the work we do in schools. This kind of support, coupled with Jane's capacity to articulate her teaching strategies, has contributed to her success.

- Notice the list of attributes that Jane uses to describe herself: organized, prepared, respectful of students, establishing goals with students collaboratively. The ability to be clear about your expectations for yourself and your students is key to having a "centered presence" in the classroom.

- As Jane gains support from peers and weekend teaching experiences, she continues to reflect upon her work and ask herself key questions about her goals and practices. As mentioned earlier, this is the best prevention against burnout.

WRITING and REFLECTION

Begin an Education Journal

Start now to keep a professional journal for yourself. This will be like Amanda's teaching journal, in which she jotted down "what I was discovering about the students and the school." Since you are beginning this activity while you are still a student, we will use the general term *education journal*.

If you have not had a lot of practice journaling, starting a reflective education journal can be daunting. You may want to begin by inserting the writing activities from Chapter 1. So, your journal can begin with the drawing of yourself as a teacher, a memory of your favorite teacher, your educational autobiography, and your experience visiting a school. You may also want to include your list of strengths and weaknesses as it relates to entering the field of education.

Being a reflective teacher is a dominant theme we will return to again and again in this text. Reflective teachers take careful note of how their teaching practice is going and modify their methods accordingly. Since you are just embarking on teaching, your reflective education journal should include how you are experiencing being an education student and what you are learning about teaching and about yourself.

Teacher education programs vary, but here are some general questions to reflect on as you begin your education journal:

- How are you experiencing the introductory education course you are taking?

- What are you discovering about the teaching profession that you did not know previously? Are there any surprises?

- If you are already in a field placement,[1] what is it like being in a school?

  - How would you describe how you feel while in the classroom?

  - What is your relationship like with your peers and with your cooperating teacher?

  - How are you experiencing the students?

  - At this point, how do you feel about a career in teaching?

  - What philosophies about teaching, if any, are you developing?

Reminder: As you write your education journal, remember that you are on your own journey of growth and change and that the journal is a good recordkeeping device for this process. Things you feel uneasy about now can become much less problematic in the future.

---

[1] *Field placement* refers to the way education students are given experience in an actual school, in the grade level of their choice. Usually they start out as observers in the classroom, and then become participant-observers, and finally begin teaching lessons themselves. Depending on the program, education students may spend as few as 10 hours a week in field placement at the beginning of the program, but by the end they will typically be spending a full school day, five days a week, in an apprenticeship, also called an internship, with one or more classroom teachers. This stage is commonly referred to as *student teaching*, and in many states it is required to obtain teacher certification.

TEACHERS AS LIFELONG LEARNERS

We are living in a rapidly changing global environment in which youngsters' and adults' lives are drastically different than they were even ten years ago. We are all experiencing the information technology revolution, which has brought access to huge volumes of information—a degree of accessibility never before experienced in human history. This explosion of information, along with the continuous connectedness that we all feel as a result of Internet and cell-phone technology, has changed the pace and progress of our daily lives.

In this ever-changing society, the activities that interest students today are necessarily different from the activities that interested you even just a few years ago. Teachers must constantly adapt and improve their skills as they respond to the recurring question: What works best in the classroom for these particular students at this period of time in our history?

Many educators today like to think of schools as **learning communities**, a term that emphasizes interaction and collaboration in the learning process. The phrase also conveys the idea that all the participants—teachers, students, and administrators—are always learning. Hence, teachers see their own continuing education as part of their work and their lives.

It is, in fact, the need for this ongoing **professional development**, as it is called, that makes many people excited about entering teaching. These individuals understand that to teach is to learn. To improve our practice requires targeted efforts at our own growth as teachers and learners. Professional development can take many forms. We will learn more about the many ways teachers extend their education in a later chapter. For now, let's hear from Amanda, Jessica, and Jane to learn how they are doing it.

learning community   A classroom, a cluster of classes, or a school organized so as to promote active engagement in learning, collaboration between teachers and students, and a sense that everyone involved shares the experience of being a learner.

professional development Teachers' lifelong effort to improve their skills and professional knowledge. Although professional development often includes advanced courses and workshops, much of your progress will depend on your own continued reading, reflection, and analysis.

TEACHING STORIES
HOW DO YOU CONTINUE YOUR PROFESSIONAL DEVELOPMENT?

AMANDA
Alongside life experience, continued schooling is needed. As I conclude my master's degree, I look toward my doctoral studies. Formal education presents important new ideas, strategies, and problems and helps your mind grow in the same way that you want your students' minds to grow.

In addition, formal education puts you in contact with professors who are experts in their fields and classmates who have a wealth of knowledge to add to your own. Being in a formal learning environment gives you a community of peers with whom you can bounce around ideas. Formal education is a wonderful resource for a teacher.

JESSICA
I continue my professional development in several ways. The school district in which I teach requires that all teachers take at least fifteen hours of in-district professional development every school year, but I tend to take much more

continued

than that because the presenters are fellow teachers or administrators who are well versed in whatever they're teaching. This year we furthered our understanding of differentiated instruction, understanding by design, and brain-based learning.

In addition to attending these courses, I participate in several other professional development opportunities, such as conferences on literacy, standards-based testing, and so on. I belong to a number of professional organizations that offer regular publications to read and conference opportunities. I have begun presenting at conferences; this requires a new level of understanding and preparation for me, so this furthers my professional knowledge.

JANE

I am always looking for conferences, classes, workshops, and news that can help me stay on top of the topics at hand. My master's program was extremely helpful in that I learned how to implement project-based learning activities in my class and how to do research on my own practice. It was very exciting, and each year I look for other opportunities to expand what I can offer myself and the students.

THE TEACHING IDEAS BEHIND THESE STORIES

Teachers are expected to keep up with the latest developments in education. In many schools and districts, in fact, teachers are offered financial incentives to continue their education though professional education courses at a college or university or through professional development courses, often referred to as *in-service* courses, offered by the school district itself. These incentives are based on how many formal graduate school credits or professional development credits a teacher earns in a given academic year. Obviously you'll appreciate the chance to earn a higher salary.

Yet, as the stories you've just read illustrate, there are other incentives for taking professional development courses. Amanda, Jessica, and Jane think of themselves as lifelong learners. They take a genuine interest in expanding their minds and improving their teaching. In fact, all of them have reached the stage of doing their own research or making their own presentations—contributing to the sum of knowledge in the field.

Professional organizations can play a major role in expanding your development as a teacher. The National Education Association (NEA) and The American Federation of Teachers (AFT), mentioned earlier in the book, offer teachers the opportunity to attend conferences, read and contribute to journals, and access professional resources. So do many other organizations; here is just a partial list.

- The National Association for the Education of Young Children (NAEYC)

- The National Science Teachers Association (NSTA)

- The National Council of Teachers of Mathematics (NCTM)

- The National Council of Teachers of English (NCTE)

- The National Council for the Social Studies (NCSS)

Many teaching resources are available at no cost online through these professional organizations; see the Resources for Further Exploration section at the end of this chapter for their websites.

Professional development takes place in informal settings as well, and this is often the most important kind. In one local school district where I have worked, teachers are encouraged to take field trips to local geological formations—by themselves, without their students—even if they do not teach science in a formal way. Imagine you are an elementary school teacher in this district. How might that type of field trip contribute to your professional development? How might it help you interest your young students in the world around them?

LEARNING PROJECT

The Induction Phase

About 40 percent of teachers leave the profession within the first five years on the job (Baldacci, et al., 2006). Well-designed teacher induction programs are successful in reducing this turnover rate. Beyond assigning a mentor, many induction programs offer weekly meetings for new teachers during which participants share stories, gain insights, and keep journals on the period of transition from novice to more experienced teacher. The goal of induction programs is not only to assist new teachers as they enter the teaching profession but also to develop reflective teachers who are responsive to the diverse cultural, social, and linguistic backgrounds of all their students.

Imagine that you are a teacher new to a school. What might be some strategies and tools an induction program could offer that would help you? Check local school districts to see if such programs are indeed available.

CONCLUDING THOUGHTS

Learning about other teachers' hopes, dreams, and experiences, as you've done in this chapter, gives you a way to consider what teaching might be like for yourself. Teaching demands so much of the individual teacher. Our emotional sides have to be expressed in order to communicate a sense of warmth and congeniality, while our intellectual selves need to maintain a sense of order, continuity, and consistency. It is a complex endeavor, requiring self-reflection and good analytical skills. One cannot overemphasize the need for personal reflection and the desire to become a lifelong learner. Luckily, teachers receive support from organizations, mentors, preparatory institutions, and sometimes from induction programs in their school districts.

Building a personal philosophy of teaching is an important starting point in your development as a teacher. Your teaching philosophy is a work in progress and will most likely change with time and exposure to new ideas about how people learn. In the next two chapters of this book, you will read about important educational philosophies that have influenced American education. Your own thinking should evolve as you engage with these ideas. What remains constant is the fact that teaching is hard work and requires that you be reflective, ever conscious, and well prepared.

CHAPTER CHALLENGE

Interviewing a Classroom Teacher

By now, you may have an idea of the grade or grade level you are interested in teaching. Are you a future elementary school, or middle school, or secondary school teacher? What is the subject area in which you specialize? Are you a future social studies, mathematics, English, science, or foreign language teacher? (Elementary school teachers can say "yes" to most of these subject categories!)

It is important to interview a classroom teacher who is working in a way you envision for yourself. Suppose you are a future social studies teacher; in that case, you will want to interview someone who has been teaching social studies for some time. Also try to choose a person who teaches at the grade level you currently aspire to.

How can you find a teacher to interview? You can request a name from a local school district. Or your teacher education program may have a field placement office that can suggest school districts with which your college or university has a relationship. Further, if your institution offers graduate programs for teachers already in the classroom, these classroom teachers can be excellent candidates for interviews. Finally, you may have a relative who is currently teaching in a context like the one you are heading for.

Be sure to thank these individuals for their time and to place a limit on the time you spend with them. Generally thirty minutes should be sufficient.

Here are some suggestions for interview questions. They include those answered by the teachers quoted in this chapter.

- How did you decide to enter teaching?
- For you, what are the most exciting aspects of the work?
- What do you think are the most difficult challenges for teachers?
- Who has given you the most support?
- How do you continue your professional development?
- How do you know you are successful?
- How would you define teaching?
- What advice would you give to a future teacher?

You will have your own questions to add to the list. For instance, you may be curious to know whether the teachers you interview are interested in National Board certification. Or you may want to learn about their personal interests or hobbies that are manifested in their teaching style (think about Ms. Outerbridge).

When you complete your interview, write about it in your journal. Respond to the following questions:

- What was the interview experience like?
- What did you learn about teaching that was new to you?

- What, if any, attributes did this teacher have that you could identify with?
- In what way(s) was this teacher different from you?

FROM THE COLLEGE CLASSROOM TO YOUR OWN CLASSROOM

Reflections for Your Portfolio

Build on your personal philosophy of teaching by reflecting on this chapter's teaching stories. Address the following questions in a document that you can add to your teaching portfolio.

- Do you think you have a "learning life"?
- How do you anticipate working with and communicating with parents?
- What did you learn from your interview with a classroom teacher that can inform your teaching philosophy?
- How does your religion or culture affect your philosophy of teaching?

RESOURCES FOR FURTHER EXPLORATION

Books

Jacqueline Grennon Brooks, *Schooling for life: Reclaiming the essence of learning* (Reston, VA: Association for Supervision and Curriculum Development, 2002). A wonderful story of what it means to be a lifelong learner.

Bobbi Fisher, *The teacher book: Finding personal and professional balance* (Portsmouth, NH: Heinemann, 2001).   This is an important book you will want to keep referring to. It shares teachers' stories as well as tips for coping with on-the-job demands.

Sam Intrator, *Tuned in and fired up* (New Haven: Yale University Press, 2003).   An inspiration in the ways the author describes ordinary people doing extraordinary teaching.

Judy Logan, *Teaching stories* (New York: Kodansha America, 1997).   An exciting book about the adventures and experiences the author shared with her students as a middle school teacher in San Francisco.

Professional Organizations

American Federation of Teachers (AFT): http://www.aft.org/
National Association for the Education of Young Children (NAEYC): http://www.naeyc.org/
National Council for the Social Studies (NCSS): http://www.ncss.org/
National Council of Teachers of English (NCTE): http://www.ncte.org/
National Council of Teachers of Mathematics (NCTM): http://www.nctm.org/
National Education Association (NEA): http://www.nea.org/
National Science Teachers Association (NSTA): http://www.nsta.org/

Lifelong Learning

eduScapes http://eduscapes.com/   A site for "lifelong learners," eduScapes offers excellent resources for teachers, parents, and students alike.

Taking Stock

Assessing Where You Are and Where You're Going

1. You now have an idea of what attributes make a good teacher and what makes teaching a profession. At this stage in reading the book, how do you assess your own goodness of fit for the teaching profession? (Your ideas may change as you read further and continue to think about the matter.)

2. Briefly, how does the way in which you experienced school influence your personal teaching philosophy?

3. In your state, are there requirements for teacher certification that pose specific challenges for you? What can you do to be better prepared for certification?

4. In Chapter 2, a teacher named Jane remarked that teaching is like starting a new job every year. Why do you think this is true?

5. Why are teachers required to be lifelong learners?

_____

_____

_____

_____

_____

6. How do you feel about the amount of preparation required for being an effective teacher? Does it surprise you? How do you think you will prepare?

_____

_____

_____

_____

_____

7. What one trait, more than others, do you need to work on to become a successful teacher?

_____

_____

_____

_____

_____

PART II

The Evolution of Schools and Teaching Practices

Where did we come from? How did we get here? These are questions children often ask their parents about their backgrounds and their beginnings. We might ask similar questions about schools. How did they get here? Why are schools this way? How did elementary, middle, and high schools develop over time? When did schooling become mandatory in America?

In the same way, we might wonder about the thinking behind today's teaching practices. From where did we get our ideas about how to teach? What is really meant by words like *pedagogy* and *curriculum*? What do we know about how people learn?

These are a few of the questions that the two chapters in Part II address as we go back in time to make more sense of the present. Knowing what and who came before us gives us a deeper understanding of our mission as we move forward.

PART OUTLINE

CHAPTER 3
An Overview of Schooling in America

CHAPTER 4
Principles of Teaching and Learning: Exploring Pedagogy, Curriculum, and Instruction

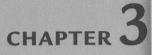

An Overview of Schooling in America

FOCUSING QUESTIONS

▶ What is your image of the earliest schools in America?

▶ Can you name some important pioneers in education?

▶ Who do you think funds public schools in America: state governments? the federal government?

▶ What different educational philosophies can you see at work in American schools today?

▶ What do you think of when you hear the term *progressive education*?

▶ What are inclusive classrooms?

▶ What is standards-based educational reform?

Schooling in America has a complex history. As we explore its roots in this chapter, take note of how the educational system has evolved to meet the needs of U.S. citizens. Also think about the descriptions of schooling in earlier times. In what ways do they remind you of teaching and learning in the twenty-first century? In what ways do these stories sound very different from the schools we know today?

A BRIEF HISTORY OF AMERICAN PUBLIC EDUCATION

As the composition of American citizenry changes over time, so do the perceived goals of schooling. Before we delve into history, consider the following question:

What do you believe to be the goals of American public education?

At different times in the development of our country, there have been varying answers to that question.

As we explore colonial America, the new nation emerging after the Revolutionary War, and the wave of immigration in the nineteenth century, you'll see how schools evolved to meet more complex demands. Look for the following themes:

▶ The role of wealth, privilege, and social capital in emerging systems of education

▶ The effect of geographic location on access to education

▶ The meaning of education for a thriving democracy

▶ The effect of immigration on the emergence of public schools

▶ The transmission of values and beliefs through public education

▶ Changes over time in the roles played by local communities, the states, and the federal government

Social Capital

From the time of the early colonies to the present, Americans have frequently debated the relationship between schools and society and the best way for government to fulfill its responsibility to educate its citizens. Historically, various traditions and forms of schooling have been mediated by the political, economic, and cultural struggles of the people. This means that, for some people, access to education has been easier than for others.

The term *social capital* refers to connections among individuals that give them access to cultural and civic events and institutions. Hence, youngsters from families with social capital are familiar with libraries, museums, and travel. Moreover, parents with social capital know how to get the best education for their children. Social capital generally comes with wealth, privilege, and other marks of social status.

The concept of social capital helps us understand how social issues were addressed as American schools

developed. Clearly, our systems of education have become more inclusive; but in the first 150 years of American nationhood, high-quality education was readily available only if you were rich, white, and male.

Do you remember my story about Mrs. Fisher from Chapter 1? She encouraged me to apply to a special high school in my city. Information about special high schools was readily available to families with social capital, but my parents were working-class immigrants who did not fully understand how to negotiate the educational system in New York City. Fortunately, my teacher helped me through the process of applying to take the entrance exam.

The issue of social capital comes up often as we explore the history of schooling in America. There has always been pressure for schools to provide more and better services for an increasingly diverse array of students.

The Colonies

Early colonial education began in the home in the 1600s when Puritans[1] established colonies in what is now the northeastern United States. In the early New England colonies, education was designed to further Puritan values and ensure that children were well versed in the Bible. The major thrust in early colonial education was the reading and understanding of scripture, so for many early colonists, religious education was synonymous with general education.

The primary responsibility for educating children was placed on the family. You may have heard about the home-schooling movement today in which parents educate their children directly, every day, in the home. We will discuss this current trend later in this text, but you can see that it has very old roots.

dame school Some colonial women transformed their homes into schools where they taught reading, writing, and computation. These schools became known as dame schools.

Many New England families could also opt to send their children to **dame schools**, which offered education to children six to eight years old. The dame school was like an informal daycare center. Parents would leave their children in the home of a neighborhood woman several days a week. The woman would go about her chores while teaching the children their letters, their numbers, and their prayers. Religious teachings, as you can see, were routinely woven into the daily lives of children. These women usually accepted a small fee for each child, and instruction often took place in the kitchen. For the most part, this was the only form of schooling offered to girls, since education was not considered important for their life's work.

Another form of education in the American colonies was apprenticeship. After young boys finished the dame school, they were sometimes apprenticed to craftsmen to learn a trade. Serving an apprenticeship allowed boys to learn a craft they could carry into adulthood. Girls, meanwhile, were usually taught domestic skills at home and learned to stitch letters and sayings onto embroidered samplers. Theirs was a second-rate education compared to what was available for boys.

Latin Grammar Schools

Latin grammar school A type of school that flourished in the New England colonies in the 1600s and 1700s. It emphasized Latin and Greek to prepare young men for college.

Realizing they needed a way to educate leaders for their communities, the Puritan colonists established **Latin grammar schools**, the first of which opened in Boston in 1635. Here, the sons of the upper social classes studied Latin and Greek language and literature as well as the Bible. To further extend the boys' education, the Puritans founded Harvard College in 1636. To enter this college, boys had to pass an entrance exam that required reading and speaking Latin and Greek.

In 1647, Massachusetts passed a law requiring formal education. Known as the "Old Deluder Satan" Act, it mandated that every town of 50 households must appoint and pay a teacher of reading and writing, while every town of 100 households must provide a grammar school to prepare youths for university. With the passage of this law, new town schools were established for the youngest students, and Latin grammar schools for older students spread through Massachusetts.

---

[1] The Puritans were Protestant dissenters in England who opposed many practices of the established church. When Charles I took the English throne in 1625, government persecution of Puritans increased. Giving up hope of reforming the English church, many Puritans emigrated, among them the early settlers of the Massachusetts Bay Colony (Boston Historical Society and Museum, 2006).

Ultimately the Latin grammar school extended into the other New England colonies and to some extent into the mid-Atlantic colonies as well. These schools were run by an elected board of townspeople and financially supported by the families of the attendees. Under this system, after finishing dame school or town school, wealthy boys could attend a Latin grammar school to prepare for college and a leadership role in society. Girls who finished the dame school or town school would continue to study their letters at home while learning domestic chores. The Latin grammar school is considered one of the forerunners of the American high school.

Geographical Differences in Colonial Education

Educational access in the early American colonies was not only determined by wealth and privilege. Where you lived also had a great impact on the type of education that was available.

In the northern colonies, largely settled by Puritans, people lived in towns and relatively close to one another. Town schools, which principally taught the Bible, became readily available after 1647. In the mid-Atlantic colonies, however, a wide range of European ethnic and religious groups established different types of schools, and various trades established apprenticeship programs. Local control was the norm. Though some Latin grammar schools existed, other private schools developed that were dedicated to job training and practical skills.

In the southern colonies, where the population was more rural, there were fewer schools during the colonial era. Wealthy plantation owners hired private tutors for their children. Many young gentlemen were sent abroad to Europe for their education.

The Late Colonial Period

By the late colonial era, in addition to the types of schools we have described so far, options for parents included:

- Schools managed by private associations, often devoted to the skills needed for a specific type of job.

- Religious schools, sponsored by churches for their members. Some churches also established charity schools for the urban poor.

- Boarding schools.

- A few private academies offering secondary education with a broader curriculum than the early Latin grammar schools. (Academies are discussed in the next section.)

Several of these options required tuitions, others were paid for by public funds, and some were funded by a combination of both.

It was still true that most girls received little schooling after the first few years. And if you were Native American or African American, you had practically no chance of formal education. The schools established for the poor typically required a family to sign a "Pauper's Oath," and hence most poor children did not attend school. Consider how you would feel if, to send your child to school, you had to sign a public document admitting your poverty. Many families chose to leave their children illiterate rather than suffer the shame of this type of public admission.

WRITING and REFLECTION

Education in the Colonies

- The assumption behind the "Old Deluder Satan" Act was that if people studied the Bible diligently, they would be less likely to fall prey to Satan's ways. What do you think of that? In our country today, does a good education protect citizens? If so, how?
- You had to be wealthy, white, and male to have access to the better forms of education in the early colonies. Does that surprise you? How has that changed, and what factors do you think contributed to the change?
- Consider the ways we have today of classifying students by their income. For instance, children of lesser means admit their status when they sign up for free or reduced-price breakfasts and lunches. Can you think of other such examples in modern schooling?
- Though women now enter professional fields formerly reserved for men, there remains a persistent gender gap in the engineering, physics, and computer science fields. What are some contributing factors to this? Why do you think more women than men pursue careers in education?

A New Nation

In the late 1700s, after the colonies gained their independence from Great Britain, efforts were made to consolidate schools and make education mandatory throughout the new nation. Congress enacted the Land Ordinance Act of 1785 and the Northwest Ordinance of 1787. These measures set aside land for public schools. Subsequently, as the popularity of sending children to school rather than teaching them at home grew, formal schools were started wherever space could be found.

Schoolhouses of that day were practical shelters: one room with benches and a stove. Desks and blackboards did not appear until many years later. No grades were given in the beginning, and one teacher worked with several age levels at the same time. Children simply learned at their own pace.

The Academy

academy A type of private secondary school that arose in the late colonial period and came to dominate American secondary education until the establishment of public high schools. Academies had a more practical curriculum than Latin grammar schools did, and students typically could choose subjects appropriate to their later careers.

Thomas Jefferson and Benjamin Franklin, among other founders of the new nation, believed that schools should move beyond the education of wealthy men for the ministry to a more broadly based education. In 1751 Franklin established a new kind of secondary school, one that would eventually replace the Latin grammar school—the **academy**. The Franklin Academy in Philadelphia offered a variety of subjects, ranging from science and mathematics to athletics, navigation, and bookkeeping. It was open to both girls and boys—if their parents could afford the tuition.

Soon after America's Declaration of Independence, other private academies were established, most of them limited to boys. These included most notably Phillips Academy in Andover, Massachusetts (1778), and Phillips Exeter Academy in Exeter, New Hampshire (1781). Academies changed the model for secondary schools by offering elective as well as required courses. It was still the case, however, that the common denominator for attendance was wealth.

Rise of the Common School

At the turn of the nineteenth century, education in the new nation was a hodgepodge of schools for basic reading and writing and grammar schools or academies for college preparation and leadership. Many young people still learned through apprenticeships or private tutoring.

Jefferson, Franklin, and others believed that the new democracy required an educated citizenry for its survival. To work properly, they thought, a democracy needs informed citizens, as well as an educational system that allows people to succeed on the basis of their skills and dedication rather than inherited privilege.

common school A public, tax-supported elementary school. Begun in Massachusetts in the 1820s, common schools aimed to provide a common curriculum for children. Horace Mann, an advocate for the common school, is often considered the "father of the public school."

These ideas gave rise to the movement for **common schools**—a system of tax-supported elementary schools. The common school is known today as the public elementary school. Horace Mann, an educational historian and reformer who championed the movement, saw common schools as promoting important civic virtues. He criticized private academies because they offered widely different curricula and perpetuated social differences between the privileged classes and ordinary citizens (Wisconsin Education Association Council, 2006).

From their beginnings in Massachusetts in the 1820s, common schools were gradually established in other New England, midwestern, western, and finally southern states. Their spread became more rapid after the Civil War.

Immigration played a key role in the thinking about public education. The 1830s and 1840s brought expansion in manufacturing and transportation. These decades also brought considerable immigration from Europe, especially in the Northeast. Immigrants were becoming an important part of the economy, and factory owners needed a trained, disciplined workforce. At the same time, as population grew in the cities, social tensions rose because of increased poverty, slums, and crime.

Prominent citizens worried about the morals of poor immigrant children and the influence their parents had on them. Many Protestant ministers looked at the rise of Catholic immigrant populations as a possible cause of

Common schools, supported by taxes, marked the beginning of public education for all.

social problems. Schools, many people believed, could offer a way to address these concerns. By centralizing the control of public education, schools could be used to uplift the poor, spread dominant national values, and assimilate immigrant children into the English-speaking American culture. State authorities, not immigrant parents, would be in control.

However, even though public schools were at this point nonsectarian, they were not necessarily nonreligious. Because common schools were seen as responsible, in part, for the moral development of children, it was believed that religion could not be completely separated from the schools. There was much debate about curriculum. Although the main thrust in common schools was the "three Rs" (reading, writing, and arithmetic), history, and science, some schools had regular readings of the King James version of the Bible. Catholic immigrants objected vehemently, and many church parishes in the late 1800s began their own church schools, known as **parochial schools**. Not until many years later, in 1963, did the Supreme Court rule that prayers and Bible readings could no longer be allowed in public schools.

With tax-supported public education in place, more and more children attended school on a regular basis (see Figure 3.1). However, because of the large size of many immigrant families, parents often needed to send their children into the workforce to help out economically. These poor working families viewed education for their children as a luxury that they could not afford. To ensure that children went to school and not to work, compulsory attendance laws came into existence. These laws were adopted by each individual state, beginning with Massachusetts in 1852 and ending with Alaska (then a U.S. territory) in 1929 (Information Please Database, 2006). Eventually, legislation restricting the employment of children in industrial settings was passed by the federal government.

> **parochial school** A school operated by a religious group. Today, in the United States, the term most often refers to a school governed by the local Catholic parish or diocese.

FIGURE 3.1

Rising School Attendance in the Nineteenth and Twentieth Centuries

The graph shows the percentage of U.S. children (ages 5 to 19) enrolled in school, illustrating the dramatic growth that began in the second half of the nineteenth century as common schools became well established and compulsory attendance laws were enacted.

Source: Data from Thomas D. Snyder, ed., *120 Years of American Education: A Statistical Portrait* (Washington, DC: National Center for Education Statistics, 1993), Table 2, p. 14.

WRITING and REFLECTION

The School as Social Control?

Horace Mann believed that all children should learn together in common schools. He lived at a time of tremendous social change when immigrants were pouring into the northeastern states, farmers were leaving rural areas to work in factories, and cities were growing rapidly, with crime and poverty on the rise. Some historians believe that Mann and other reformers, alarmed by the upheaval, promoted state-regulated public education mainly as a way to bring order and discipline to the working class. According to this interpretation, Mann and his fellow reformers felt threatened by the growing population of urban poor, and for this reason they placed a major emphasis on "moral training," standardization, and classroom drill.

Do you think that today's schools still function as institutions for social control? Be creative; think outside the box. What messages do you believe are sent to children through public schooling today? Remember the *hidden curriculum* mentioned in Chapter 2. The hidden curriculum involves messages from the teacher and the school about how the classroom and school function: the rules, the expectations, and the goals. Does this promote the kind of social control Mann envisioned? How and why?

LEARNING PROJECT

Separation of Church and State

Embedded in the Constitution of the United States is the guarantee of religious freedom for all citizens. The expression "separation of church and state" was coined by Thomas Jefferson, who opposed the use of public funds for the teaching of religion in public schools. Today the expression is often used to resist the infusion of religion into public schools. Many believe that the principle of separation of church and state is a part of our historical, legal, and political heritage, helping preserve and protect our religious liberty. As previously mentioned, the Supreme Court ruled in 1963 that prayers and Bible readings were no longer allowed in tax-supported public schools, a decision that respected the diverse religions represented by the students.

Yet the issue is far from settled. There has been much recent debate about the extent to which religious beliefs find their way into public schools. Research some of the controversies that have emerged. Some examples include the Pledge of Allegiance requirement, school prayer, and the conflicts in the state of Kansas and in Dover, Pennsylvania, about the teaching of evolution.

After reading about the different viewpoints, what do you think? Should public schools provide a forum for the opinions of religious groups? Why? Why not?

Expansion of Public Schools

By the 1870s, there was broad attendance in U.S. public elementary schools, but a large gap in available educational opportunities remained between those schools and universities. Only the wealthy continued their education at private preparatory schools for colleges and universities. Gradually, however, as society became more industrialized and laws were passed to discourage the hiring of teenage workers, parents came to view the high school as the pathway to better jobs for their children. Tax-supported public high schools slowly took hold and became the dominant form of secondary education by 1890.

The rise of the public high school led to the need for a bridge between elementary school and high school. In the early 1900s, the junior high school was established to bridge this gap, concentrating on the emotional and intellectual needs of students in grades 7, 8, and 9. In the 1950s, some middle schools were established for grades 5–8, and by the end of the twentieth

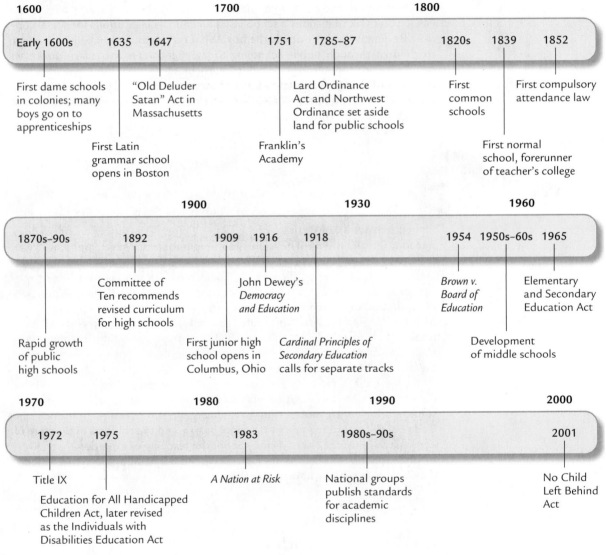

FIGURE 3.2
Some Important Events in American Education

century, the middle school was gradually replacing the junior high school (Manning, 2000). The emphasis in middle school was on interdisciplinary learning and team teaching, in which groups of students had the same teachers in common.

The timeline in Figure 3.2 summarizes many of the events we have discussed. It is remarkable to consider how many more children were educated as the common school movement took hold and public secondary schools began to flourish. In many areas of America in the early 1800s, school lasted only about 75 to 80 days a year because the entire family was needed to work the farm. By the 1830s, only about half of all children attended school and then only for this short period of time. But as the industrial revolution drew people to the cities for work and common schools flourished, more children began attending school, and by the end of the 1890s, over 70 percent of children were receiving schooling. There was such a great need for schools between 1890 and 1914 that a new high school was added every day (Krug, 1964; Wisconsin Education Association Council, 2006).

Today we can celebrate the fact that, as our nation grew, more and more people attended public schools. This does not mean, however, that we have now achieved the goal of equal educational opportunity for everyone. Later in this text, as we compare the quality of education offered to students in poor urban and rural areas with the public education available in more affluent communities, you will see that challenges remain. Still, there is no question that more diverse students—including girls and women, people of color, and the poor—are graduating from high school today and going on to postsecondary education than has ever been the case in this country.

LEARNING PROJECTS

The One-Room Schoolhouse

One-room schoolhouses dotted the American landscape for over a century. These early schools had one teacher for all the children, regardless of their ages. There is a wealth of knowledge about these early schools. You may be surprised to learn that some lasted well into the twentieth century, especially in rural areas.

Explore and describe a one-room schoolhouse. Where was it? How many children did it serve? What is its history? What type of curriculum did it have? Would you have liked to attend this school? Why or why not?

Early Schoolbooks

Generations of colonial students learned their alphabet from a device called a *hornbook*. Older students used the *New England Primer* and the *McGuffey Readers*, among other schoolbooks. Explore these early materials and describe their uses for students and teachers.

Then and Now

Many of today's educational practices began when the country was young. For example, local control, compulsory education, and tax-supported schools are

continued

premises of today's public schools, and you have seen in this chapter how early they originated.

Many of the early conflicts exist today as well. Issues concerning race, social class, and gender inequities are evident in the disparities between today's urban, suburban, and rural schools. Select one issue that dates back to America's early years and describe the ways in which it is reflected in the differences among modern-day urban, suburban, and rural schools.

Teacher Education and the Development of Normal Schools

normal school A type of teacher-education institution begun in the 1830s; forerunner of the teachers' college.

As the common school movement gained momentum, you may be wondering, Who were the teachers? Where did they come from and how were they prepared?

Once again, Horace Mann was a major influence. He promoted **normal schools**, which began shortly after the founding of the first common schools. These were two-year institutions designed to prepare teachers through courses in the history and philosophy of education and methods of teaching. Normal schools were intended to improve the quality of the growing common school system by producing more qualified teachers. The first of them, called simply the Normal School, opened in 1839 in Lexington, Massachusetts.

By the end of the 1800s, these schools became four-year colleges dedicated to teacher education. Many universities that are well known today, such as the University of California, Los Angeles, were founded as normal schools.

Normal Schools and Female Teachers

Normal schools played a major role in bringing women into the teaching profession. In the early days of American education, schoolmasters were almost always male. Women, who were mostly uneducated, were not considered suited for the job, even though the prerequisite for teaching consisted of little more than having attended school yourself. On the rare occasion that a woman did secure a job, it was with young children only. As the country expanded, common schools multiplied rapidly, but women still took a back seat in terms of employment. It was assumed that they were incapable of maintaining the discipline necessary to teach effectively.

Normal schools, however, welcomed female students and made elementary school teaching a career path for many women. By 1900, 71 percent of rural teachers were women (Hoffman, 1981).

Gender Roles in Teaching

After the Civil War and well into the 1900s, teaching became more attractive for women who wanted to find a place of employment outside the domestic sphere. Yet there were considerable constraints on women who became teach-

Having a History

Sara Evans, a historian from the University of Minnesota, once said, "Having a history is a prerequisite to claiming a right to shape the future" (1989). Learning about the earliest teachers gives us insight into how far the profession has come and into our own entitlement to consider teaching a highly significant profession.

ers, chief among them that they were not allowed to marry. The stereotype of the "spinster" was often associated with schoolteachers. It was believed that women would have divided loyalties if they were allowed to marry while being employed as teachers. (Can you imagine that happening now?) It was not until after World War II that married women were allowed to enter the teaching profession.

By the 1950s, the teaching profession, once dominated entirely by men, had become a female-dominated, "feminized" profession in many people's eyes. Young men were still attracted to educational administration as well as to secondary school jobs in mathematics and science, however. Here again, a stereotype persisted through the middle to late twentieth century: women were seen as suited to teaching young children whereas men taught math and science and ran the school.

In recent years, women have gained greater access to careers in educational administration and as teachers of mathematics and science. At the same time, however, the overall percentage of men in teaching has declined significantly since the 1960s, as we mentioned in Chapter 2. Just as it is important to have women teaching math, it is vital to have men represented in early childhood and elementary education. Breaking down gender stereotypes in schools is important—not only for teachers themselves, but also for the models they present to students. We will have more to say about gender and schooling later in this text.

The Tuskegee Normal School and the Education of African Americans

Even after the Civil War, Reconstruction, and the Thirteenth Amendment, which ended slavery in the United States, it took a long time for African Americans to achieve equal opportunity and access to a quality education. Some would argue that appropriate education remains unavailable to minority students today. As we will see in later chapters, our diverse culture and society pose many challenges and opportunities for teachers and students alike. In this respect, we can find inspiration in the story of Booker T. Washington, an African American teacher, who in 1881 became the first head of what was then called the Tuskegee Normal School for Colored Teachers in Tuskegee, Alabama. Later renamed the Tuskegee Institute, the institution today is Tuskegee University.

Under the leadership of Washington, the Tuskegee Normal School prepared African American teachers to be self-reliant and to acquire practical vocational skills, not only in teaching but in agriculture and other occupations.

Catherine Beecher

Catherine Beecher, who started the Hartford (Connecticut) Female Seminary in 1828, made a major contribution to the professional education of women. Beecher challenged accepted notions of femininity and the education of women in the nineteenth century. Born in East Hampton, New York, in 1800, Beecher believed that education should prepare women to assume roles of high responsibility in society. In particular, she thought that women should train to become teachers, a profession that would be a natural extension of their family roles. Along with her famous contemporaries, Elizabeth Cady Stanton and Susan B. Anthony, she promoted educational and political equality for women.

By the early twentieth century, the African American scholar and advocate W.E.B. Du Bois, a graduate of Harvard College and a well-known intellectual, was criticizing Washington's emphasis on vocational training at Tuskegee. Du Bois insisted that formal education in an academically rich course of study was necessary for the African American people. Regardless of these later critiques, however, Washington did a great deal to advance the education of African Americans and their representation in the teaching profession.

Drawing African Americans and other minorities into the teaching force remains an issue today. African Americans make up more than 15 percent of U.S. public school students. So do Hispanics. Yet only about 6 percent of teachers are African American, and only 5 percent are Hispanic. More than one-third of U.S. public schools have no teacher of color on the faculty (National Collaborative on Diversity in the Teaching Force, 2004; Weaver, 2004). To improve this situation, state Departments of Education and many colleges and universities are offering financial incentives to minority students for becoming teachers. An example of such a program, in existence since 1985, is the Minority Teacher Recruitment Project (MTRP) at the University of Louisville (http://louisville.edu/education/research/centers/mtrp/).

WRITING and REFLECTION

From Past to Present

- What is the history of the college or university where you are studying to become a teacher? When did teacher education programs emerge in your institution?

- What do you think it means for a profession to be "feminized?" How does that perception affect wages and social status?

- What is the racial composition of the class in which you are studying? of the schools in which you are observing?

- Who do you think was right at the turn of the twentieth century: Booker T. Washington (who advocated practical, vocational education for African Americans) or W.E.B. Du Bois (who thought African Americans should have the same rigorous academic education as other groups)? Or do you think both visionaries were correct in the ways they encouraged the development of African American teachers?

COMPETING VISIONS: EFFORTS TO RETHINK AND REFORM EDUCATION

The struggle to change or reform educational practices is as old as organized public schooling. From common school days to present times, the content and processes of education have been under continuous scrutiny. Schools, like other public institutions, are products of their times, politically, socially, and economically. Schools both reflect and influence the societal events of their day.

We are all a part of what we are trying to change. As teachers and future teachers, we seek a profession dedicated to student learning. As citizens, we know that, as Thomas Jefferson observed, it is impossible for a nation to be both free and ignorant. But we are people of diverse regions, ethnicities, and social and economic backgrounds, and to be successful educators we need to make sense of (1) who we are in the world and (2) what conditions we believe are important for learning to occur.

At different periods in our history, different philosophies have dominated our thinking about teaching and learning and about the manner in which education should proceed. In this section, we look at several competing philosophies that have shaped efforts to reform American schools since the late nineteenth century.

Many classrooms today are hybrids of several of these philosophies of education. As you read this section, think about what is happening in schools today and how the current phase of American public education will be viewed by others fifty years from now.

The High School Curriculum

From the end of the Civil War to the late 1800s, the high school curriculum kept expanding as the demand for new courses grew. There was no preset pattern for how the courses being offered should develop, and hence the high school curriculum retained old subjects like languages and mathematics and added new ones as demand arose. These new subjects included botany, physiology, anatomy, physics, and astronomy. For those students not interested in pursuing a college education, courses such as commercial arithmetic, banking, business correspondence, stenography, and typewriting were added.

By the late 1800s, opinions about the purpose of high school were sharply divided. Some believed high school should groom students for college. Others thought high school should prepare students for more practical endeavors, serving those who saw high school as the termination of their formal education.

In 1892, the National Education Association (NEA) addressed this issue by appointing the Committee of Ten, ten scholars led by Harvard University President Charles Eliot, to determine the proper curriculum for high schools. The Committee of Ten recommended eight years of elementary school and four years of high school and proposed a curriculum that was common to both college-bound and terminal students. The new curriculum featured fewer subjects, each of which would be studied for a longer period of time. The courses included foreign languages, history, mathematics, science, and English. Although these subjects offered an alternative to classical Latin and Greek courses, this was a rigorous academic curriculum, and the dominant belief was that the same subjects would be equally beneficial to academic and terminal students.

A generation later, in 1918, the NEA partly reversed course when its Commission on the Reorganization of Secondary Education issued a report called *Cardinal Principles of Secondary Education*. In this report, the commission recommended a differentiated curriculum for the comprehensive high school, offering four different tracks: college preparatory, commercial, industrial, and general academic. The commercial course of study included bookkeeping, shorthand, and typing. The industrial track included preparatory courses for domestic, agricultural, and trade endeavors.

tracking The practice of placing students in different classes or courses based on achievement test scores or on perceived differences in abilities. Tracks can be identified by ability (high, average, or low) or by the kind of preparation they provide (academic, general, or vocational).

Although high school curricula varied considerably during the rest of the twentieth century, some of the ideas set forth by the Committee of Ten and the *Cardinal Principles* continued to be dominant. The core courses—English, foreign language, science, mathematics, and history (which later evolved into social studies)—persisted in the comprehensive high school curriculum. So did the notion that high school should follow a **tracking** system, offering different courses or tracks for students with different academic aspirations.

WRITING and REFLECTION

Your Experience of Tracking

Consider your own high school education. Was there evidence of tracking—different courses available for different types of students? Explain in detail the ways in which your own high school experience reflected a type of tracking.

The Emergence of Essentialism

essentialism An educational philosophy holding that the purpose of education is to learn specific knowledge provided by core academic disciplines such as mathematics, science, literature, and history. Teachers must impart the key elements of these subjects so that all students have access to this basic or "essential" knowledge.

As you can see from the debate over the high school curriculum, educators in the early twentieth century were developing strong opinions about the proper sort of education for contemporary society. In the 1930s, the educator William Bagley coined the term **essentialism** as the name for a philosophy that had a strong impact then and continues to be influential today. According to this view, certain core kinds of knowledge are essential to a person's life in society. Essentialists believe that everyone can and should learn these key elements and therefore that the schools' primary mission is to teach them.

When you hear about teaching the "basics" or about rigorous training in the "three Rs," you are listening to an essentialist view of education. The essentials are generally embodied in the standard, time-honored subjects; in other words, essentialists believe that students should take courses in algebra and history, not in ceramics and interpretive dance. In stressing that the curriculum should remain consistent, essentialists tend to assume that a common culture should exist for all Americans. Their vision of the classroom is teacher-centered: Teachers are the dominant figures, transferring their knowledge and wisdom for the good of the students. An essentialist classroom is one in which the teacher knows best. Students listen to their teacher and learn what is taught.

To many educators in the early twentieth century, essentialism made good common sense. It was soon challenged, however, by the progressivism of thinkers like John Dewey.

Progressivism and John Dewey

progressivism An educational philosophy that stresses active learning through problem solving, projects, and hands-on experiences.

Probably the most influential educator of the twentieth century, John Dewey (1859–1952) was an educational philosopher and a professor at the University of Chicago and Columbia University in New York. He participated in a variety of political causes, such as women's rights and the unionization of teachers, and he contributed frequently to popular magazines and journals in which he connected social action in democracy with educational principles.

In Dewey's view, students should be active participants in their own learning; they learn by doing, and their interests must be a driving force behind curriculum and classroom experiences. His educational philosophy has been referred to as **progressivism** and also as *pragmatism.* It was progressive because it gave more responsibility to students and pragmatic (practical) because it embedded teaching and learning in the context of daily living. This approach contradicted the strict, top-down, authoritarian model of education that had thrived from colonial times into the nineteenth century and that continued to be reflected in essentialist approaches.

Dewey thought that schools should help children learn how to live and work cooperatively with others. Consequently, he believed that students needed to participate in decisions that affected their learning and that they should be guided by academically autonomous teachers—that is, teachers who were not bound by rigid rules about what and how to teach and who were able to build on students' strengths and talents. Dewey and his followers viewed the school as a laboratory in which the purpose of the curriculum was to integrate education with real-life experiences and a child's curiosity defined the process of learning just as much as the subject matter being taught.

John Dewey, and the progressive movement that he helped found, had a profound influence on educational thought in the United States. Progressives advocated a vibrant school setting with a curriculum that followed the interests and needs of students, encouraged active learning and problem solving, fostered deep understanding of concepts through experimentation, and supported assessment of students through close observation by well-prepared and caring teachers.

Dewey's progressivism fell out of favor, however, when it was deemed necessary that America foster stricter teaching methods during the cold war following World War II. The Soviet Union's launch of the satellite *Sputnik* in 1957—making that nation the first in space—became a symbol of what American public education had failed to achieve. Progressivism lost ground as American educators shifted again toward a more authoritarian approach and a strict adherence to lecture and rote learning. A new wave of essentialism took over, and schools focused on the task of preparing students for the technological and engineering challenges of the time.

Educational progressivism revived in the 1960s as the "child-centered" movement gained popularity in America. In the years since, various groups of

Progressivism asserted that students learned by doing and that their interests had to be a driving force of the learning experience.

educators have revisited the ideas of Dewey and his followers and revised them to address the changing needs of schools, children, and society. The philosophical influence of progressive ideas in education can be seen today in "whole language" reading programs, multiage approaches, experiential education, problem-based learning, and student-centered instruction.

WRITING and REFLECTION

Progressivism and Essentialism Today

- It is often said that Dewey's progressivism is alive and well in twenty-first century classrooms. Can you cite specific examples of how his philosophy influences classroom work today? If you are observing in the field, look for the attributes of progressive education in the classrooms you visit. If you are not in the field, reflect on your own school years: Were there any hints of Dewey's philosophy in your schooling?

- Likewise, threads of essentialism are found in many schools and classrooms. Many people believe that today's standards-oriented reform movement (discussed later in this chapter) has a "back-to-basics," essentialist feel about it. This teacher-centered model of education may be evident in your classroom observations or in your recollections of your own schooling. What do you observe or remember that relates to an essentialist approach?

LEARNING PROJECT

Reading Dewey

John Dewey thought and wrote a great deal about education. To gain greater insight into his educational philosophy, read his article "My Pedagogic Creed," written in 1897. In this article he talks about what education is and his beliefs about schools, curriculum, and pedagogy. It is available at http://www.infed.org/archives/e-texts/e-dew-pc.htm or by searching online for the article title.

In what ways does Dewey's philosophy manifest itself in what you know about schools and schooling today?

Enduring Ideas: The Influence of Perennialism

perennialism An educational philosophy that emphasizes enduring ideas conveyed through the study of great works of literature and art. Perennialists believe in a single core curriculum for everyone.

An educational philosophy related to essentialism, **perennialism** stresses the belief that all knowledge or wisdom has been accumulated over time and is represented by the great works of literature and art as well as religious texts. This educational philosophy found a strong expression in the 1980s with the *Paideia Proposal* by Mortimer Adler. In this influential call for school reform, Adler proposed one universal curriculum for elementary and secondary students, allowing for no electives. Everyone would take the same courses, and the curriculum would reflect the enduring ideas found in the works of history's finest thinkers and writers.

Like essentialism, perennialism holds that one type of education is good for all students. It differs from essentialism by placing greater emphasis on classic works of literature, history, art, and philosophy (including works of the ancient Greeks and Romans) and on the teaching of values and moral character. Essentialism can include practical, vocation-oriented courses—a class in computer skills, for instance—but perennialism leaves little room for such frivolity.

The perennialist approach has found a home at several U.S. colleges, such as St. John's College in Maryland and New Mexico, and its influence shows in the core curricula at some larger universities, including the University of Chicago and Columbia University. Threads of the perennialist philosophy are present in many parochial schools as well. Whenever you hear about a program centered on "great ideas" or "Great Books," it most likely reflects perennialist ideas.

Adler emphasized the Socratic method, a type of teaching based on extensive discussion with students. In this respect he was somewhat less teacher-centered than many essentialists. His perennialism does, however, leave little room for flexibility in the curriculum and little opportunity to reflect the changing demographics of our times.

Radical Reform Philosophies: Social Reconstructionism, Critical Theory, and Existentialism

Alongside essentialism, perennialism, and progressivism, the twentieth century gave rise to some radical reform philosophies that proposed a fundamental rethinking of the nature of schooling. Among these are social reconstructionism, critical theory, and existentialism.

Social reconstructionism is an educational philosophy that emphasizes social justice and a curriculum promoting social reform. Responding to the vast inequities in society and recognizing the plight of the poor, social reconstructionists believe that schools must produce an agenda for social change. Linked with social reconstructionism is *critical theory* or *critical pedagogy,* which stresses that students should learn to challenge oppression. In this view, education should tackle the real-world problems of hunger, violence, poverty, and inequality. Clearly, students are at the center of this curriculum, with teachers advocating involvement in social reform. The focus of critical theorists and social reconstructionists is the transformation of systems of oppression through education in order to improve the human condition.

Among critical theorists, Paulo Freire (1921–1997), a Brazilian whose experiences living in poverty led him to champion education and literacy as the vehicle for social change, has had a particularly profound impact on the thinking of many educators. His most influential work was *Pedagogy of the Oppressed,* published in English in 1970.

Another philosophy that proposes fundamental changes in education is *existentialism,* which takes student-centered learning to an extreme. Rooted in the thinking of nineteenth-century philosophers like Søren Kierkegaard, existentialism gained popular notice in the mid-twentieth century through the works of Jean Paul Sartre and others. According to this philosophy, the only authoritative truth lies within the individual. Existentialism is defined by what it rejects—namely, the existence of any source of objective truth other than the individual person, who must seek the meaning of his or her own existence.

Applied to education, existentialism proposes that students make all decisions about their choice of subject matter and activities as they seek to make meaning of their place in the world. This philosophy has not had as profound

TABLE 3.1   Key Elements of Five Educational Philosophies

Philosophy	Focus of Study	Teacher's Role
Essentialism	Core knowledge that students need to be educated citizens; this knowledge is embodied in traditional academic disciplines such as history and mathematics	Teachers are the central figures in the classroom, transferring their knowledge to students
Perennialism	Enduring ideas found in the great works of literature and art	Teachers engage in extended dialogue with students, discussing and reasoning about the great ideas
Progressivism	Integration of study with real-life experiences through active learning, problem solving, and experimentation	Teachers structure the learning activities and encourage students to explore the ideas that arise; teachers can vary the curriculum to match the needs and interests of students
Social reconstructionism/ critical theory	Schooling promotes social and political reform by focusing on social problems and the need for change	Teachers guide students to think critically about social injustice and challenge oppression
Existentialism	Students choose their own course of study as part of their effort to figure out their place in the world and the meaning of their lives	Teachers support students in exploring their own interests

an impact on American schools as the other philosophies described in this chapter have, but you can find elements of it in classrooms where teachers insist that students make their own decisions about what is important for them to know. The best-known model of existentialism is Summerhill, a school founded in England by A. S. Neill in 1921.

Table 3.1 summarizes some key features of the educational philosophies we have discussed, and the Video Case will help you explore how these ways of thinking translate into practice in actual classrooms.

VIDEO CASE

Educational Philosophies in the Classroom

How does perennialism or progressivism operate in an actual classroom? Can you see the difference between them? Find the HM Video Case "Philosophical Foundations of American Education: Four Philosophies in Action" on the student website. The video has four segments, each exploring a different philosophy in a classroom setting. The philosophies shown are essentialism, progressivism, perennialism, and critical theory.

After watching the video, compare and contrast the different philosophies—not just what they represent, but how they function in the classroom. For each philosophy, ask yourself questions like these:

- If I followed this philosophy strictly in the classroom, how would I behave?
- What learning materials would I typically use: textbooks, classic works of literature, original source materials, contemporary writings?

Finally, think about how each philosophy matches your developing thoughts about teaching. Which of these philosophies is most appealing to you? Why? Do you feel you will draw elements from different philosophies and create your own synthesis? If so, say more about which specific behaviors associated with these philosophies are most aligned with your own philosophy of teaching.

Aesthetics and Maxine Greene

We want to expand the range of literacy, offering the young new ways of symbolizing, new ways of structuring their experience, so they can see more, hear more, make more connections, embark on unfamiliar adventures into meaning.

— Maxine Greene, 2002

In this era of global interdependence and multicultural diversity, educators continue to develop their ideas about the purposes of education and the best ways to reform American schools. One influential contemporary thinker is Maxine Greene, an American philosopher, social activist, and teacher who has been an active scholar and educator at Teachers College, Columbia University, since 1965. Her belief is that the role of education is to create meaning in the lives of students and teachers through an interaction between knowledge and experience with the world.

Greene's educational philosophy is rooted in Dewey's ideas about art and aesthetics. Dewey's democratic view of education suggested that when children are able to approach problem-solving artistically and imaginatively, they grow socially and culturally through their shared experiences, insights, and understandings. Therefore, the arts are an essential part of the human experience.

aesthetic education Traditionally, this term referred merely to education in the fine arts, such as painting and music. In the broader view of Maxine Greene and other recent philosophers, however, it means education that enables students to use artistic forms and imagination to approach all fields of learning, including the sciences, and to share their perspectives with others.

Building on Dewey, Greene has contributed to the growth of a paradigm known as **aesthetic education**. She believes that the goal of education is to help students realize that they are responsible not merely for their own individual experiences; rather, they have a deep connection to, and responsibility for, other human beings who share this world. Her philosophy asks us to consider how being able to express oneself in a number of different "languages"— including imagery, music, and dance—helps us make meaning of ideas (Greene, 1995). Greene also believes that education must lead students and teachers to the discovery of their own truths and that the arts promote a type of consciousness or "wide-awakeness" (1978) in service to this process. She stresses the importance of shared perspectives in looking at the world and a respect for differences in experience.

In connection with her work at the Lincoln Center Institute for the Arts in Education in New York City, of which she was a founding member, Greene began the Maxine Greene Foundation for Social Imagination, the Arts, and Education, which prepares teachers to guide students in merging artistic expression with social justice. Its tenets focus on equity issues, quality of experiences in school, and the uses of imagination as a means of breaking down the barriers of diversity that children encounter in their daily lives. This perspective values the personal liberty of children and celebrates the imagination for its ability to open a child's mind to different possibilities and alternative solutions. An underlying assumption is that the humanities can serve as a catalyst enabling teachers and students to explore ideas more deeply and be more critically engaged with the world.

How do Maxine Greene's ideas work in an actual classroom? Consider this story:

In a sixth-grade class, Ms. Nelson is interested in her students' capacity for careful observation. She is a great admirer of many types of artists, and decorating her room are poster reproductions of famous paintings. The students move their chairs to position themselves by the poster of van Gogh's *Starry Night* (see Figure 3.3), and Ms. Nelson asks, "What do you think van Gogh was thinking about when he painted this?"

"Circles" one student responds. Another says, "dreams," and still another student offers "motion." Then Ms. Nelson asks, "What do *you* think of when you look at this painting?" Students respond with phrases like "wind blowing," "scary dreams," "day and night," and "church spires." The students really seem to like the painting, and Ms. Nelson urges them on. She asks, "What is the organizing principle behind this painting?" (This is a question she asks often when the class looks at collections of objects: what principle did the collector use to gather these objects together?)

The students decide that van Gogh was looking for images that used circles and pointy spires. Those were his organizing principles.

FIGURE 3.3
***Starry Night* (1889), by Vincent van Gogh**

Starry Night is one of the most well known paintings in modern culture.

Asked about her goals for the *Starry Night* lesson, Ms. Nelson explains, "I am interested in getting students ready to make careful observations. We are doing a science unit on mystery powders, and I want them to think about properties that objects have in common."

Can you see how this lesson represents Maxine Greene's philosophy of integrating the arts into education?

The progressive philosophies of John Dewey and Maxine Greene share a number of fundamental views:

▶ Making connections with social issues should be central to school curricula.

▶ The arts are creative tools that can expose children to new perspectives and new ways of communicating.

▶ Learning is an experiential process. Students learn by interacting with material in intellectual and sometimes manipulative ways; that is what "learning by doing" means.

▶ All forms of education should emphasize learning by **inquiry**—a process in which students ask meaningful questions and then seek their own answers.

inquiry A multifaceted activity that involves making observations, posing questions about the subject matter, and conducting research or investigations to develop answers. Inquiry is common to scientific learning but also relevant to other fields.

WRITING and REFLECTION

The Arts

• What is your own educational experience with the arts? Have you personally experienced an engagement with the arts that allowed you to think about another area of learning in a different way?

• In what ways do you think education in the arts can free students to be more personally expressive?

• How do you think John Dewey paved the way for Maxine Greene's philosophy?

Maxine Greene and Teaching

Maxine Greene believes that people who choose to become teachers should ideally be "those who have learned the importance of becoming reflective enough to think about their own thinking and become conscious of their own consciousness" (Greene, 1995). What do you think that means?

Social Justice

• Can you think of one or more examples of the use of visual or performing arts for the social good? Be specific. Would it be a poem or story that you read? a painting? a song or musical performance? a play?

• Discuss the use of the arts for furthering the causes of equity, opportunity, and fairness in our schools. How does this connect to the ideas of the social reconstructionists you read about earlier in the chapter?

continued

The Pendulum of Educational Reform

To understand the ways American public schooling has shifted emphases over the last century, imagine the swings of a pendulum. Education swung from early, rigorous, authoritarian emphasis on transmission of facts to the progressive philosophies of Dewey and others who believed in the importance of learning by doing and the interplay between experience and education. Then the pendulum swung back to a more rigid view of how schools should function. Then, once more, the rigor lessened, then it tightened again, and so on. The pendulum is continually on the move.

Which period of educational reform do you believe us to be in today? Where is the pendulum now, and which way is it moving?

FEDERAL AND STATE EFFORTS AT EDUCATIONAL REFORM: FUNDING, PRIORITIES, AND STANDARDS

Although education of the citizenry was very important to the founders of the United States, there is no mention of education for all in the Constitution. Hence, schooling became the domain and responsibility of the states, which left most of the control of schools to local communities.

Thus American schools have traditionally been run by local school boards, and the bulk of the money they need has been raised through local taxes, especially the property tax. Many critics have argued that the reliance on local property taxes is unfair, since it means that wealthier districts can raise more money for schools than poorer districts can. Yet Americans have long been reluctant to give up local funding and the control that goes with it.

As we noted earlier, however, the Soviet Union's launch of *Sputnik* in 1957 prompted a rethinking of American educational priorities. Federal and state governments increasingly began to intervene in educational matters, setting priorities and (at least sometimes) providing funds to make sure those priorities were met. The overall result of these changes is that local school districts now supply less than half of the funding for public schools, as shown in Figure 3.4. Although local schools are happy to receive government money, they are not always pleased that the funds come with strings attached, reducing local control over the way schools operate.

The following sections introduce you to several ways in which government legislation, publications, and court cases have changed the course of American public education.

Separate but Equal?

Earlier in this chapter, we discussed the fact that African Americans were denied the right to an education when this country was new and evolving. Even after the Civil War, schools were slow to develop for African Americans, and when they did, they were separate schools, only for black children. According to an 1896 Supreme Court ruling in *Plessy v. Ferguson*, "separate but equal" public facilities for different races were legal. But in time, during the first half of the 1900s, the schools serving African Americans were found *not* to be equal. They did not share equally in the resources available for public schooling; in most locations, they had fewer tax dollars and inferior conditions.

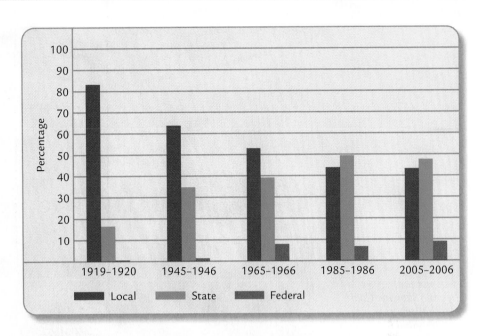

FIGURE 3.4

Percentage of School Funds Derived from Local, State, and Federal Sources

Notice how the percentage of school funds raised by local governments has decreased since the early 1900s, while the proportion contributed by federal and state governments has grown.

Source: Data from National Center for Education Statistics. (2006). *The Condition of Education 2006* (NCES 2006-071). Washington, DC: U.S. Government Printing Office; National Education Association. (2006). *Rankings and Estimates: Rankings of the States 2005 and Estimates of School Statistics 2006*. Washington, DC: Author.

Brown v. Board of Education of Topeka, Kansas
A 1954 case in which the U.S. Supreme Court outlawed segregation in public education.

The situation came to a head in 1954 with the case of **Brown v. Board of Education of Topeka, Kansas**. In this landmark case, the Supreme Court of the United States ruled unanimously that separate schools for whites and blacks were inherently unequal because the effects of such separate schooling are likely to be different. Because of this inequality, the Court decided, schools could not remain segregated.

Initially, the *Brown* decision had particular impact in the South, where schools were segregated by law (*de jure* segregation). But many northern schools were segregated informally because of separate living patterns for whites and blacks (*de facto* segregation). Over the following decades, many school systems and various court cases dealt with the challenge of eliminating *de facto* segregation, with mixed success. The efforts toward integration had a significant impact, but there was much turmoil and resistance. Numerous educators argue that *de facto* segregation still exists today in many cities and especially in suburban America.

Federal legislation, including the Civil Rights Act (1964), reinforced the importance of creating educational opportunities for all Americans regardless of race, gender, or ethnicity. The Bilingual Education Acts of 1968 and 1974 provided supplemental funding for school districts to establish programs for large numbers of children with limited English-language ability. Similarly, the

It was not until 1954, when the Supreme Court ruled that separate schools for whites and blacks were inherently unequal, that schools began racial integration.

Equal Educational Opportunities Act of 1974 provided specific definitions of what constituted denial of equal educational opportunity. These included "failure to take the appropriate action to overcome language barriers that impede equal participation by all students in an instructional program."

WRITING and REFLECTION

Your Experience with Student Diversity

- What was your schooling like in terms of student diversity?
- Does it surprise you that there was a time when black children and white children were required to attend different schools in some parts of the country?
- What is the downside of a segregated education for all parties involved? In what ways can students of various backgrounds suffer from an absence of diversity?

The Elementary and Secondary Education Act

The most extensive federal financing of schools in America was made possible in 1965 when Congress passed the Elementary and Secondary Education Act (ESEA). At that time, this legislation was seen as part of President Lyndon Johnson's War on Poverty because it ensured that federal assistance would be sent to the poorest schools and communities in the nation. Its immediate impact was to provide one billion dollars to improve the education of students from families living below the poverty line.

Every five years since its enactment, ESEA has been reauthorized; it is the single largest source of federal support for K–12 education. The federal government distributes the funds to the states, and it is the states' responsibility to

Title 1   The section of federal education law that provides funds for compensatory education.

identify the schools and districts to receive the funds. This legislation, particularly the section known as **Title 1**, has led to many important programs that fall into the general category of *compensatory education*—educational services designed specifically to create better opportunities for students with disadvantages, such as those from high-poverty neighborhoods. Examples include:

▶ Early childhood education: Head Start, the most well-known national early childhood program, helps prepare preschool children for school, focusing not just on academic skills but also on nutrition, health, and the family environment

▶ Tutoring and other supplemental academic instruction

▶ After-school centers

▶ Computer labs for poor schools

▶ Dropout prevention services

▶ Job training

▶ Parental education

▶ Professional development for teachers

The No Child Left Behind Act (NCLB) of 2001 revised the ESEA and called for states to develop content-area standards and annual testing of math and reading in grades 3 to 8. Schools with poor test results face the possibility of being closed. This revision also gives parents greater choice about where their children go to school. We discuss the implications of this act in Chapter 6 when we explore contemporary trends in education.

Title IX

Title IX   Part of the federal Educational Amendments of 1972, Title IX states that "No person in the United States shall, on the basis of sex, be excluded from participation in, be denied the benefits of, or be subjected to discrimination under any education program or activity receiving Federal financial assistance."

Title IX, part of the Education Amendments of 1972, is a federal law that prohibits discrimination on the basis of sex in any federally funded education program or activity. The main objective of Title IX is to avoid the use of federal money to support sexually discriminating practices.

Title IX was modeled on Title VI of the Civil Rights Act of 1964, which prohibits discrimination based on race, color, and national origin. However, unlike Title VI, which applies to all federal financial assistance, Title IX is limited to *education* programs or activities that receive federal financial assistance.

Title IX protects the rights of both males and females from prekindergarten through graduate school—in sports, financial aid, employment, counseling, and school regulations and policies. One impact of Title IX has been on girls' sports activities and facilities; it requires that schools provide equal opportunities, funding, and facilities for boys' and girls' teams. Unfortunately, Title IX enforcement has been fairly lax, so it is not entirely unusual to find schools in apparent violation of part of the regulation.

Two other sections of the 1964 Civil Rights Act relate to education as well, and they can be used in conjunction with Title IX to challenge discriminatory practices:

▶ Title IV authorizes federal assistance to prohibit discrimination in education on the basis of sex, race, and national origin.

▶ Title VII prohibits sex discrimination and other types of employment discrimination both in and outside of education contexts (Klein et al., 2002).

A Nation at Risk

A Nation at Risk: The Imperative for Educational Reform   A 1983 federal report that found U.S. schools in serious trouble and inaugurated a new wave of school reform focused on academic basics and higher standards for student achievement.

In 1983, the National Commission on Excellence in Education, a group of scholars and educators convened by the U.S. Department of Education, issued a report in the form of an open letter to the American people. Called **A Nation at Risk: The Imperative for Educational Reform**, this document showed deep concern about the educational system in America:

> *Our society and its educational institutions seem to have lost sight of the basic purposes of schooling, and of the high expectations and disciplined effort needed to attain them. This report, the result of 18 months of study, seeks to generate reform of our educational system in fundamental ways and to renew the Nation's commitment to schools and colleges of high quality throughout the length and breadth of our land. (National Commission on Excellence in Education, 1983).*

The report called for tougher standards for graduation, increases in the required number of mathematics and science courses, higher college entrance requirements, and a return to what was called "academic basics." It also defined "computer skills" as a new basic.

The report further recommended an increase in the amount of homework given, a longer school day, more rigorous requirements for teachers, and updated textbooks. *A Nation at Risk* inaugurated a new period of academic rigor, with increased attention to skills and standards and less emphasis on progressive concerns such as schools' role in building social understanding. The "at risk" wording implied that the United States would lose its global competitive edge if the reforms were not carried out. Even though these recommendations came from the federal government, they were implemented (or sometimes ignored) in different ways at the local, state, and district levels.

LEARNING PROJECT

The Gathering Storm

Rising Above the Gathering Storm: Energizing and Employing America for a Brighter Economic Future is the title of a report issued in 2006 by the National Academy of Sciences, the National Academy of Engineering, and the Institute of Medicine. Congress requested this report to alert the country to the fact that U.S. advantages in science and technology had begun to erode worldwide, and we were indeed losing our competitive edge in the current global marketplace.

Access the report online to learn what actions federal policy makers are recommended to take to ensure that our competitive edge is maintained. You can find it at http://www.nap.edu/catalog/11463.html∅c or by searching for the title. What are the implications of this report for education? Compare this report to the 1983 *A Nation at Risk*, which is available online at http://www.ed.gov/pubs/NatAtRisk/.

The Individuals with Disabilities Education Act (IDEA)

Individuals with Disabilities Education Act (IDEA)   The federal law that guarantees that all children with disabilities receive free, appropriate public education.

In 1975, Congress passed the Education for All Handicapped Children Act (Public Law 94-142) to ensure that all children with disabilities could receive free, appropriate public education, just like other children. This law was revised in 1990, in 1997, and most recently in 2004. It is now known as the **Individuals with Disabilities Education Act (IDEA)**.

What is so important about this act? Before 1975, there was no organized, equitable way of addressing the needs of disabled students in the public school system. Often they were marginalized, taught in separate classrooms, and provided with watered-down curricula.

As a result of the federal legislation, however, strong efforts have been made to include students with disabilities in regular classrooms. This reform, known as **inclusion**, has been implemented to greater or lesser degrees in different school districts. There are classrooms in which students with learning disabilities are integrated with general education students as much as possible. There are also classrooms in which students with special educational needs are included in the general education classroom some of the time; this arrangement is called *partial inclusion*. Some districts have a *self-contained* class as well, for students with special needs (who are often called *special education* students). Often, depending on the needs of the student population, all three models exist in the same school district. We will return to the subject of inclusion in Chapter 6.

inclusion   The practice of educating students with disabilities in regular classrooms alongside nondisabled students.

WRITING and REFLECTION

Gender, Schooling, and Title IX

- What has been your own experience of the effect of gender on educational opportunities? Do you remember ways in which your educational experience differed from that of your female or male peers? Be specific.

- Consider what Title IX says about the ways in which schools must operate. Consider, too, how far we have come as a nation from our early history when girls could not attend the early Latin grammar schools and most early academies. Do you feel we have made enough progress? not enough?

Single-Sex Schooling

Many students who have attended single-sex private schools have had very positive experiences. In fact, some public schools, for a wide range of reasons, have offered single-sex classes as well. In one public school I encountered, an all-girls physics class was thought to be a good way to engage more young women in physics. Success was measured by the achievement of the young women in the class.

Similarly, in Queensland, Australia, several high schools are experimenting with all-boys English literature and writing classes. They also are meeting with successful outcomes in terms of achievement.

Do these examples show that "separate but equal" can be a useful principle when it comes to segregation by sex? Why or why not?

Inclusion as a Model for Special Education

- Reform movements on behalf of children with disabilities have dominated special education programs for the past thirty years. What was your experience with inclusive classrooms? Were you part of a blended classroom environment of general and special education students?

- Much educational research suggests that inclusion benefits both special education students and students from the general population. Does that match your experience?

- If you have not had personal experience with inclusion, share what you have heard about it during your years in school.

Strong efforts are made to include students with disabilities in regular classrooms.

Standards-Based Educational Reform

As a response to *A Nation at Risk* and similar publications that followed, groups of scholars from content area associations developed standards for their disciplines, beginning with the National Council of Teachers of Mathematics. The first version of *Principles and Standards for School Mathematics* appeared in 1989. Language arts, science, social studies, and foreign languages followed in the 1990s, developing standards for what children at each grade level from prekindergarten to grade 12 should know and be able to do in each of the content areas. States were asked to prepare content standards based on these national guidelines and to create assessments to match the standards.

Hence the era in which we are presently living—and in which you are preparing to teach—is dominated by standards-based school reform and assessments. This movement, driven in part by the No Child Left Behind Act of 2002, is a model of considerable rigor, accountability, and strict benchmarks for student learning.

Today, teachers and school administrators often find that they have relatively little freedom to vary the curriculum or even the order in which topics are taught. Yet there are still some places where local control predominates, as the following story demonstrates:

Ms. Bennett is the principal of a public elementary school in Maryland, where children in grades 1 through 5 explore a different human-made artifact each year. The first grade studies bridges, the second grade studies elevators, the third grade investigates escalators, the fourth grade focuses on airplanes, and fifth-grade students explore the automobile. These various products of engineering design form themes that are addressed during the entire school year, regardless of what other topics are studied in that year.

How did this unusual curriculum come about? Few elementary schools have a mandate to teach students about such inventions in a formal way. When you meet Ms. Bennett, however, you learn that she entered the field of education after several years as a civil engineer. One of the first women in her college class to excel in civil engineering, she brought her passion for the work to her elementary school students. As a principal, Ms. Bennett enlisted her faculty's help to make learning about engineering design part of the school's curriculum.

In the current era of standards-driven school reform, do you think the curriculum in Ms. Bennett's school would win enthusiastic approval from the state or federal government? Later chapters will go deeper into the implications of the standards-based movement for teaching and learning.

WRITING and REFLECTION

A National Curriculum?

In the next chapter, we look at what the term *curriculum* means in practice. Before reading that chapter, stop and ask yourself this question: Given the national standards developed for virtually all school subject areas in the past twenty years, is there such a thing as a national curriculum? If you moved in the fourth grade from Montana to Illinois, would the topics addressed in school be the same? Why or why not?

Federal Mandates and Local Control

Many people believe that local control over education has eroded over the years. They say that federal legislation has intruded into the ways schools are run, often to the schools' detriment. What do you think? Are local controls more important than federal controls? Why? Why not?

CONCLUDING THOUGHTS

As you think about the history of American public education, consider all the factors that contribute to the structure and design of schooling today. In addition to geography, acts of Congress, immigration, and educational movements, we now have international events, global challenges, and a technology revolution shaping and reshaping the landscape of public education.

Today we are faced with unprecedented cultural, ethnic, and racial diversity in our schools, and although there are many local and national academic standards, *there is no standard student!* In this respect, we live in an unusual period in American education. Yet our long educational history, and the philosophies and debates that have emerged during that time, continue to influence our choices.

As you work on the Chapter Challenge of learning in detail about a local school district, think about how the district you have chosen fits into the overall pattern of American education.

JOIN THE DISCUSSION

Visit the student website and locate the Edublog for Chapter 3. Continue the discussion by responding to the following questions:

- Why is it important to diversify the teaching workforce? Why does it matter, for example, that a typical kindergarten teacher is a white female?
- How would you characterize your personal teaching philosophy at this point? Are you an essentialist? a progressive? a social reconstructionist? a mix of several types? How and why?

CHAPTER CHALLENGE

Learning About a Local School District

At this time, you'll find it useful to visit a local public school district's website. See what you can learn about the history of schooling in the area, the mission of the district, how the schools in the district are funded, and the biggest challenges facing the district today.

Write a description of this school district as if you were a real estate agent advertising the district to a future homeowner or apartment dweller. Here are some questions to guide your district profile:

- What are the key elements of the district's mission statement?
- Is the school district known for outstanding projects? What are they? How are they presented?
- Has a student or teacher from this district recently distinguished herself or himself in any special way?
- How many schools are in the district?
- How many students attend the schools?
- When was the district formed?
- How is the central administration of the district organized?
- Is there a "state of the district" report? What does it say?
- Is there a board of education for the district? If so:

  - How many members are on it? What is the duration of their terms?
  - What are the board's responsibilities? (In some states, boards are responsible for establishing the policies governing the operation of the schools.)

FROM THE COLLEGE CLASSROOM TO YOUR OWN CLASSROOM

Building Your Personal Philosophy

Add to your professional portfolio by identifying elements of essentialism, perennialism, progressivism, and other philosophies that you believe in. Use these to build on the personal philosophy that you have already begun to develop.

It is not enough to interpret what you have read. The well-prepared teacher must explain his or her rationale for designing a learning experience in a particular way.

RESOURCES FOR FURTHER EXPLORATION

Books

Mortimer J. Adler, *The Paideia Proposal: An educational manifesto* (New York: Simon & Schuster, 1998).   A now-classic statement of perennialist philosophy.

Lawrence Cremin, ed., *The republic and the school: Horace Mann on the education of free men* (New York: Teachers College Press, 1957).   This book provides original speeches and documentation exploring the contributions of Horace Mann, commonly known as the "Father of American Public Education."

John Dewey, *Democracy and education: An introduction to the philosophy of education* (Carbondale: Board of Trustees of Southern Illinois University, 1985; originally published in 1916).   Dewey describes the challenges of providing quality public education in a democratic society. He argues for the necessity of universal education for the advancement of the individual and of society.

Paulo Freire, *Pedagogy of the oppressed,* trans. Myra Bergman Ramos, 30th Anniversary Edition (New York: Continuum, 1970).   An impassioned argument for education in the service of social change.

Maxine Greene, *Variations on a blue guitar: The Lincoln Center Institute Lectures on Aesthetic Education* (New York: Teachers College Press, 2001).   This collection, which brings together lectures given over a period of twenty-five years, reflects a growing urgency for aesthetic education.

Nancy Hoffman, *Woman's "true" profession: Voices from the history of teaching* (Cambridge, MA: Harvard Education Press, 2003).   In addition to essays by Hoffman, this volume includes writings by women teachers who practiced between 1830 and 1920. The book gives terrific insight into the lives of teachers who built and transformed public education.

Anzia Yezierska, *Bread givers: A novel,* with a foreword by Alice Kessler-Harris (New York: Persea Books, 2003).   Set in the Lower East Side of New York City in the 1920s, this is a compelling story of a young immigrant Jewish woman's struggle for independence, education, and work.

Online Resources

The Informal Education Archives http://www.infed.org/archives/   A wide-ranging collection, this site offers works by John Dewey and many other writers on educational philosophy and practice.

National Dissemination Center for Children with Disabilities
http://www.nichcy.org/   This website provides data and research related to children with disabilities, explains various iterations of the IDEA, and offers helpful suggestions for teachers of students with disabilities.

School: The Story of American Public Education
http://www.pbs.org/kcet/publicschool/roots_in_history/index.html   In addition to providing a survey of famous innovators in American education, this site explores the historical roots of current educational controversies.

Title IX of the Education Amendments of 1972
http://www.usdoj.gov/crt/cor/coord/titleix.htm   Explore this website, sponsored by the Civil Rights Division of the U.S. Department of Justice, for further information about Title IX.

CHAPTER 4

Principles of Teaching and Learning: Exploring Pedagogy, Curriculum, and Instruction

FOCUSING QUESTIONS

▶ Why do most people think they can teach? Why do they suggest that teaching is easy?

▶ What have psychologists and educators discovered about the way people learn? What have scientists discovered through the study of human brain? How does such knowledge help us become better teachers?

▶ What is meant by a *curriculum*?

▶ Who decides what to teach?

▶ How does the expression "one size does not fit all" relate to education?

▶ What are the best ways to find out what students are learning?

> *If a doctor, lawyer, or dentist had 40 people in his office at one time, all of whom had different needs, and some of whom did not want to be there and were causing trouble, and the doctor, lawyer or dentist, without assistance, had to treat them all with professional excellence for nine months, then he (or she) might have some conception of the classroom teacher's job.*
>
> — Donald D. Quinn

As you consider a teaching career, you will frequently hear the terms *pedagogy, curriculum,* and *instruction*. What exactly do these terms mean? Are they all approximately the same, or are they different in important ways? How do they relate to teaching and learning? What does Donald Quinn mean when he speaks of "different needs"? How can we define professional excellence so that we can imagine what it might look like in ourselves?

In this chapter we examine the meaning of teaching and learning through an exploration of learning theories. Currently, the field of neuroscience—the study of the structure, function, development, and physiology of the brain and the nervous system—is at the forefront of understanding how people perceive and interact with the external world. Other important approaches have also contributed to the way educators think about learning today. We will examine, too, what a school curriculum is and how its content is shaped by national standards as well as by states, local school districts, local school boards, school curriculum committees, and teachers themselves.

At several points in the chapter, we will encounter parts of an interview with Dr. Jacqueline (Jackie) Grennon Brooks, a cognitive scientist and an expert in the area of learning theory. First, however, let's deal with the nature of teaching and whether it does, indeed, require special knowledge or whether it is a job anyone can do.

ANYONE CAN TEACH?

Most people have spent much of their lives as students in classrooms. Add up the years of schooling *you* have had up to this time—the number is certainly considerable, isn't it? Because people have been in classrooms for so much of their lives, there exists a common myth that "anyone can teach."

As a new teacher just starting out, I confided my nervousness about my first day of teaching to a friend, and he said to me, "Teaching is easy. You just stand up there and talk—and you like to talk." For me, that was the first of several experiences with people who *think* they know what being a teacher is all about.

As you are probably discovering for yourself, teaching and learning are complex activities. They are far from easy and automatic. As we explore the ways a teacher fosters learning, you will see that there is a lot to know about the principles behind what a teacher does. Remember, too, that the process is a dialectic. That is, it requires communication with your students, and it demands that you be an active listener, not just a talker. (My friend was right, however: I *do* like to talk.)

PEDAGOGY AND INSTRUCTION

In Chapter 2, we discussed how *who we are* comes to bear on *what we do* with our students and how we engage them in learning. In fact, who we are has everything to do with how we teach.

Pedagogy is commonly thought of today as the art or science of being a teacher. I like to think of this modern interpretation as the art *and* science of being a teacher. What makes pedagogy an art? It is a personal creative expression of oneself. I am reminded of the French philosopher and essayist Joseph Joubert (1754–1824), who said, "To teach is to learn something twice." As a teacher, you explore ways to create a lesson that will help your students understand something you already understand; this is like learning the concept again!

Yet pedagogy is more than an art. It is also a science because it relies on careful observations of (1) students' dispositions, (2) students' prior knowledge, and (3) students' responses to the activities and questions in which they are engaged. Scientists have helped us understand more clearly how students learn and how we can best promote that learning.

How, then, does *instruction* differ from pedagogy? In a conversation I had with Jackie Grennon Brooks, which I will quote from later in the chapter, she helped clarify the distinction between the two words. As Jackie explained, the root of the word *pedagogy* is the Greek stem *paid-*, meaning the child. Pedagogy began as the study of the child, and the term morphed to mean the study of teaching and learning.

pedagogy   The art and science of teaching; all that you know and believe about teaching.

instruction   The act or process of teaching; the way your pedagogy becomes enacted in practice.

In formal terms, therefore, **pedagogy** can be thought of as the belief system and the orientation that you bring to your instructional practice. **Instruction** emerges from that on a daily basis. Your pedagogy is the subtext beneath the instruction you provide in your classroom. For example, if you believe that you need to understand students' ideas and beliefs to help them gain new understanding, then that is part of your pedagogy. Your instructional decisions will emerge from that pedagogy. As teachers gain new ideas about how people learn, their pedagogical stance can shift in response to those ideas.

People often use the terms *instructional methods* and *pedagogy* interchangeably, but understanding the difference helps teachers reflect on their practice. Pedagogy is the personal teaching philosophy that gets expressed through instructional practice. It informs all the methods of instruction and decision making in the classroom. Keeping the meaning of the terms separate is important because it reminds us to revisit our personal teaching philosophy every time we plan for instruction.

Many special subject area teachers—such as math, science, social studies, language arts, and foreign language teachers—believe that they need merely to be experts in their particular areas. However, even if you are a subject area expert, becoming an expert *teacher* in your subject area requires special professional understanding. Teachers must integrate, transform, and represent subject matter knowledge in ways that are understandable to students (Toh, et al.,

pedagogical content knowledge (PCK) The understanding of how particular topics, problems, or issues can be adapted and presented to match the diverse interests and abilities of learners.

2003). This special type of knowledge is referred to as **pedagogical content knowledge**, or **PCK** for short. Being subject-specific, PCK refers to the ways particular subject matter material is best represented and communicated to make it accessible to students (Shulman, 1987, p. 4).

Now that we have clarified our terms, let's look at what some major investigators of the past century have discovered about the learning process. As you'll see, their work has led to competing theories about the way learning occurs.

LEARNING THEORIES

learning theory An explanation of how learning typically occurs and about conditions that favor learning.

The growth of the field of psychology in the twentieth century and recent advances in neuroscience have formed the foundation for learning theories that are reflected to a greater or lesser extent in schools across the country. **Learning theories** are formal ideas about how learning may happen.

There are many ways to think about learning. For some people, learning is a process; for others, it is a product; and for most people, it is both. Over the past hundred years or so, psychologists and others have used the developmental theories of their time to describe conditions that they have considered optimal for learning.

Behaviorism: A Teacher-Centered Approach

In the mid-1900s, Harvard psychologist B. F. Skinner pioneered a theory of how people learn that still has followers today. Skinner's theory of *operant conditioning* viewed learning as a response to external stimuli in the environment. For Skinner, learning was a product that could be promoted by teachers who provided the right incentives and motivation. This general approach came to be known as **behaviorism**. Behaviorists believe that all learning is shaped by the stimuli in the environment and that free will plays no role in the process.

behaviorism The theory that learning takes place in response to reinforcements (for instance, rewards or punishments) from the outside environment.

Using the behaviorist approach, teachers structured their lessons around clear objectives that stated what students would be able to do by the end of the lesson. The desired behaviors were regulated by carefully planned reinforcements and punishments. The external rewards could include good grades, increased privileges, or a special smile from the teacher. Students were seen as passive participants in the classroom who responded to the teacher's direct rewards and punishments.

Behaviorist ideas still form a backdrop for many techniques used to establish classroom discipline. For instance, teachers rely on behaviorist principles when they set up specific rewards for good behavior. Behaviorism asserts that students will modify their behavior in response to consistent delivery of rewards and punishments.

Yet there are many critics of behaviorist techniques today. Some argue that behaviorist teachers exercise too much control over their students, with the result that students tend to learn facts rather than deep concepts. Others remind teachers that rewards and punishments do not help students develop their own internal mechanisms for doing quality work and that students eventually lose interest in what they are essentially being "bribed" to do (Kohn, 1999).

Learning about students requires that teachers be active listeners.

WRITING and REFLECTION

Your Life as a Student

In what ways, if any, do your experiences as a student reflect the ideas of behaviorism? Do you remember one or more teachers who relied heavily on external rewards or punishments? Write down some specific examples of the application of this pedagogy in your past or current classrooms. Remember, we tend to teach as we have been taught, but that may not be the best approach for our future students!

Cognitive Learning Theories: The Role of Mental Processing

cognitive learning theories Explanations of the mental processes that occur during learning.

As behaviorists focused solely on students' observable behaviors as the indicators of learning, many educators and psychologists began to resist this passive view. **Cognitive learning theories** emerged to describe students' mental development. Cognitive learning theorists went "inside the head of the learner" to discover and model the thought processes that occur during learning.

A key figure in cognitive learning theory was the Swiss scholar and scientist Jean Piaget, who began conducting interviews and research studies with children in the 1920s. From these investigations, he developed the idea of *stages of cognitive development:* idea that at certain times in a child's intellectual growth different mental structures begin to emerge. He believed that most children between eighteen months and two years of age are in the sensorimotor stage, in which learning occurs mainly through sensory impressions and movement. Later, children begin to learn words and other symbols (the preoperational stage, ages two to seven); begin to generalize concepts from concrete experiences (the concrete operational stage, ages seven to eleven); and finally develop the ability to manipulate abstractions (the formal operational stage, ages eleven and older). Piaget argued that at each of these stages of maturation, a child is ready for a different type of learning. (Some critics of Piaget say that children can be in several stages at once and that the stages cannot easily be linked to certain ages.)

At each stage, Piaget decided, knowledge is not passively received but is actively built up by the learner through a process of invention or creation, not reception. This gives a great deal of responsibility to the learner. Jerome Bruner (1960, 1966), another cognitive learning theorist, took Piaget's ideas a step further by arguing that at any stage of cognitive development, teachers should allow children to discover ideas for themselves. His approach, known as *discovery learning,* remains influential today and has much in common with constructivism, which we will come to in a moment.

Social Cognitive Theories: The Role of Social Interactions

Piaget's work was soon criticized for not taking into account the learner's social contexts. After all, when children develop their understanding of the world, they do not do so in a social or cultural vacuum. Some of Piaget's critics developed forms of *social learning theory;* these over time were extended into **social cognitive learning theories**, which take into account both the learner's own mental processes and the social environment in which the learning occurs.

social cognitive learning theories Explanations that describe how learning involves interactions between the learner and the social environment.

One important social cognitive theorist, the Russian psychologist Lev Vygotsky (1962), showed how social contexts influence the ideas that people develop. As one example, the teacher and students in a classroom use language that is socially and culturally accepted in that specific environment. The ideas that children develop in the classroom conform to these socially accepted usages and meanings. When students work in groups and read each other's writing in order to critique it, for example, one student says of the other's work, "This is so cool." The meaning is that this student peer really liked the story, and the comment is readily understood. Clearly, different cultures, neighborhoods, and parts of the world would have different ways of expressing the same meaning. Since students do not learn in a cultural vacuum, studying how people learn requires consideration of the context.

Many social cognitivists stress the importance of *modeling.* For instance, if you were teaching young students how to add columns of numbers, you would probably model the process of exchanging ten ones for one ten. According to social cognitivists, students would learn, in part, by observing you; then they would learn more by doing a similar problem themselves; and they would be further served by using manipulative materials and working on exchanging units with their peers in a group.

Helping students work with others to meet common goals is an important part of teaching.

Thinking about modeling reminds us that teachers are not the only important social influence on learning. Parents, other adults, siblings, and peers have major effects on a child's intellectual development as well. A young person learns a great deal by observing various other people, communicating with them, and solving problems with them.

Constructivism: Student-Centered Learning

The work of Piaget, Bruner, Vygotsky, and others have paved the way for understanding in greater depth how people learn. The accumulated research has shown that the essence of learning is the constant effort to assimilate new information. As Carl Rogers (1983) explained, you don't merely draw in new

Carl Rogers on Learning

The well-known psychologist Carl Rogers (1983) had this to say about the learning process:

I want to talk about learning. But not the lifeless, sterile, futile, quickly forgotten stuff that is crammed into the mind of the poor helpless individual tied into his seat by ironclad bonds of conformity! I am talking about LEARN-ING—the insatiable curiosity that drives the adolescent boy [and girl] to absorb everything he [or she] can see or hear or read about gasoline engines in order to improve the efficiency and speed of his [or her] 'cruiser.' I am talking about the student who says, "I am discovering,

drawing in from the outside, and making that which is drawn in a real part of me." I am talking about any learning in which the experience of the learner progresses along this line: "No, no, that's not what I want"; "Wait! This is closer to what I am interested in, what I need"; "Ah, here it is! Now I'm grasping and comprehending what I need and what I want to know!"

I especially like the part of this quotation that talks about "drawing in from the outside, and making that which is drawn in a real part of me." That would omit the types of "learning" that include memorizing for tests!

information from the outside. For real learning to occur, you also have to make that information your own so that it becomes significant to you and you can use it for your own purposes. These ideas form the basis of a group of learning theories called **constructivism**. The constructivist approach builds on cognitive and social cognitive theories but goes further by considering how new information becomes meaningful to the learner.

constructivism   A group of theories about knowledge and learning whose basic tenet is that all knowledge is constructed by synthesizing new ideas with prior knowledge. Constructivism holds that knowledge is not passively received; rather, it is actively built by the learner as he or she experiences the world.

The Essence of Constructivism: Building Mental Schemes

Since constructivism is the learning theory most closely related to what we currently understand about how people learn, I sought an expert in the field, cognitive psychologist Jackie Grennon Brooks, to answer some questions.

> **JK:** *You have written a great deal about the learning theory called* constructivism. *How do you describe it?*

> **JGB:** Constructivism is a learning theory, and it is also an epistemology.[1] It is the study of how people learn in various contexts. It is the exploration of how people create their own knowledge using the social context around them. Learners interact with people, objects, and ideas to construct their understanding of what is happening around them.

> **JK:** *What is the main premise of constructivism?*

> **JGB:** Constructivism postulates mental schemes that change both incrementally and through big leaps. Learners see the outside world through their mental schemes. When the learner is interacting with new data and the information does not fit [an existing scheme], the learner uses what does not fit to reformulate the scheme. The learner then goes on to use this reconstructed scheme to makes sense of the new information.

mental scheme   An organizational structure in the brain; a group of foundational concepts that help the individual make sense of the world.

Let's pause a moment to examine this idea of mental schemes. A **scheme** is a sort of organizer in the brain. As the result of all your experiences during your lifetime, you have formed these organizing structures in your mind that help you make sense of the world. As Jackie notes, when you encounter new information, you try to fit it into your existing schemes. Sometimes it fits easily, as shown in the first part of Figure 4.1. Sometimes, though, it doesn't fit, as the second part of the figure illustrates.

When new information fails to match your existing schemes—when it doesn't fit your picture of the world—you have a choice. You can ignore the new information—in a sense, reject it. In that case, we can say that no new learning has occurred. Or you can remake your set of schemes to accommodate the new data—a process of truly making new information your own. That is what happens when we learn something.

To explain how people make meaning of new ideas, Jackie Grennon Brooks uses the metaphor of a "grand dance." This phrase refers to the ways each of us makes sense of the world. The "dance" involves synthesizing new experiences with what we have previously come to understand. We achieve this synthesis either by interpreting the new idea or event through our existing set of schemes about the world or by creating new schemes that better take into account the new experience, idea, or concept.

---

1 *Epistemology* is a branch of philosophy devoted to the study of knowledge. It examines the nature and scope of knowledge and philosophical questions such as: "What is knowledge?" "How is knowledge acquired?" and "What do people know?"

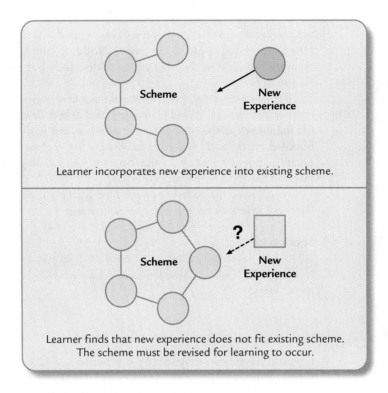

FIGURE 4.1
The Role of Mental Schemes in Learning
These simple diagrams suggest what happens when a learner tries to fit new information into an existing mental scheme. Sometimes the new material fits easily. If it doesn't, the learner must revise the scheme.

For a concrete instance of mental schemes at work, consider the following teaching story, which is not about a classroom but about an earlier context in which teaching occurs—a mother dealing with a puzzled young child.

TEACHING STORIES
MENTAL SCHEMES AT WORK

I grew up in an inner-city apartment building with six floors and twenty apartments on each floor. When I was six years old, I was allowed to use the small key to open the mailbox assigned to my family and "take out the mail." This was my daily job after school.

I had my own personal theory about mail delivery. I imagined that, when the envelope was dropped in the public mailbox on the corner, a tube carried it through underground chutes to its destination in my little mailbox. Even at the age of six, however, I was troubled by not being able to explain how the letter knew how to get to *my* mailbox.

One day, when walking with my mother, I bent down to look under the mailbox on the corner. "What are you looking for?" she asked. "I was wondering where the tubes were," I responded. "What tubes?" she asked, and I then proceeded to share my theory. Nodding, she said that she could not explain right then how the mail got to the mailbox but she would arrange a way for me to find out.

Shortly thereafter, I was home ill from school, in the care of my grandmother. My mother called from work and asked Grandma to take me down to the mailboxes at the precise time that Artie, our mailman, would arrive. She bundled me up and I was able to witness the mailman, with his special key, open the portal to all of the mailboxes in the building. One box at a time, he inserted the mail in the various boxes.

He allowed me to help him, thrilled with my curiosity about how mail "knows" where to go. He also invited me and my family to the local post office for a view of how the postal workers sort the mail for the various neighborhood routes.

I shall never forget this experience. It demonstrates, for me, what it means to reorganize my mental schemes as I set about understanding more of my external world.

THE TEACHING IDEAS BEHIND THIS STORY

It would have been easy for my mother to say, "No, Janice, mail does not travel through tubes in the ground." Instead, she honored my theory, found it quite interesting, and arranged for me to have an experience that would challenge my beliefs about underground tubes and mail delivery. By observing how the mailman opened all the mailboxes simultaneously with his large master key, I saw people as an intricate part of the mail delivery process. I began to expand my thinking and accommodate this new experience into my mental scheme.

Constructivist instruction begins with close attention to students' existing ideas, knowledge, skills, and attitudes. Just as my mother realized, these are the foundation on which new learning builds (Bransford & Donovan, 2002). Learning as much as we can about students' existing mental schemes is important if we hope to help them learn. Constructivist teachers try to activate students' prior knowledge so that, in the course of the lesson, students can build on what they already know, challenge it, rethink it, and refine it.

Because constructivists pay so much attention to students' preexisting ideas, they often face a situation similar to the one my mother encountered: the student reveals ideas that are plainly "wrong." What should a teacher do when a student has such misconceptions? Many educators believe that if teachers merely correct students' erroneous ideas verbally, those ideas may go underground—they may linger in the student's mind, unrefuted. Instead, the teacher should treat the misconception with respect and guide the student in confronting new information that contradicts it. In wrestling with the contradiction, the teacher hopes, the student will modify old mental schemes or create new ones, and in this way genuine learning will occur.

There will be many times when you will be tempted to refute a student's idea or explanation. It's certainly true that you should not allow your student to harbor misconceptions for a long time. But try to find a way to provide convincing evidence for the alternative, more accurate explanation.

Perhaps you can remember a personal theory that you held onto when you were young. How did you eventually learn, through experience and interaction with the material, that you had to adjust your thinking?

Constructivism and Teaching

A teacher's purpose is not to create students in his [or her] own image, but to develop students who can create their own image.

— Anonymous

In my interview with Jackie Grennon Brooks, she went on to explain how teachers demonstrate the constructivist approach when they help students build ideas for themselves.

JK: *OK, what does this notion of mental schemes say to us about teaching?*

JGB: It says a lot about teaching. If we can offer opportunities for students to work iteratively[2] on big concepts, the students can address those concepts over time until they can construct those concepts for themselves.

Here is an example: understanding that the order of the digits in a number tells you the value of the digits. Place value is a huge idea! Students cannot understand place value by having it explained, but when they have the opportunity to exchange bundles of units and bundle the bundles and then represent the bundles in some numerical form, then they can come to make sense of numbers.

Representing numbers as numerals is part of the convention we establish. We talk in code to one another, and students need to reinvent

Using materials, conferring with peers, and asking questions are ways that students learn math.

2 *Iteratively* means repeatedly, on multiple occasions.

that code for themselves. Then the ones, tens, and hundreds columns have meaning, and the number really represents a quantity.

This may seem like a radical idea—that individual students need to "reinvent" a basic operation we use for arithmetic. But think about what happens if students learn only the mechanical processes of mathematics. When young children are adding numbers, they can learn to "carry a 1" from one column to the next, but if they do not get the *meaning* of this procedure, they will have only a shallow and fragile understanding of what they are doing. Later on in their mathematical education, they will likely get confused because they don't fully grasp what is happening.

JK: *What is the most important message of constructivism for teachers?*

JGB: That the child's changing understandings of the world are the centerpiece, and the teacher is always trying to maximize the likelihood of that child's intellectual transformation by offering multiple learning opportunities.

By now you must see that constructivism is a very student-centered approach to teaching and learning. (See Table 4.1, which compares constructivism with behaviorism, cognitive learning theories, and social cognitive learning theories.) In this respect, John Dewey's progressive philosophy of education, which we examined in Chapter 3, provides fertile ground for teaching and learning. I asked Jackie about the link between constructivism and progressivism.

TABLE 4.1 Learning Theories Compared.

Learning Theory	Key Elements
Behaviorism	• Teacher-centered
	• Students respond to external stimuli and learn the correct responses through rewards and punishments, eventually internalizing rewards and punishments
	• Teachers are in absolute control through the stimuli they present in the classroom
Cognitive learning theories	• Somewhat learner-centered
	• Learning is active, not merely passive
	• Symbolic mental constructions in the minds of learners help them process information
Social cognitive learning theories	• Somewhat learner-centered
	• Internal mental processes are important, but we also learn through experiences shared with others; learning is as much social as it is individual
Constructivism	• Learner-centered
	• We all construct our own perspective of the world, based on individual experiences and personal schemes, which are internal knowledge structures
	• A person adjusts his or her mental model to incorporate new experiences and make sense of new information

JK: *In what ways, if any, did John Dewey's theories and the progressive era in American education anticipate current theories about how people learn?*

JGB: The progressive era was consistent with current learning theories because it invited children into a learning environment that was their life. Progressives did not talk about mental schemes, but they talked about opportunities to create a mind free to think for itself.

There was an inaccurate perception of progressivism—that it merely meant doing something physically, like a hands-on experience. Instead, Dewey referred to an active *mental* engagement. This can occur while students are listening, but it needs an attentive teacher.

Perspectives from Neuroscience: The Importance of Context

As my conversation with Jackie continued, we began to explore the ways that recent discoveries in neuroscience support what we know about learning.

JK: *How do theories about how people learn help us teach?*

JGB: Theories of learning become the data on which we base our practices of teaching. The theories of how people learn are changing. For a long time, methods of schooling were based on the behavioral theories that included stimulus-response iterations. What we know now is based on the emerging relationship between neuroscience and teaching.

The more we learn about how the brain cognitively processes, the more we realize that the way our mind works is dependent upon how the neurons in our brain are fired, and that is very dependent on the *context* that is created for learning. The progressive era had the right idea when it encouraged the active participation of students in their own learning.

JK: *How has neuroscience helped us guide our instruction?*

JGB: Problem solving involves the firing of neurons in different regions of the brain. A problem-solving event requires that multiple areas of the brain connect with each other to produce solution sets. [This is

Cookies and Brain Science

For perspective on the evolving understanding of learning, consider the effect of cookies and milk. We have always known that cookies and milk help you sleep; your great-grandmother understood that without any deep scientific exploration. More recently, though, science has added to our understanding. We now know that milk has tryptophan in it. Tryptophan is an essential amino acid and the precursor the body uses to metabolize serotonin, a neurotransmitter that regulates sleep, mood, and other physical processes. The sugar in the cookies helps catalyze the metabolism. Hence,

when you have milk and cookies, your serotonin level increases and you fall asleep. Science has provided a justification for a common practice as well as a better understanding of why it works.

Similarly, we learned many years ago that when students are actively engaged in their own learning, they understand it better. More recently, as science was able to explore neural pathways in the brain, we came to understand the physiology at work, and we see that there is a scientific reason why active engagement of the learner results in better learning.

why many scientists and educators see problem solving as a good way to learn.]

The Chicago Mastery Learning Program [implemented in the early 1980s] divided the process of reading into hundreds of different operations. What we found out was that students could decode [words] more accurately with this process than before it was broken down into hundreds of different operations, but the students were not reading or wanting to read books. We know now that there has to be a conceptual framework on which to build the parts. There needs to be a context—a reason to do the decoding. Yes, more and more data are important, but the learner still needs to *construct* the knowledge. In order to do this, he or she must have the palette on which to put the ideas. The palette must have space for mixing the colors as you need them.

Years ago we taught children that the brain is not a muscle—you cannot exercise it in order to grow. We know differently now. There are different opportunities that do create different types of neural network firing.

When Jackie talks about a "palette," she refers to the context in which the concept being learned occurs. I am reminded of a story in my own third-grade class when we were learning about the sun.

TEACHING STORIES
A PALETTE FOR LEARNING

From this large brick building in an urban area, the teacher, Ms. Schultz, walked us outside into the schoolyard and asked us to feel the sun's warmth. It was an autumn day and the air was cool, but the sun felt warm against our faces. Then she asked us to move about and explore our shadows.

Something Ms. Schultz said in the midst of this experience has stayed with me forever: "Isn't it amazing, girls and boys, that this sun is 93 million miles away and it still has the power to warm us up?" I remember thinking that the sun must be very, very hot if, after traveling all those miles, it still warmed my skin. I have thought about the sun in that way ever since.

On the next sunny day, we returned early to the schoolyard and explored our shadows again, noticing how their length changed with the time of day. Experiencing the sunlight in the context of learning about shadows made a big difference to me. I was taken with how different the size of my shadow was at noon, compared to early morning. Experiencing myself in space, responding to the sun's warmth on my body, joining with my classmates in measuring our shadows—all these activities created a palette on which my learning about the sun and shadows occurred. I have always remembered the distance of the sun from the Earth and that when the sun is overhead, around noon, my shadow is the shortest.

In these simple ways, Ms. Schultz helped create a context that shaped my learning.

WRITING and REFLECTION

The Context of Learning

Specific school memories or anecdotes often stay with us as we grow older. Can you recall an experience in which the *context* of a lesson or activity became attached to the memory of the lasting idea or concept you learned? Describe that experience and indicate how you think the context—or, as Jackie refers to it, the "palette"—made a difference.

What Makes a Fire Burn?

Read the following poem by Judy Brown (2000). Think about it as a metaphor for teaching and learning.

Fire

What makes a fire burn
is space between the logs,
a breathing space.
Too much of a good thing,
too many logs
packed in too tight
can douse the flames
almost as surely as a pail of water would.

So building fires
requires attention
to the spaces in between,
as much as to the wood.

When we are able to build
open spaces
in the same way
we have learned
to pile on the logs,
then we can come to see how
it is fuel, and absence of the fuel
together, that make fire possible.

We only need to lay a log
lightly from time to time.
A fire
grows
simply because the space is there,
with openings
in which the flame
that knows just how it wants to burn
can find a way.

How does this poem relate to constructivism as a theory of how people learn? What do the spaces between the logs represent to you?

WHAT IS A CURRICULUM?

You have read in this chapter a lot about theories of learning and instruction, but what about the actual material you will be required to teach? Educators refer to this as the curriculum. Who determines the curriculum, and how can teachers express their personal and creative selves when handed a list of topics they must address? Think about these questions as you read the following sections.

Formal, Informal, and Hidden Curricula

curriculum A plan of studies that includes the ways instructional content is organized and presented at each grade level.

The word *curriculum* derives from the Latin term meaning "running course." It is the overall plan that includes what you will teach and how the material should be arranged and presented. A curriculum may be thought of as an organizing tool for the myriad topics that are addressed at each grade level. Curricula are typically organized by content area. There are language arts, mathematics, social studies, foreign language, and science curricula. There is a curriculum associated with any subject matter taught at a given school.

informal curriculum Learning experiences that go beyond the formal curriculum, such as activities the teacher introduces to connect academic concepts to the students' daily lives.

Sometimes you will hear the official plan of studies referred to as the *formal curriculum*. There is also an **informal curriculum**, which includes all the things you do in the classroom that are not part of the official, prescribed plan. For example, you might use an important local event or news story to create a learning experience closely linked to the students' own lives. In a high school earth science class, the teacher might address an earthquake that was in the news that week and explore the causes for earthquakes, even if this was not the formal topic of study at that moment. Local news events often become the centerpiece of social studies lessons because of their relevance. Although not written into the preplanned curriculum, these informal events bring meaning to the formal curriculum and deepen students' understanding of the concepts they are learning.

In speaking of the informal curriculum, educators often include the concept of the hidden curriculum, mentioned earlier in this book. The *hidden curriculum* consists of the social rules and values schools and teachers transmit to students. Hidden curricula are communicated through the rules of conduct, dress codes, social atmosphere, and relationships among teachers, administration, and students in a given school environment. They are hidden in the sense that they are not written down, or at least not presented as part of the subject matter to be learned; but they are very much part of the school experience for both students and teachers.

The Role of National Standards and State Frameworks

In the United States, the formal curriculum in public schools is established by each state, with individual school districts adjusting it to a greater or lesser degree. Each state, however, relies heavily on the input of national groups who have been actively involved in establishing standards for their discipline. For example, the National Council of Teachers of Mathematics has a great influence on mathematics curricula throughout the country.

As we explored in Chapter 3, the standards movement has dominated public education since the early 1990s. This movement has prompted subject-area associations to state explicitly what students should know and be able to do at each grade level from kindergarten through twelfth grade, resulting in national standards for each subject. Hence, there are national standards for science, language arts, foreign languages, social studies, mathematics, technology, health, and physical education.

Many states assign statewide committees or task forces to construct curriculum frameworks based on these guidelines. The state frameworks are then adapted by the local school or district and used to develop the school-based curriculum in each subject area. Does this sound complicated? It is! But the key feature here is local control.

Local schools' control of their curricula in each area was quite broad until the federal No Child Left Behind Act was passed in 2001. The act requires that students be held accountable by means of statewide exams that assess their knowledge at various grade levels, often beginning in third grade. That change reduced local schools' control over their curricula. The statewide assessment is often thought of as a "one-size-fits-all" process because it demands a uniform statewide curriculum if students are to be successful on the tests.

The Pressure to "Cover" the Curriculum

Educators often talk about "covering the curriculum." You may hear them say, "There is so much to cover; I can never find enough time." Because of the importance of standards-based assessments, today's teachers do indeed have a great deal of material to address with their students.

In this context, it's important to remember that to "cover" can also mean to "hide." Instead of covering curriculum, constructivists would rather see teachers "uncover" it—that is, guide students to engage with the material in ways that help them reveal the key ideas and construct new understanding. Unfortunately, when there is significant time pressure, curricula often do get covered instead of revealed. We will discuss this matter further in Chapter 6.

WRITING and REFLECTION

Curriculum and Standardized Assessment

In what ways, if any, do local schools' curricula suffer as a result of the inflexibility imposed by standardized assessment? Consider this story, and respond to the questions that follow it.

A Pond in the Northeast

Several years ago, an elementary school in a northeastern suburb began an initiative to build a pond on its school property. The pond would attract birds and insects, the teachers and administrators thought, and they could build an elementary science curriculum around it. They had the pond installed and "seeded" it with a few small koi (similar to goldfish) and water plants.

Grade-level classes took responsibility for monitoring the temperature and turbidity of the pond as well as carefully noticing the life in and around it. The science curriculum in that school grew, with exploration of the properties of the pond being the centerpiece.

- Do you think it is acceptable to address the science curriculum through a study of a pond, even though standardized tests have no questions about ponds? Why or why not?

- If exploring a pond makes it difficult to "cover" all of the standards-based curriculum on which your students would be tested, how do you decide what to do?

- Do you think a curriculum can be both innovative and standards-based?

- Overall, would this pond-centered curriculum still be possible today, given the dominance of standards-driven assessments and state frameworks? Why or why not?

- How is this pond curriculum reflective of a progressive philosophy?

Curriculum as Window and Mirror

Ideally, curriculum should be both a window and a mirror. This metaphor, suggested by Emily Style in a 1996 essay, implies that:

1. Curriculum must provide windows for students into the worlds of others. That is, it should help students learn about other people, other cultures, other realities.

2. Curriculum must also offer mirrors of students' own reality. It should be connected to their lives in ways that help them see the subject matter as meaningful.

I am reminded of how I felt growing up in an inner-city environment and reading *Dick and Jane* basal readers. You are probably familiar with *basal readers,* which are textbooks used to teach reading. The *McGuffey Readers* mentioned in Chapter 3 are an early example; *The Alice and Jerry Books* are another. Typically, basal readers are published as a series of books, with each book in the series designed for a particular reading level. Dick and Jane were the main

Alice and Jerry

FIGURE 4.2
A Page from a Basal Reader
Source: Reproduced with permission of The McGraw-Hill Companies.

characters in basal readers used to teach reading from the 1930s to the 1970s. Figure 4.2 shows a typical page from a basal reader.

Dick and Jane lived in their own house with a white picket fence and a lawn sprinkler. They had a cute dog and a little red wagon. There is nothing wrong with those things, of course, but I used to ask my mother, "Where do Dick and Jane live?" I did not recognize the surroundings, and I wondered where they could be found. Certainly the private house and lawn sprinkler were not found on my block!

For me, the reading curriculum that relied on *Dick and Jane* may have been a window, but it was not at all a mirror. Many students in other areas of the United States had similar experiences with basal readers. The use of basal readers waned during the 1980s and 1990s because their stories and images did not reflect the diversity of students in classrooms across the country. Basal readers were also thought to be less authentic than other forms of writing, such as regular children's literature. Many states and local districts opted for authentic early childhood literature as a way to teach reading.

In many places today, schools use basal readers *and* authentic children's literature, offering students a language arts curriculum that includes both formats. Often, local district committees select the required literature for each grade level, and this, in conjunction with a basal reader, forms the backbone of the language arts curriculum. Many of the newer basal readers include some combination of nonfiction, biographies, adaptations of original children's books, condensations of classic children's literature, and original stories. They also feature students of many origins, not just Caucasians.

In this way, the typical language arts curriculum has evolved to function better as both a window and a mirror. Students get a glimpse into many different kinds of worlds, and more types of students see themselves in the reading material.

As a further exploration of the window/mirror metaphor, consider the following story, adapted from a wonderful paper by Linda Oxendine (1989). Remember, too, what Jackie Grennon Brooks said about creating a "palette"—a context—to help children learn.

TEACHING STORIES
SECOND GRADERS EXPLORE REGIONAL LITERATURE

In the second grade of a rural Appalachian elementary school, Ms. Bauer provides her students with rich, regional stories and uses the children's own mountain heritage and culture to teach reading. Students write their own stories based on local fables and share them with other students. They also read their classmates' stories. Every week they have a real local radio show on which they read their stories and sing songs. They ask their listeners to send them letters.

By the end of the year, the students have written many different kinds of stories, plays, and puppet shows. The stories are collected in a class storybook, which is shown to the new second-grade class as a model.

The most important benefit of this approach is that the students have developed a high motivation to read—unlike the low motivation that accompanied the basal-reader approach in the district. Every student in Ms. Bauer's class is reading avidly, none is failing, and absenteeism is down.

THE TEACHING IDEAS BEHIND THIS STORY

Do you see how the regional Appalachian stories and fables that the children read and write connect directly to their lives? They offer a mirror of the children's daily reality, and they give the students a context or palette on which to build their learning.

Note, too, that these regional stories are not part of a formal curriculum. They are an informal curriculum that Ms. Bauer developed herself. This informal curriculum carries the tacit message to Ms. Bauer's students that she cares deeply about how they live, who they are, and the heritage of the local area. Of course, she is also interested in having them learn to read and write—the object of the formal curriculum—and she realizes that this informal curriculum will help them accomplish that goal.

LEARNING PROJECT

Examining a School's Language Curriculum

Visit an elementary school close to your university or college and explain that, for a course project, you would like to examine the school's language arts basal reader and/or its literature series for grades one through three.

- What is your impression of the reading material being used for these early readers?
- Knowing what you do about the children who attend this school, in what ways do you think this reading material may act as a window? as a mirror?

Adapting the Curriculum to Your Students

One implication of what we have been saying is that you should evaluate the curriculum in light of who your students are. When presented with a curriculum in a subject area, you should ask yourself, "How can I make this curriculum more relevant to the students in this classroom at this time in their lives?" If we think of learning as a process of re-forming mental schemes, then teachers need to begin to understand their students' mental schemes in order to be successful.

This is a challenging task. One way to accomplish it is to pay careful attention to the experiences of your students. Through discussion and writing assignments, you can invite the students' authentic selves into the classroom and learn much more about them. Table 4.2 lists some questions that can help you explore the world of your students.

WRITING and REFLECTION

Curriculum as Window and Mirror

Read the 1996 essay by Emily Style called "Curriculum as Window and Mirror." You can access it online at http://www.wcwonline.org/seed/curriculum.html. In this essay, Ms. Style discusses how important it is for students to see beyond their own worlds while also seeing themselves represented in the curriculum, understanding that their experience in the world matters and that people like them have made contributions to life as we know it in the United States.

- Imagine how you can take a standard topic, such as the American Revolution, and invite students to see themselves in the experience.
- Is the metaphor of curriculum as window and mirror more aligned with a behaviorist or a constructivist view of learning? Thinking back to what you read about educational philosophies in Chapter 3, is it more likely to appeal to essentialists or to progressives?

TABLE 4.2   Questions to Ask About Your Students

- Who are my students?

- What are their interests, concerns, hobbies, beliefs, and feelings about themselves and others?

- Where do they live? Do they have siblings? Do they have both parents at home? Do both parents work outside the home? What do the students do after school?

- How can I adapt the formal curriculum to the experiences that the students encounter every day? How can I provide students with a mirror so that they will understand that their lives are part of the school curriculum?

ASSESSMENT: HOW DO WE KNOW WHAT THEY KNOW?

assessment Collecting information to determine the progress of students' learning.

Closely linked to curriculum and instruction is **assessment**, the process of collecting information to find out what students are learning. As teachers, we are always asking, "What do my students know? How are they able to demonstrate that knowledge?"

Evidence of student learning, like learning itself, is complex and takes many forms. You are probably accustomed to traditional assessments, such as paper-and-pencil tests with multiple-choice, true/false, fill-in-the-blank, and essay questions, used to evaluate students' understanding of the subject matter being taught. Typically, except for the essay questions, these tests are thought of as a measure of what students can recall at the moment, not necessarily what they have incorporated into an existing or new mental scheme.

Many students think of assessments as tests of this traditional type, given at the end of a unit. However, the more we understand about how people learn, the more we realize that an assessment is like a good instructional task and should be part of every lesson, providing feedback to both the teacher and the students about how the students are developing their understanding of the concepts in a unit. Assessments of this type are often called **embedded assessments**.

embedded assessments Classroom-based assessments that make use of the actual assignments that students are given as a unit is being taught. These can be used to evaluate developmental stages of student learning.

Many of the questions in the Writing and Reflection sections of this text are examples of embedded assessments. These questions are tools for reflection on the current instruction, as you are reading the text. Embedded assessments feel like a natural part of the instruction, so you may not be aware you are being assessed!

When we ask students to maintain a journal, write a research report, engage in a debate, design a project, or write an essay explaining a phenomenon, we are using embedded assessments. When these assessments relate directly to tasks or examples in the "real world" outside the classroom, they are also thought of as **authentic assessments**. Activities of this type ask students to perform tasks through which they can express their own ideas. You can see how different these are from tests in which students check true or false, circle a correct choice, or guess at a word for a fill-in question, relying on their recall abilities instead of demonstrating understanding.

authentic (performance) assessment An assessment that asks students to perform a task relating what they have learned to some real-world problem or example.

Often authentic assessment involves some kind of student *performance*; hence, this type of assessment is also called *performance assessment*. One type of performance assessment was pioneered by a group of scholars at Harvard University's Graduate School of Education. In an effort called Project Zero, the educators and psychologists were interested in teaching for understanding and in

A student makes a presentation to her class—demonstrating her understanding of a particular topic. The students then ask questions.

designing assessment tasks called *understanding performances* or *performances of understanding* (Perkins, 1993). Understanding performances are activities that require students to use what they know in new ways or in ways that build their understanding of unit topics. In these performances, students publicly demonstrate their understanding by reshaping, expanding on, extrapolating from, and applying what they already know. See the sidebar for examples of understanding performances.

The Chapter Challenge at the end of this chapter is a type of understanding performance. It asks you to create a curriculum with certain parameters. It

Two Examples of Understanding Performances

For a social studies unit with the understanding goal "Students will understand that history is always told from a particular perspective and that understanding a historical text means understanding who wrote it":

Students compare two accounts of the beginning of the Revolutionary War, one claiming the British fired the first shot and one claiming the colonists did. They then discuss why the two reports might be different and how they could find out what really happened. They use some of these strategies to figure out which (if either) of these accounts is the more plausible; then they present their explanation to the class.

For a mathematics unit with the understanding goals "Students will understand how percentages can be used to

describe real-world happenings" and "Students will understand how to represent numerical information in clear graphs":

In small groups, students collect and compile data about school attendance over the course of two weeks. They calculate the percentage of students who fit various categories (percentage of students absent, percentage present, percentage tardy, and so on). They then create graphs to represent their data visually, collect feedback from the class, and revise their graphs in accordance with the feedback.

Source: ALPS: Active Learning Practices for Schools, http://learnweb.harvard.edu/alps/tour/about.cfm; retrieved April 20, 2007.

requires that you understand the content and nature of curriculum, including sequencing and planning for activities. Your teaching portfolio is another example of an authentic or performance assessment. The From the College Classroom to Your Own Classroom section in each chapter has been urging you to develop your portfolio, using the information you are exploring in your course and with this text to present concepts and challenges that represent your view of teaching and learning. The portfolio reflects the sense making in which you are engaged as you prepare to teach.

rubric A scoring guide for an authentic assessment or a performance assessment, with descriptions of performance characteristics corresponding to points on a rating scale.

Because of the open-ended nature of authentic assessments and performance-based assessments, guidelines for evaluating the final performance are important. These guidelines take the form of a checklist or rubric. A **rubric** defines the expected qualities of student performance and establishes a rating scale. Generally, rubrics specify the level of performance expected for several levels of quality. These levels of quality may be written as ratings (for example, Excellent, Good, Needs Improvement) or as numerical scores (such as 4, 3, 2, 1). Numerical scores can be added up to form a total score, which is then associated with a grade (A, B, C, and so forth).

Imagine you are assessing student understanding of two sides of a contentious issue, such as the trial of Dr. Jack Kevorkian, who was found guilty of assisting people to commit suicide. (This lesson is described in Chapter 6.) You decide to engage the students in a high school history class in a debate on the issue. Table 4.3 shows a rubric you might use. Notice that there are specific ways to describe student effectiveness and achievement. The highest score a student can achieve on this rubric is 24, indicating that she or he scored a 4 for each category described.

As we noted earlier, the No Child Left Behind Act mandates large-scale, standardized assessments in each state and requires that they address mathematics and language arts at varying grade levels. These are traditional-style assessments that may not have any particular relevance to the nature of the

VIDEO CASE

Performance Assessment

Find the HM Video Case "Performance Assessment: Student Presentations in a High School English Class" on the student website. After watching the video, consider the following questions:

- When students make a poster about the writer they are studying, how does that represent a constructivist experience?

- Why do you think the students wanted their peers' feedback on their creativity?

- How did the teacher include the students in deciding how to assess this activity?

- What role did peer assessment play in these performances?

TABLE 4.3   A Sample Rubric for a High School Class Debate

CATEGORY	SCORE			
	4	3	2	1
Understanding of Topic	The team clearly understood the topic in depth and presented their information forcefully and convincingly.	The team clearly understood the topic in depth and presented their information with ease.	The team seemed to understand the main points of the topic and presented those with ease.	The team did not show an adequate understanding of the topic.
Presentation Style	Team consistently used gestures, eye contact, tone of voice, and a level of enthusiasm in a way that kept the attention of the audience.	Team usually used gestures, eye contact, tone of voice, and a level of enthusiasm in a way that kept the attention of the audience.	Team sometimes used gestures, eye contact, tone of voice, and a level of enthusiasm in a way that kept the attention of the audience.	One or more members of the team had a presentation style that did not keep the attention of the audience.
Information	All information presented in the debate was clear, accurate, and thorough.	Most information presented in the debate was clear, accurate, and thorough.	Most information presented in the debate was clear and accurate, but usually was not thorough.	Information had several inaccuracies OR was usually not clear.
Organization	All arguments were clearly tied to an idea (premise) and organized in a tight, logical fashion.	Most arguments were clearly tied to an idea (premise) and organized in a tight, logical fashion.	All arguments were clearly tied to an idea (premise), but the organization was sometimes not clear or logical.	Arguments were not clearly tied to an idea (premise).
Rebuttal	All counterarguments were accurate, relevant, and strong.	Most counterarguments were accurate, relevant, and strong.	Most counterarguments were accurate and relevant, but several were weak.	Counterarguments were not accurate and/or relevant.
Use of Facts/ Statistics	Every major point was well supported with several relevant facts, statistics, and/or examples.	Every major point was adequately supported with relevant facts, statistics, and/or examples.	Every major point was supported with facts, statistics, and/or examples, but the relevance of some was questionable.	Not every point was supported.

Developed with RubiStar, a free online rubric tool at http://rubistar.4teachers.org/.

instruction in a given class in a specific school. Because of this, critics argue that the data gathered from these large-scale assessments are not that reliable. In any case, these tests tell you only a little of what you need to know about your students' learning. Good teaching requires that we seek multiple ways to find out what students know and are able to do in a given area of content.

LEARNING TO TEACH

There is often a disconnect between what we learn about teaching and what we are able to enact in an actual classroom. One reason is that teaching, like many other endeavors, requires practice. Another reason is that we need to examine our beliefs and become comfortable with ourselves as learners as we embark on becoming teachers.

There are no quick and easy ways to make the transition into teaching. But here are some ideas to keep in mind as you consider joining the profession:

- Be comfortable with yourself as a person and feel secure in who you are.

- Wherever possible, give students opportunities to express their own ideas and to be active thinkers.

- Interrogate your students' thinking. That is, ask them where their ideas come from.

- Make connections between what you are teaching and the students' lived experiences.

- Gain an understanding *for yourself* of the material you will teach. Using that knowledge, construct activities and opportunities that lead students to engage with the materials *for themselves.*

- Preparation is a prerequisite for successful teaching!

CONCLUDING THOUGHTS

Is your head spinning from all the theories, philosophies, and movements in American public education you have read about? If so, it is important to remember that your approach to teaching should never be "all or nothing." The boundaries between movements and learning theories can overlap and become blurred.

Understanding more about how people learn helps us know that exploring students' preconceived ideas is essential to planning for instruction. Your plan may borrow principles from learning theories other than constructivism. Naming your personal approach is less important than understanding that it is subject to revision as you grow and learn and enter classrooms in a more formal role. Your present style of teaching and learning is the result of all that came before you historically and all that you personally have experienced in school. Developing consciousness about the role of the teacher and the responsibilities you will have toward your students is important preparation for your future work.

By discussing pedagogy, curriculum, instruction, and assessment, this chapter has provided perspective on part of a big question that faces all teachers: Who are my students, and how can I best teach them? In the next chapter, we will explore in detail the nature and diversity of today's students. We will examine demographic trends in the country and consider the ways your pedagogy may be informed by who your students are.

JOIN THE DISCUSSION

Visit the student website and find the link to the Edublog for Chapter 4. We continue our discussion by responding to the following questions:

➡ What did you think about the mailbox story?

➡ Did you find that you had naïve conceptions of your own as you were growing up—misconceptions about how things really worked? Talk about them. How did you begin to revise these notions?

CHAPTER CHALLENGE

Developing a Curriculum

Select a hobby or an area of personal interest about which you can develop a curriculum—that is, a logical sequence of topics and concepts to be addressed in teaching a group of youngsters about this interest area. For example, if your hobby is figure skating and your imaginary students are in seventh grade, you may want to explore with them the history of figure skating and some biographical data about figure skaters. You may also want to provide diagrams and explanations of various skating techniques, the best skates to buy, and, of course, some cautions and guiding principles.

Your curriculum should address as many aspects of your interest area as possible, but also it should hold the attention of the chosen grade level of students for more than a few days! Use the following guide to assist you in this challenge:

- What is your area of special interest? It can be a hobby, an academic interest, or a visual or performing art.

- What are the most important things you would want young people to know about this area? Make a list.

- Organize your list of topics, starting from the most basic and moving to the most complex.

- Explain each of the topics from the perspective of someone who knows very little about your special area. (For example, I know very little about figure skating.)

- What do you think are the most prevalent misconceptions about your area? Write them down. (For instance, I happen to think figure skating is dangerous.)

- How will you help students who hold these misconceptions to reconstruct their mental schemes?

FROM THE COLLEGE CLASSROOM TO YOUR OWN CLASSROOM

Relating Learning Theories to Your Teaching Philosophy

For your teaching portfolio, reflect on the learning theories presented in this chapter and discuss a theory that can help you make sense of your personal teaching philosophy. You may use more than one theory to pull together a teaching approach that makes sense to you. Remember: it is subject to change by the end of this book.

RESOURCES FOR FURTHER EXPLORATION

John Bransford, Ann L. Brown, and Rodney Cocking (eds.), *How people learn: Brain, mind, experience and school* (Washington, DC: National Academies Press, 2000).   A good introduction to new research about the way the brain works— and the relevance of this research for teaching and learning.

Suzanne Carothers, "Taking Teaching Seriously," in William Ayers (ed.), *To become a teacher: Making a difference in children's lives* (New York: Teachers College Press, 1995).   In this essay, Suzanne Carothers captures the essence of the complexity of teaching.

John Dewey, *How we think: A restatement of the relation of reflective thinking to the educative process* (Boston: Houghton Mifflin, 1998; originally published in 1933). A classic work by the great progressive philosopher, still highly relevant today.

Jacqueline Grennon Brooks, *Schooling for life: Reclaiming the essence of learning* (Reston, VA: Association for Supervision and Curriculum Development, 1999). Inspiring stories of teachers, students, and parents provide a vision of what authentically respectful and meaningful learning looks like.

Jacqueline Grennon Brooks and Martin Brooks, *In search of understanding: The case for constructivist classrooms* (Reston, VA: Association for Supervision and Curriculum Development, 1999).   If you liked what you heard in this chapter from Jackie Grennon Brooks, read this book, which is already a classic.

Sam M. Intrator and Megan Scribner (eds.), *Teaching with fire: Poetry that sustains the courage to teach* (San Francisco: Jossey-Bass, 2003).   Do you sometimes find poetry inspiring? Each poem in this collection is accompanied by a story from a teacher explaining how the poem provided encouragement and insight.

Eric Jensen, *Teaching with the brain in mind,* 2nd edition (Alexandria, VA: Association for Supervision and Curriculum Development, 2005).   A multidisciplinary approach to teaching and learning, using research about what happens in the brain when we learn.

Alfie Kohn, *Punished by rewards: The trouble with gold stars, incentive plans, A's, praise, and other bribes* (Boston: Houghton Mifflin, 1999).   Warning! Before reading this book, be prepared to suspend your beliefs about rewards and punishments and to learn the truth about how harmful incentives can be to students' full development.

Mel Levine, *A mind at a time* (New York: Simon & Schuster, 2002).   An important book written by a pediatrician and an education expert, explaining how each student is "wired" differently and that learning is an individual and unique experience for every child.

Barbara L. McCombs and Lynda Miller, *Learner-centered classroom practices and assessments: Maximizing student motivation, learning, and achievement* (Thousand Oaks, CA: Corwin Press, 2007).   This book offers a wide range of teaching and assessment strategies, including self-assessments and personal reflection devices.

Rubistar http://rubistar.4teachers.org/   This website offers a free tool to help teachers construct rubrics for all types of performance assessments. You may edit the suggestions and create your own; however, the starting points provided here can produce quality rubrics.

Taking Stock

Assessing Where You Are and Where You're Going

1. You read in Chapter 3 about the early days of American schooling, when students of all ages were in the same class. Now, in contrast, classes are usually composed of one particular age group. What age preference do you have as you seek to become a teacher?

2. Normal schools and numerous other teacher education programs developed *after* public schools were established. This sequence suggests that the American public discovered a strong need to train its teachers. What do you think are the most important things you will learn in your teacher education program?

3. When you read about various philosophies of education, from essentialism to progressivism, how would you categorize your own education? How about the professional education in which you are now engaged?

4. In what ways, if any, do you relate your potential teaching style to the significance of aesthetic education as fostered by Maxine Greene?

5. What is your personal philosophy about how you learn best? Explain your own learning style.

6. "Teaching and learning are a dialectic: they are two sides of the same coin. Hence, when you are a teacher, you are a learner simultaneously." What do you suppose those statements mean?

7. As you consider theories of learning and what we know today about the workings of the brain, what ideas do you come away with for your own practice?

PART III

Looking at Today's Schools

Here you are, considering a career in education in the early years of a new millennium, one that has already brought a host of major events and transformations. Historians will have much to say about the years you are living through. But recent events have special meaning for you as a prospective teacher. Because schools reflect society, we need to examine the ways schools and schooling have been transformed by social, political, and technological changes.

The following chapters look at phenomena like the enormous influx of immigrant families from various parts of the world, the Internet technology revolution that has blossomed into a way of life, and the increased role of federal and state governments in setting standards to measure the performance of students and teachers. As you read, think about questions like these:

▶ What is the composition of the student body? In what ways does its great diversity pose both challenges and opportunities?

▶ What contemporary educational trends are visible in today's classrooms, and how has access to the Internet both enhanced and posed difficulties for education?

▶ In what ways has standards-based assessment affected the lives of teachers and students?

As you continue your journey toward becoming a teacher, I hope you will take advantage of the learning projects, reflections, and challenges in the chapters ahead. And remember, "goodness of fit" remains an underlying principle of this text. Keep asking yourself: Am I selecting a career path for which I am uniquely well suited?

CHAPTER 5

Who Are Today's Students?

FOCUSING QUESTIONS

▶ In your imaginary classroom:

  ▶ What is your image of the students? Are they white? students of color? Is English their primary language? Are they religious, and if so, what is their religion?

  ▶ Is there access to the Internet in the classroom?

  ▶ How do teachers account for different student learning styles?

▶ Has the student composition of the elementary school you attended changed? If yes, in what ways?

▶ What do you think "culturally relevant pedagogy" refers to?

▶ What is meant by "at-risk" students?

▶ How can you best help English-language learners achieve in your classroom?

▶ How do *you* learn best? Are you a visual learner? an auditory learner?

A person's a person no matter how small. . .
—Theodor Geisel (a.k.a. Dr. Seuss), *Horton Hears a Who!* (1954)

This chapter looks at the students in contemporary U.S. schools—children between the ages of five and eighteen. As the quotation from Dr. Seuss indicates, our schoolchildren are important people; their education is vital not only to their own future but also to the future of our country.

You may be familiar with the Dr. Seuss books—the often silly, rhyming, outrageous stories that delight many children from preschool through graduation from high school. Often they have deep meaning. In a commentary on Dr. Seuss and his influence, A. O. Scott of the *New York Times* had the following to say:

> *Rather than describe the mental world of children, Seuss labored over his verses and sketches in the hopes of replicating it. His guiding insight was that some version of his words and stories was there to begin with, and that children, in discovering his work, would recognize in it what they already knew (Scott, 2000).*

For this chapter, the significance of these comments is that the students we meet and greet in the classroom come to us with their own stories, backgrounds, and experiences. It is your task to learn about your students; what their lives are like; and what hobbies, interests, talents, and challenges they bring to the classroom. Respecting and understanding them as people with their own ideas and experiences is the first step toward becoming an effective educator. In this chapter, we address the nature of the learner, today, in the early part of the twenty-first century. Who our students are, how they differ from one another, and what types of learning styles they have—these are some of the topics we explore.

THE STUDENTS: A CHANGING LANDSCAPE

Since the mid-1990s, student enrollment in American schools has mushroomed. In fact, when the estimated population of the country surpassed 300 million people in 2006, roughly one-quarter were children under the age of eighteen (Annie E. Casey Foundation, 2006a).

Total public school enrollment reached an earlier peak in 1971, when the youngest members of the baby boom generation[1] arrived in school (Fry, 2006). Enrollment then dropped off considerably in the 1970s, but it began to climb again in the late 1980s and early 1990s. By the second half of the 1990s, enroll-

---

1 *Baby boom generation* refers to those Americans born in the quarter-century following World War II, roughly from 1946 to 1964. Some experts use slightly different dates.

ment passed the 1971 mark, and the number of students in school has continued to rise. Between 1985 and 2005, enrollment in public elementary and secondary schools rose 22 percent—more than one-fifth (Snyder, Tan, & Hoffman, 2006, Table 3). Private school enrollment grew a bit more slowly, expanding 14 percent during that same time period (National Center for Education Statistics, 2006).

Clearly, the number of students in our schools has been rising rapidly. But who exactly are these students?

Ethnic Diversity

Our era of expanding school enrollment has been marked by a significant rise in minority, especially Hispanic, populations. From the 1993–1994 school year through 2002–2003, Hispanics[2] accounted for 64 percent of the increase in student enrollment. African Americans made up 23 percent of the additional students, and Asians 11 percent. White enrollment actually declined by 1 percent (Fry, 2006).

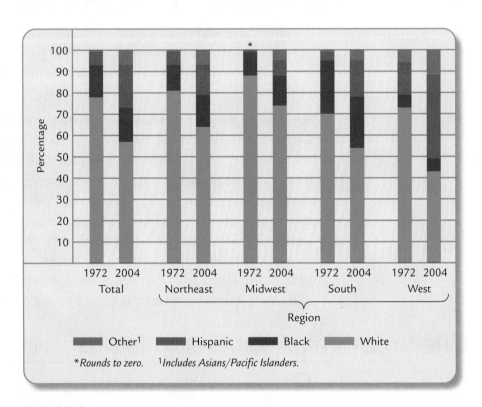

FIGURE 5.1

Minority Enrollment in American Schools

Percentage distribution of the race/ethnicity of public school students enrolled in kindergarten through 12th grade, by region: Fall 1972 and 2004.

Source: U.S. Department of Education, National Center for Education Statistics. (2006). *The Condition of Education 2006* (NCES 2006-071). Washington, DC: U.S. Government Printing Office, p. 32.

---

2 *Hispanic* refers to people whose origin is Spain or any of the Spanish-speaking countries of the Americas.

By 2004, 43 percent of public school students were considered to be part of a racial or ethnic minority group. The distribution of minority students in public schools differs across regions of the country, but minority enrollment grew in all regions between 1972 and 2004. In comparison, the number of white students decreased from 78 to 57 percent of public school enrollment during this same period (U.S. Department of Education, 2006).

As indicated in Figure 5.1, which shows percentages of minority enrollment by region of the country, the South and West have larger minority enrollments than the Northeast and Midwest. The Midwest has the smallest minority enrollment of any region (U.S. Department of Education, 2006).

Immigration accounts for a large part of the diversity among today's students. About one-fifth of youngsters under the age of eighteen are part of immigrant families. States with the highest percentage of immigrant families are New York, New Jersey, California, Texas, and Nevada—states that attract the largest number of Hispanic immigrants (Annie E. Casey Foundation, 2006b, 2007a).

Although ethnic diversity is increasing overall, recent decades have seen a new rise in *de facto* segregation—that is, whites living in different neighborhoods than minorities. Neighborhoods that are primarily white naturally have a high concentration of white students in their schools, while neighborhoods that are predominantly minority have a high concentration of minority students in the schools. In some areas, this segregation has reduced the amount of diversity teachers encounter. One report has even found that most white students continue to attend schools populated primarily by other whites, and relatively few attend schools populated primarily by minorities (Fry, 2006).

As enrollment has expanded, so has the number of schools. About half of the students attending the newer schools are white, while the white enrollment in older schools has dropped. Between 1993–1994 and 2002–2003, more than 65 percent of the increased enrollment in the older schools was accounted for by the rise in Latino[3] enrollment (Fry, 2006). From these statistics, we can see that most of the newer schools are being built in areas that are predominantly white, while the older school buildings are absorbing most of the Hispanic and other minority students.

Language-Minority Students

Between 1979 and 2004, the number of school-age children (ages 5 to 17) who spoke a language other than English at home increased from 3.3 million to 9.9 million. In terms of percentages, that is a rise from 9 percent of school-age children to 19 percent (U.S. Department of Education, 2006).

Among children who speak a language other than English at home, Spanish is the language most frequently spoken. About three-quarters of students who receive special assistance to learn English speak Spanish (American Educational Research Association, 2004). Yet hundreds of thousands of students come from homes where other languages are spoken. These include Chinese, Vietnamese, Russian, Arabic, and French Creole. Various reports emphasize that, for most of these *English-language learners* (sometimes called *ELLs*), success requires targeted and continuing intervention. As one report says,

---

3 *Latino* refers to people whose origin is the Latin American countries of Central and South America. The term is often used interchangeably with *Hispanic*.

Children who start school knowing little or no English can learn the basic skills of word recognition quickly—in about two years, if they are carefully taught. They need the same kind of reading instruction that works for native speakers, only more of it, and they need to be monitored carefully so they get help adapted to their language development needs as soon as they run into problems. (American Educational Research Association, 2004)

Bilingual Education

bilingual education
Educating English-language learners by teaching them at least part of the time in their native language.

There has been much debate over how best to boost the academic achievement of English-language learners. **Bilingual education** programs support students with limited English proficiency by teaching them at least part of the time in their native language. Since the early 1970s, these programs have taken many forms. Some teach academic subjects in the students' native language and also provide *English as a Second Language (ESL)* classes to help the students learn English. Other models, known as *two-way* or *dual-language* programs, teach fluency in both languages, so that a class of both language-minority and native English-speaking students becomes fluent in both languages. These approaches have several variations and tend to vary from school district to school district. Meanwhile, other programs *immerse* language-minority students in English-only classes without any native-language communication.

On a recent visit to an elementary school in Queens, New York, I encountered a large sign for parents that read, "We now have a dual-language program in Mandarin." I learned that 87 percent of the students in this K–5 school were from China and that those students who were native English speakers really wanted to learn Mandarin. Hence, the school began a dual-language immersion program with half of the instruction in Mandarin and the other half in English.

Non-native English-speaking students learn best in bilingual classes.

There are many other examples of schools that take pride in their bilingual programs. Yet, partly because of the large wave of Latino immigration during the past twenty years, the issue of bilingual education has become highly politicized. There are those who believe that only English should be spoken and taught in school. This has prompted some schools to adopt "English-only" programs in which language-minority students have no access to their native language in school. Criticizing this trend, many educators and linguists argue that valuing and honoring new immigrants' native languages enhances their self-esteem and their possibility for academic success.

In 2001, when the No Child Left Behind Act was adopted by Congress, all references to bilingual education as a pedagogical goal were absent. Instead of continuing to fund bilingual initiatives at the federal level, the law turned most of the responsibility over to the states in the form of block grants to assist the academic achievement of language-minority students. The way these state funds are allocated is highly variable.

LEARNING PROJECT

"English-only" vs. Bilingual Education

A 1998 initiative in California, known as Proposition 227, banned native-language instruction in the state. California, as we noted earlier, has had a particularly high influx of Spanish-speaking students. What do you think motivated voters to approve this extreme measure?

Explore the research that explains this phenomenon, and consider the issues from the standpoint of a future teacher. Did the initiative result from prejudice against Latinos and linguistic minorities, or was there a misunderstanding of bilingual education?

Are you a native English speaker yourself? What types of instruction would you imagine could help you learn another language in a way that would foster comprehension across all the academic disciplines?

Teaching English-Language Learners

You may well find yourself in a classroom with English-language learners, and it is important to use the most effective strategies to help your students grasp subject matter content while learning English. One current approach is called *Specially Designed Academic Instruction in English (SDAIE)*. Many established teachers have taken workshops devoted to this approach—one example of how being a teacher is a commitment to lifelong learning.

As we explored in Chapter 4, learning something new requires that the learner redesign her or his mental schemes. To do this, the student has to bring his or her existing knowledge into play. SDAIE pedagogy encourages this process by treating the English-language learner as a "knower," a student with lots of ideas that are temporarily inaccessible to the teacher because of the language barrier. Accessing the student's ideas involves teaching strategies like:

▶ Speaking clearly and at a slower pace

▶ Using gestures and facial expressions

▶ Using concrete materials and visuals

▶ Avoiding idiomatic expressions that are peculiar to English

▶ Engaging students in group work that is student centered (Kashen, 1994).

▶ Finding "language buddies" wherever possible—that is, pairing English-language learners with students who are more advanced in English but also fluent in the learner's native language.

If you teach a class with both English-language learners and students who are already fluent in English, your task will be to plan for *both* populations in ways that enrich the environment. Imagine that two students are using a ruler for a lesson. The native English speaker says to the student who is new to this country, "How do you say *ruler* in your language?" By sharing in this way, they both become learners. The challenge is to engage all students in helping their classmates overcome barriers to learning.

VIDEO CASE

Bilingual Education in Fourth Grade

To see how a two-way language immersion program can function, find the HM Video Case "Bilingual Education: An Elementary Two-Way Immersion Program" on the student website. As you begin watching the video, ask yourself if all the students are English-language learners. After watching the video, consider the following questions:

• Would you have liked to be a student in this program? Why or why not?

• In what ways, if any, does the two-way program level the playing field for English-language learners?

• How, if at all, were you able to tell which students were native English speakers?

• Why is communication between the Spanish and English teachers essential?

Finally, why do you think there has been so much political controversy surrounding two-way bilingual programs like this one? Consider the two sides:

• In what ways do native English speakers benefit? Explain why this kind of program has been thought of by many as a "win-win" intervention on behalf of English-language learners and native English speakers.

• What are the potential downsides of a two-way bilingual program?

Religious Diversity

As we saw in Chapter 3, religion has always played a large role in American life and American education. Today, Americans still generally see religion's influence in the world and the nation as positive. For instance, 61 percent of Americans believe that children raised with religious faith are more likely to grow up to be moral adults than those who are not (Pew Forum on Religion and Public Life, 2002). The Constitution of the United States guarantees religious freedom to all citizens, and we treasure that right. Yet, as was noted in Chapter 3, Americans are divided about how the principle of "separation of church and state" (a phrase coined by Thomas Jefferson) should apply to public schools.

Honoring diversity requires a respect for the learner and a genuine desire to bridge religious and cultural gaps.

These matters have taken on more urgency in the past few decades as new strains of religious diversity have arisen in the United States. Christians, especially Protestants, still dominate the U.S. population at large (see Figure 5.2), but other religions are growing rapidly. The total number of Americans who identified their religion as something other than Christian increased more than 32 percent between 1990 and 2001 (U.S. Census Bureau, 2007). Religions that barely registered in previous surveys, such as the Wiccan creed, now have a substantial number of adherents. Figure 5.3 shows the growth for a few selected religions. Even within the traditional affiliations of Protestant and Catholic, there are many subgroups and differences.

With such diversity in the nation's religions, teachers have much to learn about the religious beliefs of their students. Religious beliefs bring with them various expectations for an individual's behavior, including observance of customs and traditions. Remember that culture and religion are linked. Understanding who your students are and the role that religion plays in their lives is significant in helping them to learn and in "honoring" their identities.

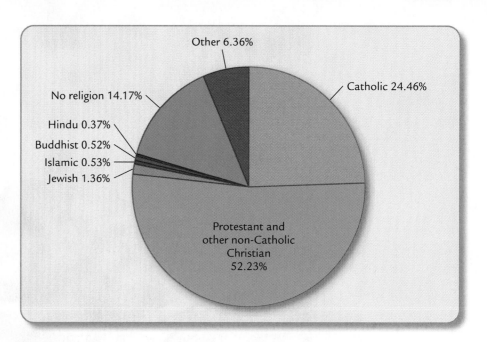

FIGURE 5.2

Major Religions in the United States, by Percentage of the Adult Population

These percentages are based on people's descriptions of their religious affiliations, not on membership in religious congregations.

Source: Calculated from U.S. Census Bureau, *Statistical Abstract of the United States: 2007* (Washington, DC: Author, 2007), Table 73.

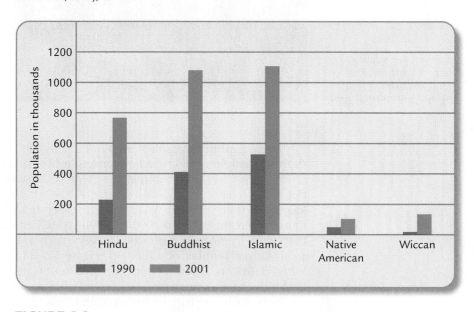

FIGURE 5.3

Growth in Selected U.S. Religions, 1990 to 2001

As in Figure 5.2, the data reflect people's self-identification.

Source: Calculated from U.S. Census Bureau, *Statistical Abstract of the United States: 2007* (Washington, DC: Author, 2007), Table 73.

WRITING and REFLECTION

Religious Diversity and You

Consider the possible extent of religious diversity in your future classroom. In this context, think about the teachings of your own religion that have influenced your life personally. How does understanding your own religious beliefs help you better serve your students?

Sexual Orientation

sexual orientation   An enduring emotional, romantic, sexual, or affectional attraction that a person feels toward people of one or both sexes.

Like religion, language, and ethnicity, **sexual orientation** is an important component of a person's identity. Schools are often the places where teens develop social skills and begin to align with peer groups. For adolescents who do not identify as heterosexual in today's culture, this process of social acceptance and approval is fraught with danger and fear of rejection and even physical harm.

Categories applied to sexual orientation typically include heterosexual, homosexual (gay and lesbian), bisexual (sexual attraction toward both sexes), and transgender (having characteristics of the opposite sex). The acronym **LGBT** is sometimes used to refer to lesbian, gay, bisexual, and transgender people as a group. Because sexual orientations are often hidden from view, LGBT individuals are often thought of as the invisible minority. In schools, fear often prevents these students from revealing their sexual identities, and it is therefore very important that schools and classrooms provide safe havens for those of our students whose sexual orientation is not aligned with the majority.

LGBT   An acronym used to represent lesbian, gay, bisexual, and transgender individuals.

Attitudes about sexual orientation are a product of individual family biases and beliefs. Students bring these to school, and gay, lesbian, bisexual, and transgender youth often have to cope with prejudice and isolation. Lack of family support for these youngsters exacerbates the problem, and there is an enormous fear of stigmatization. These students are at greater risk than others for being harassed and bullied, experiencing depression, and attempting suicide.

How widespread are these problems? The 2005 National School Climate Survey (Kosciw & Diaz, 2006), which collected information from more than 1,700 LGBT students across the country, found that bullying and harassment on the basis of sexual orientation remain common in U.S. schools. Three-quarters of the students (75.4 percent) reported that they "frequently or often" heard terms like "faggot" and "dyke." Nearly nine-tenths of the students (89.2 percent) said they frequently or often heard expressions like "that's so gay" or "you're so gay." Nearly two-thirds (64.1 percent) said they had been verbally harassed at school in the past year, and 37.8 percent reported physical harassment. In fact, during the past school year, more than 17 percent had been physically assaulted in school because of their sexual orientation. Not surprisingly, 64.3 percent of the students surveyed said they felt unsafe at school!

Because all students deserve to work in an environment that is both friendly and supportive, student groups have emerged in high schools all over the country to combat LGBT bias and discrimination. These groups or clubs are often called GSAs, for Gay-Straight Alliances; they are student-run organizations that provide a safe place for students to meet, support each other, talk about issues related to their sexual orientation, and work toward ending homophobia.

Socioeconomic Disparities

socioeconomic status (SES) A person's or family's status in society, usually based on a combination of income, occupation, and education. Though similar to *social class*, SES puts more emphasis on the way income affects status.

Another way students differ from each other is in their **socioeconomic status (SES)**, a measure of their standard of living that relates to the family's income. According to 2005 U.S. Census figures, almost one-fifth of young people under the age of eighteen live in poverty (Annie E. Casey Foundation, 2006b). Table 5.1 shows the official definition of poverty as related to family size. You may be surprised to see how much a family must earn to avoid being poor in the United States.

Here is another important, related statistic: More than 30 percent of all children in the United States live in single-parent families (Annie E. Casey Foundation, 2006b, 2007b). In most cases, obviously, one parent has less earning power than two parents do.

Socioeconomic status relates to the concept of *social capital* that we mentioned earlier in the book. The point is that the students you encounter will

TABLE 5.1   The Poverty Line: Annual Income Levels Below Which a Family Is Considered Poor

Persons in Family or Household	48 Contiguous States and District of Columbia	Alaska	Hawaii
1	$10,210	$12,770	$11,750
2	$13,690	$17,120	$15,750
3	$17,170	$21,470	$19,750
4	$20,650	$25,820	$23,750
5	$24,130	$30,170	$27,750
6	$27,610	$34,520	$31,750
7	$31,090	$38,870	$35,750
8	$34,570	$43,220	$39,750
For each additional person, add	$3,480	$4,350	$4,000

Source: U.S. Department of Health and Human Services, Annual Update of the HHS Poverty Guidelines, *Federal Register*, Vol. 72, No. 15, January 24, 2007, p. 3147.

come from various socioeconomic backgrounds. The more social capital a child's family has, the greater his or her intellectual and cultural advantages. A child with higher socioeconomic status and more social capital usually performs better than a student with little or no social capital does.

Overlapping Differences: The Social Context

The aspects of student diversity we have been considering are not isolated and independent. Often they overlap. Consider, for instance, what happens when poverty intersects with the need to learn a new language. The reality of many English-language learners is that they also represent our poorest children: they live in crowded housing environments where transportation and employment opportunities are limited and where schools are old and overcrowded. In fact, of all students who live in poverty, more than 28 percent are Latino (Aleman, 2006). Conditions of this sort cannot help but affect the students' achievement in school, putting many of these students at risk for educational failure. In the next section we will consider the term *at risk* and its full implications.

Many analysts express concern that educational policy too often ignores such individual social contexts. One criticism of the federal No Child Left Behind Act (2001), for example, is that the law's mandated standards and assessments pay little attention to ethnic- and language-minority students.

WRITING and REFLECTION

Assessing Your Own Demographics

- *Demographics* is a general term for the kind of statistics we have been discussing so far in this chapter—the characteristics of human populations. How would you describe your demographics?

- Did you attend a neighborhood school? If so, how did it reflect the composition of your neighborhood? What do you think are the advantages of attending the local neighborhood school?

- Why might a diverse student body make a greater contribution to the entire group's learning than would a homogeneous group?

STUDENTS WHO ARE AT RISK

National research has shown that children living in poor, tough neighborhoods are much more likely to drop out of school, become pregnant as teens, get in trouble with the law as juveniles, and live in poverty as adults, with their own children struggling to succeed. They are much more likely to go to prison and suffer from debilitating health conditions that further limit their ability to provide support for their children.

— Annie E. Casey Foundation (2001)

When we examine all the ways our students can differ from each other, we need to ask ourselves what combination of factors might hinder a child's becoming a successful student, graduating from high school, and

students at risk Students in danger of not completing school or not acquiring the education they need to be successful citizens.

pursuing further education or vocational training. The term **students at risk** came into widespread use after the 1983 national report described in Chapter 3, *A Nation at Risk.* This report warned that U.S. schools were becoming mediocre and that significant changes had to occur to keep the nation as a whole from declining.

Critics of this report noted that there was little mention of the role of poverty in the life of children. Many reacted to the report by citing glaring social inadequacies and saying that schools could not make up for these deficiencies. There was a "blame the victim" mentality, critics complained, in which students and parents were held to be the culprits. Indeed, schools cannot make up for many of the problems of poverty and degradation, but in turn educators must not blame their own inadequacies on the students. Both points are at work when we examine who is "at risk."

The precise definition of the term *student at risk* varies. Here are three samples:

▶ One who is in danger of failing to complete her or his education with an adequate level of skills (Slavin & Madden, 2006).

▶ One who is judged as not having the potential to participate in society in ways that are meaningful and purposeful for themselves or for society in general (McGuirk, 2001).

▶ [A student] judged to be in serious jeopardy of not completing school or not succeeding in school (Ryan & Cooper, 2007).

dropout rate The percentage of students who fail to complete high school or earn an equivalency degree.

As two of these definitions suggest, failing to complete high school is a key problem. The **dropout rate** in the United States, though it has declined recently, is still around 10 percent, meaning that one out of every ten U.S. students fails to get a high school diploma or an alternative credential (Snyder, Tan, & Hoffman, 2006, Table 106; Laird, DeBell, & Chapman, 2006, Table 6).

What puts a student at risk of dropping out or of not getting an adequate education? Social problems in our society make it difficult for even high-ability students to be successful. The greatest social risk factors include substance abuse, child abuse, poverty, homelessness, hunger, depression, and teen pregnancy. For teachers from stable homes and environments, it is often difficult to relate to these problems that affect the lives of some of America's students every day. Hence, it is essential to learn as much as possible about your students' lives.

To make the concept of risk more specific, a *family risk index* (Annie E. Casey Foundation, 2003) identifies a "high-risk child" as one who lives in a family with four or more of these risk factors:

1. Child is not living with two parents.

2. Household head is a high school dropout.

3. Family income is below the poverty line.

4. Child is living with parent(s) who is (are) underemployed.

5. Family is receiving welfare benefits.

6. Child does not have health insurance.

According to one survey, sixteen to nineteen year olds in the high-risk category were almost four times as likely to be high school dropouts as those not in the high-risk category (Annie E. Casey Foundation, 2003).

Further statistics about risk factors come from the National Youth Risk Behavior Survey (YRBS), which monitors behaviors that contribute to death, disability, and social problems among youth and adults in the United States. Conducted every two years during the spring semester, the YRBS provides data representative of ninth- through twelfth-grade students in public and private schools throughout the United States. Figure 5.4 shows some key data from a recent YRBS survey, highlighting factors that have been worrying educators and parents for several decades now: drugs, sex, and violence.

The U.S. teen pregnancy rate has gone down in recent years, but it remains the highest of any industrialized nation in the world. For young women, teen pregnancy is the major contributor to high school dropout rates. It is also significant that substance abuse crosses all socioeconomic classes. Consequently, the importance of sex education and drug abuse counseling programs in the schools cannot be overstated.

A recent report outlined several broad approaches for reducing high school dropout rates for all teens. This report, sponsored by the Annie E. Casey Foundation (2003), calls for prevention strategies that address community and school collaboration. The recommendations are summarized in Table 5.2.

In this light, think about the following Teaching Story, which describes a high school that focuses on students at risk and helps them succeed.

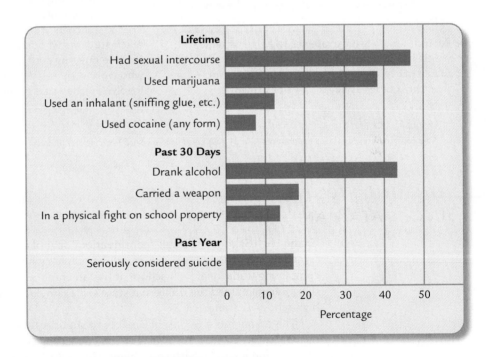

FIGURE 5.4

Risky Behaviors Among Students in Grades 9 Through 12

The YRBS survey included both public and private schools. These are just a few of the risky behaviors reported.

Source: Centers for Disease Control and Prevention, "Youth Risk Behavior Surveillance—United States, 2005," *Morbidity and Mortality Weekly Report*, 55 (no. SS-5), June 9, 2006.

TABLE 5.2   Strategies for Reducing High School Dropout Rates

Make it harder for students to drop out of school.

- Strengthen accountability.
- Offer students assistance and opportunities to stay in school.
- Gear dropout prevention efforts to the specific age and profile of the student; individualize the efforts.
- Strengthen students' understanding of the connection between education and job opportunities.

Address the underlying causes of dropping out.

- Low-income students are more likely to drop out; be aware of this.
- Monitor students' emotional condition and well-being; family stress is associated with poverty and affects the student's emotional stability.
- Watch for the presence of risk factors.
- Address minor problems, like lost eyeglasses that are not replaced or a conflict with a teacher that persists.

Address the needs of those groups at highest risk of dropping out.

- Focus intensively on strategies to help Hispanic youth stay in school; Hispanic students are more than twice as likely as black students and more than three times as likely as white students to drop out.

- Focus on dropout prevention strategies for students with disabilities and special needs.
- Provide incentives and opportunities for students in high-poverty neighborhoods to succeed.

Strengthen school readiness.

- Address families' access to economic resources and human services in children's early years.
- In particular, improve access to health care, beginning with prenatal care.
- Expand access to high-quality early education programs.

Strengthen the skills and understanding of the adults who affect teens' motivation and ability to stay in school.

- Expand access to parent education and family support programs geared to the challenges of raising adolescents.
- Use a variety of media and formats to offer more and better information to parents of teens.
- Work with schools of education to recruit and prepare teachers who are motivated and able to teach students who have a history of failure.
- Provide ongoing staff development to teachers who work with at-risk youth.
- Involve teachers and parents in planning dropout prevention programs.

Source: Adapted from Annie E. Casey Foundation. (2003). *Kids Count indicator brief: Reducing the high school dropout rate.* Baltimore, MD: Author.

TEACHING STORIES
SUCCESS AT CHANA HIGH SCHOOL

Chana High School is a small "continuation" school in Auburn, California. Designed to meet the needs of young adult students who were not successful in completing traditional high school, it has an enrollment of 250. In 2007, all of the students passed the California state exit exam, enabling them to earn a high school diploma.

The school has a wealth of services to support these youngsters, including teen parenting classes, substance abuse counseling, anger management intervention, and mental health counseling. The dedicated teachers at Chana work diligently to bolster students' academic achievement while also supporting them emotionally. The school offers five vocational programs funded by the state (including computer technology and electronics), and partnerships with technical colleges and local community colleges allow the students to earn college credit while completing their high school work.

Source: Lofing (2007).

CONTEMPORARY ISSUES RELATING TO STUDENT DIVERSITY

As you might guess, the increasing diversity of American students has led to controversy about educational priorities. In this section, we focus on three areas that have provoked much recent discussion: multicultural education, gender-fair education, and the role of religion in the schools.

Multicultural Education

You may be feeling dizzy from all the data and statistics you have read in this chapter. Why are these details about students important? As we seek to become better teachers, we must understand the origins of our students and the ways

A diverse student body provides the opportunity to learn about other ways of being in the world.

their needs can be met in the classroom. If you are not of the same culture, race, ethnicity, or social class as your students, you should make a special effort to understand their needs. You can also turn the diversity of your students into an advantage—an opportunity to share identities and cultures as you create community in your classroom.

multicultural education
Education the aim of which is to create equal opportunities for students from diverse racial, ethnic, social class, and cultural groups.

If you pursue a career in teaching, you will hear a lot about **multicultural education**, a broad term for many approaches that recognize and celebrate the variety of cultures and ethnic backgrounds found in U.S. schools. Students from groups that have traditionally been underrepresented in the school population—ethnic and racial minorities—have also been understudied. That is, until recently, most educators have not focused on what these students need to succeed in school. We now realize that these students will not be served well and will even become marginalized unless we seek answers to complex questions like the following:

▶ Whose stories are told in the classroom?

▶ How do we build community in a diverse setting?

▶ What is the role of identity formation in our work?

▶ What can we learn by hearing the stories of those from traditionally marginalized groups? (Nelson & Wilson, 1998, p. xi)

Diverse learning environments, ones in which students from several racial and ethnic backgrounds come together, offer a wonderful gift. To use Emily Style's metaphor mentioned earlier in the book, diverse learning environments provide "windows" into the worlds of people other than ourselves and create rich experiences for both students and teachers. As a result of these experiences, teachers are encouraged to develop culturally responsive teaching practices, also referred to as **culturally relevant pedagogy**. These teaching practices have several important attributes:

culturally relevant pedagogy   Teaching practices that place the culture of the learner at the center of instruction. Cultural referents become aspects of the formal curriculum.

▶ They use cultural referents—from all the cultures represented in the classroom—to develop students' knowledge, skills, and attitudes.

▶ They honor the students' life stories and belief systems and find ways to incorporate them into the curriculum and learning context.

▶ They create classroom community by granting voice and legitimacy to the experiences of students from diverse backgrounds.

▶ They encourage all students to achieve academically by acknowledging the students' personal and cultural identities.

As an example of culturally relevant pedagogy, consider the following story from Ms. Petersen's classroom.

TEACHING STORIES
CULTURALLY RELEVANT PEDAGOGY IN AN URBAN EIGHTH-GRADE MATH CLASSROOM

We are in Ms. Petersen's eighth-grade math classroom. It is room 303 in an old, overcrowded school building in an urban area. Ms. P. is exploring geometry with a diverse class of students. The topic centers around the different types of symmetry that may be found in shapes using several patterns. About one-third of her students are Latino, and the rest are of many racial and ethnic origins.

This unit in geometry considers what happens to shapes when they are moved through space. Ms. Petersen has examined the basic concepts in many different ways with her class, emphasizing that symmetry may be found in patterns in everyday life and having the students create symmetrical patterns with more than one shape. For instance, she brought in men's ties with many patterns on them and asked students to decide what type of symmetry each pattern represented. She then invited them to explore their native countries' flags. The classroom has three networked computers that students used to print pictures of their flags. The flag designs were examined for geometric shapes and symmetry (see Figure 5.5). It was a lesson that engaged all the students.

After the students had experience with several types of symmetry, Ms. Petersen posed a challenge. In groups of two, the students were to design and create a classroom flag incorporating their room number. The flag had to be in the shape of a rectangle, include two types of symmetry; and appropriately represent the students in the classroom. Students were excited about designing patterns, and they selected the colors from the flags of their various countries of origin to represent themselves. Colors from the flags of Colombia, El Salvador, Mexico, Puerto Rico, Guatemala, South Korea, and the United States adorned the design of Room 303's classroom flags.

THE TEACHING IDEAS BEHIND THIS STORY

What do you think of Ms. Petersen's lesson? Can you imagine how excited the students were that their countries' flags were part of their study of mathematics?

Flag of Mexico   Flag of Puerto Rico   Flag of South Korea

Flag of El Salvador   Flag of Guatemala   Flag of Colombia

FIGURE 5.5
Flags Used in a Culturally Relevant Geometry Lesson
What types of symmetry are revealed in these flags?

The concepts of rotation, reflection, and translation are quite complex in geometry, but by using materials her students could relate to, Ms. Petersen engaged them in a personal way.

We know from research in cognitive science, as reflected by the interview with Dr. Brooks in Chapter 4, that learning occurs best when students are fully invested in the process—when they can interact with the materials, "play" with them, explore and reexamine the concepts, and then individually make those concepts their own. Do you see how culturally relevant pedagogy helps make this possible?

WRITING and REFLECTION

Culturally Relevant Pedagogy

- How would the students' learning have been affected if Ms. Petersen had simply taught the math concepts without reference to her students' different cultural backgrounds?

- What was the point of Ms. Petersen's bringing in men's neckties?

- What other materials might you use as examples of geometrical patterns in our daily lives?

Educating Girls and Boys: Separate or Together?

You may recall from Chapter 3 that Title IX, part of the Education Amendments of 1972, prohibits discrimination on the basis of sex in any federally funded education program or activity. That law might seem to discourage single-sex schooling—the practice of educating girls in separate schools from boys—on the grounds that separate is inherently unequal. In 2006, however, the U.S. Education Department officially ruled that Title IX does not make single-sex schooling discriminatory as long as it is voluntary and takes place in an environment that also includes comparable coeducational schools and classes. As a result, single-sex schooling is expected to become more prevalent in public schools and public-supported charter schools.

One model for quality single-sex schooling exists in a high-minority area of New York City—the Young Women's Leadership School of East Harlem sent all of its 2006 graduating class to college. Yet there is much debate about single-sex schooling. In the past, all-female schools were typically private schools for the wealthy, and their principles included giving females leadership roles and creating opportunities for them to excel. Many educators feel that if a gender-fair curriculum were commonplace—if it highlighted the lives and accomplishments of women as well as men and used teaching strategies that gave voice to female students as well as to males—the advantages of all-girl environments could be accessible in coeducational environments. That is, females would not need to be separate if indeed they were treated equitably.

Because more single-sex schools will now be available to children from lower socioeconomic classes, many applaud the Department of Education's ruling. Advocates for single-sex schooling argue that girls in these separate schools will have opportunities for leadership and verbal expression often squelched in coeducational environments. Others worry, however, that single-sex environments may promote stereotyping and discrimination. In fact,

gender-fair education
Teaching practices that help both females and males achieve their full potential. Gender-fair teachers address cultural and societal stereotypes and overcome them through classroom interactions.

many advocates for girls and young women believe that same-sex schools for females will be less authentically rigorous.

These are complex problems, at the intersection of gender, race, ethnicity, and social class. Overall, the movement for multicultural education also advocates **gender-fair education**, encouraging teachers to address the needs of females and males in their classrooms in ways that help both genders realize their full potential. With this concept in mind, consider the following story from Ms. Logan's classroom.

TEACHING STORIES
GENDER STEREOTYPES AND A TRIP BACK IN TIME

In Ms. Logan's sixth-grade class, the students are closing their eyes and thinking back to their earliest memories. Ms. Logan says, ""To begin, step out of your body and see yourself at your desk with your head down. Now, travel back in time until you are in fourth grade, then third grade. What are you wearing? Who is your teacher? What are you doing? See yourself at home. What does your room look like? Who are your friends? What do you do after school? Now, see yourself as a kindergartner; see how you are playing. What do you love to do? Travel back again until you are a baby. Look around your room. Notice things around you. Now travel back again and here you are—ready to be born! Everyone is so excited, so happy, waiting for your birth. But this time, imagine you are born as the opposite sex.

"Hence, if you are boy, pretend you are born a girl. If you are a girl, pretend you are born a boy. See yourself as a baby, coming home, learning to walk, starting school, attending elementary school. Look at your room and your friends and your activities. Without talking to anybody, create a list of how your life seems different since you were born a person of the opposite sex."

Ms. Logan really likes this activity because, as the students reveal their beliefs about their lives as a member of the opposite sex, they confront stereotypes. Ultimately they learn that they are really more similar to their classmates of the opposite sex than they are different!

Adapted from J. Logan (1999). *Teaching stories.* New York: Kodansha Press.

THE TEACHING IDEAS BEHIND THIS STORY

What do you think of the activity Ms. Logan designed? As students respond to this exercise, they find they hold various misconceptions: for example, about the paint colors girls or boys would have in their rooms, or how they would have to behave if they were of the opposite sex. The discussion gives students a chance to see the ways they are similar, dispelling stereotypes.

In Ms. Logan's class, boys said that if they were female, they would have to get up extra early to fix their hair. A few of the girls objected to that remark and pointed out that they never get up early to fuss over their hair. Girls felt that if they were male, they would be able to stay out later—only to learn that the boys in their class also had curfews. Some boys insisted that they would do better in writing if they were female, but other boys argued that they were good writers! In the end, these middle-school girls and boys agreed that they both loved sports and a lot of different subjects, and that they were probably more the same than different; however, it was clear that the boys had more personal freedom and privileges than the girls.

It's important to remember that treating students *equitably* is not the same as treating them *equally*. **Equity** stands for being fair and just. Since students come from such diverse experiences, identities, and backgrounds, you cannot be fair by treating everyone in exactly the same way. To ensure equality in the learning goals we hope to achieve for each student, we need to notice of the differences among our students and use strategies to help each student reach maximum success in the classroom. In a science class, equity may mean asking yourself how to encourage more females' interest. One of the many ways may be to post pictures of female as well as male scientists. In a language arts classroom, equity may mean asking yourself how to engage the boys in more reading experiences. One way may be to integrate action heroes into the literature. In each case, the tacit message is: We are here to support all our students, and we will work to counter any stereotyping and biases in the classroom.

equity The act of treating individuals and groups fairly and justly, free from bias or favoritism. *Gender equity* means the state of being fair and just toward both males and females, to show preference to neither and concern for both.

WRITING and REFLECTION

Connections Between Gender and Learning

- Did you attend a same-sex school for any part of your education? In what ways, if any, was that a positive or negative experience?

- Research tells us that teachers often address girls and boys differently in the classroom. Without meaning to, they tend to call on boys more frequently than girls and often, in the lower grades, use this tactic as a means of maintaining control in the classroom. Can you remember a time when you were treated in a certain way in school because you were male or female? What was that like for you? What did you think about it? What do you think now?

Religion and Schools

In 1995, President Bill Clinton sent material containing guidelines on student religious expression to every school district in the United States. The letter accompanying these guidelines declared:

> *Nothing in the First Amendment converts our public schools into religion-free zones, or requires all religious expression to be left behind at the schoolhouse door. While the government may not use schools to coerce the consciences of our students, or to convey official endorsement of religion, the public schools also may not discriminate against private religious expression during the school day. . . . Religion is too important in our history and our heritage for us to keep it out of our schools. . . . [I]t shouldn't be demanded, but as long as it is not sponsored by school officials and doesn't interfere with other children's rights, it mustn't be denied.*

That message seems clear enough. Yet issues concerning religion and the schools continue to cause controversy. If you did the Learning Project on separation of church and state in Chapter 3, you discovered how many arguments there have been regarding prayer, Bible readings, religious displays on school property, and similar matters. Many people want schools to promote religious values more openly, or at least allow students to do so; others, just as vehemently, demand that schools keep strictly out of religious affairs.

One conflict about religious beliefs and the school curriculum involves the teaching of evolution in science classes. A landmark court case (*Tammy Kitzmiller, et al. v. Dover Area School District, et al.*) occurred in the town of Dover, Pennsylvania, where the school board insisted that students be required to hear a statement about intelligent design before ninth-grade biology lessons on evolution. (Proponents of intelligent design believe that the diversity of living things can be explained as the work of a designing intelligence; they do not insist on calling that intelligence God.) The statement read to students said that Darwin's theory is "not a fact" and has inexplicable "gaps." Science teachers objected that science class is not the domain to discuss the presence of an all-powerful being, and some parents brought the case to federal court.

In his ruling in December 2005, Judge John E. Jones asserted that the school board's requirement was unconstitutional. The judge said: "We find that the secular purposes claimed by the board amount to a pretext for the board's real purpose, which was to promote religion in the public school classroom." He said that the policy "singles out the theory of evolution for special treatment, misrepresents its status in the scientific community, causes students to doubt its validity without scientific justification," and "presents students with a religious alternative masquerading as a scientific theory." Hence, he concluded, it was unconstitutional to teach intelligent design as an alternative to evolution in a public school science classroom.

In another recent case in a New Jersey public high school, an eleventh-grade history teacher told his students that evolution and the "Big Bang" theory of the universe's origin were not scientific, that dinosaurs were aboard Noah's ark, and that only Christians had a place in heaven. The teacher was audiotaped by a student, and the student's family is now considering a lawsuit on the grounds that the teacher promoted religious views in a public school history classroom. The incident has divided and shocked this New Jersey community (Kelley, 2006).

In the midst of such controversies, teachers often receive conflicting messages about what they can and cannot teach regarding religion. The best understanding is to recognize that you *cannot* teach religion in public schools. Similarly, you cannot encourage or participate in student religious activity. However, you can teach *about* religion and can honor the privacy of religious ritual as long as it does not interfere with the functioning of the school or classroom and it is not forced on any other student. The following statement, posted on the website of the First Amendment Center (http://www .firstamendmentcenter.org/), was agreed on by a broad range of religious and educational groups:

> *Public schools may not inculcate nor inhibit religion. They must be places where religion and religious conviction are treated with fairness and respect. Public schools uphold the First Amendment when they protect the religious liberty rights of students of all faiths and none. Schools demonstrate fairness when they ensure that the curriculum includes study about religion, where appropriate, as an important part of a complete education.*

Teaching Values

Though schools may not teach religious doctrine, they may teach civic values, including honesty, good citizenship, and respect for others. Schools may even teach sexual abstinence or contraception. Since most religions also teach such values, why is it not unlawful to teach them? How can you draw the distinction between civic values and religious values?

MULTIPLE INTELLIGENCES: WHAT DOES IT MEAN TO BE "SMART"?

theory of multiple intelligences The theory that intelligence is not a single, fixed attribute but rather a collection of several different types of abilities.

This section deals with another type of diversity: the variation in intelligence—or perhaps a better way of expressing it, *intelligences*. Until the 1980s, psychologists believed—and many still believe—that intelligence is a fixed and measurable attribute, testable by an IQ test. Now, though, most experts, drawing on the work of psychologist and neuroscientist Howard Gardner, accept the **theory of multiple intelligences**. That is, instead of having a fixed, single intelligence, each of us is intelligent in several different ways.

From the research of Gardner and others, we now know that babies are born with many capacities. Their intelligences evolve and are expressed in multiple ways. These different ways, or different intelligences, may be more or less dominant in a particular individual. Each individual usually expresses several intelligences, to different degrees. At the beginning of his work, Gardner posited a total of seven intelligences. Later he added an eighth and a ninth, and he has proposed that other types of intelligence may also exist (Gardner, 1993, 2003, 2006). Table 5.3 describes the nine types that he considers definite and two that are tentative.

intelligence profile An individual's unique combination of relative strengths and weaknesses among all the different intelligences.

According to Gardner, each individual has all of the intelligences, but no two human beings have the same profiles of intelligence. In other words, we all have these different intelligences in differing strengths and capacities for expression. Each learner's **intelligence profile** consists of a combination of relative strengths and weaknesses among the different intelligences. Moreover, intelligences are not isolated; they interact with one another in an individual to yield many types of outcomes (Moran, Kornhaber, & Gardner, 2006).

Gardner's argument leaves educators with an important mission: finding out how to access all the types of intelligences so that all students can learn to their maximum potential. It is clear that schools traditionally have valued the first two of Gardner's categories—linguistic intelligence and logical-mathematical intelligence—and paid little attention to the others. As teachers, we need to change this emphasis; we need to explore topics in multiple ways to reach more students. When schools stress memorization of key terms without exposing students to other ways to learn about a subject, for example, students who are high in linguistic intelligence will grasp the material, but other students may lag behind and be labeled as underachieving—even though these low-achieving students would do much better if they were given the opportunity to learn and express themselves by other means. The Teaching Story on page 148 illustrates this point.

TABLE 5.3   The Multiple Intelligences Proposed by Howard Gardner

Intelligence	Explanation	Examples of People Who Display This Intelligence
Linguistic intelligence ("word smart")	Ability to use and manipulate languages	Poets, writers, lawyers, public speakers
Logical-mathematical intelligence ("math/science smart")	Capacity to analyze problems, think logically, and carry out mathematical operations	Mathematicians, scientists
Musical intelligence ("music smart")	Ability to recognize and appreciate musical patterns, pitch, rhythm, and timbre; skill in performing and perhaps composing music	Musicians, composers
Bodily-kinesthetic intelligence ("body smart")	Ability to move one's body and its various parts in a coordinated way and to handle objects skillfully; capacity to use the body to create a performance or solve a problem	Athletes, dancers
Spatial intelligence ("art smart")	Ability to recognize patterns and relationships in physical space and manipulate them mentally	Architects, surgeons, artists
Interpersonal intelligence ("people smart")	Capacity to understand other people's moods, intentions, motivations, and desires	Educators, salespeople, counselors, religious and political leaders
Intrapersonal intelligence ("self smart")	Capacity to understand your own feelings, motivations, strengths, weaknesses	People who are good at regulating their own lives
Naturalist intelligence ("nature smart")	Sensitivity to the natural world; ability to make distinctions among and classify features of plants, animals, and other aspects of the environment	Ecologists, botanists, zoologists
Existential intelligence	Concern with ultimate issues, such as philosophical beliefs about life and death; related to spiritual intelligence	Philosophers and religious leaders
Spiritual intelligence (tentative)*	Capacity to explore the nature of existence in all of its manifestations	Religious leaders
Moral intelligence (tentative)*	Concern with rules, behaviors, and attitudes that govern the sanctity of life; connected to spiritual and existential intelligence	May be present with the other intelligences

*The data for the existence of spiritual and moral intelligence are controversial, and often these are not thought of as separate intelligences.

Source: Based on Gardner (1999).

TEACHING STORIES
A MOON-PHASE JOURNAL AND MULTIPLE INTELLIGENCES

Mr. Slomin's sixth-grade science class includes a unit on the moon in which students study the moon's phases—how it appears from Earth at different times of the month. Here are Mr. Slomin's instructions for this unit:

> You are required to keep a moon-phase journal over a period of five weeks. Each day, you need to record the shape of the moon, the time that you see it, and other information about the moon that can include: how you felt watching the moon; moon poems (original or found); moon facts; or other relevant data about the moon. All these belong in your moon journal. There may be some days, due to weather or other reasons, when you cannot see the moon. Please explain your own theory about why you cannot see it and keep observing until you see it again.

Mr. Slomin's class is accustomed to receiving open-ended assignments. The students trust that he will examine their products as individual creations based on their own interests.

At the end of the five weeks, the students are asked to present their moon journals and talk about how they felt during the experience of keeping them. To everyone's surprise and delight, Dan, a shy young man who does not participate much in class, created a beautiful painting on each of the nights he could see the moon. Neither his classmates nor his teacher knew how gifted he was. His entries included a relatively small number of words, but his pictures showed close and accurate observations.

WRITING and REFLECTION

Multiple Intelligences

- In what ways does Mr. Slomin's science assignment reflect an awareness of multiple intelligences?
- If Mr. Slomin had given the class a more conventional assignment about moon phases, would Dan have learned as much? Would Mr. Slomin have been aware of Dan's learning?
- What intelligences do you think a skillful waiter combines? Justify your response.
- What intelligences do you recognize as being dominant in yourself? Describe the ways you demonstrate them.

LEARNING STYLES

learning style   The dominant way in which we process the information around us. Different people have different learning styles.

Gardner's theory of multiple intelligences has had a profound effect on how we think about the ways people perceive the world. A related idea is that people have various **learning styles**. In Chapter 4, we described learning something as a process of drawing it in from the outside and making it your own. *Learning style* refers to the particular way you take in the new idea, event, or concept.

Some people learn best by reading and writing—the traditional approach taken in schools. But researchers (Felder & Silverman, 1988, 2002; Felder and Brent, 2005) have identified other basic learning styles as well:

▶ *Auditory learners* learn best through verbal lectures, discussions, talking things through, and listening to what others have to say. For these people, written information may have little meaning until it is heard. Such learners often benefit from reading text aloud and using a tape recorder.

▶ *Visual learners* need to see the teacher's body language and facial expression to fully understand the content of a lesson. They may think in pictures and learn best from visual displays, including diagrams, illustrated textbooks, overhead transparencies, videos, flipcharts, and handouts.

▶ *Kinesthetic learners* learn best through a hands-on approach, actively exploring the physical world around them. They may find it hard to sit still for long periods and may become distracted by their need for activity and exploration.

When you study for a test, is reading the book enough for you, or do you have to take notes on what you read to remember the ideas? Most people who need to do something physical in order to make the concepts their own are kinesthetic learners. If you are one, quick—take notes on this chapter! There is so much to know!

Together, the research on learning styles and multiple intelligences has a strong message for teachers: *Don't present activities, materials, ideas, and concepts in just one way!* Because people learn in different ways and through different personal strengths, it is important to plan your lessons with multiple ways of knowing in mind.

Meeting the needs of students with a wide range of learning styles requires teachers to have more than one way to approach a topic.

VIDEO CASE

Teaching to Students' Strengths

To explore how one teacher accounts for his students' varying intelligence profiles and styles of learning, find the HM Video Case "Multiple Intelligences: Elementary School Instruction" on the student website. The video examines a class writing assignment about the passengers' experience during the ocean voyage of the *Mayflower*. This traditional social studies lesson is transformed by Mr. Won Park as he asks fourth-grade students to think about the voyage in many different ways and then to write a first-person account from a passenger's point of view.

- In what ways is this lesson informed by multiple intelligences theory?
- If you did not know about multiple intelligences and different learning styles, what would you think of this lesson?
- Why do you think Mr. Won Park asked the students to touch their faces and their clothes and to smell their clothes? What do you think he was hoping for?
- What aspects of this lesson used intrapersonal intelligence? interpersonal intelligence? kinesthetic learning?

TEACHING THE BROAD RANGE OF DIVERSE STUDENTS

The prevailing question before us is not about what children need to succeed. The research is clear. They need supportive environments that nurture their social, emotional, physical, moral, civic, and cognitive development. Instead, the question becomes, who bears responsibility for creating this environment?
— Gene Carter (2006)

New teachers often draw upon their own experiences as learners, and those experiences become the default mode for what is presumed "normal" or "expected" in the regular classroom. As we have seen, however, students today bring to the classroom a wide range of ethnic backgrounds, languages, religions, sexual orientations, learning styles, and intelligences. All of these are embedded in their culture and upbringing. You also have your own identity, embedded in a particular culture with norms and traditions that are dear to you.

To be a successful teacher, you need to become a *student of your students*. Start to view "difference" from the point of view of a learner, and ask yourself, "How am I enriched by learning more about my students? How does that contribute to my understanding of the human condition?" In this way, teaching becomes a never-ending story, a new adventure every year, just as Jane remarked in Chapter 2. Part of your job each year will be to learn about your students and the ways in which they and their backgrounds, languages, learning styles, sexual orientations, and lifestyles prepare them for your classroom.

CONCLUDING THOUGHTS

The most important theme of this chapter is that differences among students are a gift to welcome in your classroom, not a barrier to overcome. They are a gift both for you and for your students. Unless we meet and interact with people from many walks of life and with different ways of being in the world, we run the risk of closing our minds to all that is possible in the human condition.

This chapter may leave you with more questions than answers, but you can "live into" the questions. Ask yourself: Can I do this? Can I examine my pedagogy and develop teaching strategies that help the young girl from the homeless shelter, the boy from Nicaragua with limited English, the suburban youngster who has more than she will ever need, the musically gifted eighth grader who hates history, the logical/mathematical young woman who wants to be a physicist? Can I learn from them and with them and help them be all they can be, as others have helped me?

That is the message of this chapter. In Chapter 6, we explore current trends in education. Some of these trends will feel like stumbling blocks, others like welcome boosts. The following anonymous quotation sums it up:

Teachers who inspire realize there will always be rocks in the road ahead of us. They will be stumbling blocks or stepping stones; it all depends on how we use them.—Anonymous

JOIN THE DISCUSSION

Visit the student website and locate the Edublog for Chapter 5. Let's continue the discussion by responding to the following questions:

- Which areas of student diversity pose the most challenges for you as a future teacher?

- How will you meet those challenges?

CHAPTER CHALLENGE

Developing a Multiple Intelligences Survey

Imagine you want to learn more about your students. What types of questions could you include in a survey to give you an indication of each student's intelligence profile?

If you were making a survey for adult students, you might include items like these:

- Circle the activity you like best: watching a movie, reading a book, doing a sudoku puzzle.
- Which type of activity do you find more satisfying to complete:
  - Writing a term paper
  - Running a marathon
  - Designing an article of clothing

Now choose an approximate age level for your imaginary class, and develop a survey that will help you learn more about your students.

FROM THE COLLEGE CLASSROOM TO YOUR OWN CLASSROOM

Reflecting on Student Diversity

For this chapter, the addition to your teaching portfolio should be very full. What is your reaction to the various types of student diversity we have discussed and to the ways our students can be the same and different from each other?

Reflect on where you see yourself headed as a teacher. Do you have a calling, for instance, to work with at-risk students? Are you motivated to create a gender-fair classroom?

This chapter has an important message: *Different is just different; it is not lesser.* Can you teach those who are different from you in ways that do not make their difference "lesser"?

RESOURCES FOR FURTHER EXPLORATION

Print Resources

Howard Gardner, *Multiple intelligences: New horizons* (New York: Basic Books, 2006). One of Gardner's provocative and influential books.

Laurie Hansen, "Strategies for English-language learning success," *Science and Children,* 43(4) (2006), 23–25.   This article explores how best to engage English-language learners in science learning using the inquiry process.

Ana Martinez Aleman, "Latino demographic, democratic individuality, and educational accountability: A pragmatist's view," *Educational Researcher,* 35(7) (2006), 25–35.   This is a very important analysis of how Latino students are marginalized by the current accountability systems.

Films

The Color of Fear   This documentary film, first released in 1994, is a ground-breaking discussion of race relations in America by eight men of different ethnic backgrounds. Directed by Lee Mun Wah, it is used extensively by educators.

Eyes on the Prize   This award-winning documentary film tells the story of the civil rights movement from 1954 to 1965. In fourteen parts, it has been aired over public broadcasting stations since 1987. It has also been used extensively in education to teach students about the civil rights movement and the victories won through nonviolent tactics. A PBS website, http://www.pbs.org/wgbh/amex/eyesontheprize/index.html, provides information about the film and support materials for teachers.

Online Resources

Center for Research on Education, Diversity, and Excellence
http://www.crede.ucsc.edu/   This center at the University of California is a clearinghouse for research reports and briefs about teaching language-minority students.

Language Policy Research Unit http://www.language-policy.org/   Arizona State University hosts this website that addresses bilingual education and the politics of the English-only movement.

Migration Information Source http://www.migrationinformation.org/   This website, sponsored by the Migration Policy Institute, offers insights into immigration trends as well as the debate over bilingual education.

NCELA: National Clearinghouse for English Language Acquisition and Language Instruction Educational Programs http://www.ncela.gwu.edu/   This website provides a comprehensive overview of bilingual education in the United States.

The Pew Forum on Religion & Public Life, Americans Struggle with Religion's Role at Home and Abroad http://pewforum.org/publications/reports/poll2002.pdf   This downloadable document examines the conflicts surrounding the role of religion in daily life that are encountered by many segments of the American public.

What's YOUR Learning Style? http://www.usd.edu/trio/tut/ts/style.html   This website allows you to take a survey to reveal your own dominant learning style.

CHAPTER 6

Contemporary Trends and Issues in Education

FOCUSING QUESTIONS

▶ If you entered an inclusion class, in what ways, if any, would it appear different from other classes?

▶ What do you think "education for the gifted and talented" refers to? Can an inclusion student be gifted and talented?

▶ What is meant by "differentiated instruction"?

▶ What does problem-based learning involve? How about project-based learning?

▶ What has been the impact on teachers and students of the No Child Left Behind Act?

▶ What alternatives exist to traditional public and private schools?

▶ What kinds of legal rights do students have in school? What are teacher's legal rights and responsibilities?

There are always many "trends" in education, and we could spend four or five entire books discussing current ones. In this chapter, we will concentrate on several major trends and issues affecting schools across the nation:

▶ Approaches to teaching students with special needs.

▶ The use of authentic problems and projects for student learning.

▶ The impact of the No Child Left Behind Act and the emphasis on standards-based testing.

▶ The rising interest in alternative forms of schooling—specifically, public charter schools and home schooling.

▶ The changing ideas about middle schools and education of young adolescents.

▶ The impact of school violence on students and teachers.

▶ The rights and responsibilities of students and teachers.

For you as a prospective teacher, the most significant question behind all these trends and issues is the same one we focused on in Chapter 5: How can the learning needs of so many different learners be met in one classroom in one school?

THE INCLUSION CLASSROOM

Inclusion involves all kinds of practices that are ultimately practices of good teaching. What good teachers do is to think thoughtfully about children and develop ways to reach all students. . . . Inclusion is providing more options for children as ways to learn. It's structuring schools as community where all children can learn.

— Chris Kliewer, University of Northern Iowa (quoted at http://www.uni.edu/coe/inclusion/philosophy/philosophy.html)

In the preceding chapter, we explored ethnic, social class, and learning profile diversity among students; but those are only a few of the ways students can be classified. In this chapter, we examine the extremes on the spectrum of learning—students with disabilities and students who are considered gifted and talented. Both of these groups of students are considered **exceptional learners**. Teaching exceptional learners requires that teachers stretch themselves and their thinking to consider what works best for these students in their classroom settings.

exceptional learners
Students who require special educational services because of physical, behavioral, or academic needs.

Earlier in the book, you read about the Individuals with Disabilities Education Act (IDEA) and its various amendments. The law guarantees that children with disabilities receive a "free appropriate public education." But more than just providing access to education for students with disabilities, the law calls

Inclusion classes give students with disabilities equitable access to an education.

for improved results for these students and the implementation of programs to ensure their continuous progress. In fact, guidelines established by the U.S. Department of Education's Office for Special Education Programs call for improved *performance* of students with disabilities, through an alignment with the No Child Left Behind Act (2001).

The question educators must answer for each student with a disability is: What does free and appropriate public education (FAPE) look like for this child? To comply with the law, this education must take place in the **least restrictive environment** appropriate for each particular student. Hence, to the greatest extent possible, students with disabilities must be educated with children who are not disabled.

Originally, this mandate led to the *mainstreaming* of students with disabilities. Generally, mainstreaming involved having those students participate in general education classes for part of the school day and spend the remainder of the day in a separate, self-contained classroom for students with disabilities. Today, the prevailing concept is **inclusion**, which goes further than mainstreaming. Inclusion involves a commitment to educate students with disabilities in the general education classroom for the entire school day. Any special services the students need are brought to them in the inclusion classroom. Sometimes this arrangement is called *full inclusion* to emphasize that the students stay in the regular classroom full time. If students spend only part of the day in the regular classroom, the arrangement is called *partial inclusion.*

The field of **special education** focuses on the services and instructional practices needed by students with disabilities. You may be interested in becoming a special education teacher. Today, because of inclusion, that often means working in tandem with a general education teacher in the same classroom. In addition to having at least two teachers, an inclusion classroom may also have

least restrictive environment A learning environment that, to the maximum extent possible, matches the environment experienced by nondisabled students.

inclusion The practice of educating students with disabilities in regular classrooms alongside nondisabled students.

special education The branch of education that deals with services for students with disabilities or other special needs that cannot be met through traditional means.

a teacher's aide, who may be specially assigned to a student in the class with special needs.

The following Video Case features a general education class that uses the services of an inclusion specialist. Often, an inclusion specialist works with more than one teacher in a school.

VIDEO CASE

Teaching Strategies for the Inclusion Classroom

Find the HM Video Case "Inclusion: Grouping Strategies for Inclusive Classrooms" on the student website. In this classroom, the students are studying the Caribbean, working in groups at different centers. The teacher has designed the centers in specific ways so that the students gain several perspectives on the countries of the Caribbean.

As you watch this video, notice how the classroom teacher has decided where specific groups of children should begin their unit study. After watching the video, think about the following questions:

- In what ways does the general education teacher, Sheryl Cebula, employ teaching strategies that use multiple intelligences theory? (If you need to, look back at Chapter 5 for a review of this theory.)

- Although more than one teacher is in the classroom, who is in charge? How can you tell?

- How would you describe Ms. Cebula's personal pedagogy in her role as the general education teacher?

- The inclusion specialist, Ms. Jordan, intervenes in many ways. How would you describe her role in the classroom?

- What is the major difference in the way these two teachers function in this classroom?

Controversy About Inclusion

There has been a great deal of controversy about inclusion. Parents of general education students worry that their child's education may be compromised by the presence of students with special needs. They fear, for instance, that the teacher may have to spend so much time with the "special" students that "regular" students get less attention. Other people, however, believe that inclusion helps general education students appreciate people who are different from themselves.

On the opposite side of the coin, there are many critiques of self-contained classrooms for students with disabilities. Many educators worry that students in such classrooms are "labeled" for life. Applied at an early age, the disability label persists over time and limits the students' potential. Other critics point out the disproportionate number of minority boys in self-contained special education classes, especially in urban areas. How do these children get placed in such settings? Why is there a larger number of students from one ethnic group and gender than from others? Who is advocating on behalf of students with special needs?

These and other questions contribute to raging controversies surrounding special education and its implementation in public schools. Wherever you stand on this controversy, the chances are high that you will have an inclusion classroom at some stage in your teaching career.

Types of Disabilities

learning disability (or specific learning disability) A disorder in the basic psychological processes involved in learning and using language; it may lead to difficulties in listening, speaking, reading, writing, reasoning, or mathematical abilities.

Approximately half of all students with disabilities—more than 4 percent of U.S. students as a whole—have **learning disabilities** (U.S. Department of Education, 2005). These are students who have difficulty with reading, listening, speaking, writing, reasoning, or mathematical skills. Students with learning disabilities can be good in one subject area but perform poorly in other areas. For students with learning disabilities, hyperactivity and the inability to follow directions are typical problems.

In many cases, students with learning disabilities have social and behavioral problems. Sometimes the learning disability leads to behavioral distress, low self-esteem, and inappropriate behavior in the classroom.

Some other types of disabilities recognized under the IDEA are (in order from most to least frequent):

▶ Speech or language impairments

▶ Mental retardation

▶ Emotional disturbance

▶ Hearing impairments

▶ Orthopedic impairments

▶ Visual impairments

▶ Autism

(U.S. Department of Education, 2005)

Individualized Education Programs

After my son is out of public school, he'll be living and working with a diverse population of people. I want him to be accepted after he's out of school as much as when he's in school. For me, that is why inclusion is a key while he's in school.

— Parent of a child with disabilities, Waverly, IA (quoted at http://www.uni.edu/coe/inclusion/philosophy/philosophy.html)

individualized education program (IEP) A plan, required for every student covered by the Individuals with Disabilities Education Act, specifying instructional goals, services to be provided, and assessment techniques for evaluating progress.

Because there are so many types of disabilities with so many different representations within the individual child, the IDEA legislation mandates that, in order for each student to have a free and appropriate public education, each student with disabilities be provided with a learning plan. Known as the **individualized education program** or **IEP**, this plan outlines long- and short-range goals for the individual student. It also includes a description of the instructional services that will be provided to meet the goals as well as the assessment techniques that will be used to understand the student's progress.

Figure 6.1 shows a few sections from a sample IEP form. This type of form is usually completed by the general education teacher and the inclusion teacher, working together. In addition to these teachers, other people typically have input into the child's program, including the school psychologist, school administrators, and the student's parents or guardians. A successful inclusion model depends on the collaboration of all these people.

**PRESENT LEVELS OF ACADEMIC ACHIEVEMENT,
FUNCTIONAL PERFORMANCE AND INDIVIDUAL NEEDS**

Current functioning and individual needs in consideration of:

- the results of the initial or most recent evaluation, the student's strengths, the concerns of the parents, the results of the student's performance on any state or districtwide assessment programs;

- the student's needs related to communication, behavior, use of Braille, assistive technology, limited English proficiency;

- how the student's disability affects involvement and progress in the general education curriculum; and

- the student's needs as they relate to transition from school to post-school activities for students beginning with the first IEP to be in effect when the student turns age 15 (and younger if deemed appropriate).

Academic Achievement, Functional Performance and Learning Characteristics:

Current levels of knowledge and development in subject and skill areas, including activities of daily living, level of intellectual functioning, adaptive behavior, expected rate of progress in acquiring skills and information and learning style.

Social Development:

The degree and quality of the student's relationships with peers and adults, feelings about self and social adjustment to school and community environments.

FIGURE 6.1

Sections from a Sample IEP Form

Source: Excerpted from New York State Education Department, "School-Age Individualized Education Program (IEP)," Form NYSED-IEP-SA 12-05, http://www.vesid.nysed.gov/specialed/publications/policy/iep/schoolageiep.htm.

Physical Development:

The degree or quality of the student's motor and sensory development, health, vitality and physical skills or limitations that pertain to the learning process.

Management Needs:

The nature of and degree to which environmental modifications and human or material resources are required to enable the student to benefit from instruction. Management needs are determined in accordance with the factors identified in the areas of academic achievement, functional performance and learning characteristics, social development and physical development.

MEASURABLE ANNUAL GOALS

Annual Goal: What the student will be expected to be able to do by the end of the year in which the IEP is in effect.

Evaluative Criteria: How well and over what period of time the student must demonstrate performance in order to consider the annual goal to have been met.

Procedures to Evaluate Goal: The method that will be used to measure progress and determine if the student has met the annual goal.

Evaluation Schedule: The dates or intervals of time by which evaluation procedures will be used to measure the student's progress.

Annual Goal:	
Evaluative Criteria:	
Procedures to Evaluate Goal:	
Evaluation Schedule:	

FIGURE 6.1
Sections from a Sample IEP Form (continued)

VIDEO CASE

Collaboration Between the General Education Teacher and the Inclusion Specialist

Find the HM Video Case "Inclusion: Classroom Implications for the General and Special Educator" on the student website. This video explores a third-grade inclusion class in which several specialists address the needs of students with disabilities. Examine how this process works in this reading and writing lesson.

After watching the video, address the following questions:

- How does the general education teacher help the students with diverse abilities in this inclusion classroom?

- What interventions are implemented for students with apparent hyperactivity disorders?

- In what ways was the general education teacher's preparation insufficient for her current position?

- What types of students are helped by occupational therapists?

- What is the best way for teachers to learn about the nature of their students' learning disabilities?

WRITING and REFLECTION

Attributes of a Successful Inclusion Teacher

Make a list of attributes that people seeking to become inclusion teachers need to have to be successful with students with special needs.

LEARNING PROJECT

The Controversy Surrounding Inclusion

As we mentioned earlier, inclusion has brought with it a lot of controversy. For this project, you need to do some additional research on the education of students with special needs. (See the Resources for Further Exploration section at the end of this chapter for a starting point.)

Imagine that you are the parent of a child with a learning disability.

- What type of person would make the ideal teacher for your child?

- Would you want your child in an inclusion classroom or a segregated setting with special services? Why?

- What do you believe are the pros and cons of inclusion? of a segregated setting?

THE EDUCATION OF GIFTED AND TALENTED STUDENTS

A teacher asked a class what color apples are. Most of the children said "Red". . . a few answered "Green," and one child raised his hand with another answer: "White." The teacher patiently explained that apples were red or green or yellow but they were never white. The student persisted. Finally, he said, "Look inside."

— Adapted from Tara Bennett-Goleman (2001, p. 43)

This quotation reminds me of how students with "out-of-the-box" thinking often are not rewarded in school because their ideas are not aligned with conventional questioning or expected answers. Sometimes these thinkers are really gifted or talented students.

Most of us typically have less compassion for gifted and talented students than we do for students with disabilities. Conventional wisdom tells us that gifted students always land on their feet, and some of us even feel jealous of their exceptional skills and abilities. Research, however, indicates that gifted and talented learners are in as much need of special educational services as are students with disabilities (Davis & Rimm, 2004). Often their needs are not met in traditional school settings, and that situation frequently causes depression, lack of interest in school, and underachievement.

Further, among students from minority groups or of low socioeconomic status, fewer gifted and talented students are identified than in white, middle- and upper-middle-class populations. Part of this discrepancy stems from parent advocacy—parents of higher social status are more likely to push for their children to be included in gifted programs. The discrepancy also relates to the issue of social capital introduced earlier in this book. Parents with social capital understand how to get their children into special programs. In addition, social capital exposes the learners themselves to a variety of educational and cultural experiences that poorer students often do not gain access to. That early and consistent cultural exposure outside of school contributes to a sense of "giftedness."

As you might guess, the attempt to define *giftedness* has led to controversy. For much of the twentieth century, giftedness was usually measured by IQ tests: people who scored in the upper 2 percent of the population were considered gifted. Critics pointed out, however, that those tests emphasized a narrow range of skills and tended to discriminate against minority groups. Today, giftedness is defined not so much by test scores as by consistently exceptional performance.

Federal legislation has generally referred to gifted and talented children as those who show high performance capability in specific academic fields or in areas such as creativity and leadership, and who require special services by the school to develop these capabilities. To select students for such services, a variety of measures is often employed, including recommendations by teachers, test scores, and an understanding of certain identifying features of gifted and talented students, such as the pace at which they learn and the depth of their understanding (Maker & Nielson, 1996).

Services for the gifted and talented learner can provide *enrichment* (broadening the curriculum) or *acceleration* (speeding up the student's progress through the curriculum). Enrichment activities for the gifted are usually classroom-based, while accelerated programs may allow students to skip grades or graduate early from high school. Accelerated programs range from segregated grade-level classes to high school programs such as the International Baccalaureate (IB) program and advanced placement courses. The IB program is a rigorous course of study concentrating on mathematics, science, and foreign language and is internationally recognized. Advanced placement (AP) courses offer college credit while students are still in high school.

Finally, many people now recommend "gifted inclusion." Can you suppose what that might be? If you think it means designing regular classroom activities that offer gifted and talented students opportunities to expand on the unit of study, you would be correct.

WRITING and REFLECTION

Labels, Labels, Everywhere

This chapter has explored some ways students in today's classrooms are classified or "labeled": students can have gifts, talents, learning disabilities, speech or language impairments, and so on. Remember, too, some of the labels we considered in earlier chapters: English-language learners, whites, ethnic minorities, immigrants, poor, wealthy, word smart, music smart—the list could go on and on.

- In what ways are labels helpful in education?
- Where, if at all, do labels cause harm?
- Were you labeled in any way? How did that affect your life at school?
- What famous people were labeled as having learning, physical, or speech disabilities in school?

Who Is Gifted?

According to the National Association for Gifted Children (NAGC), there is no universally agreed-upon answer to the question of who is gifted. Nevertheless, the NAGC offers its own definition: A gifted person is "someone who shows, or has the potential for showing, an exceptional level of performance in one or more areas of expression."

Some gifted people have general abilities like leadership skills and the ability to think creatively. Other gifted people have more specific abilities, such as special aptitudes in mathematics, science, or music. By these standards, approximately 5 percent of the student population in the United States is considered gifted (National Association for Gifted Children, 2006).

In many cases, gifted students learn differently from their classmates in at least five important ways:

- They learn new material in much less time.
- They tend to remember what they have learned, making reviews of previously mastered concepts a painful experience.
- They perceive ideas and concepts at more abstract and complex levels than do their peers.
- They become passionately interested in specific topics and have difficulty moving on to other learning tasks.
- They are able to operate on many levels of concentration simultaneously, so they can monitor classroom activities without paying direct or visual attention to them. (Winebrenner, 2000, p. 54)

Helen Keller, No. 8

Helen Keller (1880–1968) was deaf and blind; however, despite enormous odds against her, she was able, with the help of her teacher, Anne Sullivan, to graduate from college, become a prolific writer and tour the world. It would have been infinitely easier for her today.

DIFFERENTIATED INSTRUCTION

Thus far in this chapter and in the preceding one, we have been exploring the diversity of students you will find in your classroom. We have focused on students who have exceptional learning needs, special learning profiles, language and ethnic differences, and cultural and socioeconomic differences. Sometimes, strategies for meeting the needs of these learners are developed through collaboration with a specialist, someone who has been trained in a field like special education, gifted education, or bilingual education.

Whether in collaboration with a fellow teacher or not, you will be responsible for developing teaching strategies that can accommodate the learning experience to a wide range of student abilities. Teaching to diversity has a name. **Differentiated instruction** or **differentiation** has become an important educational philosophy recognizing students' varying background knowledge, learning profiles, abilities, interests, and language. It is the basis for developing instructional practices that engage all learners through multiple approaches, tasks, and activities.

Differentiated instruction contrasts with the notion that all children should be taught in the same manner. The movement for gender-fair education, for example, identified the different needs of girls and boys in the classroom resulting from the different ways they are socialized (Sadker & Sadker,

differentiated instruction or differentiation The practice of using a variety of instructional strategies to address the different learning needs of students.

1995). The movement first focused on the needs of girls but then went on to consider new ways to help boys succeed. Overall, the important message for teachers is that equality of treatment does not guarantee equity. Equity is what we should strive for, because it provides equal opportunities for all students to succeed.

What we ask our students to do on behalf of their own learning must be geared to their individual needs and strengths. Our approach must be designed to help them achieve to their fullest potential. In other words, one size does not fit all. One type of activity or lesson will probably not reach all of your students. When you approach teaching a topic, ask yourself questions like these:

▶ In how many different ways can I engage my students in this unit of study?

▶ How can I support students with learning disabilities and challenge the gifted learner, while at the same time exciting all learners to find their strengths?

According to Carol Tomlinson (2000, p. 6), differentiated instruction is based on the following set of beliefs:

▶ Students who are the same age differ in their readiness to learn, their interests, their styles of learning, their experiences, and their life circumstances.

▶ The differences among students are significant enough to make a major impact on what students need to learn, the pace at which they need to learn it, and the support they need from teachers and others to learn it well.

▶ Students learn best when supportive adults push them slightly beyond where they can work without assistance.

▶ Students learn best when they can make a connection between the curriculum and their interests and life experiences.

▶ Students learn best when learning opportunities are natural.

▶ Students are more effective learners when classrooms and schools create a sense of community in which students feel significant and respected.

▶ The central job of schools is to maximize the capacity of each student.

WRITING and REFLECTION

It All Comes Together

• How is differentiated instruction compatible with: multiple intelligences theory, special education, inclusion, bilingual education, and gifted education?

• Look back at the curriculum you developed in the Chapter Challenge for Chapter 4. In what ways does it represent attention to diverse learners? In what ways would you have to modify it for a gifted student? an inclusion student? an English-language learner?

THE POWER OF PROJECTS AND PROBLEMS FOR STUDENT LEARNING

Looking for a history teacher, a suburban high school ran the following advertisement in the local newspaper:

Responsible for implementing curriculum specializing in the time period of 1500–1700 by designing lessons reflecting the theory of multiple intelligences, integrating with other domains using project-based learning and technology.

The phrase toward the end of the ad, "project-based learning," is one you will hear frequently. Both project-based and problem-based learning are contemporary trends aimed at ensuring that students address content areas with depth and skill. Students with diverse needs and learning profiles have been shown to benefit from the use of these strategies.

One major characteristic of both these approaches is that students work in groups, with three to five students organized around a central learning task. This technique had its beginnings in the **cooperative learning** movement, which became popular in the 1990s. Every member of each group is assigned a task, and each task is important for the goal to be reached. The students in the group are responsible for their individual learning as well as the group's learning. They work toward the common goal of promoting each other's and the group's success.

cooperative learning
An instructional approach in which students work together in groups to accomplish shared learning goals.

Project-Based Learning

To see what project-based learning looks like, consider this Teaching Story:

TEACHING STORIES
A CHALLENGING PROJECT FOR SIXTH-GRADE MATH

In Mr. Roberts's sixth-grade math class in an urban middle school, a visitor is immediately struck by what the students are doing. Students are working in groups of four to construct a model classroom, using cardboard boxes, glue guns, poster board, markers, and construction paper. Centimeter sticks and measuring tapes are scattered around each work station. When asked about their work, students eagerly show their sketches, which indicate the scale of their model and use principles of ratio and proportion. Clearly, this class is learning about mathematical concepts through a design project.

Mr. Roberts is convinced that the students will develop a deeper understanding of the concepts of ratio and proportion as a result of designing and constructing the model classroom. He is preparing a written assessment on this topic in order to more fully understand what the students know.

The *design challenge,* a term from engineering design, began with certain specifications. The ratio was stated in advance, using proportional units of 2 cm = 1 foot. The challenge also specified that the classroom contain (1) seating for 18 students, (2) a teacher's desk, (3) a discussion area with a couch and arm chairs and an area rug, and (4) ample board space. Certain constraints were imposed as well: The students may not use materials other than those supplied by the teacher, and the final model should be no larger than 40 cm long x 40 cm wide x 18 cm high. The materials provided include foam board, cardboard, construction paper, markers, glue guns, cutting tools (handled by the teacher and other adults), and assorted recyclable materials, such as wooden spools from sewing thread, cardboard paper-towel tubes, cereal boxes, and other assorted containers.

Working in groups of four, the students present their designs to the entire class after completing their model. They demonstrate how they have met the specifications and constraints of their design challenge and explain why their model classroom contains objects that are in appropriate proportion to the rest of the room. They provide a rationale for the arrangement of the students' and teacher's desks. Throughout this performance, each member of the working group has the opportunity to present his or her understanding of the project and of ratio and proportion. All the students get feedback from their classmates.

project-based learning
A teaching method that engages students in extended inquiry into complex, realistic questions as they work in teams and create presentations to share what they have learned. These presentations may take various forms: an oral or written report, a computer-technology-based presentation, a video, the design of a product, and so on.

This story demonstrates how **project-based learning** adds creativity and depth to a curriculum, promoting more meaningful learning than rote memorization or worksheet activities. Projects can be designed for any subject area, and they often embrace concepts from several disciplines. They also accommodate students with different learning profiles and abilities, helping students work from their own strengths. Everybody becomes engaged in completing the task or constructing the final product. As the newspaper advertisement indicated, projects typically reflect the theory of multiple intelligences and help students integrate knowledge from different domains.

In project-based learning, students work together to meet shared learning goals.

Projects are challenging for teachers because they require more time and more materials than a more traditional lesson does. A project is a carefully planned and organized experience involving carefully selected groups. Although classrooms engaged with projects can be noisy at times, the students are usually very self-directed and invested in their work.

Problem-Based Learning

problem-based learning Focused, experiential learning (minds-on, hands-on) organized around the investigation and resolution of messy, real-world problems.

Closely related to project-based learning is **problem-based learning**. Both strategies emphasize connections to real life, but project-based learning usually results in the construction of something, whereas problem-based learning focuses on a problem, the solutions to which may take many different forms. Problem-based learning is often more open-ended. The following Teaching Story shows problem-based learning in action.

TEACHING STORIES
How Much Milk Are We Wasting?

In Ms. Rhodes's fourth-grade Vermont classroom, a unit on recycling and conservation prompted the class to consider the amount of milk wasted in their school cafeteria during lunchtime. Ms. Rhodes introduced the problem by explaining to the class that the custodian had mentioned how many half-full milk cartons were tossed into the trash during lunch. "So many children—wasting so much milk," he said. Ms. Rhodes asked the class to consider the challenge of finding out just how much milk is wasted in a typical day in the cafeteria.

The students' problem was twofold: (a) how to calculate the volume of milk wasted and (b) how to enlist all the students in the school's help in curbing this waste.

The class enlisted the help of the custodian, who brought discarded, but not empty, milk containers to the classroom each day for a week. Working in groups of four and using graduated cylinders, the students measured the amount of milk wasted each day. They constructed a huge bar graph titled "Milk Waste" outside their classroom, labeling the axes with "day of the week" and "liters of milk wasted." Under the graph, they posed the question "What can YOU do about the amount of milk we waste in our school?"

The students also visited classrooms, talked about the problem, and gathered suggestions. By the end of the school term, there was a 70 percent decrease in the amount of milk wasted!

As this story demonstrates, problem-based learning can help students make connections between school subjects and the world outside of school. Conservation takes on new meaning when students relate it to their own lunchtime habits.

ill-structured problem A problem that lacks clear procedures for finding the solution.

Notice, too, that that the problem the students faced was not a simple one. They were not *told* how to measure the amount of milk wasted. Instead, they faced an **ill-structured problem**, one for which they had to figure out their own approach to the question. With ill-structured problems, the solutions and the steps for reaching them are not clearly defined. In this way, they resemble real-life problems, which are usually complex and messy and require creative and critical thinking skills. To solve ill-structured problems, students need to make decisions based on the facts they gather and their beliefs about the best way to proceed. Solutions emerge from the process, and there may be more than one solution to a single problem.

Karen Rasmussen (1997) describes how a twelfth-grade geology teacher designed his entire course around six ill-structured problems. Each unit lasted six weeks. His goal was to teach students that scientific findings have a lot of relevance outside the school building. In one unit, for example, students received a letter stating that a volcano in Yellowstone Park was showing signs of activity. If it erupted, the middle third of the United States could be wiped out. The students were asked what should be done. In response, they worked in groups to study volcanoes, determine the probability that such an event would occur, and describe the effect a major natural disaster would have on jobs and politics in the region. The teacher encouraged his students to locate information on the Internet. Students prepared a final paper for this unit and also presented oral reports. Their suggestions included:

▶ Drilling into the volcano to relieve the pressure.

▶ Developing evacuation plans.

▶ Not informing the public at all because, some students reasoned, the volcano was unlikely to erupt, there was no way to predict or prevent an eruption, and widespread panic would lower property values and scare industry away from the area.

Project-Based Learning in History and Geography

Here are two interesting examples of project-based learning.

(1) Third-grade students in northern California take a class trip to nearby Rush Ranch, which includes part of the Suisun Marsh. Once a Native American village, the area was later used for ranching by settler Hiram Rush. Now the remaining buildings have been converted into an information center and blacksmith shop, where students learn about marsh ecosystems, local history, and blacksmithing. Their teacher sees the process as building *geo-literacy*: "an in-depth understanding—or 'literacy'—of geography, geology, and local history."

For this purpose, the students need to do more than simply look and listen. Before the field trip, they established a question to answer: "Why is the preservation of Rush Ranch important?" They formed groups, researched the ranch in books and on the Internet, and planned what they would do on their visit. Once on the site, they take photos and videos as documentation, and they conduct interviews with the docents. Analyzing and distilling the material they have gathered, they will create an informational multimedia website (Ball, 2003).

(2) Working in groups of three, seventh-grade history students design and construct a model for a sarcophagus that would be fitting for an ancient Egyptian ruler. (The sarcophagus was the external tomb for the royal mummy in the coffin inside.) Each group of students is studying a particular ruler, and the students decorate their sarcophagus with symbols and images representing the time in which that ruler lived as well as his or her attributes, likes, and dislikes. Through this design project, students learn a great deal about their specific Egyptian leader and about the culture of the period. Then they present the sarcophagus to the class, explaining what life in Ancient Egypt was like at the time of the ruler's death.

None of these suggestions was right or wrong, but each had to be supported by the students' research (Rasmussen, 1997).

Again I want to emphasize that project- and problem-based learning can be applied in any subject area. The next Teaching Story focuses on a high school course in government in which students consider a controversial social and political issue.

TEACHING STORIES
DIFFICULT QUESTIONS ABOUT A CONTEMPORARY SOCIAL ISSUE

In a senior-level high school government course, students are shown a video of the trial of Jack Kevorkian, a doctor who was given a ten- to twenty-five-year prison sentence in Michigan for assisting in the suicide of a terminally ill patient. As is made clear in the video case, Dr. Kevorkian dismissed counsel and represented himself. He had been acquitted of similar charges several times earlier, but in this case, he was found guilty of second-degree murder.

At the point when students are studying the case, Dr. Kevorkian is very ill. After serving less than ten years in jail, he has appealed for parole to the governor of Michigan. The students are asked to make the case for or against granting Kevorkian parole, using data they collect from news reports, the video case, and their own research.

Students must present an argument with no fewer than five supporting pieces of information to support their claim. Their teacher encourages them to learn as much background information about this case as possible, including the ways this case differs from previous cases in which Kevorkian was brought to trial. Students are also required to understand the parameters of second-degree murder and to decide why or why not they believe the verdict to be just and fair.

In this class of twenty-four high school seniors, opinions are almost evenly spit. Three groups favor granting parole, and three favor refusing parole. Students' arguments cover a wide range of topics, from the techniques for assisted suicide to the actual poisonings Kevorkian helped perform. Although no one is clearly "right or wrong" in the conventional sense, the quality of the problem solving influences some students to reconsider their original decisions when they have heard all the arguments.

In a conversation with the teacher, Alex Winter, I was struck by the following remark: "When students are engaged in determining solutions to problems that exist in their real world, they use all of their mental resources to contribute to the solution. I find that I have to say very little. My role is that of a mediator—organizing presentations and moderating the conversations."

Have you ever thought of teaching in the way that Alex Winter suggests? His technique reminds us, as mentioned earlier in the book, that we may tell our students many things in our classrooms, but teaching is *not* telling.

To sum up our discussion of project-based and problem-based learning, we can note that these two approaches have several characteristics in common (Torp & Sage, 2002, pp. 15–16):

▶ Students are engaged problem solvers.

▶ Students work in groups and collaborate to find the best solution to a problem.

▶ Teachers are coaches and guides, modeling interest and enthusiasm for learning.

▶ Projects or problems deal with real-life issues that students care about.

▶ Students use interdisciplinary resources.

▶ Students acquire new skills as they work on different tasks.

▶ Students struggle with ambiguity, complexity, and unpredictability.

WRITING and REFLECTION

Your Own Projects and Problems

• Do you have a memory of a class in which you were engaged in a project or problem that required group work to determine a solution or produce a product? Describe the experience and what, if any, value it added to your education.

• In this text, you have seen a number of Learning Projects. How do they meet the criteria of problem-based or project-based learning?

• It has been said that project- and problem-based learning bring creativity and depth to an area of study. Support that statement with your own ideas.

NO CHILD LEFT BEHIND: CLOSING THE ACHIEVEMENT GAP

The No Child Left Behind (NCLB) Act of 2001 (actually signed by President George W. Bush in January 2002) was the most dramatic federal education legislation since the 1965 Elementary and Secondary Education Act (ESEA). Although NCLB was a reauthorization and revision of ESEA, it went beyond the earlier act in several important ways. It emphasized increased funding for less wealthy school districts and higher achievement for financially poor and minority students. It also introduced new measures for holding schools accountable for students' progress. Most controversially, NCLB set new rules for standardized testing, requiring that students in grades 3 through 8 be tested every year in mathematics and reading.

Many educators see NCLB as an example of the trend toward competency-based education, a movement that began in the 1970s in vocational education. The phrase *competency-based education* implies that the main focus of education is on outcome, not process. But because NCLB requires one standardized test per subject area administered at a given time in each grade level, and because these tests vary from state to state, there is controversy over how well this standardized measure can assess any sort of competency. Moreover, in the standardized tests mandated by NCLB, the competencies exist apart from the social context of schooling, as we will see in the following sections.

Teaching to the Test?

The most immediate effect of the NCLB legislation has been the emphasis on testing. Although accountability is necessary to assess student, school, and system progress, many argue that a single standardized test in mathematics and reading at each grade level, 3–8, creates a culture of test preparation that often leaves little room for creative and in-depth teaching. Teachers may be pressured, directly or indirectly, to "teach to the test"—that is, to focus narrowly on the precise skills and information students need to do well on the exam. In these circumstances, teachers often resort to old-fashioned drill-and-practice exercises, trying to cram the knowledge into their students. There may be little time left for critical thinking, delving into a subject deeply, or exploring the students' own questions.

Some educators argue that teachers do not have to *drill* students for the tests. Strategies like problem-based and project-based learning might produce

The Main Provisions of NCLB

The bold intention of No Child Left Behind was to close the achievement gap between students in poor and minority school districts and those in predominantly white, middle-class school districts by the year 2014. To achieve this goal, the legislation contained four major provisions, summarized as follows by the U.S. Department of Education.

Stronger Accountability for Results

Under No Child Left Behind, states are working to close the achievement gap and make sure all students, including those who are disadvantaged, achieve academic proficiency. Annual state and school district report cards inform parents and communities about state and school progress. Schools that do not make progress must provide supplemental services, such as free tutoring or after-school assistance; take corrective actions; and, if still not making adequate yearly progress after five years, make dramatic changes to the way the school is run.

More Freedom for States and Communities

Under No Child Left Behind, states and school districts have unprecedented flexibility in how they use federal education funds. For example, it is possible for most school districts to transfer up to 50 percent of the federal formula grant funds they receive under the Improving Teacher Quality State Grants, Educational Technology, Innovative Programs, and Safe and Drug-Free Schools programs to any one of these programs, or to their Title I program, without separate approval.

This allows districts to use funds for their particular needs, such as hiring new teachers, increasing teacher pay, and improving teacher training and professional development.

Proven Education Methods

No Child Left Behind puts emphasis on determining which educational programs and practices have been proven effective through rigorous scientific research. Federal funding is targeted to support these programs and teaching methods that work to improve student learning and achievement.

More Choices for Parents

Parents of children in low-performing schools have new options under No Child Left Behind. In schools that do not meet state standards for at least two consecutive years, parents may transfer their children to a better-performing public school, including a public charter school, within their district. The district must provide transportation, using Title I funds if necessary. Students from low-income families in schools that fail to meet state standards for at least three years are eligible to receive supplemental educational services, including tutoring, after-school services, and summer school. Also, students who attend a persistently dangerous school or are the victim of a violent crime while in their school have the option to attend a safe school within their district.

Source: U.S. Department of Education (2006).

equally good test results. At one middle school in Hahnville, Louisiana, that champions project-based learning, scores have indeed gone up. One teacher states: "Part of [the rise in scores] is probably due to project-based learning, because the knowledge does get across to them. I've had kids come back to me and tell me, 'Remember that project we did?' They have never, ever, come back to me and said, 'Remember that test we did?'" (Ball, 2004).

However, few educational systems are willing to give up test-driven teaching in favor of more flexible and creative approaches to content. There is too much at stake when the scores of the students are tallied, summarized, and publicly reported.

Does One Size Fit All?

In addition to the problem of teaching to the test, there is a big question about whether one size fits all in educational testing. Under NCLB, a single standardized test is administered to all students in the state, regardless of their individual learning contexts. Many educators believe that stripping away context denies the authenticity of the assessment—that is, it takes away any possible connection to the students' lived experience. Remember what you read in Chapter 4 about *authentic assessment*. Do test results that are unrelated to students' lives have any real meaning?

Many educators also object to the one-size-fits-all mandate based on what we know about cultural diversity and multiple intelligences. In this view, a single measure of progress is inadequate to evaluate students' understanding of content. Accurate assessments can be achieved only through *multiple* types of assessments and student performances. Many believe that schools and students are better off when local schools and districts have the "flexibility to create innovative solutions to meet their own unique situations" (Guilfoyle, 2006).

Consider Rhode Island, where annual assessments are only a small part of a student's graduation requirements. Students there demonstrate their proficiency in multiple ways:

- Portfolios, which include selected examples of student work.

- Capstone projects, which often involve in-depth research, reports, and oral presentations.

- Public exhibitions, such as posters showing the student's accomplishments in a given content area.

Authentic Assessment

In the practice of *authentic assessment,* as we discussed in Chapter 4, students demonstrate their understanding of a content area by performing a task or solving a problem in the real-life context of their classroom or their world. This demonstration often involves some kind of student *performance;* hence, this type of assessment is also called *performance assessment.* The performance can involve anything from conducting an experiment to writing a report to designing a Web-based presentation. The products of project-based and problem-based learning are often used as a form of authentic assessment.

Imagine what this approach would mean for NCLB. If testing were just one piece of an innovative, comprehensive assessment and accountability system, we would have a more accurate picture of each school's strengths and weaknesses as well as more information to help schools and individual students succeed (Guilfoyle, 2006).

Variation Among States: Are the Standards Really Standard?

Within each state, NCLB mandates standardized tests. Yet as states develop their own standards and tests for subject areas, there is enormous variability from one state to the next. In fact, students in some states perform better on the state standardized tests than they do on national math and reading tests. Some educators believe these states are setting the achievement bar too low. Because schools—and the states responsible for them—face financial consequences if students fail to show adequate progress, there is some incentive to make the standards easy to meet.

As a result of this problem, a grassroots movement is gathering momentum to coordinate state standards, at least for certain subjects. Nine states (Pennsylvania, New Jersey, Arkansas, Kentucky, Indiana, Maryland, Massachusetts, Ohio, and Rhode Island) have formed a consortium to create a common set of standards and a common test for all their students taking Algebra II (Zuckerbrod, 2007). Proponents argue that standards for a subject like algebra should not vary across state lines. If this effort succeeds, it will be one step toward genuine standardization.

The Achievement Gap

What might happen if we paid less attention to outcomes, as measured by test scores, and more attention to how children learn, which is one of the most important processes of education?. . . Studying the ways in which children learn could help us focus on cultural differences between and among the children who sit in the same classroom, and on how those cultural differences might be used to empower learning rather than to stand in its way.

— Ellen Condliffe Lagemann (2007)

Perhaps the most discouraging effect of the NCLB legislation has been its effect on low-achieving schools and districts, precisely the constituents it had hoped to serve. After the first five years under the NCLB legislation, the gap between high- and low-achieving students had actually widened (Tough, 2006). Meanwhile, the law has created a test-preparation culture that narrows the view of knowledge by focusing heavily on reading and mathematics scores (Cawelti, 2006). Although accountability is terribly important, the implementation of one high-stakes test per grade level has forced many teachers to ignore the types of creative, problem-based teaching strategies that we have discussed in this chapter—strategies that engage students in their own learning. Consequently, the very students we are hoping to "hook" become discouraged by a lifeless curriculum.

Moreover, many teachers themselves are discouraged by the effects of high-stakes testing on their teaching. "In a study of 376 elementary and secondary teachers in New Jersey, teachers indicated that they tended to teach to the test, often neglected individual students' needs . . . had little time to teach creatively, and bored themselves and their students with practice problems as they prepared for standardized testing" (quoted in Cawelti, 2006).

A basic assumption of NCLB was that maintaining high expectations is necessary for improving achievement. This is, however, only one part of a potential solution. Achievement gaps between ethnic groups and groups of differing socioeconomic status are not *caused* by schools. They are caused by powerful social and family characteristics that affect children long before they start school and continue to operate as they enter school (Hart & Risley, 1995; Brooks-Gunn, et al., 2000; Lareau, 2003). This does not mean that social and economic disadvantages—the absence of social capital—cannot be overcome in schools. But NCLB's goals cannot be achieved by enforcing a standardized testing program that few low-income students can become invested in.

VIDEO CASE

Educators Discuss IDEA and NCLB

Look for the HM Video Case, "Foundations: Aligning Instruction with Federal Legislation," on the student website. In this video, a school principal, teachers, specialists, and a school intern discuss the challenges and problems of meeting the requirements of two important pieces of educational legislation you have read about in this chapter: IDEA and NCLB. Examine this video and respond to the following questions:

- What is the best advice for a new teacher who finds himself or herself in an inclusion classroom as a general education teacher?

- How does the inclusion specialist express the sentiments behind this chapter's idea that one size does not fit all?

- What do you think the principal means when he refers to teaching as "the profession of hope?"

ALTERNATIVES TO TRADITIONAL SCHOOLS: MORE CHOICES IN AN ERA OF ACCOUNTABILITY

Under the NCLB law, if schools do not meet state standards for two consecutive years, parents may move their children into other, higher-performing schools. Essentially, NCLB obligates school districts to replace low-performing schools. This requirement has given a boost to charter schools, which are an alternative kind of public school.

Another alternative to traditional schools is homeschooling. More and more parents dissatisfied with public schools have begun to investigate the options for teaching their children at home. What do you think is behind this movement?

As a teacher, you may end up working in a charter school, or you may teach children who have been homeschooled in the past. In this section, we'll take a look at these two alternatives to traditional public and private schools.

The Rise of Charter Schools

charter schools Publicly funded elementary or secondary schools that are granted a special charter by the state or local education agency.

Since the first charter school opened in Minnesota in 1991, the charter school movement has grown to nearly 4,000 schools with more than 1.15 million children enrolled (Education Commission of the States, 2007a). A **charter school** is a public school that has a specific, written charter from the school district, the state, or another governing agency. The charter typically exempts the school from selected rules and regulations that apply to other schools. In exchange for these exemptions, the school agrees to be accountable for producing certain results, set forth in the charter, in a specified period of time. Every three to five years, a school's status is reviewed; the school's right to exist can be revoked if the school has not met the standards promised in the charter.

By 2007, forty states, the District of Columbia, and Puerto Rico had established charter school laws. This means that concerned citizens, educators, or government officials can bring a plan for a charter school to the local or state education agency and, if the plan meets the established requirements, there is a strong possibility that the school can be established.

The belief is that charter schools have the potential to develop new and creative teaching methods and that these innovations can thrive in a system that is not constrained by the usual rules and regulations. Many educators also hope that charter schools will foster a positive spirit of competition, encouraging traditional public schools to reform their practices.

What evidence is there that charter schools can fulfill this promise? On the positive side, there is a correlation between states having strong charter school laws and achievement gains for students (Center for Education Reform, 2005). Also, when charter schools are successful, there has indeed been a "ripple effect" for the public schools. Increasingly, members of the traditional public school system are turning to successful charter schools for examples of "best practices" regarding everything from curriculum to staffing and teacher retention (Mitchell, 2004).

On the negative side, there is no clear evidence that charter schools as a whole are significantly more successful than traditional public schools. The National Assessment of Educational Progress, for example, found no significant advantages for charter schools in reading or math performance (National Assessment of Educational Progress, 2005; Braun, Jenkins, & Grigg, 2006). For low-performing students in particular—the focus of many reform efforts—no studies definitively suggest that the charter school system is more successful than what is already in place.

Because many different groups of concerned citizens can start charter schools, often without any prior training in education, professionals who do research in the area of learning and teaching are concerned about the charter school movement. Analyzing the success or failure of charter schools is complicated, however, because there are so many different types serving so many kinds of students. As one team of researchers explains:

> One of the most important difficulties in studying charter schools is that many of them are targeted specifically at particular student populations and thus serve dramatically different kinds of students than regular public schools do. Although most states require charter schools to have open enrollment policies, charter schools can

still target specific populations by describing themselves as schools for a particular kind of student or by otherwise encouraging a certain kind of student to apply for admission. A study by the U.S. Department of Education found that one quarter of charter schools are targeted toward certain populations. Many people familiar with charter schools would find this a very conservative estimate. (Greene, Forster, & Winters, 2003).

Similarly, the National Education Association (2007) comments:

It is difficult—not to mention scientifically invalid—to make blanket comparisons of charter schools to traditional public schools. However, because charter schools promise to improve student achievement as a condition of relief from some of the rules and regulations that apply to traditional public schools, it is appropriate to evaluate their effectiveness.

This is a reminder that teaching and learning are highly complex activities and that schools are complicated organizations functioning on behalf of diverse students with a broad range of differences.

Who Teaches in Charter Schools?

Of the forty states with charter school laws, almost half of them stipulate that charter school teachers must be state certified. For the remainder, the requirements vary. In some states, individuals may apply for a waiver to the certification requirement. In the District of Columbia, teachers do not have to be certified at all. In still other states, special guidelines apply. Illinois, for example, requires that charter schools be able to employ noncertified teachers if they have a bachelor's degree, five years' experience in the area of degree, a passing score on state teacher tests, and evidence of professional growth; for all such noncertified teachers, mentoring must be provided (Education Commission of the States, 2007b).

Most professional educators, like the author of this book, believe that a formal program in learning to become a teacher is vital for anyone who wants to teach. For this reason, we hope that all charter schools will eventually require certification. This will ease some of the doubts about the value of charter schools for American education.

A Case Study: The Russell Byers Charter School

If you have never attended or visited a charter school, a case study may help you understand what the charter school movement is about. Begun in 2001, the Russell Byers Charter School in Philadelphia houses 400 students from kindergarten (including 4K, a kindergarten for four-year-olds) through sixth grade. The school is named after a long-time *Philadelphia Daily News* columnist who devoted much of his writing to the cause of public education and school reform. After he was murdered in a robbery attempt at a convenience store, his widow and their two children spearheaded the effort to open this charter school in his memory.

Open to all children living in Philadelphia, the school draws students from more than thirty-five neighborhoods. Because there is a long waiting list, new students are selected by lottery. The school has committed itself to small class sizes, academic excellence, civic responsibility, and community service.

All classrooms have networked computers and follow Pennsylvania state standards in the various subject areas. However, the school's educational approach, Expeditionary Learning Schools Outward Bound (ELS), based on the Outward Bound model of outdoor education, emphasizes experiential learning.

This means that students spend up to twelve weeks studying a single topic both inside and outside the classroom. Located in a downtown area, the school can draw on many nearby cultural resources, such as the Franklin Institute science museum. The cross-disciplinary subjects of study have included insect life, community gardens, the explorers Lewis and Clark, and life in a village in Ghana. When a learning unit is completed, students share their knowledge through performances featuring essays, poems, photos, theater, song, and paintings. Also central to the Byers School experience is a community service project related to the topic of study and selected by the students.

The goals and methods of this school give you some idea of why charter schools have attracted more and more American families. Keep in mind, though, that no one school is typical of this broad-ranging movement in American education.

Homeschooling: Another Nontraditional Option

In 1997, a thirteen-year-old named Rebecca Sealfon won the 70th National Spelling Bee. What was remarkable about Rebecca's performance was that she had never gone to school! Having been taught at home exclusively, her performance turned a national spotlight on **homeschooling**.

homeschooling Educating children at home rather than in a school; parents typically serve as teachers.

A few decades ago, homeschooling represented a fringe part of the educational landscape, but currently it is a fast-growing trend. In 1999, an estimated 850,000 U.S. students between the ages of five and seventeen were being homeschooled (Bielick, Chandler, & Broughman, 2001). By the year 2009, according to some estimates, the number of homeschooled children will have doubled as more families question the efficacy of traditional schools in preparing their children academically and socially for a global economy and a highly competitive marketplace. (In these statistics, students are considered to be homeschooled if their parents report them as being schooled at home for at least part of their education and if their part-time enrollment in public or private schools does not exceed twenty-five hours a week.)

Although many different types of families engage in homeschooling their children, the majority tend to be white, middle or upper-middle class, religious, and well educated. Often they select homeschooling primarily for religious and cultural reasons, eager to protect their children from "a popular culture overflowing with images of sexual rebellion and promiscuity" (Anderson, 2000). Figure 6.2 shows statistics from a survey sponsored by the National Center for Education Statistics. In this survey, the most frequent reason parents gave for homeschooling their children was concern about schools' "environment," which included worries about safety, drug use, and peer pressure. Nearly a third of parents mentioned this reason, and almost as many cited a desire to give their children religious or moral instruction. Fewer parents, but still a significant percentage, expressed dissatisfaction with academic instruction in schools (Princiotta & Bielick, 2006).

Clearly, some elements of homeschooling, including the lack of pressure to perform and a freedom of choice concerning the curriculum are appealing alternatives to mandated curriculum that is based on standardized testing. Keeping children at home also keeps them out of harm's way and, for some parents, allows religious training that, by law, their children would not receive in public school.

Some critics of homeschooling worry that most parents cannot provide the academic support their children need to learn a wide range of subjects.

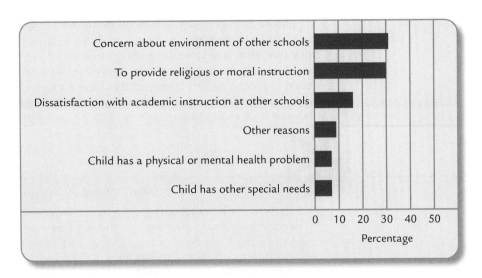

FIGURE 6.2
Reasons Parents Give for Homeschooling Their Children
Source: Princiotta, D., and Bielick, S. (2006). *Homeschooling in the United States: 2003*. NCES 2006-042.
Washington, DC: U.S. Department of Education, National Center for Education Statistics.

After all, certified teachers are trained in educational methods and in curriculum content areas, and most parents are not. However, a growing number of companies cater to parents who homeschool by providing curriculum materials. In addition, the Internet now offers an abundance of educational resources that were not available a decade ago. Many previously reluctant parents now choose to homeschool their children because of the wealth of materials available online.

Another worry about homeschooling is that students miss the socialization that occurs in schools. The entire experience of "going to school" is comprised of much more than lessons, athletics, and theatrical and musical performances. It is a daily and annual ritual event that defines the growth and development of our children. As we saw in earlier chapters, many cultural beliefs and social values are transmitted through the "hidden curriculum" of schools. Students meet peers who represent a cross section of their community—students with different learning styles, abilities, opinions, strengths, weaknesses, and ways of being in the world. Are homeschooled children denied all these opportunities?

Proponents of homeschooling point out that homeschooling parents have formed networks to engage their children in social and musical events outside the home. Homeschooling does not mean isolation. In addition, some studies indicate that very few homeschooled children are socially deprived and that homeschooled children in general have a better self-concept than conventionally schooled children do. For instance, a study conducted in 2003 (Ray, 2004) gathered data from over 5,000 adults who had been homeschooled for more than seven years. The study reported that 71 percent of these graduates were active and involved community members and participated in service activities regularly, as compared with 37 percent of U.S. adults of similar ages from traditional education backgrounds. Further, 76 percent of those surveyed, ages 18 to 24, reported voting within the last five years, compared with 29 percent for the corresponding U.S. populace.

Most state governments regulate home schooling to at least some degree. In some of these states, parents merely have to notify the educational authorities that they are schooling their children at home. In other states, parents must submit their children's test scores or other professional evaluations of academic progress. The strictest states have further conditions, such as requiring that parents file a plan or program of study before they can gain permission to homeschool their children.

WRITING and REFLECTION

Your Beliefs About Homeschooling

Supporters of homeschooling describe the movement as designed to enable students to learn freely, meaning that they are free from the constraints of teachers' plans, school schedules, peer abilities, and school disruptions. Many homeschooling groups help families support each other and network socially. Still, critics worry that homeschooling deprives children of vital learning experiences.

- Do you believe students miss important experiences by not attending a public or private school? What experiences in particular?

- Can you name one specific area of study that you believe cannot be managed successfully at home? Explain your choice.

MIDDLE SCHOOL: A MOVEMENT IN TRANSITION

In the early 1900s, the dominant school configuration was eight years of primary school followed by four years of secondary school. This "8-4" model was called into question as more and more students attended public school. In 1899, the National Education Association issued a report calling for secondary school to begin in the seventh grade, citing that time, the beginning of adolescence, as a "natural turning point in a pupil's life" (National Education Association, 1899). Nevertheless, it was another fifteen to twenty years before the junior high school model of grades 7 through 9 emerged and began to proliferate.

Originally, junior high schools were thought of as preparatory grounds for the academic rigor of high school. By the late 1960s and early 1970s, however, various models for reorganization of school district grades were being considered to meet desegregation requirements. Further, many junior high schools were seen as focusing on content mastery rather than on the psychological and emotional needs of early adolescents.

By the 1980s, many school reformers endorsed a new "middle school" concept intended to create an educational experience more appropriate for young adolescents. The goal was to make the old junior high school more developmentally responsive by changing the grade configuration from grades 7–8 or 7–8–9 to grades 6–7–8 and designing new organizational structures such as interdisciplinary teams (Juvonen, et al., 2004). The teams would ensure that a group or cluster of students would be taught by the same four or five subject area teachers, thus creating a sense of community and closeness.

In the following decades, many school districts converted their junior highs to middle schools, but the process was far from uniform. As Figure 6.3 on page 182 shows, there are still several ways of organizing the middle grades.

Middle schools are being assessed according to how well they meet the needs of preteens and young teens in transition.

Critiques of the Middle School Model

Despite well-intentioned and committed educators, middle schools do not yet fully serve the needs of young teens. The history of the middle school movement suggests that the middle school became the norm because of societal and demographic pressures and not because of hard evidence to support the need for a separate school for young teens. In fact, research in 1989 showed that seventh and eighth graders schooled in a K–8 model performed better in all areas of achievement and psychological wellness than did their peers at middle school (Eccles and Midgley, 1989; Eccles, Lord, & Midgley, 1991).

For these reasons, organization of the middle grades is still in flux. A comprehensive study of middle schools conducted by the RAND Corporation recommends that states and school districts seek alternatives to the now-typical 6–8 structure of middle school, for a number of significant reasons:

▶ National school-safety statistics suggest that physical conflict is especially problematic in middle schools.

▶ Social norms in middle school may foster antisocial behavior.

▶ Academic progress for middle schools is uneven and lackluster.

▶ Adequate state and federal supports to meet the new standards set by the NCLB legislation are unavailable for middle schools.

▶ Middle schools do not do enough to foster parental involvement.

▶ Many middle school teachers do not have certification in the subject areas they teach or specific training in the development of young adolescents. (Juvonen, et al., 2004)

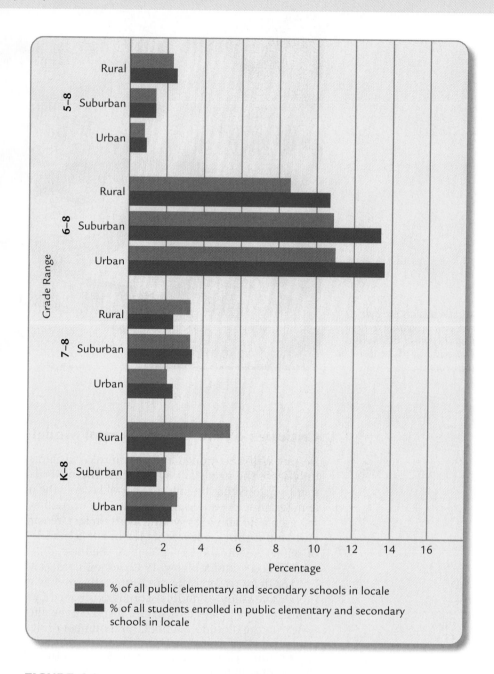

FIGURE 6.3

Frequency of Different Models for Organizing the Middle Grades

Source: J. Juvonen, V. Le, T. Kaganoff, C. H. Augustine, & L. Constant, *Focus on the Wonder Years: Challenges Facing the American Middle School* (Santa Monica, CA: Rand Corporation, 2004), Figure 1.1, p. 3.

A Framework for Effective Middle Schools

In the 2003 document *This We Believe: Successful Schools for Young Adolescents,* the National Middle School Association describes eight characteristics of an effective middle school culture:

▶ Educators who value working with young adolescents

▶ Courageous, collaborative leadership

▶ A shared vision

▶ An inviting, supportive, and safe environment

▶ High expectations for all

▶ Active learning by both students and teachers

▶ An adult advocate for every student

▶ Family and community partnerships

Further, *This We Believe* identifies and describes six critical program characteristics:

▶ Curriculum that is relevant, challenging, integrative, and exploratory

▶ Multiple teaching and learning approaches that respond to students' diversity

▶ Assessment and evaluation that promote learning

▶ Organizational structures, such as interdisciplinary teams, that support meaningful relationships and learning

▶ School-wide policies that foster health, wellness, and safety

▶ Comprehensive guidance and support services

Reading this list of fourteen characteristics makes us pause and ask: Why can't these characteristics simply be implemented? What does it take? The answers to these questions lie at the heart of every educational reform movement. They are not simple; they require an investment of time and energy on the part of administrators, teachers, parents, school districts, local school boards, and state agencies.

One example of the difficult problems of middle schools is the issue of school safety, which we have mentioned in passing several times in this chapter. When people talk about school safety today, they are referring to the outbreaks of violence that have become all too common in our schools. This is the subject of the next section.

CREATING A SAFE SCHOOL CLIMATE: THE CONCERN ABOUT VIOLENCE IN SCHOOLS

Although the vast majority of the country's students will never be touched by peer violence in their K–12 school careers, serious isolated incidents of school violence have rocked the headlines and shaken confidence in our schools. In 1999, the Littleton, Colorado, high school, Columbine, was the scene of a violent school attack by two students that claimed the lives of fourteen students and a teacher. This was the most violent school attack in U.S. history until it was eclipsed by the 2007 rampage at Virginia Tech University in Blacksburg, Virginia, which claimed thirty-two lives, including twenty-seven students.

These incidents of targeted violence, thankfully, are rare. As Figures 6.4 and 6.5 suggest, the number of violent incidents in our nation's schools has, in fact,

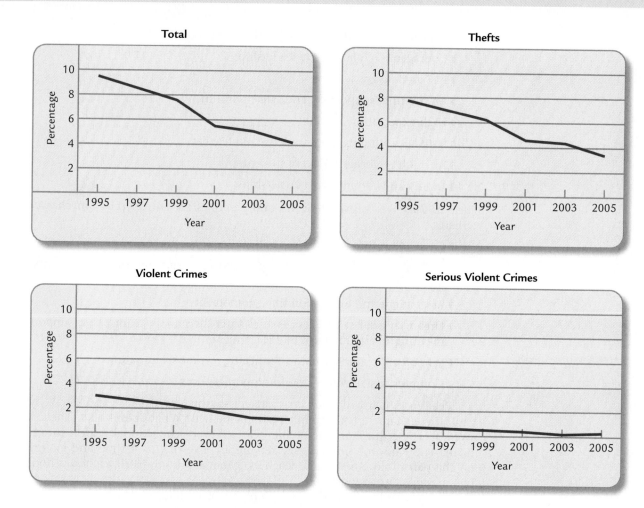

FIGURE 6.4

Crimes Against Students at School

The graphs show the percentage of students, ages twelve to eighteen, who reported criminal victimization at school during the previous six months. The category of "violent crimes" includes "serious violent crimes."

Source: Dinkes, R., Cataldi, E. F., Kena, G., and Baum, K. (2006). *Indicators of School Crime and Safety: 2006.* NCES 2007-003/NCJ 214262. Washington, DC: U.S. Departments of Education and Justice. Figure 3.1, p. 15.

been declining since the mid-1990s. Yet the highly publicized shootings of the last decade have prompted educators to examine how, if at all, these incidents, and other less serious ones, could have been prevented (Fein, et al., 2002).

Earlier in this text, we discussed school climate and the ways it is evident when you enter a school as a student or teacher. It may even be evident to a regular visitor. The school climate is a result of the relationships that exist among the students, teachers, parents, and administrators within the school community. In a school with a *climate of safety,* adults and students respect each other and, importantly, students have a positive connection to at least one adult in authority. When a climate of safety is created, you can sense it in a school; there is a feeling of emotional wellness. In this type of school climate,

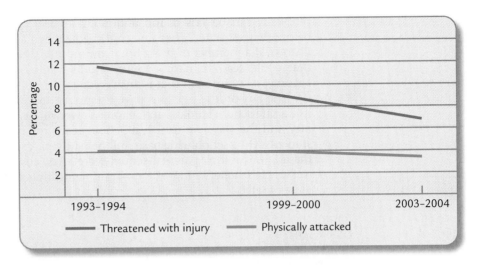

FIGURE 6.5
Violence Against Teachers

This graph shows the percentage of public and private school teachers who reported being threatened with injury or physically attacked by a student from school during the previous twelve months.

Source: Dinkes, R., Cataldi, E. F., Kena, G., and Baum, K. (2006). *Indicators of School Crime and Safety: 2006*. NCES 2007-003/NCJ 214262. Washington, DC: U.S. Departments of Education and Justice. Figure 5.1, p. 21.

Creating a School Climate That Promotes Safety and Connectedness

Working together, the U.S. Department of Education and the Secret Service have produced a guide to help schools create a climate of school safety. According to this document, the major components and tasks for creating a safe school climate include:

Assessing the School's Emotional Climate

- How do the students and teachers experience the daily life of the school?

- Is there a culture of respect?

- Are students' emotional needs being met?

- Is everyday teasing and bullying dealt with immediately?

Creating Connections Between Adults and Students

- Do students have a positive relationship with at least one adult?

- Does each student feel there is an adult she or he can talk to about problems and concerns?

Breaking the Code of Silence

- In many schools, students believe that revealing another student's pain or problems breaks a special peer code. This belief often forces troubled students to go it alone.

- In a safe school climate, students are willing to break the code of silence to get help for a peer.

Involving Everyone

- Are all members of the school community involved in creating policy and practices that help each member respond to stressful and potentially harmful events?

Source: Fein, R. A., Vossekuil, B., Pollack, W. S., Borum, R., Modzeleski, W., & Reddy, M. (2002). *Threat Assessment in Schools: A Guide to Managing Threatening Situations and to Creating Safe School Climates*. Washington, DC: United States Secret Service and United States Department of Education.

problems can be raised and addressed in peer groups and with counselors before they escalate. It becomes noticeable when a student is disturbed and in distress. If a member of the school community shows enormous personal pain that could lead to harm—to the student him- or herself or to others—it becomes a cry for help that is answered.

The box on the previous page lists some important factors that help establish a safe school climate. In Chapter 9, we will discuss the classroom community and the ways we can think about teaching as forging relationships with students. On a schoolwide basis, all the participants in the school community—the administrators, parents, school secretaries, custodians, groundskeepers, as well as the teachers and students—must contribute to the establishment of a climate of safety.

WRITING and REFLECTION

Safe Schools

- Was there ever a time in your school experience when you did not feel safe? Describe what that was like and how you handled it. What was the outcome?

- Imagine a sixth-grade student coming to you to report that a classmate has been very depressed since the death of her dog. The informant describes a conversation in which this student said she wanted to kill herself. What would you do?

PROTECTING THE RIGHTS OF STUDENTS

Clearly, students have a right to be safe in school. That is one basic right that cannot be denied. What other rights do students have?

In most states, education of children has been compulsory for more than a century. Children must go to school or (as we discussed earlier in this chapter) to a reasonable home-based alternative to school. Obviously, though, schools cannot do whatever they like with this captive audience. Along with schools' obligation to educate students, students deserve to have certain rights, but exactly what those rights should be isn't always evident. A number of recent laws and court cases have raised serious questions about the subject. Let's explore some of the issues that have come to the fore.

Before reading further, stop a moment and think: What kinds of student rights do you suppose are covered by law? And how do you suppose the recent concern about school safety has affected students' rights?

The Right to Privacy

Do you know where all of the information about your educational history is kept? Are your health records in the same place? Does the file contain records of your student loans and other information you might not like to share with everyone? What if you have a learning disability—is that documented in your file? *Who has access to this file? What are your rights?*

Family Educational Rights and Privacy Act (FERPA) or the Buckley Amendment
A federal law requiring educational agencies to protect the confidentiality of students' educational records.

The **Family Educational Rights and Privacy Act (FERPA)** of 1974, also known as the **Buckley Amendment**, is a federal law that requires educational agencies and institutions to protect the confidentiality of students' educational records. It applies to all school systems and individual schools, including colleges and universities, receiving federal financial assistance or funding.

FERPA allows students and their parents to have access to the student's records kept by educational institutions. The law also states that no one outside the institution may have access to a student's educational records, nor can the institution disclose any information from the records without the written consent of the student, or in the case of students under the age of eighteen, their parents. The U.S. Congress passed this act in response to instances of parents or students being denied access to their records or information about students being improperly used.

FERPA clearly states that parents of students in attendance at a school have the right to inspect and review the education records of their children. Further, if the parents (or students over the age of eighteen) challenge the contents of the records, they must be given a hearing. At this hearing, the parents and student have the opportunity to insert their own written explanation into the record. The intent is to make sure the records are not inaccurate, misleading, or otherwise in violation of the student's privacy or other rights.

As a college or university undergraduate or graduate student, you should have knowledge of what is in your personal records at your institution. Once you are eighteen years of age, your parents have no inherent right to inspect your educational record; that right becomes yours alone. Parents may, however, gain access to so-called directory information, which includes simple facts that would not compromise a student's privacy, such as enrollment status, major field of study, degrees received, and so on.

Recent Challenges to FERPA

Until 2001, there were no cases involving violations to FERPA brought to the U.S. Supreme Court. In 2001, however, the Court heard a case concerning the oral reporting by peers of student grades. In Oklahoma, in the Owassa Independent School District, a mother was disturbed when her son's teacher asked the class to grade each other's quizzes and then had students call out the grades so she could record them. This mother felt that the calling out of grades by his peers was a violation of her son's right to privacy. She lost the case; the Supreme Court ruled that peer grading did not violate FERPA.

A second case was brought to the Supreme Court by a college student at Gonzaga University in Washington state. The teacher certification officer at that university overheard a student discussing a teacher candidate's alleged

Students' and Parents' Rights Under FERPA

- The right to inspect and review educational records.
- The right to request amendment of educational records.
- The right to exercise some control over the disclosure of information from educational records.
- The right to file a complaint with the U.S. Department of Education if a school or other educational agency fails to comply with the act.

sexual harassment of another student and proceeded to conduct an investigation, place remarks about it in the student's record, and deny teacher certification to that student. The supposed victim of the sexual harassment denied that it occurred and never pressed charges. The alleged offender sued the university for violating FERPA. This case made its way through various levels of the state court system and finally reached the U.S. Supreme Court in 2002. The Justices ruled that FERPA did not give "enforceable rights" to individuals. Rather, it was up to the Department of Education to enforce FERPA by denying funding to educational institutions that violated the law.

Although this Supreme Court ruling may prevent individual students from collecting damages for violation of their privacy, FERPA still offers protection through the power of the purse. Because educational institutions do not want to lose their federal funding, they will be careful about allowing practices that infringe on rights established by FERPA.

Compromises on Privacy

In this age of readily accessible data, it often feels as though anyone can gain access to another person's information just by having Internet access. It is not quite that easy to get educational records. Unfortunately, however, since the Columbine High School shooting in 1999 in Colorado, educators and police agencies have felt an increased need to identify, collect, and share information in a coordinated effort to prevent a recurrence of this type of student violence. Events such as the terrorist attacks at the World Trade Towers and the Pentagon have also made the sharing of information seem more imperative.

The scope of student data collected has expanded greatly since FERPA was passed in 1974. For example, student records now include data relating to the student's needs for specific educational services. Moreover, requests for student information now come from a growing number of sources inside school systems (including counselors, principals, school social workers, special education personnel, classroom teachers) and outside school systems (military recruiters, university researchers, law enforcement officers, the courts, college admissions personnel, the media, social services agencies, and others).

WRITING and REFLECTION

Impact of FERPA on Students' Files

Imagine that you are a middle school teacher and you are having serious difficulty relating to one of your students. On occasion, this student is rude and disruptive. You have placed descriptions of these incidents in the student's file, expressing yourself both professionally and honestly.

• What will you do if the student's parent asks to see his record?

• Will you modify your statements, knowing that parents have legal access to their children's files?

• Do you think that most teachers consider FERPA when making comments in students' permanent school files?

Some additional laws do help protect the new wealth of information. Individualized education programs are protected under IDEA; parents must have ready access to student IEPs, but the information is considered confidential and schools are restricted from releasing it to people who do not have a legitimate educational interest in the child. Similarly, NCLB ensures the right to privacy of individual students' scores. Nevertheless, the USA PATRIOT Act of 2001 created the possibility that, with a subpoena, authorities could gain access to a student's confidential information without the knowledge of the student or the parents (Vacca, 2004).

Clearly, educational institutions need to exercise careful monitoring of when and to whom student data are released. As a teacher, you, too, should be sensitive to your students' rights to privacy.

First Amendment Rights of Students

Congress shall make no law respecting an establishment of religion, or prohibiting the free exercise thereof; or abridging the freedom of speech, or of the press; or the right of the people peaceably to assemble, and to petition the Government for a redress of grievances.

— The First Amendment to the U.S. Constitution

It is commonly accepted that, in schools and classrooms, the need for legitimate teaching and learning requires rules of behavior that, at times, restrict the speech of students. Yet the Supreme Court tells us in *Tinker v. Des Moines* that "students do not shed their constitutional rights when they enter the schoolhouse door." In this 1969 ruling, the Supreme Court upheld the First Amendment right of high school students to wear black armbands in a public high school as a form of protest against the Vietnam War. Wearing the armband was considered symbolic speech. According to the Court, school administrators could prohibit the armbands only if the administrators showed that the protest would cause a substantial disruption of the school's educational mission. (Do you think the case would have come out differently if school administrators had demonstrated that the armbands caused loud debates to break out in class?)

Similarly, in the 1973 case of *Papish v. the Board of Curators of the University of Missouri,* the Supreme Court ruled in favor of the First Amendment rights of Barbara Papish, a graduate student, after the university expelled her for distributing a controversial leaflet containing profanity and a cartoon of policemen raping the Statue of Liberty.

Other Court decisions, however, have supported schools in their attempts to restrict students' speech. In 1986, the Court ruled in favor of the right of Washington state high school administrators when they disciplined a student for delivering a campaign speech that was full of sexual innuendo at a school assembly. In this case, *Bethel School District No. 403 v. Fraser*, the Court expressed the view that school administrators had the right to punish student speech that violated school rules and that interfered with legitimate educational objectives. As another example, in the 1988 case of the *Hazelwood School District v. Kuhlmeier*, the Court upheld the right of school administrators to censor materials in a student-edited newspaper that concerned sensitive issues such as student pregnancy and that could be considered an invasion of privacy.

The right to express ideas and individual beliefs is fostered through responsible class activity.

Also accepted is the school district's right to impose dress code restrictions on students—and teachers. Schools may require that students wear uniforms, and they may also impose reasonable grooming and dress codes for their teachers.

Overall, it seems that the Supreme Court has tried to strike a balance between the right to free expression and schools' need to maintain a productive learning atmosphere. In day-to-day terms, teachers and administrators make their own decisions on the basis of established school policies as well as common sense. Think back to the speech and dress policies of the schools you have attended. Do you think a reasonable balance was struck between individual rights and an orderly learning environment?

The First Amendment also addresses freedom of religion, and here the issues become even thornier and more confusing, as we noted in Chapter 5. There are many legal questions surrounding the separation of church and state and the First Amendment's clause about free exercise of religion. In general terms, public schools must remain neutral about religious beliefs, but does this mean, for instance, that a student-led religious group cannot meet on school grounds? Does it mean that teachers cannot lead their students in reciting the Pledge of Allegiance, which includes the phrase "under God"?

The courts have been actively tackling these issues, and decisions made over the next few years may affect your classroom. Right now, to sum up the impact of various laws, court cases, and federal guidelines, it is fair to say that the following rules apply:

1. Prayer cannot be a regular part of the school day.

2. Worship services, including Bible readings, may not be practiced in public school.

3. Public schools may not intrude on a family's religious beliefs.

4. Teachers and administrators in public schools may not advocate religious beliefs.

5. Extracurricular religious groups may meet on public school grounds as long as they are not led by a teacher or school official.

6. Many states require that schools include the Pledge of Allegiance in their daily schedules, but the practice remains the subject of court challenges. Individual students may not be forced to salute the flag if this conflicts with their religious beliefs.

WRITING and REFLECTION

Prayer at a Football Game

The case of *Santa Fe Independent School District v. Doe* (2000) concerned a group of students at a Texas high school who offered a prayer over the public address system before a football game. The U.S. Supreme Court ruled that this practice constituted a violation of the Establishment Clause and should not be permitted.

• What is the Establishment Clause? (*Hint:* Look back at the wording of the First Amendment.)

• What do you suppose was the basic reasoning behind the Court's ruling? Think about whether the people who heard the prayer had full choice about whether to participate. Also consider the extent to which football games are sponsored and supported by schools.

THE RIGHTS AND RESPONSIBILITIES OF TEACHERS

Like students' rights, teachers' rights are protected by the U.S. Constitution. As agents of the government, public school teachers are protected by state constitutional provisions, statutes, and regulations as well. They are also held accountable to these regulations and may be dismissed if they are not meeting their obligations. This section gives a brief overview of the legal rights and responsibilities attached to the teaching profession.

Teachers' Rights

Although private school teachers do not enjoy as much protection as public school teachers, both are protected by the Civil Rights Act of 1964, which prohibits racial, sexual, or religious discrimination in employment. Teachers'

due process   A formal process, such as a legal or administrative proceeding, that follows established rules designed to protect the rights of the people involved.

tenure   A status granted to a teacher, usually after a probationary period, that protects him or her from dismissal except for reasons of incompetence, gross misconduct, or other conditions stipulated by the state.

employment rights are further protected by the due process clause of the Fourteenth Amendment to the U.S. Constitution, which provides that no state may "deprive any person of life, liberty, or property, without due process of law." This **due process** requirement means that school boards and state agencies must follow established rules when deciding to dismiss or discipline a teacher.

In most states, teachers are also protected by **tenure** statutes. These statutes define a probationary period during which a teacher's performance is evaluated. If the performance is deemed acceptable, a teacher may receive tenure, and then his or her contract is automatically renewed each year unless there is a specified cause for dismissal.

Legitimate causes for dismissal vary from state to state. In Illinois, as one example, a teacher's certificate may be revoked or suspended for immorality, a health condition detrimental to students, incompetence, unprofessional conduct, neglect of duty, willful failure to report child abuse, or "other just cause" (Illinois School Code, section 21-23a).

Teachers have a number of other rights, such as freedom of expression and the right to personal privacy, as outlined in the sidebar "Teachers' Rights: A Brief Summary." All of these are limited, however, by the teacher's responsibility to students. In his book *A Different Kind of Discipline,* Tony Humphreys (1998) talks about the ways teachers must be aware and respectful of students' rights and their own rights. He offers the following list of rights that a teacher should expect and be prepared to uphold when necessary:

▶ *I have the right to physical, emotional, social, intellectual, creative and sexual safety.*

▶ *I have the right to respect from students, colleagues, leaders and parents.*

▶ *I have the right to teach in an atmosphere of order and attention.*

▶ *I have the right to demand social structures within the school that guarantee respect for my rights.*

▶ *I have the right to ask for help when needed.*

▶ *I have the right to fair, just and effective leadership on the part of the school principal and vice-principal.*

Teachers' Rights: A Brief Summary

Teachers are generally thought to possess all of the following rights. The precise extent of these rights has been the subject of numerous court cases.

Freedom from Discrimination

The Civil Rights Act of 1964 prohibits racial, sexual, or religious discrimination in employment.

Academic Freedom

By tradition, a teacher is reasonably free to teach according to his or her best understanding of subject matter and instructional methods. But the content taught by the teacher must be relevant to and consistent with the teacher's responsibilities; a teacher

cannot promote personal or political agendas in the classroom.

Freedom of Expression

Protected by the First Amendment, teachers can express their personal opinions. However, they must not use this freedom to undermine authority and adversely affect the working relationships in a school.

Privacy Rights

Teachers enjoy limited rights to personal privacy. A teacher's personal life may lead to disciplinary action only if it affects the integrity of the school or district and hampers the teacher's effectiveness.

▶ *I have the right to express any need or grievance I may have.*

▶ *When any of my rights are violated, I have the right to have recourse to social structures within and outside the school that protect those rights.*

Teachers' Legal Responsibilities

Teachers have many ethical and professional responsibilities to their students, the parents, the school, and the district. They also have certain legal responsibilities, established by state law or by court cases.

For example, teachers must take reasonable precautions to keep their students safe. If such precautions are neglected, the teacher or the school may be held legally responsible. Teachers and schools have been sued when students were injured in the classroom, on the playground, or on field trips.

One very important legal requirement is that teachers report child abuse and negligence when they believe they have noticed it in their classrooms. Child abuse is a state crime, and each state has specific reporting guidelines. Consider North Carolina's statute:

> *Any person or institution who has cause to suspect that any juvenile is abused, neglected, . . . or has died as a result of maltreatment, shall report the case of that juvenile to the director of the department of social services in the county where the juvenile resides or is found. The report may be made orally, by telephone, or in writing. The report shall include . . . the name and address of the juvenile . . . ; the nature and extent of any injury or condition resulting from abuse [or] neglect . . . ; and any other information which the reporter believes might be helpful in establishing the need for protective services or court intervention. (quoted in Smith & Lambie, 2005).*

In some states, teacher candidates must complete child abuse seminars in which they learn the symptoms of child abuse, sexual abuse, emotional abuse, and neglect. In many school systems across the country, there are support

VIDEO CASE

Teachers Discuss Their Ethical and Legal Responsibilities

Find the HM Video Case, "Legal and Ethical Dimensions of Teaching: Reflections from Today's Educators," on the student website. After watching the video and considering the discussion about rules and rights, respond to the following questions:

- In the video, one administrator says, "If you don't know, ask. If you're not sure, don't." What does this mean?
- What did you think of the teacher who reported "disturbing things" she heard during after-school conversations among students? Would you have done the same thing? Why? Why not?
- How does a classroom teacher function as an agent of the government?
- In what ways are the "rules of the classroom" meant to support students' First Amendment rights?

services to help teachers by providing inservice classes on child, sexual, and emotional abuse and neglect.

Many districts also have specific procedures for reporting bullying and sexual harassment among students. Teachers cannot sweep these incidents "under the rug"; they must report them in a timely fashion. In Chapter 9, we return to this subject because it is a crucial part of building classroom community.

CONCLUDING THOUGHTS

From inclusion to gifted education, and from problem-based learning to test preparation, public schools in America struggle to find the best way to educate all of their students. *Complex, diverse,* and *challenging* are good adjectives to describe our students and the world in which we seek to educate them. Pursuing a career in education requires that you consider all these factors, but it also holds the promise of making a difference for the most vulnerable of our citizens—our children.

There is a strong possibility that the school or district in which you teach will have inclusion classrooms, as nearly 10 percent of all students in public schools (more, by some estimates) have a disability. You will be exposed to approaches like project- and problem-based learning that can make your students' school experience truly challenging and rewarding. At the same time, you will need to deal with the standards-based accountability movement, which is now a dominant trend in American education. You will also be asked to protect the rights of your students as you seek to contribute to a climate of safety and equity.

You may be drawn to the charter school movement, which seeks alternative ways to educate students who are often ignored by traditional schools. You may be part of an anti-bullying task force in your school. Wherever contemporary trends lead, there will be new ones to catch up to, especially as the technology revolution continues to challenge the way we think about teaching and learning.

There are contradictions here—forces pulling you in different directions. Being a teacher means finding your own way of reconciling these various demands. The following Chapter Challenge gives you another opportunity to think about some of these issues.

In the next chapter, we'll explore information technology, a trend so important that it needs a chapter of its own. It, too, brings both demands and significant benefits for both you and your students.

JOIN THE DISCUSSION

Visit the student website for this text and locate the Edublog for Chapter 6. To continue our discussion, respond to the following questions:

➡ Do you think you would like to teach in an inclusion classroom, either as the general education teacher or the inclusion specialist? Why or why not?

➡ The charter school movement and the home school movement are both gaining students. Why do you think that is so? What might be done to stem the exodus from conventional public education?

CHAPTER CHALLENGE

The Achievement Gap

Examine the work of sociologists and psychologists who have studied the effects of social class, family structure, and race on the achievement gap between poor children and wealthier children. Identify three causes for the differences in achievement results and suggest research-supported remedies that can help close the achievement gap. See the Resources for Further Exploration section for sources that will help you get started.

Charter Schools

As an alternative challenge, explore the charter school movement and describe the ways in which it holds promise for remedying the achievement gap. Specifically, investigate one of the following charter schools and describe the qualifications required to teach there.

The KIPP TRUTH Academy in Dallas, Texas: http://www.kipptruth.org/

The CHIME charter schools in Los Angeles County, California:
http://www.chimeinstitute.org/

Compass Montessori Charter School in Jefferson County, Colorado:
http://www.compassmontessori.org/

The Charter School of Wilmington in Delaware: http://www.charterschool.org/

- What unique instructional strategies are found in the charter school you explored?

- In what ways are these schools designing their goals for curriculum and instruction by taking into account the nature of their specific student bodies?

FROM THE COLLEGE CLASSROOM TO YOUR OWN CLASSROOM

The Trends You Find Appealing

There is so much to think about as you continue your professional portfolio! Write about the current educational trends you find most appealing as a future teacher. Explore the ways you can see yourself involved in this type of change.

RESOURCES FOR FURTHER EXPLORATION

Print Resources

Jeanne Brooks-Gunn, Greg J. Duncan, and J. Lawrence Aber (editors), *Neighborhood poverty. Volume 1: Context and consequences for children* (New York: Russell Sage Foundation, 2000).   The researchers assess the combined effects of individual, family, and neighborhood characteristics on the development of children and adolescents.

Gordon Cawelti, "The side effects of NCLB," *Educational Leadership* 64(3), November, 2006, pp. 64–88.   This article discusses the skewed curriculum, discouraged teachers, and manipulation of numbers that have been three unfortunate side effects of NCLB.

Charles C. Haynes, Sam Chaltain, John E. Ferguson Jr., David L. Hudson Jr., and Oliver Thomas, *The First Amendment in schools* (Alexandria, VA: Association for Supervision and Curriculum Development, 2003).   This book is an excellent resource for the comprehensive exploration of court cases and decisions about students', teachers', and administrators' First Amendment rights.

Annette Lareau, *Unequal childhoods: Class, race, and family life* (Berkeley and Los Angeles: University of California Press, 2003).   Through an in-depth study of a variety of families from different social backgrounds, anthropologist Lareau identifies the strategies of middle-class, working-class, and poor families as they interact with their children.

Lori Likis, "How a strong school faced 'failure,'" *Educational Leadership* 64(3), November, 2006, pp. 80–85.   This article describes one of the oldest charter schools in Massachusetts, the Benjamin Banneker Charter School, and its interventions for improving test score results while maintaining teacher and student morale.

Carol Tomlinson, *How to differentiate instruction in mixed-ability classrooms* (Alexandria, VA: Association for Supervision and Curriculum Development, 2001).   This text provides steps to guide teachers in differentiating instruction. It is a rich and user-friendly resource.

Online Resources

All Kinds of Minds http://www.allkindsofminds.org/   This site is designed to help users understand differences in learning. It provides helpful tips and activities to parents and educators on behalf of students with learning differences.

Buck Institute for Education http://www.bie.org/   The nonprofit Buck Institute is dedicated to improving teaching and learning. Its website offers guidelines and other resources for classroom project-based learning.

Council for Learning Disabilities http://www.cldinternational.org/   This site provides explanations of common learning disabilities, an overview of research in this area, and an international perspective on students and learning differences.

First Amendment Center Online http://www.firstamendmentcenter.org/   This site provides a comprehensive view of First Amendment issues and topics. Featuring daily updates, it offers a wealth of data about challenges to our First Amendment rights.

Keep Schools Safe: The School Safety and Security Resource http://www.keepschoolssafe.org/   This site provides resources and suggestions for students, schools, and parents to help prevent school violence.

Learn in Freedom! http://www.learninfreedom.org/   Offers parents links to many resources on homeschooling and provides profiles of famous people who learned without a public school system, including the founders of the United States.

Learning Disabilities Online http://www.ldonline.org   This website answers frequently asked questions and provides information on a wide range of learning disabilities.

National Association for Gifted Children http://www.nagc.org/   This website provides information and resources for parents and educators of gifted children.

National Middle School Association http://www.nmsa.org   This website offers current knowledge, recommended projects, and advice to all who work with youngsters of middle school age.

University of Northern Iowa Inclusion Resources http://www.uni.edu/coe/inclusion/   Designed for teachers, parents, and school staff, this site has good suggestions for inclusive classrooms.

CHAPTER 7

The Information Technology Revolution

FOCUSING QUESTIONS

▶ What do you think of when you hear the term *revolution*?

▶ Do you remember a time when you did not use a computer?

▶ Did you have access to the Internet in your high school, middle school, or elementary school classes? How was it used for learning?

▶ Have you ever done a WebQuest?

▶ Are you a blogger? Do you think blogging could be useful in the world of schools?

▶ How does the use of computer technology promote experiences that can help students learn?

▶ If all the information we could ever want to know about a topic is a few mouse clicks away, then what is the role of the teacher?

The following definitions for the word *revolution* emerge from a quick search on the Internet:

▶ A drastic and far-reaching change in ways of thinking and behaving.

▶ The overthrow of a government by those who are governed.

▶ Rotation: a single complete turn (axial or orbital) (from Word-Net, at http://wordnet. princeton.edu/).

It is the first definition, of course, that characterizes the role of computer technology, connectivity, and access to the Internet in the past generation. The information technology revolution has brought about a drastic and far-reaching change in our ways of thinking and behaving, leading us into a period that some are calling the Digital Renaissance (Jukes, 2006). As you might have noticed, I sought the definition of *revolution* on the Internet instead of in a traditional dictionary. When was the last time you went to a printed dictionary? Even your access to the Web-based videos cited in this textbook is testimony to ways in which the world has altered.

One big question for you as a future teacher—for all of us in education—is this: while all aspects of daily life have changed so dramatically, why have the design and conditions of classroom learning and teaching remained somewhat unchanged? I say "somewhat" because we do now find networked computers in many public and private school classrooms, and some teachers do seize the opportunity to engage their students in new learning experiences. By and large, however, teaching has lagged far behind the advances in technology.

This chapter addresses more than the integration of new software tools into teaching and learning. It addresses the ways information, knowledge, communication, and understanding can be redefined in this Digital Renaissance. It also underscores the fact that the same inequities that have dogged American education since its earliest days persist in the digital age.

WHAT DOES TECHNOLOGY MEAN FOR THE CLASSROOM?

digital natives People who have grown up using the digital "language" of computers, video, games, and the Internet.

Most likely, your future students will spend a good deal of time online. In fact, they will be **digital natives**, a term that commentators like Marc Prensky (2001) coined to refer to people who have used digital technology all their lives. One educator explains the situation this way:

Adults used to be able to ignore, resist, or fool ourselves about the realities going on in children's lives. Once they reached our classrooms, we paid attention to their engagement with our subject matter and their classmates—the world could and did, for the most part, stay out of school. But now, these digital natives . . . cannot keep their digital selves out of the classroom. . . . The one thing we cannot do is ignore the fact that many kids are playing around creatively, finding friends, watching videos, listening to music, communicating online whether we like it or not, whether we talk about it in school or not. (Ganley, 2006)

In this context, technology is no longer just an interesting option for teachers. It is an integral part of their students' lives, and more and more, it is part of the work teachers do as educators in the twenty-first century.

The Flat Classroom

Despite the fact that many of today's students are digital natives, the structure of most classrooms remains unchanged. A shift has gradually begun, however, in the way we think about teaching and learning. To borrow an idea from Thomas Friedman's bestseller *The World Is Flat* (2006), this shift involves seeing the classroom as "flat."

flat classroom A classroom in which students, like the teacher, have ready access to information, so that the teacher is not the lone expert.

The term **flat classroom** refers to the ways information access levels the playing field—or should I say learning field?—in the classroom. The teacher no longer must be seen as the keeper of the true truth, the source of all that is valuable to know. A typical student, through the Internet and other digital resources, has virtually limitless access to information on any topic.

If learners are accessing the Internet from home, at night, outside of the school buildings, then it stands to reason that those same learners will ultimately influence the direction of learning at school. Immediately we can see that, in a flat classroom, the teacher must be a filter, a guide, the one who directs the learning events and helps students develop their understanding as they gain access to more and more information. Later in this chapter, you will begin to see how this process works.

WRITING and REFLECTION

The Role of Education in the Information Revolution

Citing former Secretary of Education Richard Riley, a book declared in 2004 that "none of the top 10 jobs that will exist in 2010 exist today" (Gunderson, Jones, & Scanland, 2004). The point is that technology is changing so rapidly that many new jobs will appear while many old ones disappear. As teachers, we must prepare students for jobs that do not yet exist—jobs in which they will use technologies that have not been invented in order to solve problems that we don't even know are problems yet (Gunderson, Jones, & Scanland, 2004).

As a future teacher, this has to give you pause. What should the role of education become in this age of the Information Revolution? (*Hint:* Think about skills, abilities, and dispositions.)

The Connected Classroom

Should we be preparing our students for the world as it looked when we were 18, or for the world as it's going to look when they are our age?
— Karl Fisch (2006a)

Do you use the Internet every day? Do you check your e-mail? access a weather site? shop? participate in an online discussion? Because our lives have been transformed by the information technology revolution, it follows that the life of the classroom is transformed as well.

Although schools often resist change, the past twenty years have brought a significant increase in the use of technology in U.S. schools. In the early 1990s, there was one networked computer available for every twenty students. By 2005, U.S. schools as a whole possessed more than one instructional computer with Internet access for every five students in primary and secondary schools (Wells & Lewis, 2006). As we will see later in this chapter, though, there are significant disparities in many urban and rural areas.

Imagine you are in a connected classroom—a room with high-speed Internet access for all the students—and your class is doing research in social studies on the causes of the Civil War. Or perhaps students are exploring a science problem related to global warming. Or they may be checking real-time weather all around the world in preparation for a report on climate trends. In a connected classroom, the ease with which students can access a wide variety of information—and the "seamlessness" with which this information gathering can be integrated into the rest of their work—makes it possible for you to be truly creative as a teacher.

The Problem of Information Overload

Do you ever experience problems with the wealth of information available via the Internet? Is there simply too much of it out there?

"It's estimated that a week's worth of the *New York Times*," Richard Wurman wrote in 2000, "contains more information than a person was likely to come

What Internet Resources Do Schools Have?

In a 2005 survey conducted by the National Center for Education Statistics (Wells & Lewis, 2006), schools reported the extent and type of their Internet connections. At that time:

- 97 percent of public schools with Internet access had broadband (high-speed) connections.
- 45 percent of public schools with Internet access had wireless connections, and 15 percent of all individual public school classrooms had wireless Internet connections.

In addition:

- 83 percent of public schools with Internet access reported that their school or school district had recently offered teachers professional development guidance for integrating Internet use into the curriculum.
- 89 percent of public schools used the Internet to provide data to inform instructional planning.
- Secondary schools were more likely than primary schools to use the Internet for professional development through online courses.
- Compared with teachers who had twenty or more years of experience, newer teachers were more likely to report that they used computers or the Internet "a lot" to create instructional materials.

Laptops have become commonplace in classrooms in many schools. With Internet access, computers are a resource for research and a vehicle for expression.

across in a lifetime in the 18th century" (Wurman, 2000). That statement seems almost quaintly dated. Today, a week's worth of the *New York Times* is available instantly online, plus the contents of hundreds of other newspapers—and these all together are only a smidgen of what the Internet holds. You can probably access more raw information in a day than an eighteenth-century scholar could in a lifetime.

Information used to be scarce, and having more of it was considered a good thing. Now, for many of us, it feels as though we are at a saturation point, with more knowledge than we will ever need. One of the disadvantages of this information overload is that it is easy for some students to get overwhelmed. Many teachers who use the Internet for project- and problem-based learning caution that students need to be taught how to use inquiry-based methods powered by technology.

The following story gives one example of the benefits of a connected classroom; you can also see how the teacher avoids the problem of overloading her students with too much irrelevant information.

TEACHING STORIES
A THIRD-GRADE CLASS DOES RESEARCH ON CHINA

Ms. Frank's inner-city, third-grade class is studying China—a fact evident from the Chinese lanterns hanging along clotheslines overhead. In the current portion of the unit, the students are being challenged to design and construct a model of a Chinese hanging scroll. They must meet certain specifications; for instance, each scroll must provide three pieces of information about the inventions and customs of China. Today the students are beginning the research process for completing this design challenge, and Ms. Frank is discussing how to do research on the Internet.

The students sit at rapt attention and are visibly excited about beginning the project. They listen carefully to the directions for accessing three specific websites they will need to do their research. Ms. Frank has chosen these sites in advance because they provide easy access to the information the students need, they are at the right reading level for her class, and they do not include anything inappropriate or overly distracting.

Ms. Frank announces that students will work in groups of four, and she assigns group names based on the work students have already done on this unit. The groups are called Great Wall, Yeh-Shen, Chinese New Year, Red Envelope, Chinese Lantern, and Dragon. The students nod and smile in recognition of the group names.

From a cabinet in the classroom, the students get their laptop computers, each of which is wirelessly connected to the Internet. There is one laptop for every two students. The groups work well together, carefully accessing the websites Ms. Frank has instructed them to go to. It is clear that they have done this kind of work before; using these laptops for research on the Internet is second nature to them. As they gather data, you can hear comments like "The Chinese invented the compass!" and "Scroll down." Students read aloud statements about the invention of paper money and kites. In each group, the students jointly decide on the information to select from the websites, and they record their data in design portfolios.

Within a few minutes, they have collected plenty of information, and they move on to the next step in designing a hanging scroll.

THE TEACHING IDEAS BEHIND THIS STORY

When a class is researching a topic on the Web, the teacher should filter the websites in advance, as Ms. Frank did, so that students do not waste their time on unproductive sources. In that way, teachers help students manage the information available and avoid problems of information overload.

As you prepare units for your students, look for websites with useful links for many different topics or themes. That will make it easier for you to identify good resources for particular units. The sidebar "Guidelines for Internet Research" offers some additional hints for maximizing the Web's potential as an information source for your students.

Guidelines for Internet Research

- Research is not simply a list of questions for which students find answers. Students' research should focus on finding the information they need to solve a problem or complete a project.

- As they use technology, students need to stay focused on the problem they are trying to solve or the area they are exploring.

- Guide students in interpreting and using the data they find.

- Guide students in finding creative and innovative ways to present their information.

- Encourage students to use the information they gather on the Internet to further other students' understanding of the topic.

- Invite students to collaborate with other students in designing a final product.

VIDEO CASE

Teaching with Technology

Find the HM video case "Expanding the Definition of Literacy: Meaningful Ways to Use Technology" on the student website. This video provides glimpses of classrooms in which teachers at varying grade levels are using technology to enhance the literacy skills of their students.

- What methods do these teachers use to keep their students "on track" during their Internet research?

- What is Ms. Sweeney, the high school history teacher, hoping her students will gain through the use of technology? What are some of the skills she hopes students will acquire?

- In what ways does the approach of the elementary school teacher, Ms. Cebula, differ from that of Ms. Sweeney?

- How does the middle school language arts teacher, Ms. Brion-Meisels, express her pedagogy through the use of technology?

- How does the integration of technology foster critical thinking skills?

TECHNOLOGY AND LEARNING

In Chapter 4, we saw that learning requires active engagement of the learner with the material to be learned. Many educators believe that technology encourages this process. In fact, in a national survey, more than half of the participating teachers said that technology helped them engage their students in learning, and 75 percent believed that technology use in schoolwork had increased students' achievement (Project Tomorrow, 2007).

But how exactly does technology help get students involved in learning? Entire books have been written on this subject, but here is one key point: because new technologies are *interactive,* it is easier to create environments in which students can learn by doing, receive feedback, and continually refine their understanding (National Research Council, 2000). Through this process, students take charge of their own learning. By integrating technology into the classroom, you promote students' passionate involvement in their own learning, allowing them to be adaptable and flexible and to go beyond "education as usual" (Fisch, 2006b).

Three Ways Technology Supports Learning

The interactivity of computer-based technologies takes many forms, but from my perspective, there are three paramount ways it supports learning: by allowing students to deal with real-world problems as part of the curriculum; by expanding the possibilities for simulations and modeling; and by creating local and global communities of learners.

Real-World Problems

Technology fosters the use of real-world, exciting problems in the classroom curriculum. Imagine you are working with middle school students on a unit

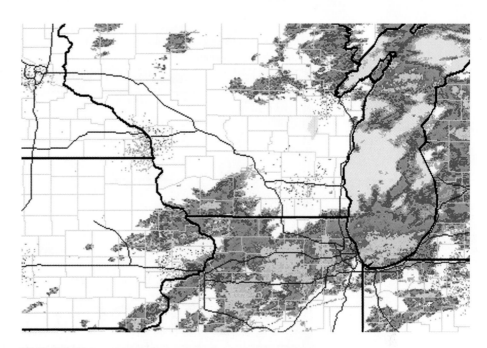

FIGURE 7.1
An Interactive Weather Map
Online, interactive maps allow students to study weather developments in
real time. This one from the National Weather Service shows a rainstorm in
the Midwest.

about weather and global warming. Using the Internet, students can find real-
time weather data about present conditions as well as archival data showing
trends over time (see Figure 7.1). They can focus on a given part of the world or
compare different areas. (See the Resources for Further Exploration section for
sample websites that offer weather data.)

Now imagine that a high school social studies class is exploring world population, comparing the number of births per day in China, India, and the
United States. From the Internet, students gather the most current information
related to population growth in these countries—data that have far-reaching
implications for consumption of natural resources. This kind of real-world context makes the unit come alive for students. Yet the data retrieval requires only
about as much time as it takes to read this paragraph!

Simulations and Modeling

simulation A computer
program or other procedure
that imitates a real-world
experience.

Students can learn a great deal through simulations. Often these imitate real-
world activities that would be impossible to bring into the classroom. Say you
want your students to understand the movements of planets in the solar system. Obviously you can't bring Mars and Venus to class, but you can use simulation software that shows the planets in motion and allows students to view
the system from different positions. As another example, if you are teaching
biology, your school system may not want to use dead animals, like frogs, for
dissections, but you can turn to computer simulations of a frog dissection. In
Net Frog (http://frog.edschool.virginia.edu/), one of the most famous such
tools, students can perform a simulated dissection online.

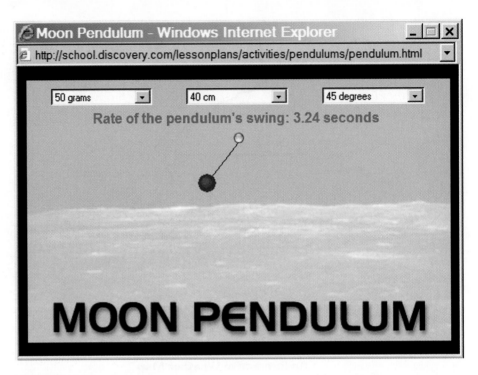

FIGURE 7.2
A Pendulum Simulation

In this online simulation, students can adjust the pendulum's weight and length and the maximum angle of its swing.

Source: Pendulums on the Moon, Discovery School Lesson Plans Library, http://school.discovery.com/lessonplans/activities/pendulums/.

Figure 7.2 shows an online simulation of a pendulum that allows students to experiment with the way different factors influence the pendulum's speed. A similar experiment using a real pendulum would be difficult to set up in the classroom, and students' measurements of the speed would be tedious and inexact. With the simulation, they can change the weight, length, and maximum angle of the pendulum and instantly see the effect on the speed.

model   A representation of a system or an object, such as a small physical structure that imitates a larger structure or a computer program that parallels the workings of a larger system.

Similarly, students often learn by creating models. For years, science students have created models of atoms and molecules, usually static ones made of plastic or Styrofoam pieces. With a computer, students can create atomic models in which the electrons move in cloud-like orbitals, and the software provides feedback about the correct number of protons and neutrons.

Do you suppose that simulations and models are useful mainly in the physical sciences? That's far from true. In social science, for example, simulations can model social dilemmas and engage students in finding their own creative solutions (see Figure 7.3). One software tool, Clover, was developed to provide middle school students with a way to look at important issues such as social justice, honesty, and conflict resolution. With Clover, students construct their own animated story and share it with their peers (Tettegah, 2006).

FIGURE 7.3
Simulating the Writing of the U.S. Constitution

This screenshot is from *The Constitution,* part of the *Decisions, Decisions* software series from Tom Snyder Productions. In this simulation, students prepare a constitution for a fictional republic that mimics the United States in the 1780s.
Source: http://www.tomsnyder.com/products/product.asp?SKU=DECCON.

Besides giving immediate feedback to users, many simulation and modeling technologies also provide opportunities for later reflection and discussion—and this point leads us to the third key benefit of technology.

Communities of Learners

Many classes have their own webpage, a site where teachers communicate with students and create an online extension of the classroom. The shared class webspace has many uses; announcements and schedules can be posted, and areas for more informal communication can be created.

On any given topic, teachers can promote focused discussions online through the use of discussion boards or forums. You may already have participated in such reflective discussions using Blackboard courseware or a similar tool in your college classes. Later in this chapter, we'll discuss the rising use of weblogs, or blogs, in educational settings. Such technology-supported conversations can help students refine their thinking, and they help build a sense that everyone is working together in a learning community.

In fact, technology can easily extend the learning community beyond the immediate classroom. In Chapter 8, we examine the rise of global networks in which students from around the world collaborate to solve problems and share their cultures. Using technology, students from different places can work on the same projects with multiple solutions and collaborate with each other via shared classroom websites and e-mail. A deep sense of community is created as the groups work toward shared goals and communicate with one another about the strategies needed to solve a mutual problem.

VIDEO CASE

Integrating Technology to Teach Literacy in the Middle School

Find the HM video case "Middle School Reading Instruction: Integrating Technology" on the student website. In the classroom shown in the video, Mr. Lawrence is exploring a Greek myth with his inner-city students. After watching the video, think about these questions:

- Mr. Lawrence talks about creating a community in the classroom. How do you think he does that through his interactions with the students?

- How does the students' use of technology—an online discussion forum where they post their thoughts about the question of the day—help create community?

- How does the online discussion forum foster literacy skills?

Using WebQuests

WebQuest A learning activity in which students investigate a question or solve a problem with information they gather from websites.

WebQuests provide an excellent example of active learning fostered by technology. A **WebQuest** is an inquiry-oriented activity in which most or all of the information used by learners is drawn from the Web. WebQuests are designed to help learners focus on using information rather than merely on looking for it. WebQuests also support learners as they analyze, synthesize, and evaluate the information.

A WebQuest activity poses a real-life problem and provides the learner with an array of websites that can be accessed to solve the problem. Students work on WebQuests as teams, usually dividing up the necessary tasks among the members.

Typically, students begin at the WebQuest's own home page, from which they can access elements such as the following:

- An Introduction that sets the context of the problem.

- A Task section that describes the challenge or the problem to be solved.

- A Process section that describes how groups of students can approach the task and divide the labor.

- A Resources section that provides links to appropriate websites to consult.

- An Evaluation section that usually contains a rubric or set of criteria by which the solution will be assessed.

- A Conclusion section that summarizes the adventure and helps students reflect on the results.

See the sidebar for a description of the multidisciplinary WebQuest called "Chocolate."

Chocolate: A Multidisciplinary WebQuest

For this WebQuest, designed for grades six through eight, students work in teams to research the history of chocolate. In the course of their quest, the students:

- Create a timeline showing the history of chocolate.
- Explore the life cycle of the cocoa plant by creating a flowchart.
- Discover how companies mass-produce chocolate by reporting on one major company.
- Think about starting their own chocolate business by brainstorming a "mindmap" of ideas.
- Learn to budget by making a spreadsheet.
- Create a business card for themselves.

An online trivia puzzle and assessment rubrics are also included.

The problem is introduced in the following scenario:

Prepare yourself for a mind-expanding and mouth-watering chocolate experience!

Here is something I bet you don't know . . .

Our class's favorite visitor, Uncle Tim (business-shrewd, multizillionaire), has a very good memory. Think about our weekly class-brainstorm sessions. Do you remember talking about ways you could make money while in school and deciding to start a chocolate business? Uncle Tim remembers. And Uncle Tim is very impressed by your ingenuity. In fact, Uncle Tim is so delighted that you chose the chocolate business (yep, Uncle Tim loves chocolate!) that he will finance this business venture for the first six months.

Uncle Tim would like you to work in teams of four, each team experimenting with a different chocolate product. He will give each team $1,000 to buy supplies. He has even arranged for each team to use one of his fully equipped hotel suites—complete with kitchen, computers, adult supervision, the works. Your parents and your school also support you in this venture. Of course, Uncle Tim expects you to keep up with your other school assignments while you turn into chocolate entrepreneurs. Wow! Can it get any better than this?

Well, there is a slight catch . . .

Even though the $1,000 is an outright gift, before Uncle Tim hands over a penny, he wants you to become very knowledgeable about your product—chocolate. He requires that each team create a presentation—in portfolio or digital format—as evidence of your chocolate smarts. This presentation will consist of four tasks, or "processes," which are labeled on the navigation menu. Finally, each of

you must complete the chocolate trivia puzzle. Completing this WebQuest will be an exciting way to meet Uncle Tim's requirements. You will be surprised by what you learn and by how much more you will want to know!

In addition to Uncle Tim's requirements, each of you must create a list of chocolate trivia questions and answers. You will use these trivia questions next term to create a Microsoft PowerPoint Chocolate Jeopardy game.

As you can see, this WebQuest activity incorporates concepts from art, business, English, math, science, social studies, and technology. Figure 7.4 shows just one of the many sites that students explore for information. You can explore this WebQuest further at http://www.btcs.org/tutorials/WebQuests/chocolate/.

Source: Sara Mazeroff, Chocolate: A Multidisciplinary WebQuest, http://www.btcs.org/tutorials/WebQuests/chocolate/.

The Sweet Lure of
CHOCOLATE   Page Eight

"FEEL GOOD" FOOD
One of the most pleasant effects of eating chocolate is the "good feeling" that many people experience after indulging. Chocolate contains more than 300 known chemicals. Scientists have been working on isolating specific chemicals and chemical combinations which may explain some of the pleasurable effects of consuming chocolate.

Caffeine is the most well known of these chemical ingredients, and while it's present in chocolate, it can only be found in small quantities. Theobromine, a weak stimulant, is also present, in slightly higher amounts. The combination of these two chemicals (and possibly others) may provide the "lift" that chocolate eaters experience.

Phenylethylamine is also found in chocolate. It's related to amphetamines, which are strong stimulants. All of these stimulants increase the activity of neurotransmitters (brain chemicals) in parts of the brain that control our ability to pay attention and stay alert.

REALAUDIO
Researcher Daniele Piomelli explains why his group decided to study chocolate.

FIGURE 7.4

A Research Site from the "Chocolate" WebQuest

This is part of a webpage from the Exploratorium Magazine Online, one of the many sources students reach through links in the "Chocolate" WebQuest.

Source: http://www.exploratorium.edu/exploring/ exploring_chocolate/choc_8.html.

VIDEO CASE

Active Learning in High School Social Studies

Find the HM video case "Integrating Internet Research: High School Social Studies" on the student website. As you watch this class explore the civil rights movement, think about the following questions:

- How does the technology allow students to take ownership of their own learning in this classroom?

- Why does the teacher believe it is useful for students to learn about the civil rights movement by using Internet resources?

- How would you describe the role of the teacher in this social studies unit? Is the teacher imparting information or acting as a guide and facilitator?

- In this unit, what is the role of primary sources on the Internet?

- How does the teacher deal with the disparity between her own level of computer knowledge and that of the students?

The Current Wave: Web 2.0

Web 2.0 is a term that loosely refers to a second generation of Internet services that are leading us toward even more open communication. One feature of Web 2.0 that you have probably already experienced is the rise of social networking sites, such as MySpace (http://www.myspace.com/) and Facebook (http://www.facebook.com/). According to high-tech commentator Dion Hinchcliffe (2006), some of the key aspects of Web 2.0 are:

▶ Data and software are continuously and seamlessly updated, often very rapidly.

▶ User interfaces are rich and interactive.

▶ There is an "architecture of participation" that encourages user contributions.

To put it simply, a fundamental characteristic of Web 2.0 is this: a user can readily input information that then becomes an important source of content for other users. Blogs and wikis are two excellent examples of this trend.

Blogs

Blogging . . . is about reading what is of interest to you: your culture, your community, your ideas.
— Stephen Downes (2004)

blog (short for weblog) An online journal using software that makes it easy for the user to create frequent entries; typically, visitors can add their own comments and responses.

Most likely you're aware of the rapid proliferation of **blogs**, online journals on which a writer posts frequent observations and others respond with their own comments. It seems that everyone, from music fans to politicians, now has a blog. Blogs are becoming increasingly popular with teachers, too, because they offer a forum for expression for students as young as the second grade.

Blogging is not the same as using an online discussion board or discussion forum. Blogs are about "centered communication"—centered on the individual (Ganley, 2006). Blogs require a personal presence, unlike online discussion boards, which can be relatively impersonal as students respond to the questions posed by the teacher. While discussion boards are very directed and require specific, focused postings, blogging is open-ended, allowing users to add content through links called tags. Blogging also invites comments from online users outside of the immediate classroom community.

Blogs can be used for almost any subject. Students write about how they attacked a tough math problem, post observations about their science experiments, or display their latest art projects (Selingo, 2004). For teachers, blogs are attractive because they require little effort to maintain, unlike more elaborate classroom websites. Helped by templates found at a number of online sites (see the Resources for Further Exploration section at the end of this chapter), teachers can build a blog or start a new topic in an existing blog simply by typing text into a box and clicking a button.

Educational blogging, guided and monitored by the teacher, invites students to publish their work on the site. A related-comments link allows readers to post comments. Hence educational blogging gives students an opportunity not only to publish their writing but also to receive and respond to comments from their classmates and *the rest of the world!*

Imagine, for example, a fifth-grade class where students are working on writing projects. They publish their writing in online blogs, and teachers link these blogs to other Internet items that relate to the same topic. Students visit each other's blogs and learn more about their classmates, and they also receive comments from a much larger community than their own classroom. Compare this situation to the traditional model in which the audience for students' written work consists only of the teacher.

Students learn from comments on their work and from their own reflection on those comments. Downes (2004) tells the story of students who posted a review of a circus and were amazed when a member of the circus read the review and responded. When the students in this class realized that a lot of people might react and become a part of the conversation, they refined their writing.

Overall, blogging can help students:

▶ Reflect on their writing and thinking.

▶ Persist in their writing over time.

▶ Engage readers of the blog in a sustained conversation that leads to further writing and thinking (Downes, 2004).

Why Use Blogs for Education?

Charlie Lowe (2002), a professor of writing, made the following observation about blogs in educational settings. (He was writing in his own blog, of course!)

About a year ago, I asked my first- year composition students whether they did much reading and writing outside of class. Most of them said, "No." But when I asked them if they wrote e-mails, used AOL IM, and surfed the Internet, they almost unanimously said, "Yes."

To them, the Internet and other forms of electronic discourse were not associated with their concept of "reading and writing" in the school sort of way. I imagine that this difference might be because one is "fun" and the other is "work." But regardless, I've come to feel that reading and writing the Web is a way for me to tap into a writing space that students already use—and more importantly, want to use.

Wikis

wiki An online site that allows visitors to add, remove, and otherwise edit or change the available content.

Wikis are another major feature of Web 2.0. A **wiki** is a website or other online resource that fosters collective authoring by allowing many users to add content or edit the existing content. The most famous example is Wikipedia (http://www.wikipedia.org/), the online encyclopedia that bills itself as "the free encyclopedia that anyone can edit." At the time of this writing, Wikipedia offered almost 2 million articles in English, not to mention Dutch, Spanish, French, Italian, Portuguese, Swedish, and other languages. Theoretically, anyone in the world can contribute his or her expertise to the effort. In case you were not sure about the arrival of "information overload," Wikipedia may convince you that it is here!

Implications of Web 2.0

Think about the implications of blogs, wikis, and similar developments. In this new wave of communication via the Internet, the end user of the content or information is also an author of content, along with everyone else who is interested in a given topic. This situation challenges our thinking about information and its reliability and veracity. With Web 2.0 technology, not only "experts" have access to cutting-edge information; there is increasing reliance on communities of "experts" that are redefined to include us all.

This is the flat classroom on a global scale, and it has important implications for the way we teach and learn. Again we are reminded that the most meaningful learning involves inquiry processes, reflection, and active, committed participation by the learner.

WRITING and REFLECTION

Are Schools Out of Touch with Our Lives?

Some educators who reflect on the information technology revolution tell the following story:

> Rip Van Winkle awakens in the 21st century after a hundred-year snooze and is, of course, utterly bewildered by what he sees. Men and women dash about, talking to small metal devices pinned to their ears. Young people sit at home on sofas, moving miniature athletes around on electronic screens. Older folk defy death and disability with metronomes in their chests and with hips made of metal and plastic. Airports, hospitals, shopping malls—every place Rip goes just baffles him. But when he finally walks into a schoolroom, the old man knows exactly where he is. "This is a school," he declares. "We used to have these back in 1906. Only now the blackboards are green." (Wallis & Steptoe, 2006)

The authors go on to say that, compared with other institutions, U.S. public schools seem like "throwbacks."

- What do you think of this story?
- Does it resonate with your experience as a student?
- Do you have ideas about how the classroom of today should reflect the technology of today? What changes do you think are needed?
- Can you imagine starting a weblog with your students in your classroom? What topics might be discussed? How would it contribute to student learning?

STANDARDS FOR THE USE AND UNDERSTANDING OF TECHNOLOGY

A s you have seen throughout this chapter, technology offers exciting ways for teachers to teach and students to learn all kinds of subject matter, from history to physics. But with the increased role that technology plays in our lives, knowledge about technology itself also becomes important. Today's students are expected to develop a strong degree of **technological fluency** during their schooling. Without it, they would find themselves lost in the contemporary workplace.

technological fluency
Proficiency in the use of technology, including an understanding of the way technology systems operate and the ability to use technology to access information from a wide variety of sources.

The International Society for Technology in Education® (ISTE), which has more than 85,000 members, has developed the National Educational Technology Standards (NETS), guidelines describing what students should know and be able to do. Many students develop technological fluency as a consequence of the time they spend on the Internet: blogging with friends, checking out the latest movie, shopping, writing e-mail, as well as researching school topics and participating in discussion forums. Some students, though, may require extra support.

Even if your students have a lot of technological savvy, you need to understand how to capitalize on this know-how and connect with your students through technology-powered education. For this reason, ISTE has created a separate set of NETS for teachers, listed in Table 7.1. What do you think of these standards? Have you achieved them already? Do you have more work to do to qualify as a technologically fluent teacher?

Computer-based projects can include artifacts downloaded from the Web. The potential to expand upon student learning is part of technology integration.

TABLE 7.1 National Educational Technology Standards (NETS) for Teachers

According to the International Society for Technology in Education, all classroom teachers should be prepared to meet the following standards and performance indicators.

Technology Operations and Concepts

Teachers demonstrate a sound understanding of technology operations and concepts. Teachers:

- demonstrate introductory knowledge, skills, and understanding of concepts related to technology.
- demonstrate continual growth in technology knowledge and skills to stay abreast of current and emerging technologies.

Planning and Designing Learning Environments and Experiences

Teachers plan and design effective learning environments and experiences supported by technology. Teachers:

- design developmentally appropriate learning opportunities that apply technology-enhanced instructional strategies to support the diverse needs of learners.
- apply current research on teaching and learning with technology when planning learning environments and experiences.
- identify and locate technology resources and evaluate them for accuracy and suitability.
- plan for the management of technology resources within the context of learning activities.
- plan strategies to manage student learning in a technology-enhanced environment.

Teaching, Learning, and the Curriculum

Teachers implement curriculum plans that include methods and strategies for applying technology to maximize student learning. Teachers:

- facilitate technology-enhanced experiences that address content standards and student technology standards.
- use technology to support learner-centered strategies that address the diverse needs of students.
- apply technology to develop students' higher-order skills and creativity.

- manage student learning activities in a technology-enhanced environment.

Assessment and Evaluation

Teachers apply technology to facilitate a variety of effective assessment and evaluation strategies. Teachers:

- apply technology in assessing student learning of subject matter using a variety of assessment techniques.
- use technology resources to collect and analyze data, interpret results, and communicate findings to improve instructional practice and maximize student learning.
- apply multiple methods of evaluation to determine students' appropriate use of technology resources for learning, communication, and productivity.

Productivity and Professional Practice

Teachers use technology to enhance their productivity and professional practice. Teachers:

- use technology resources to engage in ongoing professional development and lifelong learning.
- continually evaluate and reflect on professional practice to make informed decisions regarding the use of technology in support of student learning.
- apply technology to increase productivity.
- use technology to communicate and collaborate with peers, parents, and the larger community in order to nurture student learning.

Social, Ethical, Legal, and Human Issues

Teachers understand the social, ethical, legal, and human issues surrounding the use of technology in preK–12 schools and apply those principles in practice. Teachers:

- model and teach legal and ethical practice related to technology use.
- apply technology resources to enable and empower learners with diverse backgrounds, characteristics, and abilities.
- identify and use technology resources that affirm diversity.
- promote safe and healthy use of technology resources.
- facilitate equitable access to technology resources for all students.

Source: International Society for Technology in Education. (2002). *National Educational Technology Standards for Teachers: Preparing Teachers to Use Technology.* Washington, DC: Author.

INTERNET SAFETY

So far in this chapter, we have talked about the many advantages that students can reap from ready access to the Internet and ease of connectivity. But teachers must also consider students' safety in online communication.

Experts agree on several areas of concern (National School Boards Foundation, 2007):

1. Young people may accidentally stumble onto websites that are violent, pornographic, or objectionable due to inappropriate language and content.

2. "Cyberstalking" and threats from online predators pose threats to children and teenagers' safety. Drawn to social networking, students may reveal personal identifying information to predators without realizing it.

3. Online marketing aimed directly at children and teens influences young peoples' decisions about products and brands. This can undermine parental authority in much the same way that television advertising can. The difference is that Internet advertising is not regulated by the government, and exposure is often more intense.

4. The interactive, two-way nature of the Web gives marketers the ability to collect data about individual computer users. Companies collect personal information about children and teens as their websites encourage youngsters to share their hobbies, interests, and other personal preferences. This invasion of privacy is commonplace on the Internet.

Chapter 9 addresses an additional concern, "cyber-bullying," and its consequences.

All of these are important issues, and school districts have taken steps to address them. Most school districts and libraries have installed blocking and filtering technologies to safeguard against offensive websites. Schools and districts are also implementing "Net safety" workshops and discussions. As a teacher, you need to be aware of the potential problems in students' Internet use and make sure there are sufficient safeguards.

THE DIGITAL DIVIDE

Although all students are expected to develop technological fluency, some struggle if they come from schools and home backgrounds in which technology is not widely accessible. Later in life, they will be at a disadvantage for technology-based tasks, and they may even miss out on educational opportunities that involve technological resources (Kim & Bagaka, 2005, p. 319). In a world that is so information-rich, we have to remember that technology access is not equal.

digital divide   The division between people who are "rich" in technological access and expertise and those who are "poor" in this respect.

According to Wikipedia, the **digital divide** is "the gap between those with regular, effective access to digital technologies and those without." On one side of the divide, people have easy access to technological resources and know how to use them. On the other side, people have substantially less access, less experience, and correspondingly less knowledge. It was the U.S. Department of

Students with Internet access at home have an advantage over those whose families are not able to afford it. This creates a digital divide.

Commerce that first coined the term *digital divide*. The distinction is not only between those who have computer access at home and those who do not. The digital divide also refers to the *quality* of hardware, software, and connectivity that is available to users across social classes.

Who are those with less technological access and experience? Students living in poverty are almost twice as likely as other students to access the Internet from school only (DeBell & Chapman, 2003, Table 3). In addition to this gap between social classes, educators worry about a geographical divide: students in suburban schools spend significantly more time on computers both at home and at school than do rural and urban students.

The ratio of students to instructional computers with Internet access is actually higher in schools with the highest poverty concentration than in schools with the lowest poverty concentration (Parsad & Jones, 2005, p. 7), but this abundance of computers at school does not fully make up for less access at home. Access to computers at home has been found to be an important factor in students' ability to use computer resources for word processing, information processing and presenting, and other types of communication (Kim & Bagaka, 2005). For many students in poor urban areas, public libraries provide a free option for Internet access, and there may be nearby Internet cafés as well. Still, people are more likely to make regular use of an Internet connection at home than anywhere else. And for students in poor rural areas, Internet-enabled public libraries and coffee shops may be only a rumor.

To help underserved populations develop technological fluency, we must find a means of closing this technology gap caused by lack of access at home. The mere existence of computers in a school does not mean they are being used productively. Many educators have pointed out that professional development for teachers is vital in ensuring that computers in schools are used purposefully and with an eye toward improving students' higher-order skills, not just basic skills.

Studies have revealed that when teachers have positive beliefs about technology and their own proficiency in using it, they can better integrate technology tools and practices into their teaching, which results in a narrowing of the digital divide (Kim & Bagaka, 2005). What does this mean for you as a future teacher? You can best serve your students if you make full use of technology; to do that, you need to believe in its potential and in your own comfort and knowledge level. This is a reminder that, as stated earlier in this book, "we teach who we are." The following Writing and Reflection section invites you to think about this idea.

WRITING and REFLECTION

Your Beliefs About Computers in Education

Examining your own computer use and your beliefs about its role in your education is a good way to start formulating a personal approach to integrating technology in your teaching. To reflect on this topic, think about questions like these:

- What would your life be like if you did not have ready access to the Internet?
- What is the most important use you make of the computer and the Internet?
- How much of your time is spent on social networking sites such as MySpace?
- In your view, what are the most important reasons for integrating technology in schools?

Learning How to Learn: The $150.00 Laptop Project

The One Laptop Per Child Project (OLPC)—founded by Nicholas Negroponte, former chairman of the MIT Media Lab, and other faculty members from this lab—is based on the premise that a laptop would be the single most useful learning tool for poor children living in remote places. In addition to providing Internet access, a laptop would enable them to form learning communities. After analyzing what those children most needed from an educational laptop, the group decided to design a new model from scratch, with the goal of making it available for around $150. Investment for the project was secured from companies like News Corporation, Google, and eBay.

The philosophy behind the project maintains that if young people are given computers and allowed to explore, they will "learn how to learn" (Seymour Papert as quoted by Markoff, 2006). The idea is that each laptop will have wireless capacity, a small 7.5-inch screen, and an external manual generator to recharge the battery. As prototypes come off the assembly line, Negroponte seeks to convince governments of third-world countries that the laptops will be a positive force for social development. Satellite links could be used to extend the wireless Internet to rural areas (Markoff, 2006).

The larger issue at stake is whether a networked laptop equipped with a word processing program, a simple Web browser, and a number of learning programs can become an effective learning tool even if a school lacks sufficient technology expertise and students have little prior exposure to technology. This is a real test of the possibilities of technology itself for closing the digital divide. You can explore OLPC further at http://www.laptop.org/.

VIDEO CASE

Computers and Classrooms

Find the HM Video Case "Educational Technology: Issues of Equity and Access" on the student website. This video case explores some of the complexities a school district faces in attempting to provide equitable access to technology for all of its students.

- In this school district, what is the educational technology coordinator's main challenge in providing equity?
- How can new teachers gain the technological knowledge they need?
- What is the advantage of having a computer lab in the school? How do you think that facilitates learning?

ASSISTIVE TECHNOLOGY

assistive technology (AT) A device or service that increases the capabilities of people with disabilities.

A chapter on technology would not be complete without a brief discussion of assistive technology. The term **assistive technology (AT)** refers to devices that promote greater independence for people with disabilities by enabling them to perform tasks that would otherwise be difficult or impossible. AT can take many forms, from simple to complex. For students with visual impairments, for example, a simple type of AT is a keyboard with large symbols that makes it easier for the students to type. A more complex form is speech recognition software that converts the student's spoken words into text on the screen. Similarly, screen reader software can read aloud the information displayed on a computer screen.

In the past, for blind students who read by means of Braille (a writing system that uses raised dots identifiable by touch), curriculum materials were usually converted through a lengthy process that required two to four weeks' lead time. Now, with computer technology, relevant materials can be converted at the time they are needed. With a computer program, text that the teacher types into a word processing document is transformed into Braille and printed on a Braille printer within seconds. This technology makes it possible for the teacher to include blind students in the same activity as the rest of the class, at the same moment.

For disabled students whose fine motor skills do not allow them to write easily and without pain, note taking is an arduous task. Teachers with interactive whiteboards in their classrooms can save the notes written on the board and print them for these students. An **interactive whiteboard**, typically the size of a regular chalkboard, is linked to a computer. Teachers can project images from the computer onto the board. When students or the teacher write on the board with a special marker, the notes can be saved as text in the computer.

interactive whiteboard A whiteboard that works together with a computer to display and save information.

In the following story, students with a wide range of learning disabilities experience a lesson on maps using a SMART Board, one brand of interactive whiteboard.

A Smart Board assists a student with disabilities by providing interactive technology controlled by the student and displayed for the class.

TEACHING STORIES
A SECOND-GRADE LESSON ON MAPS

On the day that I visit their classroom, the ten students in Ms. Mandel's self-contained special education second-grade class are learning about maps. Seated on a carpeted area in front of a SMART Board, they tell me that a map is a bird's-eye view of the earth from above.

Ms. Mandel chats with the children about maps that are found on the subway, on trains, in the mall, and at a major sports complex. She uses the SMART Board to display different types of maps. One map has roads and street names and stores and gas stations and houses. There is a produce map with images relating to fruits and vegetables grown in New York state, where the school is located. Still other maps show weather changes, vacation spots, and geographic features.

The children can manipulate a pointer and direct it to different images on the map. By manipulating the image of a car or a plane, they can take a ride from one destination to another. Taking turns with the pointer, the students respond to questions on cards located in a wall "pocket" next to the SMART Board. Each card has a number corresponding to the map type and a question like "How would you get from Amy's house to Home Depot?" or "What is the name of the town closest to the dairy farm?"

Deeply engaged in this activity, the students do well manipulating objects and moving them to destinations on the SMART Board. They are using the technology very creatively. One student tells me, "We are having a great time."

continued

The questions on the cards involve the class in interpreting symbols, locations, and directions, and I am struck by the way these students with various learning disabilities are making sense of the maps and are developing higher-order thinking skills.

This story highlights ways technology can reduce or eliminate the barriers to learning experienced by students with disabilities. But don't suppose that only "special" technology is suitable for these students. The technology you use with all your other students—the same technology that enhances meaningful learning, reflection, and discussion—also provides benefits for those who are disabled. For instance, a student who struggles to write with pen or pencil may find it much easier to write on a computer.

CONCLUDING THOUGHTS

Living through a social and educational transformation like the information technology revolution is both exciting and challenging. Although we look forward to new ways of teaching our students, many challenges face us as we imagine how the traditional classroom will be transformed to reflect the high-tech world around us.

In the flat classroom, the traditional hierarchy is broken down. Many students can find information as quickly as we can, and that means our role as teachers must change accordingly. We should take full advantage of the ways technology can promote independent learning through real-world projects, simulations, and collaborative investigations. At the same time, we have to guide students in negotiating the overload of information so that they use their time wisely.

We should make sure that students gain the technological fluency they will need in later life. To do so, we need to meet high standards ourselves in our understanding of technology and its uses in education. Further, we need to seek ways to use technology to "level the learning field," so that all of America's students are served equitably by our schools. The Chapter Challenge will help you begin a deeper exploration of the promises and challenges of educational technology.

JOIN THE DISCUSSION

Visit the student website for this text and locate the Edublog for Chapter 7. True to the theme of this chapter, you can add your own thoughts about technology and education.

- Are you a digital native? a digital immigrant (someone who did *not* grow up with technology)?

- In your opinion, what is the greatest promise of technology for teaching and learning?

CHAPTER CHALLENGE

Computers in the Classroom

Arrange an interview in a local school with either the technology specialist or an assistant principal. This can be an elementary, middle, or secondary school. Explain that you are doing a college or university project designed to help you more fully understand the ways schools integrate technology and learning.

Here are some suggested questions for your interview. You may have many more!

- Does the school have computers in every classroom? Does it also have a separate computer lab?
- How many networked computers are there in the average classroom?
- Do the computers access the Internet via a wired or wireless connection?
- Who oversees the maintenance and upgrade of the computers and software?
- Does the school have a philosophy or list of guidelines governing the use of the computers in the classroom?
- In what ways are the networked computers used by teachers in the school to promote learning?
- What do you think the next step is for this school to become a more technologically current environment?
- After the interview, reflect on what you have learned. What uses for computers in this school most impressed you? What are some of the glaring problems associated with technology integration—in this school and elsewhere?

FROM THE COLLEGE CLASSROOM TO YOUR OWN CLASSROOM

Your Thoughts About Using Technology in Teaching

As you continue to develop your teaching portfolio, describe the ways you anticipate integrating your life as a technology user into the work you will do with your students. What are the possibilities?

RESOURCES FOR FURTHER EXPLORATION

AccuWeather http://home.accuweather.com/ National and international weather information, satellite photos, and more.

Clover Authoring Software http://orchid.cs.uiuc.edu/projects/clover/ Clover is an authoring tool—software that helps teachers and students create multimedia vignettes. Designed to help middle school students learn to deal with bullying, it demonstrates some of the potential for using simulations in the social sciences. This site offers a description of the software and a free download.

Blogger http://www.blogger.com/ This website offers easy-to-understand information about blogging and can help you create your own blog in minutes.

Childnet International http://www.childnet-int.org/safety/teachers.aspx This kid-friendly site, designed for children and teens, has important tips for Internet safety.

eMINTS http://www.emints.org/   eMINTS is a professional development site for educators that focuses on technology. The site includes links to WebQuests developed by participating teachers.

International Society for Technology and Education: National Educational Technology Standards http://cnets.iste.org/   This website provides the National Educational Technology Standards for teachers, students, and administrators, combined with a wealth of supporting materials. This will help you understand what it means to learn with technology.

Kathy Schrock's Guide for Educators http://school.discovery.com/schrockguide/   An annotated compilation of websites useful for teachers, divided into subject areas.

Moveable Type Publishing Platform http://www.movabletype.org/   Designed for business but easily applicable to education, this website provides an easy-to-use software platform for blogging.

National Weather Service http://www.nws.noaa.gov/   Here students can collect actual data on climate conditions ranging from snowstorms to air quality.

NetSafeKids http://www.nap.edu/netsafekids/   Sponsored by the National Academies, this site is a valuable resource for adults and children who are seeking ways to stay safe in cyberspace.

Net Frog http://frog.edschool.virginia.edu/   A well-known simulation of frog dissection.

Population Connection: Education and Action for a Better World http://www.populationconnection.org/   A website dedicated to examining the effects of world population growth on the earth's resources.

Will Richardson, *Blogs, wikis, podcasts, and other powerful web tools for classrooms* (Thousand Oaks, CA: Corwin Press, 2006).   This book has cutting-edge ideas and illustrations for transforming the classroom with Web 2.0 tools.

tBlog.com http://www.tblog.com/   A website for those who are interested in creating their own blogs or visiting blogs that address a wide range of topics.

Weather.com http://www.weather.com/   Statistics, maps, photos, and explanations of weather events throughout the country.

Weblogg-ed http://www.weblogg-ed.com/   Will Richardson introduces the reader to educational blogging via this website.

The WebQuest Page http://webquest.sdsu.edu/   Explanations, examples, and training materials from Bernie Dodge, the originator of the WebQuest concept.

Wikipedia http://www.wikipedia.org/   Described as the free encyclopedia that anyone can edit, this website contains entries on events and places that any print encyclopedia would have, but it also includes a related dictionary, thesaurus, and much more.

CHAPTER 8

Globalization and Education

FOCUSING QUESTIONS

▶ Where have you heard the term *globalization*?

▶ What comes to mind when you think of the "knowledge economy"?

▶ How is the globalization of education related to the flat classroom?

▶ What does it mean to suggest that *what* we learn is not as important as *how* we learn?

▶ What are the attributes of a "global student"?

In this chapter, we examine one of the many ways the technology revolution has changed student experiences in the classroom. As a result of "seamless" access to the Internet, students and teachers from all over the world can communicate electronically, sharing their cultures, their school lives, and their larger world. Students can work side by side even if they live thousands of miles apart. Let's explore how this interaction occurs and what it means for our students.

EDUCATION IN THE KNOWLEDGE ECONOMY

knowledge economy   An economic system in which the use and exchange of knowledge plays a dominant role. In this kind of economy, knowledge is both an economic asset and a key product.

We are educating students to become part of an information society in which the creation, distribution, and manipulation of information is a significant economic and cultural activity. The **knowledge economy** is this society's economic counterpart. In the knowledge economy, businesses operate through the collaboration and shared problem solving of people across the globe, transforming information into creative innovations for a technological world.

Think about this: one of the most successful recent innovations has been the design and construction of a wireless multiport based on Universal Serial Bus (USB) technology. This device enables smart drives, digital cameras, personal digital assistants, and cell phones to be connected wirelessly to your laptop computer simultaneously.

What do such products suggest for education? Innovations like the wireless multiport are complex in their technology, and their success depends on many different people from all over the world having access to the technology. Further, people's ability to collaborate ensures that the best design will hit the market. Yet the technological skills and collaboration techniques involved in this kind of product development are not taught in most of today's public schools!

The Flat World

More people [can] collaborate and connect on more stuff than in any other time in the history of the world.
— Thomas Friedman (2006)

globalization   The increase of global connectivity, integration, and interdependence in economic, cultural, social, and technological spheres.

In his best-selling book *The World Is Flat,* Thomas Friedman (2006) uses the metaphor of a flat world to describe the leveling of the playing field on which industrialized and emerging-market countries compete. Friedman recounts many examples of **globalization** in which companies in India and China are becoming part of global supply chains that extend across oceans, providing everything from service representatives and X-ray interpretation to component manufacturing. He also describes how these changes are made possible through intersecting technologies, particularly the Internet.

In a flat world, Friedman explains, the work done by corporations is no longer conducted vertically, that is, in a structure of workers and supervisors with each person at each level having different specific tasks. Rather, much of the work has gone horizontal: corporate analysts examine each step in a process and ask whether the firm is a leader in that step; if not, they determine who in the world can best do that work at the appropriate level of quality and the lowest possible cost. The firm then contracts with providers for each service; the firm itself performs only those functions it does best. This arrangement is known as *outsourcing,* and many functions formerly performed by American workers are now being outsourced to workers in other countries who can do these jobs better, more cheaply, and faster. Remember, one does not have to be in the same geographical location to be a coworker in a company.

Like the flat classroom described in Chapter 7, the flat world creates significant challenges for teaching and learning. We are facing educational decisions that will "ultimately determine not merely whether some of our children get 'left behind' but also whether an entire generation of kids will fail to make the grade in a global economy because they can't think their way through abstract problems, work in teams, distinguish good information from bad or speak a language other than English" (Wallis & Steptoe, 2006). Yet many school classrooms still resemble the ones our grandparents attended—with the teacher front and center and the students listening and writing at their desks. Clearly, our educational system has a lot of adapting to do.

The Global Student

In the flat new world, educational opportunities are limitless, even without help from school, government, churches or business. Much of what you need to know about pretty much everything is out there on the Web somewhere.
— Doc Searls (2005)

One of the first steps in preparing ourselves and our students to function in an information-rich, global knowledge economy is to explore the attributes of people who successfully navigate this new and exciting world. Generally these are people who:

▶ Are curious and have a passion for learning.

▶ Have imagination and creativity.

▶ Have a rich sense of current events and are prepared for change, because change is the new universal constant.

Think for a moment about the way these three qualities interlink. If change has become a constant in our lives, adaptation to change will dictate our intellectual and emotional survival. But how do we prepare ourselves for change? Do we memorize volumes of data? No, because the data we memorize today may be outdated by tomorrow.

In this situation, *learning how to learn* becomes more important than *what* we learn. Thus it is the individual with curiosity, imagination, and a passion for learning who will be most successful in the global knowledge economy. Curious students work hard at learning and eagerly find new opportunities to learn.

Learning How to Learn

The kind of information teachers used to ask students to memorize is now available on the Internet, usually just a few keystrokes away. Consider this memorable anecdote:

Learn the names of the rivers in South America. That was the assignment given to Deborah Stipek's daughter Meredith in school, and her mom, who's dean of the Stanford University School of Education, was not impressed. "That's silly," Stipek told her daughter. "Tell your teacher that if you need to know anything besides the Amazon, you can look it up on Google." (Wallis and Steptoe, 2006)

Working together to accomplish a task can be face-to-face or virtual.

Because simple facts are easy to locate, today's students require what educators refer to as more *depth* of understanding and less *breadth*. In other words, key ideas and topics should dominate the curriculum, not lists of facts that can be found easily enough on the Web.

metacognition The understanding of your own thinking and learning processes.

Educators also talk about the importance of **metacognition**, the understanding of one's own learning processes. Students with metacognitive skills know how to approach a learning task. They have good learning strategies. In other words, they have learned how to learn.

The projects and problems described in Chapter 6 and 7 illustrate some ways of developing metacognitive skills and depth of understanding. As students work in teams, both in their classrooms and online, they risk making mistakes on their journey to finding solutions and consensus. They develop critical thinking, making connections between ideas and events, and they learn how to keep on learning.

VIDEO CASE

Learning How to Learn

Find the HM Video Case "Metacognition: Helping Students Become Strategic Learners" on the student website. This video shows a middle school class trying to make sense of a newspaper article about China. The way the teacher, Ms. Craven, asks students to think about the words they encounter in the newspaper provides a glimpse into metacognition.

To get the full benefit of the video, watch it more than once and then respond to the following questions:

- Ms. Craven requires the students to make personal comments about what they are reading, right on the paper itself. How is this helpful for learning?
- How does writing a comment like "What does this mean?" on the newspaper article represent metacognition?
- What metacognitive strategies, if any, do you employ when reading this textbook?

Skills for the Twenty-first Century

If you are not prepared to be wrong, you will not come up with anything original.

— Sir Ken Robinson (2006)

A recent report by the New Commission on the Skills of the American Workforce (National Center on Education and the Economy, 2006) issues this warning:

This is a world in which a very high level of preparation in reading, writing, speaking, mathematics, science, literature, history and the arts will be an indispensable foundation for everything that comes after for most members of the workforce. It is a world in which comfort with ideas and abstractions is the passport to a good job, in which creativity and innovation are the key to a good life, in which high levels of education—a very different kind of education than most of us have had—are going to be the only security there is. (New Commission on the Skills of the American Workforce, 2006)

The report goes on to offer a blueprint for rethinking American education to prepare students for the global economy. It describes, among other things, what might be called twenty-first century skills important for students as they enter the global marketplace. Let's explore several of these.

Knowing More About the World. Kids are global citizens now. They need to understand the world economy, be able to identify the nations in the developed and developing world, become sensitive to foreign cultures, and learn foreign languages.

Thinking Outside the Box. Students need to think creatively to solve problems, seeing patterns where others may see chaos. As the report confirms, it is interdisciplinary combinations—such as design and technology, mathematics and art, music and science—from which really innovative ideas and products for the global economy emerge. Creativity expert Ken Robinson (2006) believes that "we get educated out of creativity" in school. It is essential, therefore, to foster creative problem solving by providing students with challenging problems and guiding them to find solutions.

Managing New Sources of Information. Students need to develop skills that help them manage the vast amount of information to which they are exposed. For one thing, they must learn to distinguish between reliable and unreliable information. Karen Bruett, who serves on the Partnership for

21st Century Skills, explains that students have to *manage, interpret, validate,* and *act* on the overflowing information and the proliferating media that characterize this century (Wallis & Steptoe, 2006). I like to abbreviate these terms as **MIVA**.

MIVA   Acronym for *manage, interpret, validate,* and *act*—terms describing what students must learn to do with the vast amount of information they access on a daily basis.

Developing Good People Skills. With so much being accomplished online, we can get the mistaken notion that good people-to-people communication is unnecessary in today's marketplace. However, as noted earlier, most recent innovations involve collaboration among teams of people. The ability to work and communicate with others—often people from different cultures—is essential.

The "Essential Cognitive Backpack"

Another way of describing the thinking skills and habits today's students require is provided by Mel Levine, a pediatrician, professor, and founder of an organization called All Kinds of Minds. In an article called "The Essential Cognitive Backpack," Levine (2007) discusses the capacities for interpretation, instrumentation, interaction, and inner direction:

- *Interpretation* refers to students' ability to analyze material, not just memorize facts about it. To interpret information, students not only have to grasp it, but they also need to understand it in many different ways. This requires conversation and discussion, as seen in the Video Case about Ms. Craven's class.

- By *instrumentation,* Levine means students' skills in effectively using their time, managing their responsibilities, and establishing their priorities.

- *Interaction* refers to students' ability to form and sustain productive and fulfilling relationships that enable them to collaborate with others, retain their individuality, and communicate effectively.

- *Inner direction* refers to some of the ideas that have pervaded this text: in particular, the capacity for self-reflection and knowing one's strengths and weaknesses.

Levine's "essential backpack" skills are similar to the MIVA skills described by Karen Bruett's group. All of these skills are increasingly important as the world grows flatter, information is more abundant, and the pace of change is ever more rapid.

WRITING and REFLECTION

Twenty-first-Century Skills

Imagine how differently we live now than did teachers in the first decade of the twentieth century.

- Reflecting on your own education, inside and outside the classroom, describe your exposure to world geography and foreign cultures.

- Describe a time when an interdisciplinary unit prompted you to "think outside the box."
- Describe strategies you have developed for managing, interpreting, validating, and acting on the many pieces of information that come your way on a daily basis.
- In what ways do you take responsibility for your own learning?

LEARNING PROJECT

Globalization: Arguments For and Against

Globalization used to be widely celebrated as a new birth of freedom. The inference was that better connections in a more open world would improve people's lives by making new products and ideas universally available, breaking down barriers to trade and democratic institutions, resolving tensions between old adversaries, and empowering more and more people (Friedman, 1999). Now, however, globalization is itself a topic of global debate.

As someone seeking a career in education, you may want to examine some of the causes of this debate. One place to start is the website of the International Monetary Fund, where you can find an article called "Globalization: Threat or Opportunity?" (http://www.imf.org/external/np/exr/ib/2000/041200.htm). You may have your own ideas about whether globalization is a "good thing." As you read and think about this subject, consider the following questions:

- Who benefits most from globalization?
- Why are some people suspicious of globalization?
- How might this debate find its way into the classroom?
- How can schools reflect a global marketplace?

VIDEO CASE

A Global Classroom

Find the HM Video Case "Diversity: Teaching in a Multiethnic Classroom" on the student website. In this video, a Japanese language teacher, a classroom teacher, and all the students in a second-grade class learn an ancient Japanese art form. Students in the class hail from the United States, Japan, Russia, New Zealand, and Africa. Although they are not using the Internet, this lesson has many attributes of appropriate education for the global classroom.

- In what ways does this American classroom feel like a global classroom?
- Think back to what we said in Chapter 4 about curriculum as both a window and a mirror for students. How does this activity act as a window and a mirror for the students in the class?

continued

- Why might some people criticize the use of an ancient Japanese art form for storytelling?
- How does this activity foster an appreciation of global differences?
- How does this art activity relate to Ms. Frank's class activity in Chapter 7? (Look back at the Teaching Story called "A Third-Grade Class Does Research on China.")

TEACHING IN THE GLOBAL CLASSROOM

After all that we have said so far about the flat world, the global student, and the needs of a technology-driven world, you must be wondering, What does this mean for teaching?

First of all, it means that your job as a teacher is to demonstrate a love and a passion for learning. In the words of Thomas Friedman (2006), "You can't light the fire of passion in someone else if it does not burn in you to begin with" (p. 305). You can't expect your students to become curious and inventive if you don't display those qualities yourself.

Second, it means that you should help students develop the necessary areas of understanding and skills we have mentioned: knowledge of the world; the ability to collaborate; metacognitive skills; the MIVA skills of managing, interpreting, validating, and acting on information; and the willingness to think outside the box to come up with new solutions.

This may be a very different scenario for you, as a teacher, than you imagined based on your own schooling. But as you'll see from the following Teaching Stories, this approach ties in with the themes we have been developing throughout this book.

TEACHING STORIES
COMMUNICATING WITH A CLASS ACROSS THE OCEAN

Recently students in a fifth-grade class on the Eastern Shore of Maryland used their handheld Palm computers and keyboards to communicate with students in a fifth-grade class in South Africa. Each student e-mailed a message to a student "buddy" in the class in South Africa. The students exchanged information about their personal interests and about what they were learning in mathematics.

Then the teachers set up an international telephone link between the classrooms using Skype, a free Internet phone service. The Maryland students used their math skills to calculate what time it would be in South Africa during their call. In this Skype conversation and in further communications, both classes learned about life and culture in each place, the languages spoken and understood, and the role of homework and studying in their lives.

THE TEACHING IDEAS BEHIND THIS STORY

This story offers a small example of the ways global communication can foster the development of skills necessary for the twenty-first century. The students develop an awareness of students in another part of the world as well as a sensitivity to another culture and lifestyle. They become better communicators, too, as they adapt to the global terrain. This simple form of globalization can lead to many long-lasting relationships.

A number of websites can help you set up similar "buddy" exchanges with classes from distant countries and cultures. One example, the ePals Global Community (http://www.epals.com/), has linked students in two hundred countries as cross-cultural learning partners and friends. To find partner classes on this site, you can select a country from a map (see Figure 8.1), and then you can specify options such as the type of school, the age range of the students,

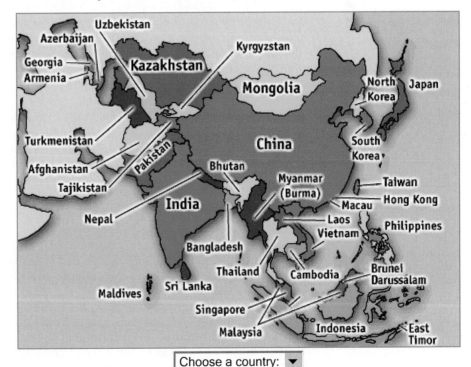

FIGURE 8.1
The Asia Map from the ePals Site

At the ePals website, clicking on a world map takes you to a regional map like this one. With another mouse click, you choose a country to find a list of schools interested in cross-cultural learning exchanges.

Source: http://www.epals.com/search/maps/asia/.

and the language(s) spoken. Your class may also join any of the global discussion boards and projects hosted by ePals.com.

If you have the resources and opportunity to create this type of global communication, be sure to embed it in a larger learning context. For example, if your middle school class is studying Asia, you can use the ePals site to locate a middle school class in India whose students can become e-mail partners with your students. Guide your students in deciding what types of questions they can ask to learn about their partners' interests, hobbies, lifestyle, and goals. Be sure, too, that your students are aware of their responsibilities in such an exchange, such as responding in a timely manner and using appropriate customs for polite and acceptable communication.

The next story describes an even more ambitious cross-cultural collaboration.

TEACHING STORIES
A CHALLENGING PROJECT FOR SIXTH-GRADE MATH

"Good Evening Earthling!" says the greeting on a website called Artificial Intelligence: Manufactured Minds. This site provides links and animations that address the history and uses of artificial intelligence as well as the ethical questions involved. Its topics range from neural networks to the meaning of consciousness. The site is an impressive achievement, especially when you realize that it was designed by high school students—and that the students are from New Hampshire, South Australia, and India.

You can find this site in the library at ThinkQuest.org (http://library .thinkquest.org/05aug/01158/index.html). For a window into the world of global high school collaboration, look at the Colophon section of the website, where the creators describe their backgrounds and their process of teamwork. I loved reading about the creators and learning how they learned from each other as they worked on this project. You will, too.

THE TEACHING IDEAS BEHIND THIS STORY

In addition to being an amazing example of cross-cultural collaboration, this story demonstrates the use of project-based learning to foster the type of creative thinking students need in a knowledge economy. ThinkQuest, sponsored by the Oracle Education Foundation, offers a project-based learning experience to students and teachers around the world. It is a competition in which nobody loses. The challenge is for students, grades 4 through 12, to work in teams to design and build innovative and educational websites to share with the world. Teachers and students select from a broad range of educational categories and topics. The teams that work on the website collaborate electronically via e-mail, Internet chat, and online forums. Global perspectives are encouraged.

Collaboration of this sort—students from diverse areas of the world working on a project that requires multiple ways of thinking and knowing—can become cumbersome and complex without a well-organized structure. Luckily, in addition to ThinkQuest, other educational foundations, organizations, and corporations have developed websites dedicated to this kind of networked project-based learning. See the Resources for Further Exploration section at the end of this chapter.

LEARNING PROJECT

Investigating ThinkQuest

Visit ThinkQuest (http://www.thinkquest.org/) and select a topic that interests you from the library. The broad range of categories includes Arts & Entertainment, Books & Literature, History & Government, Science & Technology, and much more.

Choose one student-created website to examine in detail. Respond to the following questions as you explore it:

- What kinds of students were involved in this website design team?
- Who were the coaches and teachers?
- How does the website design reflect creativity? innovation?
- Why is the collaboration involved in designing this website in the best interests of student learning?

TEACHING STORIES
MIDDLE SCHOOL STUDENTS PREPARE A NUTRITION AND EXERCISE PLAN

Groups of middle school students work together to create a nutrition and exercise plan for a person with particular needs. Each group chooses its subject from the following list:

- A person with hypertension
- A strict vegetarian
- A pregnant woman
- A person who is lactose intolerant
- A diabetic
- An athlete in training
- An astronaut in space

The students begin by watching a video. Sponsored by the National Space and Aeronautics Administration (NASA), the thirty-minute program shows how scientists use mathematics to study astronauts' loss of bone calcium and muscle mass while they live in space. Then students set out to make similar calculations to design the proper diet for their own subject. A NASA website offers links to research information, and another online page provides an exercise-related activity in which students collect and analyze data on heart rate.

This project, "Better Health from Space to Earth," is part of the NASA CONNECT series. Students in one middle school can collaborate with students from another to create the optimal diet and exercise plan for their chosen person.

THE TEACHING IDEAS BEHIND THIS STORY

NASA CONNECT presents several new programs each year for students in grades six to eight. Each program tries to establish connections "between the mathematics, science, and technology concepts taught in the classroom and the mathematics, science, and technology used everyday by NASA researchers." This series is another good example of project-based learning that involves collaboration, creative thinking, and problem-solving skills.

Notice, too, that each NASA CONNECT project explores an intersection of two or more subject areas. Consider how many subject areas are relevant in creating the nutrition and exercise plans described in the story. Figure 8.2 shows just one of the student handouts from this project.

5TUDENT hANDOUT

What is a Serving Size?

Serving Size: "Nutrition Facts" Labels

1. Look at the copy of the "Nutrition Facts" labels of the foods. Write the name of each of the foods under the Food Name column in Table 2 below. Find the serving size recommendations on each "Nutrition Facts" label. Write the recommended serving size listed on the "Nutrition Facts" label for each food in the appropriate space.

2. Take the paper plates and cup marked "Food Label" to the food station. Measure out the appropriate amounts of each food based on the "Nutrition Facts" labels. Put each portion on a paper plate or in the cup.

Table II. Estimates

FOOD NAME	"Nutrition Facts" food label (recommended serving size) Use cups as a measure

FIGURE 8.2

A Student Handout from the "Better Health from Space to Earth" Project

Source: NASA CONNECT. (2003). *Better Health from Space to Earth: An Educator Guide with Activities in Mathematics, Science, and Technology.* Hampton, VA: Langley Research Center, National Aeronautics and Space Administration.

Journal Write: Write a short paragraph to answer each of the following questions:

1. Compare your serving size estimates to the serving sizes recommended by the "Nutrition Facts" labels. Describe any differences.

2. Based on the information you collected, why do you think it might be important to look at the serving sizes listed on food labels?

3. Estimation skills are an invaluable tool to scientists, engineers, and researchers. What are some other ways you can use estimation skills on a daily basis?

If twenty-first century skills require "out of the box" thinking, one of your responsibilities as a twenty-first century teacher is to create problem-solving projects that give students the opportunity to be creative and to make connections to their daily lives. Perhaps a student has a friend or a family member who is an athlete; if so, completing the diet and nutrition plan may include interviewing a friend.

Videoconferencing

videoconferencing Real-time audio and video communication allowing individuals or groups at different locations to talk in a face-to-face setting.

Videoconferencing is a telecommunications medium that allows individuals or groups at different locations to transfer video and audio in real-time, face-to-face settings. Videoconferencing via the Internet is a readily available extension of your classroom.

Many teachers are already accustomed to "virtual field trips," which use videoconferencing technology to enable students to visit a museum, zoo, or other remote location. Now, students can use similar technology to "visit" other students and work collaboratively with them. With videoconferencing, students can exchange ideas in face-to-face discussions. Through such interactions, students develop their social and communication skills while preparing and presenting their joint projects (Townes-Young & Ewing, 2005).

Here's one example of videoconferencing: The Kenosha Unified School District in Wisconsin organizes "History Mystery" projects in which a fourth-grade class pairs with another fourth-grade class elsewhere in the state. Each partner class prepares a ten-minute presentation with clues about a significant event, person, invention, activity, or location from Wisconsin's history. The classes videoconference with each other to experience these presentations "live." The students may use pictures, songs, and skits in their presentations. After each class presents its "History Mystery," students in the other class work as a team to research the clues. After a set amount of research time, students have the opportunity to ask their partners three "yes" or "no" questions. This, too, happens in real time, in a videoconference. If necessary, a re-evaluation period is allowed before the mysteries are revealed (Roehre, 2007).

In addition to addressing multiple learning styles, this kind of project fosters a multitude of skills, including but not limited to creativity, in-depth thinking, good communication, and the ability to interpret events.

You may also want to investigate the videoconferencing offered by the NASA Digital Learning Network (http://nasadln.nmsu.edu/dln/). During these videoconferences, teachers and students exchange ideas with NASA experts in science and engineering. Interacting with experts gives students the sense that they are working on real-world questions and that their insights are significant. To help classes make best use of these interactions, NASA provides pre- and postconference instructional materials that teachers can use to develop and extend the lesson (see Figure 8.3).

Videoconferencing is another tool in the quest for real-life collaborative learning among students in different locations. A number of websites can help you get started with videoconferencing; see the Resources for Further Information section at the end of the chapter.

Virtual Classes in High School

distance learning Education in which students and teachers are not physically present at the same site.

You are probably familiar with online courses at the college level. In this widespread form of **distance learning,** college and graduate students take certain

FIGURE 8.3
Illustration of the Sun and Planets from a NASA Digital Learning Network Activity

This beautiful image comes from a PowerPoint presentation made available to teachers to prepare students for a videoconference on asteroids.

Source: NASA Digital Learning Network, Asteroids PowerPoint Presentation, http://nasadln.nmsu.edu/dln/content/catalog/details/?cid=67.

courses without ever visiting a physical classroom. You may be surprised to learn, however, that online courses are growing more and more common at the precollege level, as the following story demonstrates.

TEACHING STORIES
THE VIRTUAL CLASSROOM

David, a high school senior in Pennsylvania, has already taken every social science course his small private school can offer. Rather than take electives he does not need, David has enrolled in two Advanced Placement courses online: macroeconomics and microeconomics.

In nearby Collingswood, New Jersey, many such Advanced Placement courses are offered online through the district's virtual high school. "Ten years ago," says the director of the Collingswood program, this type of education "was a niche. It was something only kids who were geeks did. Now, it's something everyone does."

Collingswood collaborates with Virtual High School in Massachusetts, a nonprofit organization that offers more than 200 online courses to 7,500 students worldwide in 400 participating schools. As the CEO of Virtual High

School explains, this arrangement "gives kids the opportunity to learn in a way that is more in tune with how they exist as citizens; in a class of 25, you may have 25 students logging on in 25 different locations, learning global citizenship skills."

Sources: K. A. Graham, Virtual classes opening worlds, *Philadelphia Inquirer*, September 7, 2006; VHS Member Profile, website of Virtual High School, http://www.govhs.org/, retrieved January 2, 2007.

THE TEACHING IDEAS BEHIND THIS STORY

Already, millions of high school students take distance learning courses to supplement traditional courses offered at their brick-and-mortar schools. These virtual classes are becoming more and more popular. In *synchronous* distance learning, students are virtually present through the Internet at the same point in time. More commonly, though, the learning environment is *asynchronous*— that is, students from different geographical areas work at different times.

One of the significant advantages of virtual schools is that they can provide courses otherwise unavailable to a local student. This is especially important in rural areas, where one school often serves all students from prekindergarten to twelfth grade and the financial resources for extensive enrichment courses are unavailable. Some school districts form partnerships with a distance learning firm that tracks open seats in distance learning courses and offers them to school districts at discounted rates (Graham, 2006).

In the typical arrangement, students who take courses online communicate daily with the teacher, who may be in some other part of the country or even in another nation. Yet students do much of their course work independently, on their own schedule. Usually a school guidance counselor keeps in

Students are learning over a large distance through videoconferencing. Technology makes virtual classrooms possible.

touch to make sure students are keeping pace with the work required from the online course. Naturally, some students are better at independent work than others; for some students, online courses at the precollege level are not the best choice. The value of an online course depends in part on the individual's maturity, work habits, and motivation.

Online courses can enroll students from many localities and even from many countries. In these situations, collaborative problem solving, as we saw earlier with the ThinkQuest collaborations, entails communication among students from widely different cultures, socioeconomic classes, and geographical regions. Learning to work with such diverse students enhances precollege students' abilities to be team problem solvers and to appreciate the contributions of people from radically different environments.

What does an online environment mean for teaching? When teachers are asked to develop an online course from a course they are used to teaching face to face, the challenge is often transformative. Imagine that you have developed lesson plans for a unit of study and now you are going to use these lessons online with fifteen to twenty students who are working at different paces and at different times around the globe. To make this leap, you have to ask some soul-searching questions, like the ones listed below in "Questions for Teaching an Online Course." In fact, research shows that teaching an online course leads many teachers to reexamine some of their beliefs about teaching and learning. The concepts of teacher-student and student-student communication, as well as student accountability and assessment, change in the online environment. Many teachers improve their skills as they think more deeply about their subject area as well as the nature of communication with and among their students (Lowes, 2005).

Perhaps you will be asked to be part of a virtual high school when you are teaching a face-to-face classroom. You may find it challenging to do both—teach face to face and teach online. The intellectual "space" of the online class requires a different type of preparation. You will be happy to know, however, that most students who take online courses feel like they are part of a learning community and value the experience. The Chapter Challenge at the end of this chapter invites you to examine how you will communicate ideas and controversies and conduct discussions in an online environment.

Questions for Teaching an Online Course

To prepare for teaching an online course, you need to ask yourself questions like these:

- What do I hope the online students will get out of this course?

- Why have I been teaching this course in this particular way?

- What needs to change for the online environment? Which elements of my lesson plans do I keep? Which do I leave out?

- How do I substitute an online activity for something I have done face to face?

- How can I foster group work and collaboration among students who are physically far apart?

- How can I improve the way I communicate with students?

Source: Adapted from Pape, et al. (2005).

WRITING and REFLECTION

The Online Community

Chapter 9 explores the important concept of the classroom as a learning community. To be an effective teacher, you need to build a sense of community in the classroom. Take a moment to think about your own experience with online communities, either in coursework or in other areas such as chatrooms, blogs, social networking sites (MySpace, Facebook), and the like.

- What factors help an online group function as a real community?
- In what ways is an online community similar to a classroom community? How is it different?

The Teacher's Role in a Global Classroom

At this point in the chapter you may be wondering, "Why am I going into teaching if students can get so much information elsewhere and connect so readily to the rest of the world?" That is a legitimate question. The answer lies in the importance of your passion, your curiosity, your capacity to listen to and accept students, to gently challenge their ideas and guide them—these are the qualities that will make you a successful teacher.

Your expertise in your content area must be apparent, but it is less important than your ability to help students navigate the flood waters of information available to them. Your challenge is to become a teacher who helps students become discriminating consumers of information, capable of validating data by doing research and formulating well-supported opinions. In other words, your message to students is, "Now that you know what the raw information says, how do you process it?" As a teacher, you will help students make meaning

A teacher addresses several groups of students separated by large distances in a virtual classroom.

from the data they find; you will help them draw out the big ideas or core concepts in ways that connect to the real world.

Remember as well that you are your students' guide through group learning, collaboration, conflict resolution, and socially acceptable communication. You can help them become lifelong creative learners by challenging them with problems and projects that require them to collaborate and share in this new, open-source world. That sounds like a tall order, but more and more it is how we live our lives.

CONCLUDING THOUGHTS

Why do some things take root and grow while others barely break the surface? How long does something have to be around before we can declare that it's here to stay? What has to happen in order to transform an oasis of change into an entire landscape?
— Ronald Thorpe (2003)

The twenty-first century challenges us to understand more about how people learn, communicate, and do business in a global environment or what Friedman calls the "flat world." Who we become as teachers will reflect the times in which we live—our global interconnectivity and our unending access to information and media.

It is difficult to predict the world in which your students will take part as adults. Think about this: in the years many of today's college-aged students were born, there were hardly any cell phones or digital cameras, no iPods or MP3 players, very few Internet sites, no GPS devices in cars, and no TIVO or Google. Now try to think twenty years into the future. Can you even begin to imagine what further changes will occur?

Connectivity, communication, and collaboration have become this century's reading, 'riting, and 'rithmetic—three Cs to replace the traditional three Rs of the twentieth century. Of course, we need the three Rs to become adept at the three Cs. Yet the world into which you must guide your students is more complex and demanding than ever before.

Clearly, to teach in this environment, we must be students of history and of current affairs, and very much able to keep pace with constant change. Further, the global community challenges us to see beyond our own world and into the worlds of others as a way to make the planet a more tolerant, more sustainable, and safer place. As teachers, our personas are revealed in the classroom: how generous of spirit we become, how capable we are of listening to and learning with our students.

JOIN THE DISCUSSION

Visit the student website for this text and locate the Edublog for Chapter 8. Share your answer to this question: At this point in the text, how, if at all, has your image of teaching and learning changed? Be specific!

CHAPTER CHALLENGE

Creating an Online Course

Imagine you are teaching this chapter of the book in an online environment. You have seventeen students, all of whom are high school seniors taking an elective course in globalization. The students come from seven different high schools in various regions of the United States as well as in India, Belarus, and China.

- How will you organize the materials for this course?
- What "big ideas" or major concepts will you want the students to learn?
- Provide examples of four topics that would stimulate discussion and get the participants to reflect on the material.
- How will you assess the students' discourse?
- How will you foster a learning community online?
- Are you currently part of an online learning community? Explain.

FROM THE COLLEGE CLASSROOM TO YOUR OWN CLASSROOM

Designing an Activity to Promote Twenty-first-Century Skills

As you continue your teaching portfolio, imagine you are teaching at a grade level of your choice. Think of *one activity* you could undertake with your class to enhance your students' capacity to use twenty-first century skills. Describe this activity as specifically as possible.

RESOURCES FOR FURTHER EXPLORATION

Educere http://www.educere.net/   Educere connects K–12 students and schools with a wide array of distance-learning courses.

ePals Global Community http://www.epals.com/   A good resource for connecting your class with students in other countries.

Friends Across the Sea: Salisbury and Bloemfontein http://www.wcboe.org/programs/oit/glen/hastings.html   A Web record of the exchanges described in this chapter between students in Maryland and South Africa.

Intercultural E-mail Classroom Connections (IECC) http://www.iecc.org/   IECC maintains several mailing lists that help teachers link their classes with partners in other countries for e-mail exchanges or collaborative projects.

International Education and Resource Network (iEARN) http://www.iearn.org/   iEARN connects teachers and students around the world in collaborative projects that emphasize a social justice theme.

Kidlink http://www.kidlink.org/   A global, multilingual e-mail network for young people between the ages of ten and fifteen. Through the associated KIDPROJ, adult mentors organize curriculum projects.

NASA CONNECT http://connect.larc.nasa.gov/   NASA's series of integrated math, science, and technology programs for middle school students.

NASA Digital Learning Network http://nasadln.nmsu.edu/dln/   NASA's umbrella site linking its many educational programs and activities.

ThinkQuest http://www.thinkquest.org/   A project-based learning initiative in which students from around the world participate in designing websites that may be used for reference by other students.

The United Nations Association of the United States of America (UNA-USA) http://www.unausa.org/   This website provides information about the Model UN program as well as about global curriculum, consultants, and annual conferences.

Videoconferencing: A Digital Handbook for Teachers and Students http://www.d261.k12.id.us/VCing/   This site provides a good deal of information about educational videoconferencing, including strategies for implementation and ideas for curriculum.

The Videoconferencing Cookbook http://www.videnet.gatech.edu/cookbook.en/   A useful introduction to the uses of videoconferencing and the technology involved.

Wide Angle: Lesson Plan Index http://www.pbs.org/wnet/wideangle/classroom/   An excellent resource for teachers, this site includes lesson plans and accompanying videos on global issues, from growing up in other countries to conflicts resolved and challenges to be faced. Sign up for the newsletter to keep abreast of offerings.

Taking Stock

Assessing Where You Are and Where You're Going

1. What are your thoughts about teaching in an inclusion classroom? Would you welcome a partner teacher? How would it feel to share your classroom with another teacher?

2. When you reflect on your own cultural and ethnic background, how do you feel about teaching students whose cultures and backgrounds are very different from yours? What is the greatest challenge for you in that scenario?

3. Have you, or has anyone you know, struggled as a result of being a non-native English speaker? How can you make such a journey easier for your students?

4. How would you describe your own learning style? (*Hint:* You can have more than one.) For example, is this writing exercise a struggle, or do you like putting thoughts on paper?

5. People who seek a career in teaching often think that it is fair to treat all students in the same way. How does it feel to know (as you read in Chapter 5) that treating all children the same is *not* equitable?

6. For you, what would be the pros and cons of teaching in a charter school?

7. When you think of technology and schooling, do you consider yourself a digital native or the opposite, a digital immigrant?

8. In your ideal classroom, what types of technology would be available (both hardware and software)?

9. Which of the twenty-first century skills that we hope to foster in students are you most adept at? How will that help you as a teacher?

Classrooms, Communities, and You

Part IV addresses the pressing question of how to create classroom environments that are welcoming, caring, and ultimately effective for teaching and learning. The personal nature of teaching distinguishes it from many other professions. Teaching keeps you on your toes and requires self-awareness and a special mindfulness of your actions and intentions. You need this level of consciousness to become an effective teacher. Remember, teaching is about building relationships.

In this part of the book, we also explore the importance of instilling a sense of belonging among your students—a feeling that everyone in the classroom belongs to the same community. This sense of community not only enhances students' learning experiences; it also acts as a buffer against some of the problems in today's schools, such as bullying and sexual harassment.

Finally, Part IV offers several tools to assist you in analyzing—once again—whether teaching is the right career for you. Thinking about the "goodness of fit" between yourself and the profession is a crucial step in preparing for a fulfilling and successful teaching life.

PART OUTLINE

The Classroom as Community

FOCUSING QUESTIONS

▶ When you think of a community, what do you picture?

▶ What does it mean to really *belong* to a group?

▶ Why are students' social and emotional dispositions important for learning?

▶ What comes to mind when you think of classroom management?

▶ How can we use formal meetings in the classroom to create community?

▶ What are some of the attributes of a learning community?

▶ How can we prevent sexual harassment and bullying in the classroom and online?

This chapter considers the issue of "community" in conventional classrooms—where students are gathered, physically face-to-face, with a teacher for a specified period of time. Many of the principles described here also relate to the online classrooms we discussed in the previous chapter. Whatever the domain in which you teach, your primary function is to ask, "How do I create an environment in which students have respect for themselves and for the other members of the classroom community?"

In the current era, in which schools focus intensely on the academic proficiency of their students as recorded by standards-based tests, it is important to recognize that academic proficiency is only one of the major goals of education. There are social and emotional goals as well. Students should become learners with the capacity to love, work, and be active community members (Cohen, 2006). Along these lines, the philosopher John Dewey urged educators to have a sympathetic understanding of learners as individuals in order to have an idea of what is actually going on in their minds (1938, p. 39).

BUILDING COMMUNITY IN THE CLASSROOM

John Dewey (1916–2004) asserted that the aim of education is to support the development of the skills and knowledge needed for responsible and caring participation in a democracy. In a sense, then, the question this chapter seeks to answer is, "How do students become engaged, responsible participants in a democracy, and how does that process start with the environment created in their classrooms?"

Classroom Management and Classroom Community

classroom management The ways teachers create an effective classroom environment for learning, including all the rules and conditions they establish.

New teachers often seek to understand more about what is typically called **classroom management**. By *management,* they mean the ways the teacher can get students to do what the teacher wants them to. Classroom management has been defined as "the set of teacher behaviors that create and maintain conditions in the classroom permitting instruction to take place efficiently and effectively" (Ryan & Cooper, 2007, p. 499). Other educators believe that good classroom managers "carefully arrange their classrooms to minimize disturbances . . . and make sure that instruction can proceed efficiently" (Sadker & Zittleman, 2007, pp. 398–399).

Among many progressive educators, though, the term *classroom management* is frowned upon because it can imply that teachers use the power differential between themselves and their students to force students to follow a certain set of rules. Recently, educators interested in classroom management have begun to focus instead on the creation, through various strategies, of a **classroom community** in which each participant is invested in the smooth operation of the whole and all participants have an interest in outcomes. In this way of looking at the matter, rules and conditions are not established by the teacher alone, but by the group as a whole.

classroom community A sense of common purpose and values shared by the teacher and students in a classroom, so that they see themselves as working together in the process of learning; a classroom atmosphere that emphasizes trust, care, and support.

Although we do need structures, routines, and class rules to guide the teaching and learning in our classrooms, the way we arrive at these guidelines is crucial.

Different teachers have different ways of establishing classroom expectations. When I was chatting with Meredith, who has been in the classroom for two years, we explored her experiences as a first-year teacher in an urban school known for its discipline problems. She taught a second-grade class of thirty students, and she felt her first year had been successful and satisfying. I asked her how she felt before the first day of school.

> I was scared. I wanted to meet the children and I was excited, but before the first day of school, I was told that I had behavior problems in my class. But, after the first five minutes with the class, I was fine. My classroom management skills kicked in, and I was on my way.

When I asked Meredith where she got those skills, she said, "From my mother." I was stunned because I know there are many teaching courses with the title "Classroom Management." Was her mother wiser than professional educators? She elaborated on what she had learned from her mother:

> My mother always expected the best from me, and she was strict and demanding, but I knew she really cared about me and had my best interests at heart. Still, she was a "no-nonsense mom" who set goals with me and had clear expectations. She checked with me to see how I felt about how I was meeting my goals. I do the same thing with the children in my classroom.
>
> I ask them what type of classroom will help them learn. I have strict policies, but we discuss each policy and why it makes sense for their learning environment. I hold out the expectation that they will abide by the rules, and I keep my door open. I explain to them that anyone passing our classroom should be able to see a model of students busy with their work and their class discussions. Of course, when they work in pairs or groups, there is some noise, but that is necessary for them to collaborate with their classmates.

I asked if she used any little tricks to keep students focused and productive. Yes, she said, she had hand signals to get their attention when they were working in pairs or groups; she introduced those signals on the first day of school. Also, during a group conversation, she would quietly walk over to students who were not paying attention, and her body language helped amend their behavior.

Mostly, Meredith explained, she genuinely cares about her students and expects them to be successful. She wants a classroom that works for both the students and the teacher, and sometimes that means she has to alter her plans. For example, if she notices that the second graders are very engaged in a topic and working diligently on task, she extends the lesson, altering her own routine to allow them to go further in an area of study that *they* find compelling:

> Everything is a collaboration; there is no such thing as "teaching" separate from "learning." It is not always possible to know what curriculum areas will set an entire class on fire—and when one comes up, I hate to let it go just because my plan book says I should.

Good teachers live for those moments when the students are "on fire" (Intrator, 2003), carried away and enthused by a topic, a project, an experience, or a story. It is at these times, when students are fully communicating with each other, responding to peers and to you, that you think, "Wow, this is why I came to this work!" These experiences engage students' thinking and enthusiasm so completely that they "forget" they are supposed to resist school and get carried away by the excitement of the moment.

Can you remember a time in your own history as a student when that happened? At these moments, you understand that the classroom is "managed" by the quality of the learning experience, the engagement of the students, and the appreciation of the teacher for the intellectual work that is going on. This is a learning community. It is "managed" by everyone in it. Let's look at another story that can tell us more about the foundations of a classroom community.

TEACHING STORIES
MY FIRST YEAR OF TEACHING EIGHTH-GRADE GENERAL SCIENCE IN NEW YORK CITY

In an old school building in the east Bronx, in New York City, I am trying to bring eighth-grade physical science to life. As part of a unit on the properties of mixtures, we are studying solutions. For this lesson, I want to show the students that, in a solution with water, even though the particles of a solute (the substance that dissolves) seem to disappear, they can be reclaimed. If you boil off the water, the original solute remains at the bottom of the flask. In fact, if you collect the steam and condense it back into water, you can end up with the solute and the water in separate containers—exactly the way they started before the solution was made.

To do this, I set up an apparatus called a Liebig condenser, made popular by the German chemist Justus Baron von Liebig, which makes it possible to collect vapors and turn them back into a liquid. The condenser has an inner tube and an outer tube. The entire apparatus connects to the lab sink in my classroom.

We start with blue crystals of copper sulfate. We stir them into water, making a copper sulfate solution. Then we try to reverse the process. We place the flask containing the solution on a tripod over a bunsen burner, connecting the open end of the flask to the Liebig condenser with rubber tubing. When the copper sulfate solution boils, the water vapor is collected in the condenser's inner tube, and cold water from the lab sink swirls around the outer tube. Slowly, clear water—the steam turned back into liquid—drips from the condenser into a collecting beaker. The students sit in rapt attention, enthralled.

I ask the class if this process would work if the tube were hooked up to the hot water faucet. All the students shout, "No, it's the cold water that does it!" They seem to understand that the cold turns the steam back into water by removing the heat from the vapor. I do not mind that they are shouting: "Mrs. Koch—look inside the flask—look—the blue crystals are coming back!" "Yes," I remark, "and how many thought they were gone for good?" Many students raise their hands. They are smiling; they "get it."

They ask if we can try another solution tomorrow. "Sure," I reply . . . and tomorrow we will try it with salt water. When the students file out at the end of class, some of them call out, "That was so cool, Mrs. K."

continued

I leave the school building elated. I know the students have had a learning experience. They now know more about evaporation, condensation, and the entire process of distillation. As I drive home with a big smile on my face, I am reminded that it is just for days like this that I keep teaching. I say to myself: it's worth all the preparation!

THE TEACHING IDEAS BEHIND THIS STORY

Think about what is happening behind the scenes in this eighth-grade classroom. For one thing, the students have learned that I go to a good deal of trouble on their behalf. I have taken the time to set up this complex apparatus and have it ready for their class. They appear to understand that I am deeply invested in their learning and in providing a good science experience. Today will tide us over other days that may not be as exciting; but the students will expect a similarly exciting lab demonstration at some future date.

Over time, as I continued to show my commitment to these students, they never cut science. They were interested. They were well behaved. They managed themselves.

But there are other factors at work here as well. By saying that the students managed themselves, I don't mean that we had no classroom rules. We did in fact have rules in which everyone was invested. This leads us to our next topic.

Rules, Procedures, and Routines: A Collaborative Effort

To create classroom community, teachers must provide opportunities and structures that can encourage students to help and support one another. To do so, teachers need to offer explicit instruction so that students learn *how* to support one another (Hittie, 2000).

Rules, procedures, and routines are a good example. Effective teachers use these to manage their classrooms. Too often, however, the decisions are solely in the hands of the teacher, and the students have no voice in, and hence no responsibility for, the way their classroom is managed. To build classroom community, a teacher needs to involve the students in establishing the rules and procedures. Remember what Meredith said: "I ask [my students] what type of classroom will help them learn. I have strict policies, but we discuss each policy and why it makes sense for their learning environment."

Now think about my eighth-grade science classroom. The students were all fired up about the distillation experiment, but their behavior stayed well within the limits of appropriate classroom decorum. What rules do you think the class and I developed?

The students and I developed a chart guiding behavior for watching complex demonstrations. As we made up the chart, the students were creative and inventive, and the result was a true collaborative effort, shown in Figure 9.1. As the story reveals, there *was* some calling out, but it never progressed to the point of jumping and screaming, and it was a fitting expression of the students' excitement.

The point is clear. A classroom that functions well allows students to provide input about the ways it should be run. Classroom rules and procedures result from a collaborative effort. Building a community honors all the participants, and the value of creating community is that each participant is invested in the outcomes.

Rules for Observing Demonstrations

✓ Check that you can see prior to the start of the demonstration.

✓ Find a place in the room where you have a clear view of the experiment.

✓ Do not crowd around the front by the lab desk.

✓ Do not jump up and down and scream.

FIGURE 9.1
Rules That Students and I Developed for Class Demonstrations

Is a Well-Managed Classroom Silent?

Many new teachers, and veteran teachers as well, confuse a well-run classroom with pervasive silence. As the distillation experiment reveals, appropriate noise related to the activity or experience in which the students are engaged is a healthy aspect of a well-managed classroom. In fact, classrooms in which teachers insist on quiet all the time run the risk of students becoming disengaged and not really "present" in the social and emotional ways required for learning. Consider this excerpt from a student teacher's journal about his experience in a first-grade classroom:

I have noticed a trend in many elementary classrooms, and it is especially prevalent in my current first-grade placement. That trend is the overemphasis put on silence in the classroom.

It seems that no matter what activity the children are engaged in, it is expected to be done in silence, or with whispers at the most. My cooperating teacher often reprimands the children for being too loud and is constantly telling them to be quiet. She even sometimes uses an electronic traffic light that detects the volume of sound in the classroom and sounds an alarm when it gets too loud. If the alarm goes off, the class is penalized by losing recess time.

Here, in first grade, there is an emphasis on silent, individualized work. This is a contradiction to how children learn. They need hands-on, stimulating learning experiences and those activities are often noisy . . . but they need them! They need to move and to have peer interaction. They should be going to centers and working with others toward mutual goals.

When it comes down to it, there is not a single time of the day when it is OK for the class to be noisy and lively. I think it is a shame and I believe that it is directly related to the behavior problems in the classroom. The children in my placement have a lot of trouble staying seated and quiet all day. But you cannot blame them when the only outlets for their energy are at lunch and gym!

At certain times, the classroom needs to be very quiet with students listening attentively. Good classroom management also allows for the active engagement of students, encouraging the thinking process and creating engaged learners.

Everything we know about how people learn reminds us that learning requires the active engagement of the learner—through social contexts, collaboration with other students and the teacher, and personal metacognition. The stereotype of the teacher in the front of a room full of rows of silent children runs counter to this understanding. Today, classrooms have many configurations: students may be seated at tables, in groups of desks, or, yes, even in rows. But however the classroom is arranged, learning cannot happen in silence.

Being Fully Conscious

As a teacher, you are "on" from the moment your school day begins. Everything you say and do may have an effect on your students. For that reason, it's impossible to overstate the importance of being fully aware and in control of your own behavior. As you read the following story, note the reactions of the student, the teacher, and the parent. What was the effect on classroom community?

TEACHING STORIES
THE WAY YOU HOLD YOUR PENCIL

At the end of a school day in third grade, my nine-year-old daughter Robin came off the school bus, made eye contact with me, and started to sob. She had held back tears all afternoon and had to struggle to compose herself to tell me about her humiliation by her third-grade teacher.

It appears that left-handed Robin was holding her pencil in an awkward way. Mrs. Owens held her hand up to the class and said, "Class, do you all see the way Robin is holding her pencil? You must never hold your pencil that way." Well, that was it for Robin for the rest of the school day. Humiliated, she retreated quietly into herself and returned home bruised by this criticism.

I visited Mrs. Owens the following day, and before I could recount the episode she showered me with compliments about Robin. When I shared my concern about the pencil incident with her, she said, "Oh, that was nothing; I didn't mean anything by it. I just want her to hold her pencil correctly."

THE TEACHING IDEAS BEHIND THIS STORY

This was an impulsive, unconscious moment on the part of Mrs. Owens. One of her students was hurt by the exchange. Teachers cannot afford to "shoot from the hip." They must be careful to explore ways to change students' habits by engaging in constructive and caring dialogue.

Among the essential qualities teachers need to be successful, one is a clear sense of their own adulthood and a grounded sense of who they are. When you teach, your personality and needs are on display at all times. If you are very needy, your students will sense that. You should make certain that your students' needs come before your own needs.

Teachers have different personalities, but what they have in common is that the teacher is usually the responsible adult in the classroom. As the adult, the teacher is obligated to create a safe, secure, and organized learning environment in which routines and expectations are consistent and respectful.

WRITING and REFLECTION

The Teacher as the Adult in the Classroom

Teachers are always learners; we learn constantly about ourselves, our students, and our content areas. As we return to the theme of "we teach who we are," it is important that you seek the inner understanding that is a hallmark of really wonderful teachers. Think about these questions:

- What does it mean to act like an adult in the classroom? What attributes does that involve?
- What behaviors are inappropriate for teachers?
- Do you remember teachers who were ineffective because of behaviors that were not responsible?

   Then, on a personal level, ask yourself:

- Am I the type of person who tends to speak without thinking?
- Do I tend to "shoot from the hip"?
- Even though I am well meaning, has there been a time when I hurt somebody's feelings because I was overly blunt?

VIDEO CASE

Teachers Building Community

Find the HM Video Case "Classroom Management: Best Practices" on the student website. In this video, several teachers demonstrate and talk about the ways they conduct their classrooms. Notice that, in the first segment, the elementary teacher talks about investing time in helping the children understand the routines of the classroom. The middle school teacher explicitly addresses the building of a community with shared expectations. The seventh-grade student reminds us that the teacher must be a "listener" before he or she jumps to judgment, and the guidance counselor reminds teachers that if a student is "acting up," it is often not a personal response to the teacher.

continued

- What do you think the elementary school teacher means when she says that she waits at least six weeks before giving her young students independent activities?
- How does the middle school drama teacher create community?
- Why do you suppose the seventh-grade student urges his teachers not to react first but to listen first?
- Why do you think Ms. Miller spends two hours on grouping students? How does that effort contribute to classroom community?

The Classroom as a Safe Place

In Chapter 6, we discussed the importance of creating a safe school climate. In many ways, a classroom community is a microcosm of the larger school climate. You may not be able to control the climate elsewhere in the school, but there is a lot you can do in your own classroom.

To foster a sense of community in the classroom, teachers must ensure that the classroom is a safe place—not just a physically safe environment, but also an emotionally safe place where students are treated with respect, both by the teacher and by each other. In such a place, everyone is held accountable for what happens. Students come to rely on the teacher's sense of fairness and the consistency with which she or he upholds classroom rules and guidelines.

Some teachers establish a classroom meeting time to help build the sense of community. Some teachers have "Morning Meeting," while others have class meetings to discuss a particular event or to handle a problem. Each type of meeting serves a different purpose and contributes to the shared sense of community. The following teaching story illustrates how the meetings work in one fifth-grade classroom.

TEACHING STORIES
CREATING COMMUNITY WITH MORNING MEETING

In a fifth-grade inclusion classroom, Ms. Sanders, who has been teaching for five years, has established the practice of daily Morning Meetings. This is a critical part of the day that fosters relationships among students. The inclusion students, in particular, comment that this is their favorite part of the day.

The four parts of the Morning Meeting are the greeting, the share, announcements, and the news. The meeting takes place at the beginning of each school day on a rug at the rear of the classroom, where students sit on pillows in a circle facing each other, with the teacher positioned in a prominent spot in the circle.

Ms. Sanders views Morning Meeting as a critical event of the day, a time when students are recognized, life stories are heard, and all individuals are valued. She explains, "I make sure I greet each child, even if he or she is going out to a band lesson or early math. I make sure that I talk to them all and they are greeted by name. I look at Morning Meeting as a place to talk about what is on the kids' minds and what is going on in their lives. Morning Meeting gives the students a place to share with the whole class, not just me. I love it! It really brings us together as a community, and I learn so much about the students as people from this daily exchange."

The students regard Morning Meeting as an important opportunity to share their life outside of school, learn about their classmates, and celebrate their differences. One boy remarks, "We do Morning Meeting, and I especially like the sharing part when you get to bring in something and share it with the class. I always like to see what other people bring in, and when I bring in something, people always come up to me at snack and want to see it. Then when I have a play date they will ask to see the thing I shared, like my arrowhead or rock collection. It makes me feel good inside and kind of special."

Another student says, "I like Morning Meeting the best because you get to hear about current events and what is going on in the world. You also get to hear what is going on in other people's lives during sharing. I really like that."

Ms. Sanders explains: "I think that the personality of the teacher helps the classroom become a warm and caring atmosphere. I think that I am very easygoing and laid back. I am always happy and smiling, and I try really hard to make the class a fun place for all kids. If I come in and I tell the kids a story that happened to me yesterday or a story about my life, then they will share with me. That creates a nice warm environment in which to learn. I try to make the class like a community. I stress that from day one. I promote an environment where they are free to take risks. They can treat each other like friends, and they can count on each other for help."

The students in this class are aware that they are a part of a special classroom community. Their sense of belongingness is not necessarily the norm outside of their classroom. They talk about bullying, ridicule, and aggressive behavior by students from other classes—experiences that occur regularly on the playground, in the lunchroom, and on the bus. Some express outrage at the social injustice experienced by their peers. The students in this class feel a sense of responsibility toward each other, reflecting the care and concern embodied by their teacher, Ms. Sanders.

In this classroom, clearly, the management is handled by everyone.

THE TEACHING IDEAS BEHIND THIS STORY

Ms. Sanders is quite aware of the various ways she encourages a sense of community. She mentions her easygoing personality; her storytelling, which connects her life experiences with those of the students; and her vigilance in promoting a risk-free environment and a safe place for friendships to grow. All of these are critical components in developing a caring classroom.

Morning Meeting in itself is a structure that can build a sense of community and acceptance among the members of a classroom. The daily exchanges among students allow them (1) to feel validated and an important part of the classroom community, (2) to make meaning out of new concepts, (3) to assist themselves and others in the learning process, and (4) to celebrate personal differences. If you establish a Morning Meeting in your classroom, you may find that students rush to the rug each morning to engage in this community-building ritual.

In this era of high-stakes testing mandated by the No Child Left Behind law, too many teachers are preoccupied with students' academic achievements as recorded on standardized tests. Research studies have discovered, however, that if students do not feel emotionally and socially safe, the opportunities for them to learn are limited. According to research, a sense of belongingness—of

Creating community in the classroom often starts with a Morning Meeting.

being connected in important ways to others—is one of three basic psychological needs essential to human growth and development, along with autonomy and competence (Osterman, 2000, p. 325). In simple terms, students' learning improves when teachers integrate social and academic learning in the classroom (Bickart et al., 2000; Rimm-Kaufman, 2006). Hence, building classroom community is an intrinsic part of creating academically competent students.

VIDEO CASE

Using Classroom Meetings to Create Community

Find the HM Video Case "Elementary Classroom Management: Basic Strategies" on the student website. The teacher in this video, Ms. Moylan, uses Morning Meeting to create community in her classroom. In particular, the video shows a meeting in which she helps prepare students for a busy field trip the following week. As you watch the video, think about these questions:

- How does Ms. Moylan use the "fair crayon can" with names inside it? How does this device promote fairness?

- How does she engage students in community problem solving?

- When she engages her students in role playing, what is she trying to accomplish?

- After viewing this teacher in action for a few minutes, how would you describe her classroom management style?

- What is the significance of consistency and fairness, especially for the new teacher?

The Responsive Classroom Approach to Community Building

Responsive Classroom
An approach to teaching and learning, developed by the Northeast Foundation for Children, that seeks to bring together social and academic learning.

A group of educators from the Northeast Foundation for Children (NEFC) has developed a program called the **Responsive Classroom**, which introduces teachers to the theory and practice of sound classroom management through democratic principles and practices. The Responsive Classroom approach rests on principles like these (Northeast Foundation for Children, 2007; Rimm-Kaufman, 2006):

▶ The social curriculum and the academic curriculum are equally important.

▶ How children learn is as important as what they learn.

▶ Social interaction facilitates cognitive growth.

▶ Children need to learn cooperation, assertion, responsibility, empathy, and self-control if they are to be successful socially and academically.

▶ Knowing children individually, culturally, and developmentally is essential to good teaching.

▶ Knowing children's families is essential to good teaching.

▶ The working relationships among the adults in a school are critically important to students' learning.

Notice that many of these principles align with what we have said previously in this book. These ideas rest heavily on the understanding that teaching and learning are about building and fostering relationships—relationships among teachers and students; among students and their peers; and among teachers and other teachers, administrators, and the community at large.

Following these principles, the developers of the Responsive Classroom model recommend a number of specific teaching strategies. They advocate Morning Meeting, for instance. They suggest "guided discovery," an approach to learning similar to the project- and problem-based methods discussed earlier in this text. They also recommend "academic choice," a term that highlights the importance of activities in which students make their own choices, solve problems, and work collaboratively. They even propose strategies for arranging materials, furniture, and displays to encourage independence, promote caring, and maximize learning. You can read more about Responsive Classrooms at http://www.responsiveclassroom.org/.

Tips for Creating a Classroom Community

From what you have read in this chapter, you should already have some good ideas for creating community in your classroom. The most basic suggestion I can offer is to take a genuine interest in your students. Authenticity "outs itself." Students can sense when you are honestly interested in them as people as well as learners.

The sidebar "Creating a Classroom Community and Maintaining Appropriate Behavior" offers more detailed guidelines. Remember, it is often the little things you do that build a sense of trust among your students. In the following Teaching Story, the first- and second-grade teacher tells how she discovered that her youngsters were very capable of managing many of the classroom routines—and that doing so gave them a sense of community and responsibility.

TEACHING STORIES
CLASSROOM WORKERS FORM COMMUNITY

This is the easiest way I've found to do classroom jobs. I was doing a lot of tidying up and organizing each day after school and thought that my first/second graders could do most of these things with a little training. I gave every student in my class a job. This builds community and responsibility. Children have a new job assignment every month, so I have to assign new jobs only eight times each year. I keep track of the assignments on a class list on my computer. We have ten minutes at the end of the day for "job time" and don't line up for dismissal until the room is clean and jobs are done.

Creating a Classroom Community and Maintaining Appropriate Behavior: Guidelines for a New Teacher

- Teachers can never be overprepared. The first key to a successful teaching experience is to plan, plan, and plan!

- Understand your expectations for students' behavior and share those with them. Show them and tell them what you are hoping for.

- To build a sense of community, develop rules collaboratively with your students, and be very clear about these.

- Establish both continuity and consistency. Keep rules to a minimum but enforce them. Always have clear consequences for breaking a rule, and never threaten to take a particular action if you are not willing to carry it out.

- Be prepared to admit your mistakes. Use humor when appropriate.

- Monitor students frequently so that unacceptable behavior is detected early and can be addressed before it becomes a serious disruption.

- Redirect students' inappropriate behaviors by asking them to do something constructive at that moment.

- Make respect central to your classroom culture. The only way to hold students to high expectations is to gain their respect by making it clear that you care about them and that your class will lead to real learning that will benefit them.

- Minimize the power differential in everyday communication.

- Keep calm in all situations. Calmness allows you to make rational decisions. If a student is confrontational, it never works to react with anger. Let the situation cool down; wait, and then approach the student calmly.

- Whenever possible, connect your classroom discussions and curriculum to students' lives, communities, and culture. Learn as much as you can about your students and make connections to their lived experiences.

- Build students' confidence in their own intelligence and creativity. Talk about multiple intelligences, if appropriate, and how people can be smart and creative in many ways.

- Have engaging activities prepared for the students when they walk into the classroom. You may play a piece of music, put an appropriate puzzle on the board, or have materials available for students to explore.

- Keep lecturing to a minimum. Engage students in group projects, centers, presentations, discussions, or role plays. Place the students at the center of the learning experience. Make the classroom about *them*.

- Remember, the best and most appropriate consequences for students are positive ones—the intrinsic joy that comes from success, accomplishment, social approval, good academic performance, and recognition. Create experiences that enable all students to feel good about themselves.

Sources: Adapted from Miller, L. (2004), 12 tips for new teachers, in K. D. Salas, R. Tenorio, S. Walters, & D. Weiss (Eds.), *The new teacher book: Finding purpose, balance, and hope during your first years in the classroom* (Milwaukee, WI: Rethinking Schools, Ltd.); and from "Tips for Creating a Peaceful Classroom," *Teacher Talk* (http://education.indiana.edu/cas/tt/v2i3/peaceful.html; retrieved May 29, 2007).

We also do some "job-sharing," in which two children do a big job together. I have two mail carriers, two scrap monsters (to pick up scraps from the floor), a supply shelf manager, a library helper, a center inspector, a desk inspector, a pencil sharpener, an overhead projector cleaner, two lunch menu helpers, a table washer, a reading corner helper, a plant monitor, a chalkboard cleaner, a whiteboard cleaner, a sink cleaner, a math shelf helper (organizes math materials), a door holder (holds the door when we line up to go to special activities and for the chalkboard helper when he/she goes outside to clap erasers), and a substitute helper who does jobs of children who are absent.

I do have to assign jobs carefully; mail carriers and lunch menu helpers need to be able to read, and I often choose very active children to be scrap monsters and board cleaners. If you look around your room to see what kinds of things need to be done daily that your students can help with, your students will probably suggest some other jobs, too!

Source: Adapted from "A Classroom Job for Every Child," at http://atozteacherstuff.com/pages/5055.shtml.

THE TEACHING IDEAS BEHIND THIS STORY

A great deal of psychological research indicates that people, even young children, experience feelings of well-being and happiness when they have a sense of purpose and are of use. Psychologists suggest that this sense of well-being rests on individuals' ability to use their strengths and virtues in the service of something larger than themselves (Seligman, et al., 2005).

Enlisting your students in service to the classroom community gives them a sense of purpose and allows them to make a contribution to the whole. Even

When students have specific jobs, they feel more responsible to the class.

service learning A teaching and learning strategy that integrates meaningful community service with instruction and reflection to enrich the learning experience, teach civic responsibility, and strengthen communities.

in middle and high school, when your time with the students is of shorter duration, you can make this happen.

Beyond the classroom, your students may have the opportunity to engage in **service learning**—that is, community service done in collaboration with a larger project at the school. This type of learning not only connects students with the larger community, but it also forges bonds among the students as they collaborate to make a difference in their own neighborhoods.

WRITING and REFLECTION

Student Roles and Responsibilities

Think back to your own middle and high school experience.

- In what ways, if any, did students contribute to the management of the daily classroom routines and protocols?
- Did you have any service learning experiences? If so, reflect on what those experiences taught you.

Establishing Boundaries

Developing good relationships with your students requires setting appropriate boundaries. You want the classroom to belong to everyone; yet, as we noted earlier, you are the adult in the room, and you have a particular responsibility to make sure the environment is conducive to learning. You are not one of the kids. Sometimes new teachers, afraid of becoming their students' "friend," become overly authoritative and defeat their own attempts at creating community. Think about your own personality in this respect.

- Are you very authoritative, or are you shy?
- Do you anticipate having a difficult time reprimanding students or implementing the rules of the classroom?
- How can you act as the adult in the classroom and at the same time respect your students and make them feel valued and important?

PREVENTING HARASSMENT AND BULLYING

Successful teachers invite their students' lives, languages, and cultures into the classroom. They start building a classroom community on the first day of school. They care about their students, and they create an environment where social justice is both a goal and a reality.

In this type of environment, injustices toward individuals or groups of students become readily apparent. Two prominent examples of social injustice in today's schools are sexual harassment and bullying. This section explores these topics and discusses how you can help prevent them from endangering your classroom community.

Sexual Harassment in School

Under the guidelines established by the federal Office for Civil Rights, sexual harassment is considered a form of sex discrimination and is therefore prohib-

sexual harassment Unwelcome sexual advances, requests for sexual favors, or other physical and expressive behavior of a sexual nature that interferes with a person's life.

ited by Title IX of the Education Amendments of 1972. Generally speaking, **sexual harassment** is any "unwanted and unwelcome sexual behavior" that interferes with a person's life. Sexual harassment does not include "behaviors that you like or want (for example, wanted kissing, touching, or flirting)" (AAUW Educational Foundation, 2004, p. 11).

Sexually harassing behaviors happen in school hallways, stairwells, and classrooms, and they have a negative effect on the emotional and educational lives of students. In a 2000 federal survey, more than 36 percent of U.S. public schools reported at least one incident of sexual harassment (Dinkes, et al., 2006, p. 84). Eight in ten students experience some form of sexual harassment during their school lives. Eighty-five percent of students in grades eight through eleven say that students harass other students at their schools, and "almost 40 percent of students report that teachers and other school employees sexually harass students in their schools" (AAUW Educational Foundation, 2004, 2001).

On May 24, 1999, the Supreme Court ruled that school districts can be liable for damages under federal law for failing to stop a student from subjecting another student to severe and pervasive sexual harassment (Koch, 2002, p. 262). Title IX also guarantees that hostility and ridicule toward gay and lesbian students that is not immediately acted upon by the school or district may be grounds for a lawsuit against that district. See Table 9.1 for a simple checklist that you can apply to your school or district.

As a teacher, you need to learn about your school or district's policies concerning sexual harassment and teach them openly to your students. Make sure students know the sanctioned procedures for reporting abuse so that they do not needlessly suffer victimization by others. Many schools use role-playing scenarios or videos to prompt student discussion of sexual harassment issues.

TABLE 9.1   Sexual Harassment Checklist for Schools or School Districts

- Does your school/district have a specific policy against sexual harassment?
- Does your school/district foster an atmosphere of prevention by sensitizing students and staff to issues of sexual harassment?
- Is your school/district prepared to receive and respond to complaints?
- Does your school/district have a grievance procedure for sexual harassment?
- How effective has your school/district been in implementing its anti-harassment policy?

Source: Adapted from AAUW Educational Foundation. (2004). *Harassment-free hallways: How to stop sexual harassment in school.* Washington, DC: American Association of University Women Educational Foundation.

Types of Sexual Harassment

According to the Office for Civil Rights of the U.S. Department of Education, sexual harassment falls into two basic categories.

Quid pro quo sexual harassment occurs when a school employee causes a student to believe that he or she must submit to unwelcome sexual conduct to participate in a school program or activity. It can also occur when a teacher suggests to a student that educational decisions such as grades will be based on whether the student submits to unwelcome sexual conduct.

Hostile environment harassment occurs when unwelcome verbal or physical conduct is sufficiently severe, persistent, or pervasive that it creates an abusive or hostile environment for the affected student (Office for Civil Rights, 1997, 2001).

Establishing a sense of community with your students is a vital means of preventing harassment in school. When students feel responsible for one another and care about their learning community, harassing behaviors are less likely to occur—and when they do, they are less likely to persist. If your classroom community fosters an atmosphere of risk-free communication, your students will be better able to talk about alleged harassment and determine what to do.

Beyond the general principle of making respect central to your classroom culture, you should consider specific guidelines for student behavior that will help prevent sexual harassment. Often, well-meaning teachers ignore certain behaviors, especially in middle and high school, as long as they seem socially acceptable to the students themselves. For instance, teachers may decide that name calling and excessive flirting are "normal" for the students' age, when in fact these behaviors can be very disruptive to the victim's well-being. It is important to know how to respond to this type of occurrence. There are many surveys and checklists that help teachers and students recognize sexually harassing behavior. A checklist for teens might suggest, for example, that acceptable flirting makes you feel flattered, while harassment makes you feel unattractive or ashamed. The particular guidelines you adopt should take into account your students' age, the cultures represented in your classroom, and your school and district policies. See the Resources for Further Exploration section for some useful starting points.

LEARNING PROJECT

Supreme Court Decisions and Sexual Harassment

Explore the following Supreme Court cases: *Franklin v. Gwinnett* (1992), *Gebser v. Lago Vista Independent School District* (1998), and *Davis v. Monroe* (1999). (You can find information on the Web and also in the book by Nan Stein and Lisa Sjostrom listed in the Resources for Further Exploration section.) For each case, ask yourself:

• What were the circumstances of the case?

• What decision was reached by the High Court?

• What are the damages to be paid by the school or district?

• What are the implications of this case for sexual harassment in schools?

Bullying and Teasing

While creating community in the classroom is an important deterrent to negative student behaviors, teachers cannot be everywhere. Let's go back to Ms. Sanders's classroom, described earlier in this chapter. Despite the warm and caring environment promoted by her use of Morning Meeting, one of the students reported bullying and teasing in the playground at lunchtime. Because there is a longstanding tradition of the classroom or school bully, this problem is often overlooked. In fact, half of America's schoolchildren report being bullied at least once a week, and ten thousand children nationwide report staying home from school once a month because of a bully (Corcoran, 2002).

bullying Repeated cruelty, physical or psychological, by a powerful person toward a less powerful person.

Bullying implies repeated harmful acts and an imbalance of power. It can involve physical, verbal, or psychological attacks or intimidation directed against a victim who cannot properly defend him- or herself because of size or strength or because of being outnumbered or less psychologically resilient. Bullying includes assault, tripping, intimidation, rumor spreading and isolation, demands for money, destruction of property, theft of valued possessions, destruction of another's work, and name calling (Sampson, 2002). Figure 9.2, which focuses on teenagers, shows statistics about some of the prevalent types of bullying.

The most likely targets of bullies are gay students or students who are perceived to be gay (Corcoran, 2002). Homophobia, the fear of and intolerance toward homosexuals, is very much part of the culture of secondary schools.

Many antibullying programs have been put in place, including procedures that students can follow if they feel they are being bullied. Most of the time, however, students do not reveal that they are being bullied, and witnesses tend not to come forward. Although there are more male bullies and male victims, the numbers of female bullies and victims are on the rise (Olweus, 2003). Victimization by bullying has been linked to student depression, eating disorders, and even suicidal tendencies (Sears, 1991).

In classes where a strong sense of community has been created, the bullying victim is more likely to come forward, as are the witnesses. The emphasis is on the common good and on care and respect for one another.

Cyber-Bullying

In Chapter 7, we discussed the concept of Internet safety. Social networking is a way of life for our nation's youth. They are part of myriad online communities,

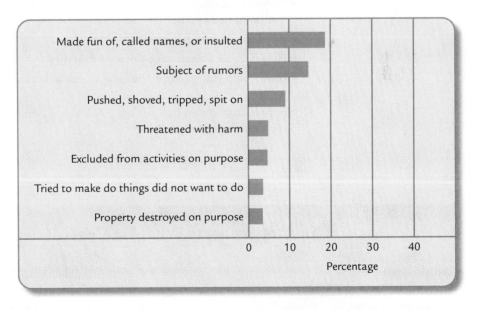

FIGURE 9.2

Percentage of Students, Ages 12 to 18, Who Reported Bullying Problems at School During the Previous Six Months

Source: Data from Dinkes, R., Cataldi, E. F., Kena, G., Baum, K., & Snyder, T. D. (2006). *Indicators of School Crime and Safety: 2006.* NCES 2007-003/NCJ 214262. Washington, DC: U.S. Government Printing Office.

and with all these opportunities to communicate online, there are hidden dangers. In chatrooms, people can pretend to be someone they are not and entice unknowing youngsters to meet them. This is a major source of Internet child and teen abuse, and many schools are adopting programs to warn their students about online sexual predators and establishing ways to report online solicitations. Internet crime is a crime like any other and should be reported to proper local, state, or federal authorities.

More prevalent than sexual predation, however, are nasty e-mails, texts, or website postings about an individual student. This phenomenon, known as **cyber-bullying**, can constitute a computer crime if it reaches a serious level. It is a federal crime to anonymously annoy, harass, threaten, or abuse any person via the Internet or a telecommunications system. Even at a less-than-criminal level, cyber-bullying can lead to the same traumatic effects as physical bullying does.

The most important action a student can initiate if she or he is experiencing cyber-bullying is to tell someone immediately. Many schools are promoting Internet safety programs, and a number of websites offer helpful tips for students (see the sidebar "Tips for Students Who Are Cyber-Bullied"). Creating a safe and trusting classroom community extends to protecting your students from online abuse. See the Resources for Further Exploration section at the end of this chapter for some useful research sites.

cyber-bullying Bullying or harassment through electronic means such as e-mail, website postings, text messaging, blogs, mobile phones, or pagers; also called *online bullying*.

WRITING and REFLECTION

Personal Reflections on Bullying and Harassment

- Do you remember a time when you or someone you knew was bullied or sexually harassed in school?
- What was the experience like?
- How did you or your acquaintance deal with it?
- How would you recognize bullying or sexual harassment in your own classroom?
- Females sometimes bully in less physical ways than do males. How would you describe female bullying?

Tips for Students Who Are Cyber-Bullied

- Tell a trusted adult.
- Never open, read, or respond to messages from people you know to be cyber bullies.
- If the problem is school related, tell your school. All schools have bullying solutions.
- Do not erase the messages. They may be needed to take action.

- If you are bullied through chat or instant messaging, the bully often can be blocked.
- If you are threatened with harm, call the police.

Source: Adapted from "Beware of the Cyber Bully," iSAFE America, http://www.isafe.org/imgs/pdf/education/CyberBullying.pdf; accessed May 29, 2007.

CLASSROOM COMMUNITY AND GOODNESS OF FIT

As we mentioned earlier, good classroom management requires that you be "fully conscious" in the classroom. It requires what Jacob Kounin (1970) called "withitness," a concept sometimes interpreted as having "eyes in the back of your head" to ward off any undesirable behavior. I prefer to think of "withitness" as a broad awareness that you have about yourself and your students together. Do you have a centered presence in the classroom? Are you aware of the students' dispositions on any given day as they enter your room? At any moment, do you know whether the principles of classroom community that you and the students have developed are working?

These are important matters to take into consideration when deciding on the "goodness of fit" between yourself and the teaching profession. Think about the following questions:

▶ Are you interested in learning more about students?

▶ Are you interested in learning more about yourself?

▶ Are you organized? Do you plan ahead?

▶ Do you have ideas about how you will act in front of a class?

▶ Can you foster an environment in which all voices can be heard and valued?

▶ Does the idea of checking in with your students at a Morning Meeting or a similar ritual sound appealing?

▶ Can you be fully conscious or "with it" in a large group of students?

▶ Do you believe you have the potential to be a role model for a younger, less empowered person?

▶ Can you give up center stage in order to have others share power with you?

▶ Are you willing to work hard and plan meaningful lessons, activities, and experiences so you can be prepared, even overprepared, for your students?

If your answers to all of these questions are "yes," then you are on your way to serving your students well.

CONCLUDING THOUGHTS

Clearly, good communication and collaboration with your students are vital for creating a classroom in which everyone feels responsible for managing the environment and working toward the common good. As a teacher, you should identify the most effective rules for your classroom and seek the students' assistance in establishing these as classroom priorities. When you involve your students in setting guidelines for everyone to follow, you help them buy into an environment where everyone can learn and occurrences like bullying and sexual harassment are stopped in their tracks.

Classroom community relates to the principles of teaching and learning we have discussed throughout this book. When you have your students work in groups, develop their own strategies for solving problems, and apply their concepts to meaningful real-world projects, you not only help them learn individually but you also foster their sense of the classroom as a learning community. When you honor diversity and use culturally relevant pedagogy, you create the same effect. All of these practices are good teaching methods *and* good classroom management strategies.

Finally, your ability to be honest with your students and to show your interest in their lives will go a long way toward earning their trust and turning the classroom into a safe place and a genuine learning community.

JOIN THE DISCUSSION

Visit the student website for this text and locate the Edublog for Chapter 9. Respond to the following questions:

➡ How does a new teacher establish a sense of authority in the classroom?

➡ In your judgment, what is the most important thing you can do to establish classroom community

CHAPTER CHALLENGE

An Ideal Classroom Community

Think of a classroom environment in which you would feel comfortable and respected, encouraged to learn and to participate. Make a list of the arrtibutes of that classroom. Next to each attribute, indicate the role the teacher would play in creating the environment.

- Do you think your teaching style and personality will affect your success in creating this kind of community? Why or why not?
- What physical structure do you imagine your classroom will have? How will it be arranged? How will that structure help you build community?
- What strategies will you employ to promote respect among your students?

FROM THE COLLEGE CLASSROOM TO YOUR OWN CLASSROOM

Your Plans for Creating a Classroom Community

There is a great deal of content to digest in this chapter. In your portfolio, include your plans for creating classroom community. Think deeply about how you will translate the principles we have discussed into your own practice. Be honest with yourself; if you have concerns, write about them.

RESOURCES FOR FURTHER EXPLORATION

Books

Kelley Dawson Salas, Rita Tenorio, Stephanie Walters, and Dale Weiss (Eds.), *The new teacher book: Finding purpose, balance and hope during your first years in the classroom* (Milwaukee, WI: Rethinking Schools, Ltd., 2004).   Compiled by new and beginning teachers, this is an excellent resource for establishing classroom communities.

Lisa Sjostrom and Nan Stein, *Bullyproof: A teacher's guide on teasing and bullying for use with fourth and fifth grade students* (Wellesley, MA: Wellesley College Center for Research, 1996).   This book helps teachers create classroom environments that involve students in making the classroom a safe space.

Nan Stein, *Classrooms and courtrooms: Facing sexual harassment in K–12 schools* (New York: Teachers College Press, 1999).   In addition to describing significant court cases involving school sexual harassment, this book addresses the responsibilities of schools and districts in preventing harassment.

Nan Stein and Lisa Sjostrom, *Flirting or hurting: A teacher's guide on student-to-student sexual harassment in schools (grades 6 through 12).* (Washington, DC: National Educational Association, 1994).   This is a helpful guide for understanding offensive peer interactions that create hostile environments in the classroom and the school. Nan Stein has also collaborated on a series of three short videos called "Flirting or hurting: Sexual harassment in schools."

Online Resources

Bullying: Facts for Schools and Parents http://www.naspcenter.org/factsheets/ bullying_fs.html   Sponsored by the National Association of School Psychologists, this page offers an overview of bullying and strategies for responding to bullying incidents. Also see the section of the site called "Behavior & Discipline."

It's My Life: Building a Classroom Community and Bully-Free Zone http://pbskids.org/itsmylife/parents/lesson_plans/bullies_classroom _community.html   From PBS, this website offers lessons and suggestions for building safe classroom spaces.

Harassment-Free Hallways: How to Stop Sexual Harassment in School http://www.aauw.org/ef/harass/pdf/completeguide.pdf   This downloadable booklet offers full guidelines for preventing and responding to sexual harassment.

Kidscape: Helping to Prevent Bullying and Child Abuse http://www.kidscape.org.uk/childrenteens/onlinesafety.shtml   This website provides important tips for staying safe in chatrooms, when using e-mail, and in text or video messaging.

Responsive Classroom http://www.responsiveclassroom.org/   This website describes the Responsive Classroom model and provides access to a number of other resources to foster social and academic learning.

What's the Most Important Thing I Can Do to Have a Well-Managed Classroom? http://www.nea.org/classmanagement/hwong.html   Harry Wong addresses your first day as a teacher and what you can do to establish classroom procedures and expectations.

Nancy Willard, *Educator's Guide to Cyberbullying and Cyberthreats* http://www.cyberbully.org/docs/cbcteducator.pdf   This brief online guide discusses common types of cyber-bullying and what to do about them.

CHAPTER 10

Making the Decision to Become a Teacher

FOCUSING QUESTIONS

▶ Why is public education vital to a thriving democracy?

▶ What are the most important roles of the teacher in the twenty-first century?

▶ What does the dictum that "one size does not fit all" say about teaching and about learning?

▶ What attributes do you have that make teaching the right choice for *you*?

▶ How much have you thought about your "goodness of fit" with the teaching profession?

▶ If you decide to pursue a teaching career, what steps lie ahead?

At this point in your journey, you would be correct to conclude that modern classrooms are complex places, that teaching is a highly sophisticated activity, and that a career in education requires careful planning, the capacity for spontaneous decision making, and actions based on careful personal reflection.

In this final chapter, we examine some of the tools you can use to decide if, in fact, teaching is a career you personally should be considering. There is rarely a moment of absolute certainty, but there are signs that can help you make your choice.

REFLECTING ON TEACHING

You have to love kids and want to connect with them—because if you don't connect with the kids, you will never be able to convey the materials; if you cannot feel the music, you cannot play the music. . . . I can teach anyone about pedagogical strategies but I cannot teach a person to love kids. And you can feel it in a classroom as soon as you walk in.

— Christopher Day (2004)

Take a few minutes to work through the sidebar inventory called "My Aptitude for Teaching." Your responses to questions like those in the inventory may change over time; however, it is important to address them and reflect on your own personal attributes as you consider a teaching career.

Research has found that people are often happier when they are making a contribution to others (Seligman, 2002), and that is certainly true of teaching. But there is also considerable evidence that people are more successful when they are engaged in work that plays to their strengths. If teaching does not play to your own strengths, perhaps it is not the best profession for you.

VIDEO CASE

Effective Teaching

Find the HM Video Case "Teaching as a Profession: What Defines Effective Teaching?" on the student website. In this video, several teachers and administrators talk about what makes an effective teacher. Consider their remarks and respond to the following questions:

- What theme recurs throughout the video?
- What types of intelligence are required to be effective in the classroom?
- Terms like *flexible, thoughtful, spontaneous, caring,* and *knowledgeable* emerge as significant attributes of teachers. How would you rank these in order of importance?

continued

- What is the role of a sense of organization and efficiency for the teacher?
- What skills do you think students need to be successful?

The Purposes of Public Education and the Role of the Teacher

Above all things, I hope that the education of the common people will be attended to, convinced that on their good sense we may rely with the most security for the preservation of a due degree of liberty.

— Thomas Jefferson, in a letter to James Madison, 1787

Chapter 3 described the vital role public education has played in American democratic society since the early days of the nation. As the preceding quotation from Thomas Jefferson indicates, American public schools have always been expected to fulfill certain public missions that go beyond the purely academic.

My Aptitude for Teaching: An Inventory

Many teachers fail to consider critical questions before becoming a teacher. Here are a few key questions you should be asking yourself.

- Do I like being around children and teenagers?

This sounds obvious, but many prospective teachers do not think about this question!

- Am I a listener or a talker?

If you are unsure, monitor yourself or ask friends and family. Listening and talking are both important to being an effective teacher. Sometimes, though, teachers talk too much; would that be your tendency?

- How good am I at listening to myself and others?

Personal reflection is a major requirement for becoming an effective teacher. So is the ability to listen carefully to what students have to say.

- Do I enjoy making a contribution to the social good?

Do you have a prior history of community or volunteer work?

- Do I like to be in control in social situations?

A strong need for control in group settings may be a danger signal for a prospective teacher.

- Do I like to participate in discussions and argue thoughtfully?

Willingness to engage in discussions is an important attribute for an effective teacher. This does not mean getting your own way but rather being a full participant.

- Do I like to help others even at an expense to my own convenience?

Successful teachers need generosity of spirit. After all, you are doing your work on behalf of others.

- Do I take pleasure in other people's success?

A generous spirit leads to authentic joy when others you care about achieve success.

- Am I comfortable working on projects in groups?

The ability to compromise and work with others toward a common goal is important for working with colleagues as well as students.

- Do I feel comfortable going along with the consensus of a group?

Many people are comfortable with teamwork as long as they get their own way, but when the group reaches a decision they do not like, they have a very different reaction. Because teachers often work in grade-level or disciplinary teams, group decisions influence their daily activities and routines in the classroom.

- Do I believe there are things I can learn from the students?

Teachers often like to position themselves as the "keeper of the true truth." Students, however, have many things to teach us, and now is a good time to think about what they might be.

Communication, collaboration, and connection are the hallmarks of twenty-first-century teaching and learning.

public education   Education that is publicly financed, tuition-free, accountable to public authorities, and accessible to all students. The term covers various types of public schools, including traditional schools, charter and magnet schools, vocational schools, and alternative schools.

Today, as you have seen throughout this book, **public education** serves the basic function of preparing young people to lead productive lives by increasing their academic achievement and improving their readiness to secure jobs in an increasingly global economy. In addition, however, public education helps equip our youth to become responsible and active citizens in a democratic society. In other words, it prepares them to participate in decisions that contribute to the social good (Center on Education Policy, 2007).

Although the current era of standards-based assessments emphasizes quantifiable academic achievement, it is useful to envision your career in education as serving a broader purpose. The Center for Education Policy (2007) describes the mission of public education in terms of six main themes:

1. To provide universal access to free education.

2. To guarantee equal opportunities for all children.

3. To unify a diverse population.

4. To prepare people for citizenship in a democratic society.

5. To prepare people to become economically self-sufficient.

6. To improve social conditions.

In Chapter 9, we explored how classrooms can create a sense of community, a social group mindful of the needs of each of its members. In this sense, creating classroom community becomes more than a tool for effective teaching and learning; it becomes a model for social justice and social participation in the microcosm of the classroom. Clearly, the important goals of education include helping students develop their abilities to think critically, appreciate diverse cultures, maintain curiosity about the world, and show confidence in expressing their own ideas.

In Chapter 1, we described teaching as an essential profession and reviewed a code of ethics developed by the National Education Association. Now that we have come to the end of this text, I invite you to think about the profession of teaching as requiring an overriding commitment by its members to the well-being of their students. Teaching is not an ordinary job. It is a profession that establishes our identities and reveals our values.

Most important, the functions and responsibilities of teachers are not confined to the classroom. Central to your work as a teacher is devoting time and energy to professional communities, activities, conferences, and workshops. Teaching is an opportunity for intellectual development, both through professional teacher development courses and through your own intimate contact with new books, ideas, and technologies. Actually, few teachers are successful who are not also intellectually curious.

Further, as you have seen in this text, teaching in the twenty-first century requires guiding students through the huge quantity of information that enters their lives on a daily basis. It is your job to help them understand what is valid and what needs to be discarded. These contemporary teaching needs make the teacher's role more complex and ever-changing than has been the case in any previous era. Luckily, you can find support through various professional organizations, such as those described later in this chapter.

One Size Does Not Fit All

In Chapter 3, when we explored the history of American public education and the many reform movements that have dotted the landscape of teaching and learning, we saw that American education is a large mosaic. Methods are varied, and successes and failures weave their way through each successive period of history. There is no one right way to teach; there are many right ways—and many incorrect ways as well. Just as there are multiple learning styles and learning profiles, teaching is as variable as the types and personalities of teachers.

The challenge is to imagine you are on a journey of both inward and outward exploration. You will explore your own personality traits, subject areas of expertise, capacity for generosity, and schooling stories. Try to remember the special moments that made you feel like school was the best place in the world. Also recall those times when being a student was painful or you were victimized by a teacher, knowingly or unknowingly.

One way to explore your thoughts about teaching is to examine artifacts you have saved from your school years—objects that symbolize "the teacher" to you. The following story by Mike Keany tells of one such artifact belonging to a school principal whose mother was a teacher.

TEACHING STORIES
AN ARTIFACT

Recently I had the opportunity to visit a wonderful new principal in her office. There, prominently and lovingly displayed on a bookshelf, was a true artifact of education. It was a chalk staff liner—a device in which five pieces of chalk were inserted and then drawn across the chalkboard to create lines on which to practice penmanship. (I understand music teachers still use this to create a musical staff.) Upon closer examination and explanation from the new principal, I came to learn that this was used by her mother for thirty-plus years in the same school in which this new principal first taught. We talked about its importance as an artifact and as a treasured keepsake. The principal explained that many curious young teachers who come into her office have no understanding of the device and often ask many questions about its use.

Over the weeks since that visit I find myself thinking often about that device and the connection it provides between generations. Despite our protestations, education really does connect the generations. Education is about handing down the knowledge of society from those who created it to those who will inherit it. . . .

As I reflect on that chalk staff liner, I know that some of the students you touch may accomplish great things for our world. Some will become poets, some doctors, and some will become caring parents. If we are lucky, and I think we will be, some will become the same type of wonderful educators [you strive to be] and the cycle will be renewed. It may not be a chalk staff liner that is cherished but your words, your deeds, or just your lessons.

Source: Keany, M. (2006). A message to the electronic community. From the Departmental Science LISTSERV (departmental-science@nassauboces.org), cosponsored by the Nassau Board of Cooperative Educational Services and the Long Island School Leadership Center, New York State, 12-19-06.

THE TEACHING IDEAS BEHIND THIS STORY

In the end, you will need to find your own way through the maze of information you gather about teaching. As Mike Keany's thoughtful writing suggests, one of your most useful tools is your capacity for reflection, along with your humility. It is profoundly moving to affect the lives of young people. It is also an extraordinary responsibility.

Find a way to connect with colleagues or classmates with whom you can have a conversation about teaching. Learning to teach is very much about having conversations and exchanging stories with willing colleagues. These discussions will help you discover the ways teaching will be a personal expression of yourself.

LEARNING PROJECT

A Thank-You Note

Write a letter to a teacher who inspired you, being sure to include the specific reasons he or she influenced you. Share your own desire to become a teacher, and state the ways you hope to emulate this person's practices. Because of gaps in distance or time, your letter may not actually reach the intended person; perhaps you won't even know where to mail it. You will, though, be adding to *your* story with this reflection on your desire to teach.

Creating a Culture of Caring

Many teachers talk about the importance of *caring* about students so that they see themselves as valuable and capable of learning. Creating a caring environment has a deep effect on you as well. Katy Ridnouer tells the following story, illustrating how an ethic of caring contributes to the life of a middle school teacher.

TEACHING STORIES
TEACHING WITH HEART

Although the United States trains more than enough teachers to meet its needs, the attrition rate for educators is higher than for any other professional occupation. According to a report from the National Commission for Teaching and America's Future, up to one-third of new U.S. teachers leave the profession within the first few years. I was one of them. In my second year, I taught eighth-grade language arts in a school full of challenges. I felt isolated, unsafe, and incapable, but I trudged on. I met with parents, I brainstormed with colleagues, and I discussed issues with members of the administration. Nothing changed. At the end of the year, I decided to leave teaching for the quiet solitude of the bookseller's life.

For six months or so, I convinced myself that I had made a good choice. Then the dreams about my classroom started. I was in front of my eighth graders, leading a grammar lesson. I saw their willing faces. I saw *them*. I then realized that I had expected everyone else to change while I remained the same. I expected the surly child to be pleasant, but I did nothing to encourage this behavior. I expected the underachieving child to work to his potential, but I did nothing to bring this about. I even expected the motivated child to stay motivated but did nothing to contribute to that end. My eyes opened, I returned to teaching, and I have never looked back.

I identify as a teacher. It's what I am meant to do, and it is as rewarding to me as art is to the artist, a great play is to the athlete, and the correct diagnosis is to the doctor. When I see students grapple with a concept and come away with new understanding of the material and a new respect for themselves, the long hours I invest hardly matter. . . .

Today, my guiding maxim as a teacher is to create a learning community within the four walls of the classroom. I define a learning community as a group of people who come together with a willing spirit to learn and support one another despite racial, economic, religious, and achievement differences. Learning communities promote curiosity, higher-level thinking, enhanced interpersonal skills, and confidence in both students and teachers. I have found that the key to creating a learning community is to *manage your classroom with heart*—and by that, I mean permeate the classroom atmosphere with caring concern. This involves care in interactions with students, lesson planning, seating chart decisions, discipline concerns, grading, and more. Putting care for your students first creates a learning community that inspires them to be their best selves, both in school and out in the world.

When I went back to the classroom, I changed the way I perceived my job. . . . Most significantly, I had to care about my students, which was something I hadn't really allowed myself to do before. Sure, I was friendly to them and I wanted them to succeed, but I can't say I was a caring teacher. Frankly, I saw caring as a risky venture. I worried that my feelings might be hurt if my students mocked my concern for them or if they didn't reciprocate it. I worried that I might get caught up in my students' personal concerns and neglect their academic achievement. I worried that the administration would think I had "gone soft." But on my second go-round, I decided to take the risk: to allow myself to care about my students—to nurture them and their learning. I am a happier teacher, a better teacher, and a richer human being because of it. My great hope is that by welcoming my students into my heart, I have enriched their lives.

Source: Katy Ridnouer, from the Introduction to *Managing Your Classroom with Heart: A Guide for Nurturing Adolescent Learners* (Alexandria, VA: Association for Supervision and Curriculum Development, 2006).

THE TEACHING IDEAS BEHIND THIS STORY

Katy Ridnouer's story is one of hope and resolve. She returned to the middle school classroom because she instinctively knew that was where she was meant to be. That intangible quality, that inner knowing, cannot be taught; it must be felt. She needed to revisit her desire to teach because, on the first go-around, she was not meeting with a sense of personal success.

Her story is a reminder that the early years of teaching confront us with many challenges. Working with young people is often unpredictable and can shake one's confidence. Feelings of frustration are not uncommon; however, they are often counterbalanced by a sense of profound accomplishment when students have that "aha" moment and demonstrate that they really "get it." This story reminds us that becoming proficient in our chosen profession takes time. Being patient with yourself as you begin is an important attribute.

The next story offers another perspective on a new teacher and the culture of caring she has created.

TEACHING STORIES
A NEW TEACHER, URBAN BLIGHT, AND A CULTURE OF CARING

Jaime Barron started teaching the fourth grade in an urban area where poverty is commonplace, most children are from minority backgrounds, and more than 90 percent have lived all or some of their lives in homeless shelters. The

continued

students come to school with very little social capital. Many are from single-parent families where their responsibilities include the care of younger siblings. All of the students receive free breakfast and lunch daily.

Since Jaime's experience with these fourth-grade students was very positive, she asked if she could "loop" with this class to fifth grade. (*Looping* is the process of sending an entire class together into the next grade level with the same teacher. In some school districts, it requires parental approval.) When I visited her and her class, it was the middle of the fifth grade, and the twenty-nine students were working in seven groups on projects that involved designing model ecosystems for different animals around the world.

Jaime's room is covered with print; student work hangs everywhere. There are posters hanging from clotheslines strung across the room. The posters explain group-work rules that include taking turns, listening to others, and offering ideas. For these students, working independently is a challenge, but they enjoy working on projects and accessing information on the computer, and they tell me they really like Ms. Barron.

The classroom is small and crowded, and there are not enough resources. The students have little knowledge about environments beyond their urban apartments and shelters. Doing group projects that construct environments far beyond their streets is a new experience for them. To aid their imagination, a world map hangs in the classroom. Their city is circled in red.

All the students, who range in age from ten to thirteen, appear to have a fundamental understanding that Ms. Barron cares about them. They respond to this. Each morning they bring her enormous plan book to her and ask, "What are we doing today?" They understand that she prepares for them. She is very calm and very firm; she never yells; she never takes unacceptable behavior personally. Jaime knows that the students with whom she works struggle in their environment. She reminds them of rules and structures they have developed to keep the class running smoothly and to maximize learning. The students tell me they feel safe in her class and are lucky to be with her. "She never yells." Jaime tells me there is little truancy in her class.

I ask Jaime if she will remain in this school next year, when her current students move on to middle school. Yes, she will stay, she explains, because she feels she is making a difference and she is needed here.

THE TEACHING IDEAS BEHIND THIS STORY

It will come as no surprise to you that, to Jaime Barron, teaching is much more than a job. It is an authentic commitment to working on behalf of her students. Her clarity about her purpose finds its way into the classroom community that she and her students have created. The students trust her and know she will not harm them, demean them, scream at them, or use her power over them. Her calm voice and caring manner are accompanied by classroom structures that keep the students productive and safe.

Jaime is extremely well prepared all the time. She consistently has a creative, activity-oriented experience in which to engage the class. She takes the students on field trips, monitors their homework, and works with them one-on-one during lunchtime.

Jaime also actively reflects on her teaching. For example, she was sorry that she did not begin the unit on ecosystems around the world, which was mandated by the grade-level curriculum, with an understanding of how the students' local urban ecosystem could be studied. She has some days that are worse than others, some days that are better, but throughout the ups and downs she loves her work and could not imagine doing anything else.

Looking Again at Multiple Ways of Teaching and Learning

Now that my five-year-old niece, Maren, has entered kindergarten, we have an ongoing philosophical discussion about education. "Teachers know everything," she says. "No," I say. "Teachers know some things. Nobody knows everything. There are some things you know that your teacher doesn't know." "Like what?" "Like what it feels like to be your Mommy and Daddy's oldest child, to be Gary's good friend, to be my five-year-old niece."

— Judy Logan (1997)

Throughout this text, we have visited different types of classrooms with varying approaches to teaching. As we have seen, studies in neuroscience show that, for a concept to get hooked into their prior knowledge, individuals need to construct meaning for themselves. We have explored project-based and problem-based learning as ways to place the students' own construction of knowledge at the center of their learning experience.

Many educators see "student-centered learning" as an "anything goes" method. On the contrary, student-centered environments seek to draw out students' ideas in order to deal with the misconceptions that often accompany the learning of something new. Unless we understand what students are thinking about the material in which we engage them, we cannot know if they "get it."

Do remember, however, that student-centered environments use multiple teaching strategies, ranging from direct explanations to problem-based and project-based learning. The successful teacher learns how to adapt the materials to the class in a way that reaches the individual students and asks them to do something to demonstrate their understanding. Hence, student-centered classrooms invite learners to create explanations, demonstrate meaning, and come up with their own ideas and questions related to the content area.

WRITING and REFLECTION

Demonstrating Understanding

One way to demonstrate your understanding of what it means to become a teacher is to complete an "I AM" poem. "I AM" poems ask the poet to state five different descriptions of himself or herself. We begin the poem by stating:

I AM . . . . A FUTURE TEACHER.

continued

Complete the following statements so as to reflect your understanding of becoming a teacher:

I wonder . . . . (two things you wonder about)
I hear . . . . (voices in your head)
I see . . . . (your vision for your professional self)
I want . . . . (what you hope for)
I AM . . . . A Future Teacher

Student projects become part of the fabric of the classroom.

Revisiting the Revolution in Technology

In earlier chapters, we emphasized the growing effect of technology on education. Connect, communicate, and collaborate—these are the three C's of the newest wave of technology use in the classroom. As you saw in earlier chapters, teaching can involve creating a class website the content of which is determined by collaboration among all the students. Students may use the website to publish digital videos related to a topic of study. With Web 2.0 technology, such as blogs and wikis, the user of content can readily add to the content. If you have contributed to the interactive blog set up for users of this textbook, you yourself have become a creator of important material through sharing your ideas about preparing to become a more effective educator. These are just a handful of the possibilities that technology brings to the classroom.

Technology offers two more benefits that are not always appreciated:

1. Learning is more powerful when students are prompted to take information presented to them in one form and "represent" it in an alternative way. The technology now available for teaching and learning helps students do just that. When students create their own representations of information, they provide clues about their thinking and give teachers a view of the accuracy of their conceptions.

2. You have seen the importance of recognizing that there are multiple intelligences and different learning styles. Technology can help students integrate information from multiple modalities, ensuring that all students, no matter what their learning style, have the opportunity to grasp key concepts.

The technology revolution has made collaborations across classroom, state, and country borders possible.

One way to gain insight into educators' use of technology is to visit teachers' blogs. In addition to providing helpful hints about technology use, these teachers are employing technology to further their own understanding of the profession, much as you are doing when you use the student website for this book. In the Resources for Further Exploration section at the end of this chapter, you'll find several recommended blog sites.

Consider your teaching role in a "flat" world and take an interest in other languages and the global community. Explore possibilities for linking your class with classes in different regions of the country or in foreign countries. Learn how to extend your classroom through videoconferencing, e-mail buddies, and other suggested strategies provided in Chapters 7 and 8. The opportunity to engage your students in communication on a global scale is one of the most exciting teaching challenges of the twenty-first century.

Google, the well-known search-engine company, sponsors a site called Google for Educators (http://www.google.com/educators/), which includes a number of online tools such as blog software and collaborative word-processing applications. The section on Google Earth, a satellite-mapping resource, includes suggestions for use in the classroom. Rip Van Winkle would not recognize these tools!

Get a head start and investigate technologies such as these. Look into the technological capacities of the schools or districts in which you find yourself observing and practice-teaching—and do the same when you get your first teaching job. Remember that your students will be deluged with data and that one of your critical roles will be helping them assess the value of the information to which they are exposed.

LEARNING PROJECT

Find Your Place

Explore Google for Educators (http://www.google.com/educators/) and sign up for teacher-relevant information. Examine the links on this website and respond to the following questions:

• Find your home or school on Google Earth. What do you think is the educational value of this technology?

An International Project on Global Warming

In one recent project involving Google for Educators, the company invited students and teachers to brainstorm ideas about combatting global warming. The website featured links to resources and tips on techniques for slowing the increase in the world's temperature. Participants submitted their ideas via the website. Ideas came in from upwards of eighty schools, more than half of them outside the United States. Eleven- to thirteen-year-old students at Ghana's Opoku Ware School, for example, suggested that farmers allow land to lie fallow to enable soil nutrients to regenerate. High school students in Romania suggested that scientists create hybrid plants that can survive extreme conditions.

Source: Adapted from Rhea R. Borja, "Google for Educators" unveils interactive tools for schools, *Education Week*, 26(13), November 29, 2006, p. 9.

- How could Google Apps help your school's communication matrix?
- In your opinion, which of the other tools on the Google for Educators site would be most useful for your classroom? Why?

Goodness of Fit

As you learned in Chapter 1, *goodness of fit* is a term used in descriptive statistics to mean a match between a theory and a set of observations. By using the term to refer to the match between a teacher candidate's attributes and the job of a teacher, this book has invited you to consider your own suitability for the teaching profession.

Think about what you have learned about teaching and what you have recognized about your personal attributes. Remember that there is no one definition of a "good" or "successful" teacher. There are several attributes, described in the inventory you took earlier in this chapter, that bode well for individuals seeking to become teachers. For instance, being a good listener and having generosity of spirit, as evidenced by your willingness to make a contribution to the social good, are excellent ingredients for a successful teacher. But you need to examine the realm of teaching and learning in all its complexity and consider how well it fits with your own dispositions.

The power of a teacher cannot be overestimated. You will be responsible for the education of tomorrow's thinkers and leaders, and you will learn the joy of making a contribution to other people's growth and development.

GETTING STARTED IN THE TEACHING PROFESSION

If you do make the decision to become a teacher, you will need to know about the types of field experiences that are required, professional certification and the various organizations that represent and support teachers. Although the exact process for becoming a teacher varies from state to state, the rest of this chapter will give you an overview.

The Field Experience

Your first experience in a classroom will probably be through your field placement. The field placement is an opportunity for you to serve as an apprentice and learn from the regular classroom teacher and from your own experience of working with the students.

In some field experiences, you are considered a *participant-observer*. While participating in the life of the classroom, you make careful observations and study the classroom environment to learn about child and adolescent development and teaching methods. Usually, participant-observers are not required to spend the entire school day in the field placement; rather, they must be immersed in the school for a specific number of hours each week.

In other field placements, you are considered a *student teacher*. In this arrangement, you are assigned to a teacher, usually called the "cooperating teacher," on a daily basis for a specified period of time, such as ten to twelve weeks. Student teachers at the secondary level often receive two placements, one in a middle school and the other in a high school. At the elementary level, depending on your state's requirements, you may receive one placement in grades K–2 and another in grades 3–5.

As a student teacher, you will be expected to teach the class at prearranged times. During some of these teaching experiences, you will be formally observed by a supervisor assigned by your institution. Student teaching is a special time when you develop a clear idea of what the life of a classroom teacher is all about. It is a very important part of your professional preparation.

Before you start your field experience, it is important to learn as much as possible about the school and classroom to which you have been assigned. (See "Tips for New Teachers," later in this chapter.) Be certain that you understand your role in the classroom and that you are aware of the dress code for teachers in the particular school. Ask questions. Be gracious, and be sure to thank the teacher in whose classroom you are gaining experience.

Certification and Standards

certification The process of obtaining state authorization to teach in the public schools.

Becoming a teacher in the public schools requires **certification** by your state. A state teaching certificate or license shows that you have met the state's requirements for becoming a teacher at specific grade levels and (especially for higher grades) in a certain subject area. For instance, your certificate might be for elementary education (grades K–6), for middle school social studies, or for middle school and high school biology.

Your state's Department of Education (DOE) website will describe the range of areas for which you can be licensed. Requirements for teacher certificates or licenses vary from state to state. Some states are relatively compatible with other states in their certification requirements; some states are more individualistic. Of course, your teacher education program will go a long way toward preparing you for state certification; but it is important to understand the certification requirements *beyond* completing your program.

The Praxis Tests

Praxis is the doctrine that when actions are based on sound theory and values, they can make a real difference in the world.
— Paulo Freire (1970)

the Praxis Series A series of assessments used by many states as part of the teacher certification process.

Most states require that future teachers pass a state exam or series of exams. The Educational Testing Service has developed **the Praxis Series** of professional assessments for beginning teachers. (As used by social scientists, the term *praxis* relates to action based on principles and theories that have a sound basis in research and experience.) A large number of states use this series of tests to assess your knowledge of subject matter and pedagogy.

The Praxis Series™ consists of three separate kinds of tests:

1. The Praxis I® tests measure basic academic skills in reading, mathematics, and writing. Usually you take these tests before entering your teacher education program or before your student teaching or internship.

2. The Praxis II® tests measure knowledge about specific subject areas and about principles of learning and teaching. Generally you take these tests when you complete your teacher preparation program.

3. The Praxis III® assessment focuses on actual classroom performance. In states that require Praxis III, it usually takes place in your first year of

teaching and leads to a higher level of certification. It includes direct observation of your classroom practice, review of a video or other documentation you send in, and interviews.

Several states offer their own assessments for certification and licensing, but these tests are typically similar to the Praxis tests. See the sidebar for sample Praxis test questions, and visit the Praxis website (http://www.ets.org/praxis/) to find out whether the state in which you hope to teach requires the Praxis test.

The INTASC Standards

Interstate New Teacher Assessment and Support Consortium (INTASC)
An organization that develops standards and principles to guide the preparation, licensing, and professional development of teachers. INTASC's members are state education agencies and national educational organizations.

Many of the requirements for certification are based on standards and principles developed by a national organization, the **Interstate New Teacher Assessment and Support Consortium (INTASC)**. Established in 1987, INTASC represents a combined effort by numerous state education agencies and national educational organizations to reform the preparation, licensing, and professional development of teachers. The consortium works from the premise that "an effective teacher must be able to integrate content knowledge with the specific strengths and needs of students to assure that *all* students learn and perform at high levels" (Council of Chief State School Officers, 2007).

Table 10.1 lists INTASC's model standards for beginning teachers. As you read these, remember that a large body of research supports the concepts behind what makes an effective teacher. The ten principles elucidated in Table 10.1 refer to instructional practices, personal skills associated with

Sample Questions for the Praxis II Test

The following samples illustrate the types of questions asked on the Praxis II test for the subject area called "Education of Young Children."

1. In which of the following situations is a teacher NOT behaving in a professional manner?

    (A) A teacher, when speaking on behalf of an educational organization, voices support for several of the organization's programs and policies that are in conflict with his or her personal belief.

    (B) A teacher who has identified some students who would benefit from additional exposure to literacy provides the names and addresses of those students to the subscription department of an educational magazine.

    (C) A teacher, concerned about a child's welfare, reveals confidential information to the school guidance counselor who may be able to act in the child's interest.

    (D) A teacher, having concerns about the professional behavior of a co-worker, meets informally with the colleague and attempts to resolve the matter collegially.

2. Which of the following placements for Michael, a child with extensive disabilities, is most consistent with the concept of "inclusion," as described in the IDEA legislation?

    (A) A setting that maximizes contact with other disabled children

    (B) A traditional early childhood program in which children with disabilities do not receive special services

    (C) The same educational program, with supports, that other children his age are receiving

    (D) A program that provides to each child with disabilities a trained paraprofessional who works one-on-one with the child

Source: Educational Testing Service. (2005). *The Praxis Series Test at a Glance: The Education of Young Children.* http://www.ets.org/Media/Tests/PRAXIS/pdf/0021.pdf; retrieved February 13, 2007.

Learning to teach requires observing, participating, and practicing in real classrooms.

TABLE 10.1	The INTASC Model Standards for Beginning Teacher Licensing, Assessment, and Development
Principle 1	*The teacher understands the central concepts, tools of inquiry, and structures of the discipline(s) he or she teaches and can create learning experiences that make these aspects of subject matter meaningful for students.*
Principle 2	*The teacher understands how children learn and develop, and can provide learning opportunities that support their intellectual, social, and personal development.*
Principle 3	*The teacher understands how students differ in their approaches to learning and creates instructional opportunities that are adapted to diverse learners.*
Principle 4	*The teacher understands and uses a variety of instructional strategies to encourage students' development of critical thinking, problem solving, and performance skills.*
Principle 5	*The teacher uses an understanding of individual and group motivation and behavior to create a learning environment that encourages positive social interaction, active engagement in learning, and self-motivation.*
Principle 6	*The teacher uses knowledge of effective verbal, nonverbal, and media communication techniques to foster active inquiry, collaboration, and supportive interaction in the classroom.*
Principle 7	*The teacher plans instruction based upon knowledge of subject matter, students, the community, and curriculum goals.*
Principle 8	*The teacher understands and uses formal and informal assessment strategies to evaluate and ensure the continuous intellectual, social, and physical development of the learner.*
Principle 9	*The teacher is a reflective practitioner who continually evaluates the effects of his/her choices and actions on others (students, parents, and other professionals in the learning community) and who actively seeks out opportunities to grow professionally.*
Principle 10	*The teacher fosters relationships with school colleagues, parents, and agencies in the larger community to support students' learning and well-being.*

Source: Interstate New Teacher Assessment and Support Consortium. (1992). *Model Standards for Beginning Teacher Licensing, Assessment, and Development: A Resource for State Dialogue.* Washington, DC: Council of Chief State School Officers.

communication, and commitment to the profession—all of which have been themes throughout this text.

The National Board for Professional Teaching Standards

As mentioned in Chapter 1, the National Board for Professional Teaching Standards (http://www.nbpts.org/) offers a national system for certifying teachers who meet rigorous standards. These standards are relevant to what you have already explored about teaching and learning. National Board Certified Teachers (NCBTs) embody these "Five Core Propositions":

▶ **Proposition 1:** Teachers are committed to students and learning.

▶ **Proposition 2:** Teachers know the subjects they teach and how to teach those subjects to students.

▶ **Proposition 3:** Teachers are responsible for managing and monitoring student learning.

▶ **Proposition 4:** Teachers think systematically about their practice and learn from experience.

▶ **Proposition 5:** Teachers are members of learning communities. (National Board for Professional Teaching Standards, 2002)

These are themes familiar to all those who are preparing to become teachers. The National Board has used these general propositions to establish standards for certification in many areas of teaching, from early childhood education through middle childhood education to the various academic specialties in secondary education. National Board standards are created by committees of educators who are accomplished professionals in their fields.

The process of becoming a National Board Certified Teacher is arduous and has many steps. To seek this certification, you must:

▶ Hold a bachelor's degree.

▶ Have three full years of teaching/counseling experience.

▶ Possess a valid state teaching/counseling license for that period of time, or, if you are teaching where a license is not required, have taught in schools recognized and approved to operate by the state.

Compared to an ordinary teaching certificate, National Board Certification is recognized in all states as a higher level of achievement. To obtain this certification, you must meet the requirements of a portfolio assessment that includes videotapes of your teaching, student work, and your accomplishments outside of your school experience. In addition, you must take an exam that assesses your content knowledge in your certificate area; there are test centers across the country.

Teaching Positions Here and Abroad

Teachers are in demand throughout the United States and all over the world. In the United States, the teaching areas in shortest supply include, but are not limited to, special education, bilingual education, earth science, chemistry, physics, mathematics and computer science, and foreign languages. Of course, these shortages vary by particular location and with population trends.

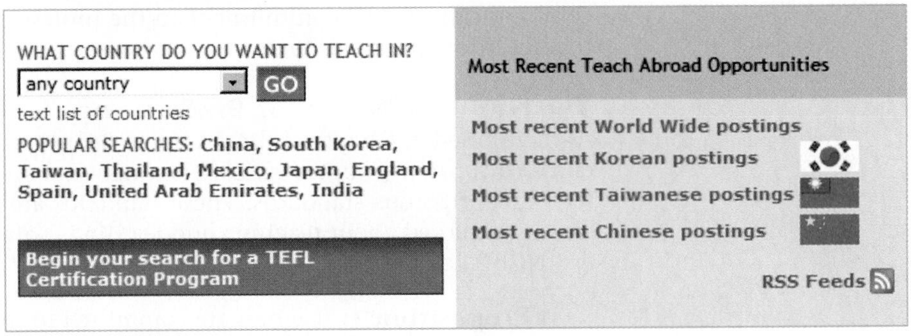

FIGURE 10.1

Part of a Screen from the Teach Abroad Website

Teach Abroad is one of a number of websites that offer information about overseas teaching positions and certification.

Source: http://www.teachabroad.com/. Retrieved April 7, 2007

As Chapter 8 indicated, though, the world has shrunk tremendously because of technology. You may want to challenge your thinking by going to a foreign country and gaining first-hand experience teaching there. If you make the decision to do this, it is wise to find others who have traveled this path before you and learn from them what the experience was like. There are groups of teachers who have taught abroad and can serve as resources for you. You can access these groups through teaching-abroad websites, such as the ones listed in the Resources for Further Exploration section at the end of this chapter.

What kinds of positions are available in foreign countries? Although there are teaching opportunities in all disciplines and languages, the majority of positions available are for native English speakers teaching English as a foreign language. To be eligible for these positions, you usually must hold a certificate for Teaching English as a Foreign Language (TEFL). Native English speakers may take an online course to become certified in TEFL. A number of websites, such as the one shown in Figure 10.1, list opportunities for teaching abroad and offer information about TEFL courses.

In addition, there are more than 300 American International Schools overseas. These are typically private, nonprofit schools based on an American or British model. Often, the schooling they provide leads to the International Baccalaureate (IB) diploma, an international credential that is offered at some schools in this country as well. To explore American International Schools, visit the International Schools Services website (http://www.iss.edu/). Half of the staff members at these schools are from North America.

Tips for New Teachers

As you begin your field work or your work in your own classroom, remember that as a teacher, you are an educational leader. Your teaching is as much a product of *who you are* as of how you implement strategies. The following list offers some tips as you get started.

▶ **Learn as much as you can about your school environment.** Do your homework. Be prepared. By that I mean learn everything you can about the school in which you will be doing your field placement work or getting your first teaching job.

▶ How long has the school been in this community?

▶ How many students and teachers are there?

▶ How many administrators are there?

▶ Who are the students? What types of homes, apartments, or other forms of housing arrangements do they live in?

▶ Can you expect a student body that is diverse ethnically? socially? economically? How many inclusion classrooms are there?

▶ How many networked computers are in each classroom?

▶ What does the school website have to say? Is this school or district known for any particular achievements?

▶ Do classes have their own websites?

▶ How do the students perform on mandated assessments? These scores are a matter of public record.

▶ If this is your field placement, from whom do you need permission?

▶ Are visitors and invited guests required to sign in? What is the correct protocol?

▶ **Keep a journal.**

▶ Write down your experiences as you begin. Include your fears and your questions. Record as much as possible about the experience of being in this particular class in this school.

▶ Remember to reflect on your days and your weeks as a teacher, and be fully conscious in the classroom. Journaling can help you stay conscious so you do not "shoot from the hip."

▶ **Join a collegial group, and find a friend.** Become part of a new-teacher group, either in your school or college or in your community. If you cannot find one that meets face to face, check for responsible groups online. In the most trying of times, it is often your colleagues who offer the most support and help you move forward. This point was made clearly by the teachers who shared their stories in Chapter 2.

If you are lucky, you will find one particular person in your new school with whom you can connect and share your experiences of teaching. This kind of relationship often builds into a lasting friendship.

▶ **Find a mentor.** Connect with an experienced teacher whom you trust, and communicate your hopes and fears to this person. Being a teacher means you are always a learner: learning about yourself, your content area, and your students. There is much to learn from mentors, so seek out a person who can fill this role for you.

▶ **Remember that teaching is not telling.** Teaching is not about you; it is about the students. Your focus should be on them. How will you engage them? What will you do on behalf of their learning?

▶ **Plan for creative experiences and activities.** Prepare lessons in which the students' active engagement is at the center, and listen to their ideas. Showing your students that you value what they think is priceless.

▶ **To create a safe environment, show that you are human.** Do not believe that you have to know everything and do everything right. Model vulnerability for your students; show them that you can laugh at your own mistakes. Students will feel more comfortable when you show that you are learning as well. This does not mean that you are not credible; it simply means that as humans we all make mistakes.

▶ **Be passionate.** Teachers express their passion for teaching in different ways, but being delighted to be with your students, coming in well prepared, and having a specific plan in mind are all ways to show the students that you care.

▶ **Differentiate instruction.** Remember that treating all students equally does not ensure equality of outcomes. Equitable and fair-minded teaching considers the ways all of our students, in all their diversity, learn best.

EDUCATIONAL ASSOCIATIONS

Dozens of professional organizations provide continuing support of one kind or another for teachers. These range from national associations that offer professional development resources to local union affiliates that may negotiate your next contract with the school district.

Professional organizations have the potential to create learning communities among their members. They offer rich resources for you to use in planning lessons and expanding your professional knowledge. Some of them also help improve your salary and working conditions and protect your professional rights.

Here we review two of the most prominent organizations, the American Federation of Teachers and the National Education Association. There are also many subject- and grade-level-specific groups that provide resources, grants, and guidance for you as you begin your professional career; see the Resources for Further Exploration section in Chapter 2 for a list.

The American Federation of Teachers

The American Federation of Teachers, a union affiliated with the American Federation of Labor and Congress of Industrial Organizations (AFL-CIO), was

The Vision of the AFT

The following passage helps explain the AFT's overall goals and principles.

As a community of professionals in unison with all working people, we are committed collectively to advancing human rights, opportunity, social and economic justice, freedom of conscience and expression, unfettered civic and political participation, fairness at work, tolerance, democracy, and security at home and abroad. The AFT stands for the right of individuals everywhere to form and participate in voluntary democratic, civic, cultural, religious, and fraternal institutions for self-help, worship, advocacy, and mutual support.

Source: American Federation of Teachers. (2007). A vision that endures. http://www.aft.org/about/vision.htm; retrieved February 7, 2007.

founded in 1916 to represent the interests of classroom teachers. Its first member, John Dewey, recognized the importance of teachers' having their own organization. Today, one visit to the organization's website (http://www.aft.org/) reveals a wealth of resources for the classroom teacher and for other education personnel as well. For example, the site provides information about professional development opportunities and grants.

In addition to being a valuable resource, the AFT directly represents teachers in many school districts around the country. The organization has 43 state affiliates, more than 3,000 local affiliates, and more than 1.3 million members. You may find, particularly if you teach in a large urban school system, that the AFT negotiates contracts for the teachers and other school employees in your district. If so, you will probably become a member of the union, and you may want to take an active role in the local affiliate.

The National Education Association

The National Education Association, founded in 1857, now has approximately 3 million members and more than 14,000 local affiliates. In addition to its Code of Ethics, described in Chapter 1, the NEA provides job searches, teaching tips and tools, important resources for your professional development, and activities and workshops of interest in your state. The organization's website (http://www.nea.org/) is a valuable point of entry to these resources.

Since the 1960s, the NEA has functioned as a union, conducting collective bargaining on behalf of teachers and working to protect teachers' rights as employees of a school district. It also acts as a lobbying organization on educational issues, and it helps set professional standards for the teaching profession.

Most teachers belong to either the AFT or the NEA, and some belong to both. Your decision about membership may be governed in part by local conditions, such as which organization represents the teachers at your school. Remember that an important benefit of membership is that it provides links with other teachers for professional collaboration.

FROM THE COLLEGE CLASSROOM TO YOUR OWN CLASSROOM: BUILDING YOUR TEACHING PORTFOLIO

Throughout this text, you have been asked to reflect on the topics addressed in each chapter as a way of compiling your teaching portfolio. Developing a portfolio is an excellent way to organize your thinking about teaching and to display some of your accomplishments on this journey. You should continue to update the portfolio each year you teach. It is your professional and personal record, and it demonstrates your knowledge and beliefs as well as your accomplishments. What you choose to include in your portfolio is a statement of what you think is important.

When you begin to look for a job, you will need a version of your portfolio to present to prospective employers. Many of the previous chapters' portfolio suggestions can find a place in this presentation version, and so can your response to the Chapter Challenge at the end of this chapter. The portfolio you show others should be concise, clear, readable, and well organized.

Here are some further suggestions for preparing your portfolio.

▶ Keep your documents in a three-ring binder; you will add or remove material as time goes on. The binder should be neat and visually appealing—not artsy-craftsy, but attractive and professional.

▶ Include a table of contents so that viewers can skip to parts that particularly concern them.

▶ Begin with a short essay introducing yourself. In a few paragraphs, describe your interest in teaching and learning and what you have accomplished. See the sidebar for a sample introductory essay.

▶ Describe your educational philosophy; that is, what you believe a good teacher needs to understand about teaching and learning.

▶ Discuss your classroom management theory. If your focus is on building community in the classroom, be specific about how you plan to do that.

▶ Describe your student teaching experience with specific mention of the grade levels you taught and the lessons and activities you prepared. If you have copies of supervisors' observations that attest to your abilities, include them.

▶ Include a few samples of student work from your field experience.

▶ If you have approved photos of yourself and a class in action, or even a brief video (about four minutes long) that you have burned on a DVD, include them. ("Approved" means that you have received consent forms from the other people shown in the photos or video.)

▶ Include your resume, certifications, awards, and letters of reference.

▶ Have all the material available electronically, either on a personal professional website that you have developed or on a CD that you give to the interviewer.

▶ Do not overdo it. We live in a fast-paced culture, and people do not have a great deal of time to read your portfolio. Be concise and to the point.

A Sample Introductory Essay for a Teaching Portfolio

I have just graduated from Hofstra University, where I majored in biology and secondary education. I have always loved science and enjoy sharing it with others. I have had experience student teaching in grades 7–9 and 10–11. My certification area in biology and general science prepares me to teach grades 7–12 in New York State. I have passed all the exams and requirements for this initial certification.

For my field experience, I have been a participant-observer in grades 8 and 11, and I feel equally comfortable in the middle school and the high school. I have also spent two summers as a counselor at an environmental education camp in Maine, where I enjoyed working with teenagers in a natural setting. I believe my organizational skills, my ability to plan, my understanding of the content area, and my passion for teaching will enable me to be a successful new teacher.

CONCLUDING THOUGHTS

A noted author (Friedman, 2006) talks about something he calls the "passion quotient" for teaching. He tells the story of a young child who receives his or her first fire truck or doctor's kit and wants to be a fireman or a doctor. That innocent passion for a certain job, without knowing the salary or the working hours or the preparation required, is what you need to get back in touch with. You need to discover your inner passion, and when you find it, you will know it.

You may already know that your passion is teaching, in which case you will be eager to explore the professional organizations described in this chapter. Or you may still be searching and wondering. If we are going to be successful, what we select as our life's work must bring us joy, especially if it is teaching. Remember, it is fine to change your mind and say, "I thought this was for me, but now I see I'm better suited to another career."

I want to remind you, though, that teaching is wonderfully satisfying work. The feeling you get when you realize that you have made a contribution on behalf of someone else's development is indescribable. I remember my first year of teaching like it was yesterday. I was nervous, overprepared, and in the end overjoyed. Although I needed the paycheck (which in 1966 was quite meager), I used to forget to pick it up at the main office of the junior high where I taught science. The school secretary used to tease me, but one day she gave me a wonderful compliment. She said, "Judging by the smile I always see on your face, I can tell that you get paid for this job in other ways." I was touched by this statement (although my landlord, of course, needed payment in cash).

Becoming a teacher is a commitment to a life of service that has the potential to bring you great joy and personal satisfaction. My best wishes to you on this journey.

JOIN THE DISCUSSION

Visit the student website for this text and locate the Edublog for Chapter 10. Respond to the following questions:

➡ How did you assess your aptitude for teaching after responding to the inventory of questions early in this chapter?

➡ What do you think of the INTASC standards? Which one(s) are you most confident that you have already achieved?

CHAPTER CHALLENGE

Your Decision About Teaching

Write a 400-word essay describing why you believe your decision to become a teacher represents a "good fit" with the profession—or not.

RESOURCES FOR FURTHER EXPLORATION

General Professional Resources

Karen A. Bosch and Katharine C. Kersey, *The first-year teacher: Teaching with confidence,* **rev. ed.** (New York: National Education Association, 2000). Available from the National Education Association's online bookstore (http://store.nea.org/), this book helps answer many questions for first-year teachers who are moving from the college campus to their own classrooms.

A candidate's guide to National Board certification. http://www.nea.org/ or http://www.aft.org/.   Available at both the AFT website and the NEA website, this booklet complements the resource materials provided by the National Board for Professional Teaching Standards.

Electronic Portfolios http://www.electronicportfolios.org/   This website gives important information about the application and development of electronic portfolios for interviewing, teaching, and continued professional development.

Katy Ridnouer, *Managing your classroom with heart: A guide for nurturing adolescent learners* (Alexandria, VA: Association for Supervision and Curriculum Development, 2006).   A fine book that discusses topics like "balancing care and discipline," "handling common challenges," and "expectations and accountability."

Teacher Leaders Network http://www.teacherleaders.org/   This network supports teachers as they explore professional development through meaningful conversations with educators from around the country. It is sponsored by the Center for Teaching Quality in Hillsborough, North Carolina.

Technology and Blogs

Cal Teacher Blog http://calteacherblog.blogspot.com/   Offering inspirations and comments from new and seasoned teachers, this website is a source of good, interesting ideas on a wide range of topics.

Google for Educators http://www.google.com/educators/   You will find a link to Google Earth, teacher blogs, and much more on this useful website.

Teacher Magazine: Blogboard http://blogs.edweek.org/teachers/blogboard/   A selection of the "new and noteworthy" in educators' blogs, with links to many educational resources.

Teachers Teaching Teachers http://teachersteachingteachers.org/   This site provides current information on the uses of blogging, podcasting, webcasting, and Skype for teachers and students.

Teaching Abroad

International Schools Services http://www.iss.edu/   This website is the primary resource for seeking teaching positions in American International Schools around the world. There are four International Recruitment Centers at different locations each year, and registering with ISS provides you with current information on job availability.

Teach Abroad http://www.teachabroad.com/   This site lists specific job opportunities abroad as well as training programs and other opportunities.

Professional Organizations

See the Resources for Further Exploration section in Chapter 2 for a list of professional organizations devoted to specific subject areas.

American Federation of Teachers (AFT) http://www.aft.org/   In addition to a wealth of resources for teachers, this site offers a brief history of the movement for teacher unions.

Association for Supervision and Curriculum Development (ASCD) http://www.ascd.org/   An international, nonprofit association of professional educators who work across all grade levels and subject areas.

National Board for Professional Teaching Standards (NBPTS) http://www.nbpts.org/   Here you can read more about the Five Core Propositions and explore the requirements for NBPTS certification.

National Education Association (NEA) http://www.nea.org/   Check the NEA's summary of current issues in education. Do you agree with the positions the NEA has staked out?

Taking Stock

Assessing Where You Are and Where You're Going

1. Describe a time when you experienced a classroom as a community. How did the teacher create it? How did it feel to belong to this community?

2. What are the greatest personal challenges you need to overcome to build community in your classroom?

3. What is the meaning behind the statement "Good teaching leads to good classroom management"?

4. Which of the ten INTASC principles will be most challenging for you as you become a teacher?

5. What level of passion do you feel about teaching? Why is that important?

6. What would be your greatest challenge in teaching abroad? How appealing is the possibility of teaching abroad for you?

7. Briefly, what have you concluded from your evaluation of your "goodness of fit" with the teaching profession?

8. Start your introductory essay for your teaching portfolio. Draft the first two or three sentences.

GOOD LUCK!

Appendix A

State Education Offices

To find out more about your state's or territory's requirements for teacher certification or licensure, contact the department of education or visit its website. Here is a list of names and addresses to get you started.

Alabama

Alabama Department of Education
Gordon Persons Office Building
50 North Ripley Street
P.O. Box 302101
Montgomery, AL 36104–3833
Phone: (334) 242–9700
Website: http://www.alsde.edu/html/home.asp

Alaska

Alaska Department of Education and Early Development
801 West 10th Street, Suite 20
P.O. Box 110500
Juneau, AK 99811–0500
Phone: (907) 465–2800
TTY: (907) 465–2815
Website: http://www.eed.state.ak.us/

Arizona

Arizona Department of Education
1535 West Jefferson Street
Phoenix, AZ 85007
Phone: (602) 542–5393
Toll-free: (800) 352–4558
Website: http://www.ade.az.gov/

Arkansas

Arkansas Department of Education
4 Capitol Mall
Little Rock, AR 72201–1071
Phone: (501) 682–4475
Website: http://ArkansasEd.org/

California

California Department of Education
1430 N Street
Sacramento, CA 95814–5901
Phone: (916) 319–0800
Website: http://www.cde.ca.gov/

Colorado

Colorado Department of Education
201 East Colfax Avenue
Denver, CO 80203–1799
Phone: (303) 866–6600
Website: http://www.cde.state.co.us/

Connecticut

Connecticut State Department of Education
165 Capitol Avenue
Hartford, CT 06106–1630
Phone: (860) 713–6543
Toll-free: (800) 465–4014
Website: http://www.sde.ct.gov/sde/site/default.asp

Delaware

Delaware Department of Education
Townsend Building
401 Federal Street, Suite 2
Dover, DE 19901–3639
Phone: (302) 735–4000
Website: http://www.doe.state.de.us/

District of Columbia

District of Columbia Public Schools
825 North Capitol Street, NE
Washington, DC 20002
Phone: (202) 442–5885
Website: http://www.k12.dc.us/

Florida

Florida Department of Education
Turlington Building
325 West Gaines Street, Suite 1514
Tallahassee, FL 32399–0400
Phone: (850) 245–0505
Website: http://www.fldoe.org/

Georgia

Georgia Department of Education
2054 Twin Towers East
205 Jesse Hill Jr. Drive SE
Atlanta, GA 30334–5001
Phone: (404) 656–2800
Toll-free: (800) 311–3627 (Georgia residents only)
Website: http://public.doe.k12.ga.us/index.aspx

Guam

Guam Public School System
P.O. Box DE
Hagåtña, GU 96932
Phone: (671) 475–0495
Website: http://www.gdoe.net/

Hawaii

Hawaii Department of Education
1390 Miller Street
Honolulu, HI 96813
Phone: (808) 586–3230
Website: http://doe.k12.hi.us/

Idaho

Idaho State Department of Education
650 West State Street
P.O. Box 83720
Boise, ID 83720–0027
Phone: (208) 332–6800
Toll-free: (800) 432–4601 (Idaho residents only)
TTY: (800) 377–3529
Website: http://www.sde.state.id.us/Dept/

Illinois

Illinois State Board of Education
100 North First Street
Springfield, IL 62777
Phone: (217) 782–4321
Toll-free: (866) 262–6663 (Illinois residents only)
TTY: (217) 782–1900
Website: http://www.isbe.net/

Indiana

Indiana Department of Education
State House, Room 229
Indianapolis, IN 46204–2798
Phone: (317) 232–6610
Website: http://www.doe.state.in.us/

Iowa

Iowa Department of Education
Grimes State Office Building
400 East 14th Street
Des Moines, IA 50319–0146
Phone: (515) 281–3436
Website: http://www.state.ia.us/educate/

Kansas

Kansas State Department of Education
120 SE 10th Avenue
Topeka, KS 66612–1182
Phone: (785) 296–3201
TTY: (785) 296–6338
Website: http://www.ksde.org/

Kentucky

Kentucky Department of Education
500 Mero Street
Frankfort, KY 40601–1957
Phone: (502) 564–4770
TTY: 502–564–4970
Website: http://www.education.ky.gov/

Louisiana

Louisiana Department of Education
1201 North Third Street
P.O. Box 94064
Baton Rouge, LA 70804–9064
Phone: (225) 342–4411
Toll-free: (877) 453–2721
Website: http://www.louisianaschools.net/

Maine

Maine Department of Education
Burton M. Cross State Office Building
111 Sewall Street
23 State House Station
Augusta, ME 04333–0023
Phone: (207) 624–6600
TTY: (888) 577–6690
Website: http://www.maine.gov/education/

Maryland

Maryland State Department of Education
200 West Baltimore Street
Baltimore, MD 21201
Phone: (410) 767–0100
Website: http://www.marylandpublicschools.org/
    MSDE/

Massachusetts

Massachusetts Department of Education
350 Main Street
Malden, MA 02148–5023
Phone: (781) 338–3000
TTY: (800) 439–2370
Website: http://www.doe.mass.edu/

Michigan

Michigan Department of Education
608 West Allegan Street
P.O. Box 30008
Lansing, MI 48909
Phone: (517) 373–3324
Website: http://www.michigan.gov/mde/

Minnesota

Minnesota Department of Education
1500 Highway 36 West
Roseville, MN 55113–4266
Phone: (651) 582–8200
TTY: (651) 582–8201
Website:
http://education.state.mn.us/mde/index.html

Mississippi

Mississippi Department of Education
Central High School Building
359 North West Street
P.O. Box 771
Jackson, MS 39205
Phone: (601) 359–3513
Website: http://www.mde.k12.ms.us/

Missouri

Missouri Department of Elementary and Secondary
Education
205 Jefferson Street
P.O. Box 480
Jefferson City, MO 65102–0480
Phone: (573) 751–4212
TTY: (800) 735–2966
Website: http://dese.mo.gov/

Montana

Montana Office of Public Instruction
P.O. Box 202501
Helena, MT 59620–2501
Phone: (406) 444–3095
Toll-free: (888) 231–9393 (Montana residents only)
Website: http://www.opi.mt.gov/

Nebraska

Nebraska Department of Education
301 Centennial Mall South
P. O. Box 94987
Lincoln, NE 68509–4987
Phone: (402) 471–2295
TTY: (402) 471–7295
Website: http://www.nde.state.ne.us/

Nevada

Nevada Department of Education
700 East Fifth Street
Carson City, NV 89701–5096
Phone: (775) 687–9200
Website: http://www.doe.nv.gov/

New Hampshire

New Hampshire Department of Education
Hugh J. Gallen State Office Park
101 Pleasant Street
Concord, NH 03301–3860
Phone: (603) 271–3494
Toll-free: (800) 339–9900
TTY: Relay NH: 711
Website: http://www.ed.state.nh.us/

New Jersey

New Jersey Department of Education
100 Riverview Plaza
P.O. Box 500
Trenton, NJ 08625–0500
Phone: (609) 292–4469
Website: http://www.state.nj.us/education/

New Mexico

New Mexico Public Education Department
300 Don Gaspar
Santa Fe, NM 87501–2786
Phone: (505) 827–5800
Website: http://www.ped.state.nm.us/

New York

New York State Education Department
Education Building
89 Washington Avenue
Albany, NY 12234
Phone: (518) 474–5844
Website: http://www.nysed.gov/

North Carolina

North Carolina Department of Public Instruction
301 North Wilmington Street
Raleigh, NC 27601–1058
Phone: (919) 807–3300
Website: http://www.ncpublicschools.org/

North Dakota

North Dakota Department of Public Instruction
Department 201
600 East Boulevard Avenue
Bismarck, ND 58505–0440
Phone: (701) 328–2260
Website: http://www.dpi.state.nd.us/

Ohio

Ohio Department of Education
25 South Front Street
Columbus, OH 43215–4183
Phone: (614) 466–4839
Toll-free: (877) 644–6338
TTY: (888) 886–0181
Website: http://www.ode.state.oh.us/

Oklahoma

Oklahoma State Department of Education
2500 North Lincoln Boulevard
Oklahoma City, OK 73105–4599
Phone: (405) 521–3301
Website: http://sde.state.ok.us/

Oregon

Oregon Department of Education
255 Capitol Street NE
Salem, OR 97310–0203
Phone: (503) 947–5600
TTY: (503) 378–2892
Website: http://www.ode.state.or.us/

Pennsylvania

Pennsylvania Department of Education
333 Market Street
Harrisburg, PA 17126–0333
Phone: (717) 783–6788
TTY: (717) 783–8445
Website: http://www.pde.state.pa.us/

Puerto Rico

Puerto Rico Department of Education
P.O. Box 190759
San Juan, PR 00919–0759
Phone: (787) 759–2000
Website: http://www.de.gobierno.pr/

Rhode Island

Rhode Island Department of Elementary and
Secondary Education
255 Westminster Street
Providence, RI 02903–3400
Phone: (401) 222–4600
TTY: (800) 745–5555
Website: http://www.ridoe.net/

South Carolina

South Carolina Department of Education
1429 Senate Street
Columbia, SC 29201
Phone: (803) 734–8500
Website: http://ed.sc.gov/

South Dakota

South Dakota Department of Education
700 Governors Drive
Pierre, SD 57501–2291
Phone: (605) 773–3134
TTY: (605) 773–6302
Website: http://doe.sd.gov/

Tennessee

Tennessee State Department of Education
Andrew Johnson Tower, Sixth Floor
710 James Robertson Parkway
Nashville, TN 37243–0375
Phone: (615) 741–2731
Website: http://www.state.tn.us/education/

Texas

Texas Education Agency
William B. Travis Building
1701 North Congress Avenue
Austin, TX 78701–1494
Phone: (512) 463–9734
TTY: (512) 475–3540
Website: http://www.tea.state.tx.us/

Utah

Utah State Office of Education
250 East 500 South
P.O. Box 144200
Salt Lake City, UT 84114–4200
Phone: (801) 538–7500
Website: http://www.schools.utah.gov/

Vermont

Vermont Department of Education
120 State Street
Montpelier, VT 05620–2501
Phone: (802) 828–3135
TTY: (802) 828–2755
Website: http://www.education.vermont.gov/

Virginia

Virginia Department of Education
P. O. Box 2120
James Monroe Building
101 North 14th Street
Richmond, VA 23218–2120
Phone: (804) 225–2420
Website: http://www.doe.virginia.gov/

Virgin Islands

Virgin Islands Department of Education
44–46 Kongens Gade
Charlotte Amalie, VI 00802
Phone: (340) 774–2810
Website: http://www.doe.vi/

Washington

Office of Superintendent of Public Instruction
Old Capitol Building
600 South Washington
P.O. Box 47200
Olympia, WA 98504–7200
Phone: (360) 725–6000
TTY: (360) 664–3631
Website: http://www.k12.wa.us/

West Virginia

West Virginia Department of Education
Building 6, Room 358
1900 Kanawha Boulevard East
Charleston, WV 25305–0330
Phone: (304) 558–2681
Website: http://wvde.state.wv.us/

Wisconsin

Wisconsin Department of Public Instruction
125 South Webster Street
P.O. Box 7841
Madison, WI 53707–7841
Phone: (608) 266–3108
Toll-free: (800) 441–4563
TTY: (608) 267–2427
Website: http://dpi.wi.gov/

Wyoming

Wyoming Department of Education
Hathaway Building, Second Floor
2300 Capitol Avenue
Cheyenne, WY 82002–0050
Phone: (307) 777–7690
TTY: (307) 777–8546
Website: http://www.k12.wy.us/

APPENDIX B

ORGANIZATIONS YOU MAY WANT TO JOIN

The following organizations provide useful resources and networking for new teachers and also for prospective teachers who have not yet started their careers. Many offer reduced membership rates for students.

General Organizations

American Educational Research Association (AERA)

http://www.aera.net/

Formed to promote the scholarly study of educational issues, AERA has 25,000 members. In addition to publishing books and several leading journals, the organization offers grants and fellowships and organizes conferences. A division called the Graduate Student Council sponsors activities especially for graduate students in education-related fields.

American Federation of Teachers (AFT)

http://www.aft.org/

With more than 1.3 million members, the AFT provides all the services of a union as well as a number of important publications and news updates.

Association for Supervision and Curriculum Development (ASCD)

http://www.ascd.org/

Designed not just for educational administrators but also for teachers, ASCD offers web seminars and online courses; publishes books, journals, newsletters, and videos; and conducts a variety of workshops and conferences.

International Society for Technology in Education (ISTE)

http://www.iste.org/

Publishes the National Educational Technology standards for teachers, students, and administrators along with a wealth of supporting materials. Members receive ISTE periodicals, get discounts on other publications, and can join special interest groups, such as one devoted to digital equity or special education technology.

National Catholic Educational Association (NCEA)

http://www.ncea.org/

An organization that serves 200,000 Catholic educators throughout the United States.

National Education Association (NEA)

http://www.nea.org/

With more than 3 million members, the NEA is the largest educational organization in the United States. Members can benefit from insurance programs, discussion forums, online professional development resources, and discounts on items ranging from magazines to rental cars.

National Middle School Association (NMSA)

http://www.nmsa.org/

This association offers periodicals, professional development opportunities, and conferences for those interested in the middle grades.

Organizations for Specific Areas and Disciplines

American Alliance for Health, Physical Education, Recreation and Dance (AAHPERD)

http://www.aahperd.org/

An umbrella organization that represents the interests of a variety of professionals working in physical or health education, AAHPERD sponsors an online career center accessible through its main website.

American Council on the Teaching of Foreign Languages (ACTFL)

http://www.actfl.org/

This association publishes periodicals, sponsors an online Career Center, and offers professional development workshops for foreign language teachers.

Council for Exceptional Children (CEC)

http://www.cec.sped.org/

Dedicated to improving education for students with disabilities or gifts, CEC publishes books and journals, offers resources for finding a job in the field, and has hundreds of local chapters.

Council for Learning Disabilities (CLD)

http://www.cldinternational.org/

This organization brings together parents and educators interested in learning disabilities. Members receive two free research journals and discounts on others, as well as the opportunity to attend conferences.

International Reading Association

http://www.reading.org/

Focusing on educators interested in any aspect of literacy, this association offers publications, meetings, and online resources.

National Art Education Association (NAEA)

http://www.naea-reston.org/

This association sponsors an annual convention for art educators and publishes periodicals in the field.

National Association for Gifted Children (NAGC)

http://www.nagc.org/

This association serves parents and administrators as well as teachers of gifted children by providing publications, professional development academies, and an Advocacy Toolkit.

National Association for Music Education (MENC)

http://www.menc.org/

This association publishes several journals, sponsors a Job Center, and acts as an advocate for music education in the public schools.

National Association for the Education of Young Children (NAEYC)

http://www.naeyc.org/

Focused on early childhood education, NAEYC publishes a regular journal as well as books and videos, sponsors an accreditation program for child-care programs, and develops standards for teachers.

National Association of Biology Teachers (NABT)

http://www.nabt.org/

This association publishes *American Biology Teacher,* sponsors conferences and workshops, and offers a wealth of online instructional resources.

National Council for the Social Studies (NCSS)

http://www.ncss.org/ or
http://www.socialstudies.org/

NCSS sponsors state and local meetings as well as a national conference; offers curriculum standards and teaching resources; publishes journals and newsletters; and tracks legislative actions relevant to the teaching of social studies.

National Council of Teachers of English (NCTE)

http://www.ncte.org/

The council publishes a dozen periodicals related to language arts education; offers professional development opportunities; and sponsors programs designed to promote the language arts among underserved communities.

National Council of Teachers of Mathematics (NCTM)

http://www.nctm.org/

NCTM develops math standards, publishes grade-specific journals, and offers online workshops for members.

National Science Teachers Association (NSTA)

http://www.nsta.org/

Focused on science teaching, NSTA publishes both books and journals related to science teaching and sponsors a New Science Teachers Academy. Online, the association offers a discussion board and a number of interactive resources.

APPENDIX C

SUGGESTED READING

The Resources for Further Exploration at the end of each chapter in this book suggest a number of sources relevant to particular topics. But if you want to read more generally about the life of a teacher, the following books can help you understand some of the issues that a teacher faces and see what it's really like to teach in today's classrooms.

William Ayers, ed. *To become a teacher: Making a difference in children's lives.* (New York: Teachers College Press, 1995). In this volume a variety of authors share their views of different aspects of teaching. Together, they help us see beyond the label of children "at risk" to the great potential of children "at promise."

Jacqueline Grennon Brooks, *Schooling for life: Reclaiming the essence of learning* (Reston, VA: Association for Supervision and Curriculum Development, 2002). A book filled with inspiring stories about teachers and learners.

Deborah A. Byrnes and **Gary Kiger,** editors, *Common bonds: Anti-bias teaching in a diverse society,* 3rd edition (Olney, MD: Association for Childhood Education International, 2005). Discussions of many forms of classroom diversity—cultural, economic, religious, and more—and how experienced teachers create an environment in which these differences are recognized and accepted.

Christopher Day, *A passion for teaching* (London: RoutledgeFalmer, 2004). A book for and about teachers who have a passion for their teaching and who love learners and learning.

Rafe Esquith, *There are no shortcuts* (New York: Anchor Books, 2003). This book describes how an inner-city teacher, a winner of the American Teacher Award, inspires his students and reflects on his practice.

Bobbi Fisher, *The teacher book: Finding personal and professional balance* (Portsmouth, NH: Heinemann, 2001). The author corresponded with hundreds of teachers to discover the sources of their greatest joy as well as their primary concerns about the teaching profession.

Sam Intrator, *Tuned in and fired up: How teaching can inspire real learning in the classroom* (New Haven: Yale University Press, 2003). As his title suggests, the author shows how powerful real learning experiences can be, for both teachers and students, and suggests ways to make them happen more frequently.

Alfie Kohn, *Beyond discipline: From compliance to community,* 10th Anniversary Edition (Alexandria, VA: Association for Supervision and Curriculum Development, 2006.) Many stories from actual classrooms support the author's argument that classrooms work best when teachers and students move beyond "discipline" and "classroom management" to a sense of classroom community. In the 10th Anniversary Edition, Kohn considers how his ideas apply to the current emphasis on school accountability and high-stakes testing.

Alfie Kohn, *Punished by rewards: The trouble with gold stars, incentive plans, A's, praise, and other bribes* (Boston: Houghton Mifflin, 1999). This groundbreaking work argues that using extrinsic rewards to encourage compliance misses the point of helping students find joy in learning. The argument remains controversial, but it has important implications for teaching.

Jonathan Kozol, *Ordinary resurrections: Children in the years of hope* (New York: Harper Perennial, 2001). For more than a generation, Kozol has been a passionate critic of American educational practices, stressing the needs of poor and socially marginalized children across the United States. In this book, he lets some of the children in an economically depressed section of the South Bronx speak for themselves.

Judy Logan, *Teaching stories* (New York: Kodansha America, 1997). An exciting book about the author's experiences as a middle school teacher in San Francisco.

Frank McCourt, *Teacher man: A memoir* (New York: Scribner, 2005). A now-celebrated writer who became famous with his earlier memoir *Angela's*

Ashes, McCourt focuses this book on his thirty years of teaching in New York City. His tales are funny, irreverent, and very moving.

Parker Palmer, *The courage to teach: Exploring the inner landscape of a teacher's life* (San Francisco: Jossey-Bass, 1998). Does your inner life—your values, beliefs, and personal goals—affect the way you teach and relate to your students? Palmer argues emphatically that it does, and he shows why and how.

Kelley Dawson Salas, Rita Tenorio, Stephanie Walters, and **Dale Weiss,** editors, *The new teacher book: Finding purpose, balance, and hope during your first years in the classroom* (Milwaukee, WI: Rethinking Schools, 2004). This handy publication, which addresses the experiences of a first-year teacher, offers some useful "how-tos" for getting off to a good start in your classroom, building community, and much more.

Sylvia Ashton Warner, *Teacher* (New York: Touchstone Books, 1963). The moving story of one teacher who helped Maori children with unconventional but effective methods.

Marilyn Watson with **Laura Ecken,** *Learning to trust: Transforming difficult elementary classrooms through developmental discipline* (San Francisco: Jossey-Bass, 2003). Focusing on Laura Ecken's classroom, this book presents many vignettes of school life, along with Ecken's reflections and Watson's sharp analysis.

Appendix D

Action Research: Professional Development from the Inside Out

Action research, also called *practitioner research, classroom research,* or *teacher research,* refers to research that you do yourself in order to examine and improve your own teaching practices. As such, it is a tool for understanding the conditions for learning in the classroom and the social context of the school.

Action research is research done *by* teachers, *for* themselves; it is not imposed on them by someone else. For this reason, it can be seen as professional development from the *inside out.* It is systematic and purposeful, and it is done because teachers want answers to questions that concern them.

The process of action research involves:

1. Identifying an area of focus: an area that you are concerned about or that you want to know more about

2. Collecting data

3. Analyzing and interpreting the data

4. Developing an action plan for putting what you have learned to use

For the data collection step, you should learn how to take meaningful field notes of your classroom experience—similar to keeping a teaching journal. You may also need to become familiar with techniques like interviews, surveys, and video recordings. However, many of the Chapter Challenges in this textbook ask you to make observations and conduct interviews. Thus you are already on your way to becoming a classroom researcher.

One good resource for action research is a book called *You and Your Action Research Project* (McNiff, 2003). This book provides specific directions but also asks broader questions. It highlights four important points about action research:

- ❯ I am the central person in my research.

- ❯ I am asking a real question about a real issue, and I am hoping to move toward a possible solution.

- ❯ I am starting from where I am.

- ❯ I am trying to bring about some improvement. (Remember: any improvement is useful, no matter how small.)

Notice the frequent use of the word "I" in that list of central ideas. This clue should help you see that action research is a long way from the kind of research that implies "distance" or "neutrality." Action research happens in the classroom or the school, where you study the conditions of learning for your own students.

■ Identifying Your Area of Focus

To determine an area of focus for action research, try the following steps:

1. Reflect on possible areas of focus in light of your values and beliefs about teaching and learning.

2. Choose a situation you wish to change or improve.

3. Describe the evidence you have that this situation represents a problem.

4. Identify the critical factors that affect this area of focus.

Sometimes, we have areas of concern in our professional work that are not good topics for an action research study. Hence, teachers need to answer further questions. Is your area of focus an issue that:

▷ involves teaching and learning?

▷ is within your locus of control?

▷ you feel passionate about?

▷ you would like to change or improve?

Your answer to all of these questions should be "yes."

Notice the question about locus of control. It is important to consider whether you can learn something about your students or your school that will affect your own practice and help you work more effectively on behalf of your students. If the area of research is one where you cannot make any changes even after collecting your data, then your research may be theoretically sound, but it will not be *action* research.

■ Sample Action Research Questions from Classroom Teachers

Here is a sampling of research questions developed by actual classroom teachers.

What are the students' perceptions of the purpose of homework? What, if any, is their preference about type of homework? A third-grade teacher developed an anonymous survey for the students and learned that they preferred a meaningful homework assignment (even if it took longer) to rote work.

What, if any, are the connections between student expectations of test difficulty and their performance? An eleventh-grade physics teacher gave the same test to two physics classes of equal ability. To one class, she stated, "This test is going to be hard." To the other class, she did not say anything before distributing the test. The class that had the "difficult" expectation did not fare as well as the other class. (She did not count this test in the students' grades.)

According to the reports of tenth-grade math teachers, are there any differences between early morning and late afternoon classes in terms of the students' ability to learn? A tenth-grade math teacher gave surveys to all of his colleagues to complete anonymously. They did, and when he analyzed their results, there was a marked difference in attitudes and dispositions between the students in the early morning classes and those in late afternoon classes. Which classes do you think were more attentive? How could the teacher use this information?

Does playing background music during chemistry lab affect students' learning, attitudes, and dispositions? A tenth-grade chemistry teacher conducted a survey to learn her chemistry students' favorite type of music. When she played this kind of music, softly, during the chemistry lab time, her students chatted less with friends and stayed on task better.

How do teachers and teaching assistants describe their roles and responsibilities in their middle-school collaborative classrooms? This teacher survey yielded valuable data. In this particular middle school, teachers assumed that their assistants understood their roles and responsibilities, when in fact many did not and were too timid to ask. As a result, an in-service course for teachers and their assistants was developed.

How can autism programs in the early grades be extended to higher grades? In one school district, the program for autistic children covered only kindergarten through second grade. As an action research project, a teacher explored other school districts that had programs for later grades. Interviewing the administrators, she gained valuable insight into how to extend the program in her own district.

■ Reporting Your Results

You have just read a small sampling of the excellent research projects that teachers have implemented to improve their practice. Usually, they express the results of their projects in the following format:

Statement of Problem: This is the area of focus selected.

Researcher Stance: This section explains why the area of focus is of interest to the teacher.

Methodology: This section describes what the teacher did to collect information (data) about the problem.

Findings: This section describes the data collected. It presents the answers to surveys, responses to interviews, the results of teacher journaling, and so forth.

Analysis and Interpretation: In this section the teacher interprets the findings, stating what she or he believes is going on.

Recommended Action: This section describes what the teacher will do about what has been learned.

■ Obtaining Consent

Action research is something you accomplish *with* your students, not something you do *to* your students. Nevertheless, when you conduct any kind of research in your classroom, you need to gain school and parental approval.

Figure D.1 shows a sample of the kind of letter you should send home to parents.

Getting Started

As you have seen, action research provides insights into the situations within a school or classroom that create a suitable context for learning. Doing such research can help you become a more reflective practitioner. The central question is always "How can I help my students improve the quality of their learning?"

Once you are situated in your own classroom, I urge you to think about beginning an action research project. Here are some guides to consult:

Dear Parents:

I will be conducting research in your child's classroom to learn more about the students' attitudes toward homework. They will be completing surveys and participating in open-ended interviews. I am looking forward to discovering ways to change the homework practices to encourage more students to find enjoyment in the process.

Thank you for your cooperation with this research. Please sign and return the form at the bottom.

Sincerely,

Ms. Smith
Class 2-301

- -

I give permission for my daughter/son
to participate in the homework study.   _____

_____
Parent/Guardian Signature

FIGURE D.1
Sample Consent Letter

Useful Sources on Action Research

Chiseri-Starter, E., & B. Sunstein. (2006). *What works? A practical guide for teacher research.* Portsmouth, NH: Heinemann.

Johnson, A. (2005). *A short guide to action research.* 2nd edition. Boston: Allyn and Bacon.

Madison, Wisconsin, Metropolitan School District. *Classroom action research.* http://www.madison.k12.wi.us/sod/car/carhomepage.html

McNiff, J. (2003). *You and your action research project.* London: RoutledgeFalmer.

Mills, G. (2003). *Action research: A guide for the teacher researcher.* 2nd edition. Saddle River, NJ: Merrill.

New Horizons for Learning. *Action research: A strategy for instructional improvement.* http://www.newhorizons.org/strategies/action_research/front_action.htm

GLOSSARY

academy A type of private secondary school that arose in the late colonial period and came to dominate American secondary education until the establishment of public high schools. Academies had a more practical curriculum than Latin grammar schools did, and students typically could choose subjects appropriate to their later careers. (62)

aesthetic education Traditionally, this term referred merely to education in the fine arts, such as painting and music. In the broader view of Maxine Greene and other recent philosophers, however, it means education that enables students to use artistic forms and imagination to approach all fields of learning, including the sciences, and to share their perspectives with others. (77)

American Federation of Teachers (AFT) An international union, affiliated with the American Federation of Labor and Congress of Industrial Organizations, representing teachers and other school personnel as well as many college faculty and staff members, health-care workers, and public employees. (19)

assessment Collecting information to determine the progress of students' learning. (112) *See also* Authentic (performance) assessment; Embedded assessments; Rubric.

assistive technology (AT) A device or service that increases the capabilities of people with disabilities. (218)

at risk *See* Students at risk.

authentic (performance) assessment An assessment that asks students to perform a task relating what they have learned to some real-world problem or example. (112)

behaviorism The theory that learning takes place in response to reinforcements (for instance, rewards or punishments) from the outside environment. (94)

bilingual education Educating English-language learners by teaching them at least part of the time in their native language. (128)

blog (short for **weblog**) An online journal using software that makes it easy for the user to create frequent entries; typically visitors can add their own comments and responses. (210)

Brown v. Board of Education of Topeka, Kansas A 1954 case in which the U.S. Supreme Court outlawed segregation in public education. (81)

Buckley Amendment *See* Family Educational Rights and Privacy Act (FERPA).

bullying Repeated cruelty, physical or psychological, by a powerful person toward a less powerful person. (265) *See also* Cyber-bullying.

burnout *See* Teacher burnout.

certification The process of obtaining state authorization to teach in the public schools. (284)

charter schools Publicly funded elementary or secondary schools that are granted a special charter by the state or local education agency. (176)

classroom community A sense of common purpose and values shared by the teacher and students in a classroom, so that they see themselves as working together in the process of learning; a classroom atmosphere that emphasizes trust, care, and support. (249) *See also* Learning community.

classroom management The ways teachers create an effective classroom environment for learning, including all the rules and conditions they establish. (249)

climate, school *See* School climate.

cognitive learning theories Explanations of the mental processes that occur during learning. (95)

common school A public, tax-supported elementary school. Begun in Massachusetts in the 1820s, common schools aimed to provide a common curriculum for children. Horace Mann, an advocate for the common school, is often considered the "father of the public school." (63)

community *See* Classroom community; Learning community.

constructivism A group of theories about knowledge and learning whose basic tenet is that all knowledge is *constructed* by synthesizing new ideas with prior knowledge. Constructivism holds that knowledge is not passively received; rather, it is actively built by the learner as he or she experiences the world. (98)

cooperative learning An instructional approach in which students work together in groups to accomplish shared learning goals. (166)

culturally relevant pedagogy Teaching practices that place the culture of the learner at the center of instruction. Cultural referents become aspects of the formal curriculum. (140)

culture, school *See* School culture.

curriculum   A plan of studies that includes the ways instructional content is organized and presented at each grade level. (106)

cyber-bullying   Bullying or harassment through electronic means such as e-mail, website postings, text messaging, blogs, mobile phones, or pagers; also called *online bullying*. (266)

dame school   Some colonial women transformed their homes into schools where they taught reading, writing, and computation. These schools became known as dame schools. (60)

differentiated instruction or differentiation   The practice of using a variety of instructional strategies to address the different learning needs of students. (164)

digital divide   The division between people who are "rich" in technological access and expertise and those who are "poor" in this respect. (215)

digital natives   People who have grown up using the digital "language" of computers, video, games and the Internet. (199)

distance learning   Education in which students and teachers are not physically present at the same site. (235)

dropout rate   The percentage of students who fail to complete high school or earn an equivalency degree. (136)

due process   A formal process, such as a legal or administrative proceeding, that follows established rules designed to protect the rights of the people involved. (192)

educational autobiography   Your own educational history, told by you. (6)

embedded assessments   Classroom-based assessments that make use of the actual assignments that students are given as the unit is being taught. These can be used to evaluate developmental stages of student learning. (112)

equity   The act of treating individuals and groups fairly and justly, free from bias or favoritism. *Gender equity* means the state of being fair and just toward both males and females, to show preference to neither and concern for both. (144)

essentialism   An educational philosophy holding that the purpose of education is to learn specific knowledge provided by core academic disciplines such as mathematics, science, literature, and history. Teachers must impart the key elements of these subjects so that all students have access to this basic or "essential" knowledge. (72)

exceptional learners   Students who require special educational services because of physical, behavioral, or academic needs. (155)

Family Educational Rights and Privacy Act (FERPA) (or the "Buckley Amendment")   A federal law requiring educational agencies to protect the confidentiality of students' educational records; also known as the Buckley Amendment. (187)

flat classroom   A classroom in which students, like the teacher, have ready access to information, so that the teacher is not the lone expert. (200)

gender-fair education   Teaching practices that help both females and males achieve their full potential. Gender-fair teachers address cultural and societal stereotypes and overcome them through classroom interactions. (143)

globalization   The increase of global connectivity, integration, and interdependence in economic, cultural, social, and technological spheres. (224)

goodness of fit   A term generally used in descriptive statistics to describe the match between a theory and a particular set of observations; in this book, it means the match between a teacher candidate's personal attributes, values, and dispositions and the demands of teaching. (11)

hidden curriculum   What students learn, beyond the academic content, from the experience of attending school. (44)

homeschooling   Educating children at home rather than in a school; parents typically serve as teachers. (178)

ill-structured problem   A problem that lacks clear procedures for finding the solution. (168)

inclusion   The practice of educating students with disabilities in regular classrooms alongside nondisabled students. (85, 156)

individualized education program (IEP)   A plan required for every student covered by the Individuals with Disabilities Education Act, specifying instructional goals, services to be provided, and assessment techniques for evaluating progress. (158)

Individuals with Disabilities Education Act (IDEA)   The federal law that guarantees that all children with disabilities receive free, appropriate public education. (84)

informal curriculum   Learning experiences that go beyond the formal curriculum, such as activities the teacher introduces to connect academic concepts to the students' daily lives. (106)

inquiry A multifaceted activity that involves making observations, posing questions about the subject matter, and conducting research or investigations to develop answers. Inquiry is common to scientific learning but also relevant to other fields. (79)

instruction The act or process of teaching; the way your pedagogy becomes enacted in practice. (93)

intelligence profile An individual's unique combination of relative strengths and weaknesses among all the different intelligences. (146) *See also* Theory of multiple intelligences.

interactive whiteboard A whiteboard that works together with a computer to display and save information. (218)

Interstate New Teacher Assessment and Support Consortium (INTASC) An organization that develops standards and principles to guide the preparation, licensing, and professional development of teachers. INTASC's members are state education agencies and national educational organizations. (285)

knowledge economy An economic system in which the use and exchange of knowledge plays a dominant role. In this kind of economy, knowledge is both an economic asset and a key product. (224)

Latin grammar school A type of school that flourished in the New England colonies in the 1600s and 1700s. It emphasized Latin and Greek to prepare young men for college. (60)

learning community A classroom, a cluster of classes, or a school organized so as to promote active engagement in learning, collaboration between teachers and students, and a sense that everyone involved shares the experience of being a learner. (49) *See also* Classroom community.

learning disability (or specific learning disability) A disorder in the basic psychological processes involved in learning and using language; it may lead to difficulties in listening, speaking, reading, writing, reasoning, or mathematical abilities. (158)

learning style The dominant way in which we process the information around us. Different people have different learning styles. (148)

learning theory An explanation of how learning typically occurs and about conditions that favor learning. (94) *See also* Cognitive learning theories; Social cognitive learning theories.

least restrictive environment A learning environment that, to the maximum extent possible, matches the environment experienced by nondisabled students. (156)

LGBT An acronym used to represent lesbian, gay, bisexual, and transgender individuals. (133)

management *See* Classroom management.

mental scheme An organizational structure in the brain; a group of foundational concepts that help the individual make sense of the world. (98)

metacognition The understanding of your own thinking and learning processes. (226)

MIVA Acronym for *manage, interpret, validate,* and *act on*—terms describing what students must learn to do with the vast amount of information they access on a daily basis. (228)

model A representation of a system or an object, such as a small physical structure that imitates a larger structure or a computer program that parallels the workings of a larger system. (206)

multicultural education Education the aim of which is to create equal opportunities for students from diverse racial, ethnic, social class, and cultural groups. (140)

multiple intelligences *See* Theory of multiple intelligences.

National Board for Professional Teaching Standards (NBPTS) A nonprofit organization that aims to advance the quality of teaching by developing professional standards for teachers. (19)

National Education Association (NEA) The largest organization of teachers and other education professionals, headquartered in Washington, DC. (14)

A Nation at Risk A 1983 federal report that found U.S. schools in serious trouble and inaugurated a new wave of school reform focused on academic basics and higher standards for student achievement. (84)

normal school A type of teacher-education institution begun in the 1830s; forerunner of the teachers' college. (68)

parochial school A school operated by a religious group. Today, in the United States, the term most often refers to a school governed by the local Catholic parish or diocese. (64)

pedagogical content knowledge (PCK) The understanding of how particular topics, problems, or issues can be adapted and presented to match the diverse interests and abilities of learners. (94)

pedagogy The art and science of teaching; all that you know and believe about teaching. (93)

perennialism   An educational philosophy that emphasizes enduring ideas conveyed through the study of great works of literature and art. Perennialists believe in a single core curriculum for everyone. (74)

performance assessment   *See* Authentic assessment.

philosophy of teaching statement   A description of your ideas about teaching and learning and how those ideas will influence your practice. It should be based on your knowledge of educational research. (9)

Praxis Series   A series of assessments used by many states as part of the teacher certification process. (284)

problem-based learning   Focused, experiential learning (minds-on, hands-on) organized around the investigation and resolution of messy, real-world problems. (168)

professional development   Teachers' lifelong effort to improve their skills and professional knowledge. Although professional development often includes advanced courses and workshops, much of your progress will depend on your own continued reading, reflection, and analysis. (49)

progressivism   An educational philosophy that stresses active learning through problem solving, projects, and hands-on experiences. (72)

project-based learning   A teaching method that engages students in extended inquiry into complex, realistic questions as they work in teams and create presentations to share what they have learned. These presentations may take various forms: an oral or written report, a computer-technology-based presentation, a video, the design of a product, and so on. (167)

public education   Education that is publicly financed, tuition-free, accountable to public authorities, and accessible to all students. The term covers various types of public schools, including traditional schools, charter and magnet schools, vocational schools, and alternative schools. (273)

reflective practitioner   A teacher who consistently reflects on classroom events (both successes and problems) and modifies teaching practices accordingly. (3)

Responsive Classroom   An approach to teaching and learning, developed by the Northeast Foundation for Children, that seeks to bring together social and academic learning. (259)

rubric   A scoring guide for an authentic assessment or a performance assessment, with descriptions of performance characteristics corresponding to points on a rating scale. (114)

scheme   *See* Mental scheme.

school climate and **school culture**   The values, cultures, practices, and organization of a school. (21)

service learning   A teaching and learning strategy that integrates meaningful community service with instruction and reflection to enrich the learning experience, teach civic responsibility, and strengthen communities. (262)

sexual harassment   Unwelcome sexual advances, requests for sexual favors, or other physical and expressive behavior of a sexual nature that interferes with a person's life. (263)

sexual orientation   An enduring emotional, romantic, sexual, or affectional attraction that a person feels toward people of one or both sexes. (133)

simulation   A computer program or other procedure that imitates a real-world experience. (205)

social cognitive learning theories   Explanations that describe how learning involves interactions between the learner and the social environment. (96)

socioeconomic status (SES)   A person's or family's status in society, usually based on a combination of income, occupation, and education. Though similar to *social class*, SES puts more emphasis on the way income affects status. (134)

special education   The branch of education that deals with services for students with disabilities or other special needs that cannot be met through traditional means. (156)

specific learning disability   *See* Learning disability.

students at risk   Students in danger of not completing school or not acquiring the education they need to be successful citizens. (136)

teacher burnout   The condition of teachers who have lost their motivation, desire, sense of purpose, and energy for being effective practitioners. (38)

teaching portfolio   A collection of documents and other items that represent your work as a teacher, your goals, and your philosophy. (24)

technological fluency   Proficiency in the use of technology, including an understanding of the way technology systems operate and the ability to use technology to access information from a wide variety of sources. (213)

tenure A status granted to a teacher, usually after a probationary period, that protects him or her from dismissal except for reasons of incompetence, gross misconduct, or other conditions stipulated by the state. (192)

theory of multiple intelligences The theory that intelligence is not a single, fixed attribute but rather a collection of several different types of abilities. (146)

Title 1 The section of federal education law that provides funds for compensatory education. (83)

Title IX Part of the federal Educational Amendments of 1972, Title IX states that "No person in the United States shall, on the basis of sex, be excluded from participation in, be denied the benefits of, or be subjected to discrimination under any education program or activity receiving Federal financial assistance." (83)

tracking The practice of placing students in different classes or courses based on achievement test scores or on perceived differences in abilities. Tracks can be identified by ability (high, average, or low) or by the kind of preparation they provide (academic, general, or vocational). (71)

videoconferencing Real-time audio and video communication allowing individuals or groups at different locations to talk in a face-to-face setting. (235)

weblog *See* Blog.

WebQuest A learning activity in which students investigate a question or solve a problem with information they gather from websites. (208)

wiki An online site that allows visitors to add, remove, and otherwise edit or change the available content. (212)

References

AAUW Educational Foundation. (2001). *Hostile Hallways: Bullying, Teasing, and Sexual Harassment in School.* Washington, DC: American Association of University Women Educational Foundation.

AAUW Educational Foundation. (2004). *Harassment-Free Hallways: How to Stop Sexual Harassment in School.* Washington, DC: American Association of University Women Educational Foundation.

Aleman, A. M. (2006). Latino demographic, democratic individuality, and educational accountability: A pragmatist's view. *Educational Researcher,* 35(7): 25–35.

American Educational Research Association. (2004). English language learners: Boosting academic achievement. *Research Points,* 2:1 (Winter).

American Federation of Teachers. (2003). *Where We Stand: Teacher Quality.* AFT Teachers Educational Issues Department, Item Number 39–0230. Washington, DC: Author.

American Federation of Teachers. (2007). A vision that endures. http://www.aft.org/about/vision.htm; retrieved February 7, 2007.

Anderson, B. C. (2000). An A for home schooling. *City Journal,* 10(3), Summer. New York: Manhattan Institute for Policy Research.

Annie E. Casey Foundation. (2001). *Where Kids Count, Place Matters: Trends in the Well-being of Iowa Children.* Des Moines, IA: Iowa Kids Count.

Annie E. Casey Foundation. (2003). *Kids Count Indicator Brief: Reducing the High School Dropout Rate.* Baltimore, MD: Author. Available at http://www.aecf.org/kidscount/indicator_briefs/dropout_rate.pdf.

Annie E. Casey Foundation. (2006a). 2000 Census data: Key facts for United States. Kids Count Census Data Online, http://www.aecf.org/; retrieved October 24, 2006.

Annie E. Casey Foundation. (2006b). *2006 Kids Count Data Book: State Profiles of Child Well-being.* Washington, DC: Author.

Annie E. Casey Foundation. (2007a). Children in immigrant families: Percent: 2005. Kids Count State-Level Data Online, http://www.kidscount.org/sld/compare_results.jsp?i=750; retrieved April 20, 2007.

Annie E. Casey Foundation. (2007b). Children in single-parent families: Percent: 2005. Kids Count state-level data online, http://www.kidscount.org/sld/compare_results.jsp?i=721. Accessed April 20, 2007.

Baldacci, L., Moore Johnson, S., & The Project on the Next Generation of Teachers. (2006). Why new teachers leave . . . and why new teachers stay. *American Educator,* (Summer): 9–21, 45.

Ball, A. (2003). Geo-literacy: Forging new ground. Edutopia-online [online]. http://www.edutopia.org/php/article.php?id=Art_1042&key=037; retrieved December 11, 2006.

Ball, A. (2004). Great team, great school. Edutopia-online. http://www.edutopia.org/php/article.php?id=Art_1142&key=037; retrieved December 11, 2006.

Bennett-Goleman, T. (2001). *Emotional Alchemy: How the Mind Can Heal the Heart.* London: Harmony Books.

Bickart, T., Jablon, J., & Dodge, D. T. (2000). *Building the Primary Classroom: A Complete Guide to Teaching and Learning.* Washington, DC: Teaching Strategies, Inc.

Bielick, S., Chandler, K., & Broughman, S. P. (2001). *Homeschooling in the United States: 1999.* NCES 2001–033. Washington, DC: U.S. Department of Education, National Center for Education Statistics.

The Boston Historical Society and Museum. (2006). Who were the Puritans? http://www.bostonhistory.org/faq.php#puritan; retrieved August 29, 2006.

Brooks, J. G. & Brooks, M. (1999). *In Search of Understanding: A Case for Constructivist Classrooms.* Reston, VA: Association for Supervision and Curriculum Development.

Braun, H., Jenkins, F., & Grigg, W. (2006). *A Closer Look at Charter Schools Using Hierarchical Linear Modeling.* NCES 2006–460. Washington, DC: U.S. Department of Education.

Brooks-Gunn, J., Duncan, G. J., & Aber, J. L. (Eds.). (2000). *Neighborhood Poverty. Volume 1: Context and Consequences for Children.* New York: Russell Sage Foundation.

Brown, J. (2000). *The Sea Accepts All Rivers & Other Poems.* Alexandria, VA: Miles River Press.

Bruner, J. S. (1960). *The Process of Education.* Cambridge, MA: Harvard University Press.

Bruner, J. S. (1966). *Toward a Theory of Instruction.* Cambridge, MA: Harvard University Press.

Carnegie Forum on Education and the Economy. (1986). *A Nation Prepared: Teachers for the 21st Century.* New York: Carnegie Corporation.

Carter, G. (2006). Supporting the whole child. *ASCD Education Update* 48(12): 2, 8. Alexandria, VA: Association for Supervision and Curriculum Development.

Cawelti, G. (2006). The side effects of NCLB. *Educational Leadership* 64(3): 64–88.

Center on Education Policy. (2007). *Why We Still Need Public Schools: Public Education for the Common Good.* Washington, DC: Author. http://www.cep-dc.org/; retrieved February 1, 2007.

Center for Education Reform. (2005). *All About Charter Schools.* Washington, DC: Center for Education Reform.

Cicourel, A. V., & Mehan, H. (1985). Universal development stratifying practices and status attainment. *Research in Social Stratification and Mobility,* 4: 3–27.

Cohen, J. (2006). Social, emotional, ethical, and academic education: Creating a climate for learning, participation in democracy, and well-being. *Harvard Educational Review* 76(2): 201–237.

Condliffe Lagemann, E. (2007). Public rhetoric, public responsibility, and the public schools. *Education Week,* 26(37): 30, 40.

Corcoran, K. (2002). Bullying slurs are rampant, nationwide survey finds. *San Jose Mercury News*, December 13.

Council of Chief State School Officers. (2007). Interstate New Teacher Assessment and Support Consortium (INTASC). http://www.ccsso.org/Projects/interstate_new_teacher_assessment_and_support_consortium/780.cfm; retrieved February 13, 2007.

Crawford, J. (2006). Hard sell: Why is bilingual education so unpopular with the American public? http://www.asu.edu/educepsl/LPRU/features/brief8.htm; retrieved October 27, 2006.

Davis, G. A., & Rimm, S. B. (2004). *Education of the Gifted and Talented.* (5th ed.) Boston: Allyn & Bacon.

Day, C. (2004). *A Passion for Teaching.* New York: Routledge.

Deal, T., & Peterson, K. (1990). *The principal's role in shaping school culture.* Washington, DC: U.S. Department of Education.

DeBell, M., & Chapman, C. (2003). *Computer and Internet Use by Children and Adolescents in 2001.* NCES 2004–014. Washington, DC: National Center for Education Statistics.

Dee, T. S. (2005). A teacher like me: Does race, ethnicity, or gender matter? *American Economic Review, 95*(2): 158–165.

Dee, T. S. (2006). The why chromosome. *Education Next,* no. 4 (Fall): 68–75.

Downes, S. (2004). Educational blogging. *Educause Review,* September/October: 14–26.

Dewey, J. (1914/2004). *Democracy and Education.* New York: Dover.

Dewey, J. (1938). *Experience and Education.* New York: Collier Macmillan.

Duckworth, E. (1991). Twenty-four, forty-two, and I love you: Keeping it complex. *Harvard Educational Review,* 61:1 (February): 1–24.

Eccles, J. S., & Midgley, C. (1989). Stage/environment fit: Developmentally appropriate classrooms for early adolescents. In R. Ames & C. Ames (Eds.), *Research on Motivation in Education,* Vol. 3. San Diego, CA: Academic, pp. 139–186.

Eccles, J. S., Lord, S., & Midgley, C. (1991). What are we doing to adolescents? The impact of educational contexts on early adolescents. *American Journal of Education* 99: 521–542.

Education Commission of the States. (2007a). Charter schools: Quick facts. http://www.ecs.org/html/IssueSection.asp?issueid=20&s=Quick+Facts; retrieved May 13, 2007.

Education Commission of the States. (2007b). StateNotes: Charter school teacher certification. http://mb2.ecs.org/reports/Report.aspx?id=93; retrieved May 13, 2007.

Evans, S. (1989.) *Born for Liberty: A History of Women in America.* New York: Free Press Publications.

Farber, B. A. (1991). *Crisis in Education: Stress and Burnout in the American Teacher.* San Francisco: Jossey-Bass.

Fein, R. A., Vossekuil, B., Pollack, W. S., Borum, R., Modzeleski, W., & Reddy, M. (2002). *Threat Assessment in Schools: A Guide to Managing Threatening Situations and to Creating Safe School Climates.* Washington, DC: United States Secret Service and United States Department of Education.

Felder, R. M., & Brent, R. (2005). Understanding student differences. *Journal of Engineering Education* 94(1): 57–72.

Felder, R. M., & Silverman, L. K. (1988, 2002). Learning and teaching styles in engineering education. *Journal of Engineering Education* 78(7): 674–681. Author's Preface by R. M. Felder, written in 2002, http://www.ncsu.edu/felder-public/Papers/LS–1988.pdf; retrieved April 30, 2007.

Fisch, K. (2006a). NECC: Fearless courage: Technology and high school transformation (eMINTS). *The Fischbowl: A Staff Development Blog for Arapahoe High School.* http://thefischbowl.blogspot.com/2006/07/necc-fearless-courage-technology-and.html; posted July 9, 2006, retrieved December 9, 2006.

Fisch, K. (2006b). This is not education as usual. *The Fischbowl: A Staff Development Blog for Arapahoe High School.* http://thefischbowl.blogspot.com/2006/12/this-is-not-education-as-usual.html; posted December 15, 2006, retrieved December 18, 2006.

Franklin, J. (2003). Reaching for results. *ASCD Education Update* 45(8): 1. Alexandria, VA: Association for Supervision and Curriculum Development.

Freire, P. (1970). *Pedagogy of the Oppressed.* M. B. Ramos (Trans.). New York: Continuum.

Friedman, T. L. (1999). *The Lexus and the Olive Tree: Understanding Globalization.* New York: Farrar, Straus and Giroux.

Friedman, T. (2006). *The World Is Flat: A Brief History of the Twenty-first Century.* (Updated and expanded ed.) New York: Farrar, Straus and Giroux.

Fry, R. (2006). *The Changing Landscape of American Public Education: New Students, New Schools.* Washington, DC: Pew Hispanic Center Research Report.

Ganley, B. (2006). Centering, connecting and creating: Transformations in blogging classrooms. Videoconference presentation. http://mt.middlebury.edu/middblogs/ganley/bgblogging/2006/06/; accessed May 18, 2007.

Gardner, H. (1993). *Frames of Mind: The Theory of Multiple Intelligences.* New York: Basic Books.

Gardner, H. (1999). *Intelligence Reframed: Multiple Intelligences for the 21st Century.* New York: Basic Books.

Gardner, H. (2006). *Multiple Intelligences: New Horizons.* New York: Basic Books.

Gay, Lesbian & Straight Education Network (2005). *The 2005 National School Climate Survey: The Experiences of Gay, Lesbian, Bisexual, and Transgender Youth in Our Schools.* New York: GLSEN.

Graham, K. A. (2006). Virtual classes opening worlds. *Philadelphia Inquirer,* September 7.

Greene, J. P., Forster, G., & Winters, M. (2003, July). Education Working Paper No. 1. New York: The Manhattan Institute for Policy Research.

Greene, M. (1978). *Landscapes of Learning.* New York: Teachers College Press.

Greene, M. (1995). *Releasing the Imagination: Essays on Education, the Arts, and Social Change.* San Francisco: Jossey-Bass.

Guilfoyle, C. (2006). NCLB: Is there life beyond testing? *Educational Leadership* 64(3): 8–13.

Gunderson, S., Jones, R., & Scanland, K. (2004). *The Jobs Revolution: Changing How America Works* (2d ed.) Chicago: Copywriters, Incorporated.

Hammerness, K. (2006). *Seeing Through Teachers' Eyes: Professional Ideals and Classroom Practices*. New York: Teachers College Press.

Haynes, C., Chaltain, S., Ferguson, J., Hudson, D., & Thomas, O. (2003). *The First Amendment in Schools*. Nashville, TN: First Amendment Center.

Hinchcliffe, D. (2006). The state of Web 2.0. *Dion Hinchcliffe's Web 2.0 Blog*. http://web2.wsj2.com/the_state_of_web_20.htm; retrieved December 10, 2006.

Hittie, M. (2000). Building community in the classroom. Paper presented at the International Education Summit, Detroit, Michigan, June 26, 2006.

Hoffman, N. (1981). *Woman's True Profession: Voices from the History of Teaching*. New York: The Feminist Press and McGraw Hill.

Humphreys, T. (1998). *A Different Kind of Discipline*. Dublin, Ireland: Gill & Macmillan, Ltd.

Information Please Database. (2006). State compulsory school attendance laws. http://www.infoplease.com/ipa/A0112617.html; retrieved August 15, 2006.

International Society for Technology in Education. (2002). *National Educational Technology Standards for Teachers: Preparing Teachers to Use Technology*. Washington, DC: Author.

Interstate New Teacher Assessment and Support Consortium. (1992). *Model Standards for Beginning Teacher Licensing, Assessment and Development: A Resource for State Dialogue*. Washington, DC: Council of Chief State School Officers.

Intrator, S. (2003). *Tuned In and Fired Up: How Teaching Can Inspire Real Learning in the Classroom*. New Haven, CT: Yale University Press.

Jackson, P., Corey, S., Kleibard H., & Gage, N. L. (1968). *The Way Teaching Is*. Reston, VA: Association for Supervision and Curriculum Development.

Joubert, J. (2005.) *The Notebooks of Joseph Joubert*. New York: The New York Review of Books. Translated and with an introduction by Paul Auster.

Jukes, I. (2006). From Gutenberg to Gates to Google (and beyond. . .): Education for the online world. http://ianjukes.com/infosavvy/education/handouts/fgtg.pdf; retrieved December 8, 2006.

Juvonen, J., Le, V., Kaganoff, T., Augustine, C. H., & Constant, L. (2004). *Focus on the Wonder Years: Challenges Facing the American Middle School*. Santa Monica, CA: Rand Corporation.

Kashen, S. (1994). Bilingual education and second-language acquisition theory. In C. F. Lebya (Ed.), *Schooling and Language Minority Students*, pp. 61–63. Los Angeles: California State University.

Keany, M. (2006). A message to the electronic community. From the Departmental Science LISTSERV (departmental-science@nassauboces.org), cosponsored by the Nassau Board of Cooperative Educational Services and the Long Island School Leadership Center, New York State; retrieved December 19, 2006.

Kelley, T. (2006). Talk in class turns to God, setting off public debate on rights. *New York Times*, December 18. http://www.nytimes.com/2006/12/18/nyregion.

Kim, S. H., & Bagaka, J. (2005). The digital divide in students' usage of technology tools: A multilevel analysis of the role of teacher practices and classroom characteristics. *Contemporary Issues in Technology and Teacher Education* 5(3/4): 318–329.

Klein, S., Ortman, P., & Friedman, B. (2002.) What is the field of gender equity in education? In J. Koch & B. Irby (Eds.), *Defining and Redefining Gender Equity in Education*. Greenwich, CT: Information Age Publishing.

Koch, J. (2002). Gender issues in the classroom. In W. R. Reynolds & G. E. Miller (Eds.), *Educational Psychology*. Volume 7 of the *Comprehensive Handbook of Psychology*. Editor-in-Chief: I. B. Weiner. New York: Wiley.

Kosciw, J. G., & Diaz, E. M. (2006). *The 2005 National School Climate Survey: The Experiences of Lesbian, Gay, Bisexual and Transgender Youth in Our Nation's Schools*. New York: Gay, Lesbian and Straight Education Network.

Kounin, J. S. (1970). *Discipline and Group Management in Classrooms*. New York: Holt, Rinehart and Winston.

Kozol, J. (1985). *Illiterate America*. Garden City, NY: Anchor Press/Doubleday.

Kozol. J. (1991). *Savage Inequalities*. New York: Crown Publishers.

Krug, E. A. (1964). *The Shaping of the American High School, 1880–1920*. New York: Harper & Row.

Kyraciou, C. (2001). *Essential Teaching Skills*. Cheltenham, United Kingdom: Nelson Thornes LTD.

Laird, J., DeBell, M., & Chapman, C. (2006). *Dropout Rates in the United States: 2004* (NCES 2007–024). Washington, DC: National Center for Education Statistics.

Lareau, A. (2003). *Unequal Childhoods: Class, Race, and Family Life*. Berkeley and Los Angeles: University of California Press.

Levine, M. (2007). The essential cognitive backpack. *Educational Leadership* 64(7): 16–22.

Lieberman, M. (1956). *Education as a Profession*. Englewood Cliffs, NJ: Prentice-Hall.

Lofing, N. (2007). Chana named model school. *Sacramento Bee*, April 5; retrieved from http://www.sacbee.com/293/v-print/story/148899.html.

Logan, J. (1999). *Teaching Stories*. New York: Kodansha America.

Lowe, C. (2002). Why weblogs? *Kairosnews: A Weblog for Discussing Rhetoric, Technology and Pedagogy*. http://kairosnews.org/why-weblogs; posted July 27, 2002, retrieved December 20, 2006.

Lowes, S. (2005). Online teaching and classroom change: The impact of virtual high school on its teachers and their schools. Teachers College, Columbia University: Institute for Learning Technologies. http://www.ilt.columbia.edu/publications/; retrieved January 2, 2007.

Maker, J., & Nielson, A. (1996). *Curriculum Development and Teaching Strategies for Gifted Learners*. (2nd ed.) Austin, TX: PRO-ED.

Manning, M. L. (2000). A brief history of the middle school. *The Clearing House*, 73(4): 288–301.

Martin, R. A. (2000). Teaching as a profession: Historic, public, union, and alternative perceptions. Available online at http://www.pathsoflearning.net/library/profession.cfm; retrieved June 9, 2006.

McBrien, J. L., & Brandt, R. S. (1997). *The Language of Learning: A Guide to Education Terms*. Alexandria, VA: Association for Supervision and Curriculum Development.

McGuire, W., Ed. (1954). *Collected Works of C. J. Jung,* vol. 17. Princeton, NJ: Princeton University Press.

Miller, L. (2004). 12 tips for new teachers. In K. D. Salas, R. Tenorio, S. Walters, & D. Weiss (Eds.), *The New Teacher Book: Finding Purpose, Balance, and Hope During Your First Years in the Classroom.* Milwaukee, WI: Rethinking Schools, Ltd.

Mitchell, S. (2004). *Charter Schools, Still Making Waves.* Washington, DC: Center for Education Reform.

Moe, T. M. (2001). *A Primer on America's Schools.* Stanford: Hoover Institution Press.

Moos, R. H. (1979). *Evaluating Educational Environments: Procedures, Measures, Findings, and Policy Implications.* San Francisco: Jossey-Bass.

Moran, S., Kornhaber, M., & Gardner, H. (2006). Orchestrating multiple intelligences. *Educational Leadership,* 64(1): 23–27.

National Assessment of Educational Progress. (2005). *America's Charter Schools: Results from the NAEP 2003 Pilot Study.* NCES 2005–456. Washington, DC: U.S. Department of Education.

National Association for Gifted Children. (2006). What is gifted? http://www.nagc.org; retrieved November 16, 2006.

National Board for Professional Teaching Standards. (2002). *What Teachers Should Know and Be Able to Do.* Arlington, VA: Author. http://www.nbpts.org/UserFiles/File/what_teachers.pdf; retrieved July 14, 2006 and February 7, 2007.

National Center for Education Statistics. (2006). *The Condition of Education 2006* (NCES 2006–071). Washington, DC: U.S. Government Printing Office.

National Center for Education Statistics. (2006). Fast facts: Enrollment trends. http://nces.ed.gov/fastfacts/; retrieved November 2, 2006.

National Center on Education and the Economy. (2006). *Tough Choices or Tough Times: The Report of the New Commission on the Skills of the American Workforce.* San Francisco: Jossey-Bass.

National Collaborative on Diversity in the Teaching Force. (2004). *Assessment of Diversity in America's Teaching Force: A Call to Action.* Washington, DC: National Education Association.

National Education Association. (1899). Report of the Committee on College Entrance Requirements. *Journal of the Proceedings and Addresses of the Thirty-eighth Annual Meeting, Los Angeles,* pp. 632–817.

National Education Association. (1975). Code of Ethics of the Education Profession. Available online at http://www.nea.org/aboutnea/code.html; retrieved July 14, 2006.

National Education Association. (2003). *Status of the American Public School Teacher 2000–2001.* Washington, DC: Author.

National Education Association. (2006a, May 2). National Teacher Day spotlights key issues facing profession. Available online at http://www.nea.org/newsreleases/2006/nr060502.html; retrieved July 14, 2006.

National Education Association. (2006b). *Rankings and Estimates: Rankings of the States 2005 and Estimates of School Statistics 2006.* Washington, DC: Author.

National Education Association. (2007). Issues in education: Charter schools. http://www.nea.org/charter/index.html; retrieved May 13, 2007.

National Research Council. (2000). *How People Learn: Brain, Mind, Experience, and School* (Expanded ed.) Washington, DC: National Academies Press.

National School Boards Foundation. (2007). Safe & Smart: Research and guidelines for children's use of the Internet. http://www.nsbf.org/safe-smart/index.html; retrieved May 30, 2007.

Nelson, C., & Wilson, K. (1998). *Seeding the Process of Multicultural Education.* Plymouth, MN: Minnesota Inclusiveness Program.

New Commission on the Skills of the American Workforce. (2006). *Tough Choices or Tough Times.* Washington, DC: National Center on Education and the Economy.

Northeast Foundation for Children. (2007). What is the Responsive Classroom approach? http://www.responsiveclassroom.org/about/aboutrc.html; retrieved May 29, 2007.

Oakes, J. (1985). *Keeping Track.* New Haven: Yale University Press.

Office for Civil Rights. (1997). *Sexual Harassment: It's Not Academic.* Washington, DC: U.S. Department of Education.

Office for Civil Rights. (2001). *Revised Sexual Harassment Guidance: Harassment of Students by School Employees, Other Students, or Third Parties.* Washington, DC: U.S. Department of Education.

Olweus, D. (2003). A profile of bullying at school. *Educational Leadership,* 60(6) (March): 12–17.

Osterman, K. (2000). Students' need for belongingness in the school community. *Review of Educational Research,* 70: 323–367.

Oxendine, L. (1989). *Dick and Jane are Dead: Basal Reader Takes a Back Seat to Student Writing.* Charleston, WV: Appalachia Educational Laboratory, Inc.

Palmer, P. (1998). *The Courage to Teach: Exploring the Inner Landscape of a Teacher's Life.* San Francisco, CA: Jossey-Bass.

Pape, L., Adams, R., & Ribiero, C. (2005). The virtual high school: Collaboration and online professional development. In Zane L. Berge and Tom Clark (Eds.), *Virtual Schools: Planning for Success.* New York: Teachers College Press.

Parsad, B., & and Jones, J. (2005). *Internet Access in U.S. Public Schools and Classrooms: 1994–2003* (NCES 2005–015). U.S. Department of Education. Washington, DC: National Center for Education Statistics.

Perkins, D. (1993). Teaching for understanding. *American Educator,* 17(3): 28–35.

The Pew Forum on Religion and Public Life. (2002). *Americans Struggle with Religion's Role at Home and Abroad.* Washington, DC: Author.

Pope, D. C. (2003). *Doing School: How We Are Creating a Generation of Stressed Out, Materialistic, and Miseducated Students.* New Haven, CT: Yale University Press.

Prensky, M. (2001). Digital natives, digital immigrants. *On the Horizon* 9(5), October, 2001. http://www.marcprensky.com/writing/Prensky%20%20Digital%20Natives,%20Digital%20Immigrants%20%20Part1.pdf; retrieved May 17, 2007.

Princiotta, D., & Bielick, S. (2006). *Homeschooling in the United States: 2003*. NCES 2006–042. Washington, DC: U.S. Department of Education, National Center for Education Statistics.

Project Tomorrow. (2007). Speak up 2006: Snapshot of selected national Findings from Teachers. http://www.tomorrow.org/docs/Speak%20Up%202006%20National%20Snapshot_Teacher.pdf; retrieved May 26, 2007.

Rasmussen, K. (1997). Using real-life problems to make real-world connections. *Curriculum Update,* Summer. Alexandria, VA: Association for Supervision and Curriculum Development.

Ray, B. (2004). *Home Educated and Now Adults*. Salem, OR: National Home Education Research Institute.

Rimm-Kaufman, S. (2006). Social and Academic Learning Study on the Contribution of the *Responsive Classroom®* Approach. Turners Falls, MA: Northeast Foundation for Children.

Rippa, S. A. (1997). *Education in a Free Society: An American History.* New York: Longman.

Robinson, R. (2006). Do schools kill creativity? Invited talk at the Education, Entertainment, Design Conference, Monterey, CA. Available online at http://www.ted.com/index.php/talks/view/id/66; retrieved May 24, 2007.

Roehre, J. (2007). 2nd annual Wisconsin History Mystery statewide 4th grade videoconference project. *Videoconferencing Opportunities for KUSD.* Kenosha Unified School District, Kenosha, WI. http://kusdevcopps.blogspot.com/; retrieved May 28, 2007.

Rogers, C. R. (1983). *Freedom to Learn for the 80s.* Columbus, OH: Charles Merrill.

Ryan, K., & Cooper, J. M. (2007). *Those Who Can, Teach.* (11th ed.) Boston: Houghton Mifflin.

Sadker, D. M., & Zittleman, K. R. (2007). *Teachers, Schools, and Society: A Brief Introduction to Education.* New York: McGraw-Hill.

Sadker, M., & Sadker, D. (1995). *Failing at Fairness: How Our Schools Cheat Girls.* New York: Touchstone/Simon & Schuster.

Sampson, R. (2002). *Bullying in Schools*. Problem-Oriented Guides for Police Series, Guide No. 12. Washington, DC: Office of Community Oriented Policing Services, U.S. Department of Justice. Available at http://www.popcenter.org/problems/PDFs/Bullying_in_Schools.pdf; retrieved January 10, 2007.

Schön, D. A. (1983). *The Reflective Practitioner: How Professionals Think in Action.* New York: Basic Books.

Scott, A. O. (2000). Sense and nonsense. *New York Times,* Nov. 26, Section 6, p. 48.

Searls, D. (2005). Getting flat, Part 2. *Linux Journal,* http://www.linuxjournal.com/article/8280; retrieved April 29, 2005.

Sears, J. (1991). Teaching for diversity: Student sexual identities. *Educational Leadership* 49(1): 54–57.

Seligman, M. E. P. (2002). *Authentic Happiness.* New York: Free Press.

Seligman, M. E. P., Steen, T. A., Park, N., & Peterson, C. (2005). Positive psychology progress: Empirical validation of interventions. *American Psychologist,* 60: 410–421.

Selingo, J. (2004). In the classroom, web logs are the new bulletin boards. *New York Times,* Circuits, August 19.

Shulman, L. (1987). Knowledge and teaching: Foundations of the new reform. *Harvard Educational Review,* 57(1):1–22.

Slavin, R. E., & Madden, N. A. (2006). *Success for All: 2006 Summary of Research on Achievement Outcomes.* Baltimore: Johns Hopkins University, Center for Data-Driven Reform in Education.

Smith, T. W., and Lambie, G. W. (2005). Teachers' responsibilities when adolescent abuse and neglect are suspected. *Middle School Journal* 36(3): 33–40.

Snyder, T. D., ed. (1993). *120 Years of American Education: A Statistical Portrait.* Washington, DC: National Center for Education Statistics.

Snyder, T. D., Tan, A. G., & Hoffman, C. M. (2006). *Digest of Education Statistics 2005.* (NCES 2006–030). U.S. Department of Education, National Center for Education Statistics. Washington, DC: U.S. Government Printing Office.

Style, E. (1996). Curriculum as window and mirror. Available online: http://www.wcwonline.org/seed/curriculum.html. Originally published in 1988 in *Listening for All Voices: Gender Balancing the School Curriculum.* Summit, NJ: Oak Knoll School Monograph, pp. 6–12.

Tettegah, S., & Bailey, B. (2006). Clover: Connecting technology and character education using personally constructed animated vignettes. *Interacting with Computers* 18(4): 793–819.

Thorpe, R. (2003). Getting the center to hold: A funder's perspective. Chapter 5 in Norris Dickard (Ed.), *The Sustainability Challenge: Taking Edtech to the Next Level.* Washington, DC: Benton Foundation and the Education Development Center. Available online at http://www.benton.org/publibrary/sustainability/sus_challenge.html

Toh, K-A., Ho, B-T., Chew, C. M. K., & Riley, J. (2003). Teaching, teacher knowledge and constructivism. *Educational Research for Policy and Practice* 3:195–204.

Tomlinson, C. (2000). Reconcilable differences? Standards-based teaching and differentiation. *Educational Leadership* 58(1): 6–11.

Torp, L., & Sage, S. (2002). *Problems as Possibilities: Problem-Based Learning for K–16 Education.* (2nd ed.) Alexandria, VA: Association of Supervision and Curriculum Development.

Tough, P. (2006). What makes a student? *New York Times Sunday Magazine.* November 26.

Townes-Young, K., & Ewing, V. (2005). Creating a global classroom. *T.H.E. Journal,* November.

U.S. Census Bureau. (2007). *Statistical Abstract of the United States: 2007.* Washington, DC: Author.

U.S. Department of Education. (1998). Achieving excellence in the teaching profession. In *Promising Practices: New Ways to Improve Teacher Quality.* Washington, DC. Available online at http://www.ed.gov/pubs/PromPractice/chapter1.html; retrieved June 6, 2006.

U.S. Department of Education, Office of Special Education and Rehabilitative Services, Office of Special Education Programs. (2005). *25th Annual (2003) Report to Congress on the Implementation of the Individuals with Disabilities Education Act.* Washington, DC.

U.S. Department of Education. (2006). Overview: Four pillars of NCLB. http://www.ed.gov/nclb/overview/intro/4pillars.html; retrieved November 30, 2006.

U.S. Department of Education, National Center for Education Statistics. (2006). *The Condition of Education 2006* (NCES 2006–071). Washington, DC: U.S. Government Printing Office.

Vacca, R. S. (2004, May). Student records 2004: Issues and policy considerations. *CEPI Education Law Newsletter.* Richmond, VA: Commonwealth Educational Policy Institute. Available online at http://www.cepionline.org/newsletter/2003–2004/2004_May_stud_records.html.

Vygotsky, L. (1962). *Thought and Language.* Cambridge, MA: MIT Press.

Wallis, C., & Steptoe, S. (2006). How to bring our schools out of the 20th century. *Time Magazine,* December 18.

Weaver, R. (2004). Diverse educators critical to quality teaching. President's Viewpoint, National Education Association, Nov. 10. http://www.nea.org/columns/rw041110.html; retrieved April 17, 2007.

Wells, J., and Lewis, L. (2006). *Internet Access in U.S. Public Schools and Classrooms: 1994–2005* (NCES 2007–020). U.S. Department of Education. Washington, DC: National Center for Education Statistics.

Winebrenner, S. (2000). Gifted students need an education, too. *Educational Leadership,* 58(1): 52–56.

Wisconsin Education Association Council. (2006). Great Schools issue paper: The common school movement. http://www.weac.org/greatschools/Issuepapers/commonschool.htm; retrieved September 9, 2006.

Wood, T., & McCarthy, C. (2002). Understanding and preventing teacher burnout. Washington, DC: ERIC Clearinghouse on Teaching and Teacher Education, ED477726.

Wurman, R. (2000). *Information Anxiety2.* New York: Doubleday.

Younger, M., Brindley, S., Pedder, D., & Hagger, H. (2004). Starting points: student teachers' reasons for becoming teachers and their preconceptions of what this will mean. *European Journal of Teacher Education,* 27(3): 245–264.

Zuckerbrod, K. (2007). 9 States united on test, standards for high school math. *Philadelphia Inquirer,* April 11, 2007.

CREDITS

This constitutes an extension of the copyright page. We have made every effort to trace the ownership of all copyrighted material and to secure permission from copyright holders. In the event of questions arising as to the use of any material, we will be pleased to make the necessary corrections in future printings. Thanks are due to the following authors, publishers, and agents for permission to use the material indicated.

Text

Chapter 1.   15: "NEA Code of Ethics," reprinted by permission of the National Education Association.

Chapter 4.   105: Excerpted from *The Sea Accepts All Rivers & Other Poems* by Judy Sorum Brown, Miles River Press, 2000. Available from Judy Brown, 3907 Calverton Drive, Hyattsville, MD 20782.   113: From Tina Blythe and Associates, *The Teaching for Understanding Guide*, Copyright © 1998 by Jossey-Bass, San Francisco. Reprinted with permission of John Wiley & Sons, Inc.   115: Reprinted by permission of Advanced Learning Technologies in Education Consortia.

Chapter 5.   138: Reprinted by permission of the Annie E. Casey Foundation.   143: Reprinted by permission of Kodansha America, Inc. Excerpted from *Teaching Stories* by Judy Logan published by Kodansha America, Inc. (1999).

Chapter 6.   182: *Focus on the Wonder Years: Challenges Facing the American Middle School* by J. Juvonen et al. Copyright 2004 by Rand Corporation. Reproduced with permission of Rand Corporation in the format Textbook via Copyright Clearance Center.   192: From Dr. Tony Humphreys, *A Different Kind of Discipline*. Copyright © 1998. Reprinted by permission of the author.

Chapter 7.   206: from *Pendulums on the Moon*, Discovery School Lesson Plans Library.   207: Permission authorized by Tom Snyder Productions.   209: Reprinted by permission of the author; by Jim Spadaccini, from *The Sweet Lure of Chocolate*, photo by Amy Snyder, © Exploratorium, www.exploratorium.edu.   214: Reprinted with permission from National Educational Technology Standards for Teachers: Preparing Teachers to Use Technology, © 2002, ISTE (International Society for Technology in Education), www.iste.org. All rights reserved.

Chapter 8.   231: Reprinted by permission of ePALS.

Chapter 9.   260: "Classroom Workers Form Community" from http://atozteacherstuff.com/pages/5055.shtml. 266: Adapted with permission from "Beware of the Cyber Bully," iSAFE America.

Chapter 10.   275: Reprinted by permission of Michael Keany, Director, Long Island School Leadership Center. 276: From the Introduction to *Managing Your Classroom with Heart: A Guide for Nurturing Adolescent Learners*, by Katy Ridnouer, Alexandria, VA; ASCD, 2006. Used with permission. The Association for Supervision and Curriculum Development is a worldwide community of educators advocating sound policies and sharing best practices to achieve the success of each learner. To learn more, visit ASCD at www.ascd.org.   285: PRAXIS materials are reprinted by permission of Educational Testing Service, the copyright owner. However, the test questions and any other testing information are provided in their entirety by Houghton Mifflin Company. No endorsement of this publication (Adobe eBooks or SafariX eBooks) by Educational Testing Service should be inferred.   286: Used by permission of The Council of Chief State School Officers. The Interstate New Teacher Assessment and Support Consortium (INTASC) standards were developed by the Council of Chief State School Officers and member states. Copies may be downloaded from the Council's website at http://www.ccsso.org. Council of Chief State School Officers (1992). *Model Standards for Beginning Teacher Licensing, Assessment, and Development: A Resource for State Dialogue*. Washington, DC: Author. http://www.ccsso.org/contents/pdfs/corestrd.pdf. 288: From http://www.teachabroad.com. Reprinted by permission of GoAbroad.com.   290: Reprinted by permission of AFT. AFT is a union of professionals which represents educators in school districts across the country.

Photos

Part I: (xxx): Creatas Images/Jupiter

Chapter 1:   2: © Elizabeth Crews;   6: © Michael Newman / PhotoEdit;   10: © James Shaffer / PhotoEdit; 18, 21:© Elizabeth Crews

Chapter 2:   26, 33: © Elizabeth Crews; 35: © Michael Newman / PhotoEdit;   40, 46: © Elizabeth Crews

Part II: 56: © Michael Newman / PhotoEdit

Chapter 3:   58: © Marion Post Wolcott/Corbis;   63, 73: © Bettmann/Corbis;   78: The Starry Night, June 1889 (oil on canvas) by Vincent van Gogh (1853–90) © Museum of Modern Art, New York, USA/ The Bridgeman Art Library; 82: © Bettmann/Corbis;   86: © Ian Shaw/Getty Images

Chapter 4:   91: © Elizabeth Crews;   95: © Christina Kennedy / PhotoEdit;   97: © Mark Garten/Corbis; 101: © David Young-Wolff / PhotoEdit;   113: © Elizabeth Crews

Part III: 122: © Elizabeth Crews

Chapter 5: 124, 128: © Elizabeth Crews; 131: © Bob Daemmrich / The Image Works; 139: © Elizabeth Crews; 149: © Michael Newman / PhotoEdit

Chapter 6: 154: © Elizabeth Crews; 156: © Dennis MacDonald / Alamy; 164: © Corbis; 167, 181, 190: © Elizabeth Crews

Chapter 7: 198: © Elizabeth Crews; 202: © Ed Kashi/Corbis; 213: © David Young-Wolff/Getty Images; 216: © Elizabeth Crews; 219: © John Birdsall/ The Image Works

Chapter 8: 223: © Elizabeth Crews; 226: © Michael Newman / PhotoEdit; 237: © Syracuse Newspapers/Dick Blume/ The Image Works; 239: © Gary Walts/Syracuse Newspapers/ The Image Works

Part IV: 246: © Mary Kate Denny / PhotoEdit

Chapter 9: 248, 254 (left): © Elizabeth Crews; 254 (right): © Michael Newman / PhotoEdit; 258: © Elizabeth Crews; 261: © Felicia Martinez / PhotoEdit

Chapter 10: 270: © Michael Wildsmith/Getty Images; 273: © Steve Smith/Getty Images; 280: © Myrleen Ferguson Cate / PhotoEdit; 281: © Ed Kashi/Corbis; 286: © Elizabeth Crews